CW01514659

Aboriginal
ENGLISH

A Cultural Study

J.M. Arthur

at
**The Australian
National Dictionary Centre**

Melbourne
OXFORD UNIVERSITY PRESS
Oxford Auckland New York

OXFORD UNIVERSITY PRESS AUSTRALIA

Oxford   New York
Athens   Auckland   Bangkok   Bombay
Calcutta   Cape Town   Dar es Salaam   Delhi
Florence   Hong Kong   Istanbul   Karachi
Kuala Lumpur   Madras   Madrid   Melbourne
Mexico City   Nairobi   Paris   Port Moresby
Singapore   Taipei   Tokyo   Toronto
and associated companies in
Berlin   Ibadan

OXFORD is a trade mark of Oxford University Press

National Library of Australia
Cataloguing-in-Publication data

Arthur, J. M. (Jay Mary), 1946– .
   Aboriginal English: a cultural study.

   Bibliography.
   Includes index.
   ISBN 0 19 554018 2.

   1. Aborigines, Australian – Languages – Dictionaries.
   2. Aborigines, Australian – Social life and customs.
   3. English language – Dialects – Australia – Dictionaries.
   4. Kriol language – Dictionaries. I. Title.

427.99403

Typeset by Egan-Reid Ltd, Auckland, New Zealand
Printed through Bookpac Production Services, Singapore
Published by Oxford University Press,
253 Normanby Road, South Melbourne, Australia

ACKNOWLEDGMENTS

This work was begun and funded almost entirely through the Australian National Dictionary Centre. Dr Bill Ramson, the first Director of the Centre, agreed to support this project, at a time when Aboriginal English was receiving little attention, either in the scholarly or general community. For his initial and continued support I am very grateful. The present Director, Dr Bruce Moore, followed the project through the last stages of editing, and his contributions and comments have been of great assistance. I am also grateful to Dr Nicholas Peterson, for his support in the final year, and his most useful commentaries on the manuscript. I would like to thank Joan Ritchie, Maureen Brooks and Hilary Kent for their extensive work at the editing stage, Julia Robinson for her comments, and Dorothy Savage and Betty Warner, who keyed in the citations and dealt with my handwriting. I am greatly indebted to three patient computer programmers, Monica Berko, Gavin Mercer and the late Harriet Michell, for their assistance.

I would like to thank those who gave linguistic and cultural advice on the material: in particular, Dr Ian Green, Dr Deborah Bird Rose, Dr Luise Hercus, Dr Alan Dench and Dr Nicholas Thieberger.

This work is much indebted to those Aboriginal and non-Aboriginal authors and editors, who, often against current publishing practice, insisted that their own words, or those of the oral testimonies they were editing, should remain in the language in which they were written or spoken—Aboriginal English. This book is a testament to their determination, and to all those authors who cared enough for language and for Aboriginal culture to record this distinctive speech.

My final and most particular thanks are to Peter Read.

For M.G.A. and D.P.A

CONTENTS

INTRODUCTION

This book is a study of some of the experiences and histories of contemporary Aboriginal people as represented through words of one of their languages. This language is Aboriginal English.

A history of Aboriginal English

At the time of the British invasion, Aboriginal Australians spoke about two hundred distinct languages. Within these languages were many dialects, so that there were about five hundred different ways of speaking in Aboriginal Australia in 1788. Many if not all Aboriginal people were multilingual, speaking two or more languages fluently and understanding several more. After the invasion and the massive social changes that followed, many of those languages were lost. Some were lost because all the people who spoke them had died, or the survivors were so few that they joined other communities and their children grew up speaking the language of those communities. Sometimes the older speakers of a language did not hand on their knowledge to the younger generation, possibly because they felt that the society their children now had to inhabit was so inimical to Aboriginal culture that such knowledge would only be to their disadvantage. In many places, speakers of different languages came to live together in government settlements and town camps, either through forcible removal from their countries by the authorities or through voluntary relocation. In such places one Aboriginal language, or a form of English, became the lingua franca, and other languages ceased to be spoken. Well into the middle of this century, government authorities actively prevented the handing on of languages to Aboriginal children through different forms of institutionalisation. In southern Australia especially, there were great assimilationist pressures placed on people not to speak their own language. Aboriginal languages are also still subject to the pressures placed upon all minority languages around the world, where the activities of the controlling society, employment, education and the media are predominantly the domain of the majority language. So of the two hundred Aboriginal languages of 1788, only about eighty are still spoken today by older people and even fewer by whole communities.

After 1788, Australia had two communities: one European, predominantly English-speaking, and one Aboriginal, speaking a great variety of languages. (A number of the Europeans were Gaelic speakers and others spoke English dialects very different from 'standard' British English.) As in all such linguistically divided communities, a 'pidgin' developed quite quickly in the early days of the occupied Gadigal and Eora countries of the Sydney area. A 'pidgin' is a form of language which provides communication between communities who cannot speak each other's language. Pidgins often develop where one community wants to trade with another ('pidgin' is in fact a nineteenth-century Chinese pronunciation of the English word 'business'). It is found where one culture has colonised another, so that around the world pidgins based on English, Spanish, French etc., followed the European colonising movements of the last three or four hundred years. Pidgins characteristically take vocabulary from both languages but are usually based more closely on one language than another; a common pattern is to take the vocabulary from the colonising language but retain some indigenous grammatical features, so that pidgins associated with English for example, may appear at first sight to be closer to the majority form of English than they actually are. They generally have a limited vocabulary with a restricted choice of words with similar senses and this vocabulary tends to focus on the areas of interaction between the two groups. This first Australian pidgin contained elements of both languages; it contained local Aboriginal words such as *cobbon*, 'head' and *budgery*, 'good'. Some of the English words it used such as *belong, all the time* and *by and by* are found in other Englishes from the area which have a similar pidgin 'ancestry', such as Tok Pisin from Papua New Guinea. There are other words such as *plenty, savvy,* and *alonga*, which also occur in areas very remote from Australia but which have had a similar British colonising experience. The English speakers took some Aboriginal words into their own language. Among those in common use today are *boomerang, corroboree, dingo, kangaroo, koala,* and *cooee.*

As the frontier advanced north from the settled areas of southern Australia, the pidgin travelled with the invaders. It did not reproduce exactly in the new areas; particular social and linguistic histories and the contribution of local Aboriginal languages created regional variations. However, there are still some similarities between the language of Aboriginal people in north and central Australia today and the language of people in nineteenth-century New South Wales, because of the time lag in the process of colonisation.

Over time, this colonial language changed. It became no longer a restricted form of communication, a pidgin, but a complete and sufficient form of English, although it still differed to a greater or lesser degree from the English spoken by non-Aboriginal people. The period when this happened varied throughout Australia, as it took over a hundred years for the non-Aboriginal occupation of Australia to be complete. This form of Australian English, which is often still called 'pidgin', is more accurately described as 'Aboriginal English'. It is a dialect of Australian English, that is, a form of Australian English which is significantly different from the general form but still more or less intelligible to other speakers of the language.

There are many forms of Aboriginal English. The linguistic history and experiences of Aboriginal people from different areas of Australia have varied enormously. In some areas colonisation is still relatively recent and many people in such areas speak their own Aboriginal language as a first language. In other areas there are no local languages still spoken and Aboriginal people are a very small minority of the population. People differ in the amount of educational exposure to non-Aboriginal Australian English they have received. So Aboriginal English is not really one dialect but a continuum, a series of 'Aboriginal Englishes'; at one end a language which differs in only a few words from other Australian speech, and at the other a language which has become so different from other

Australian Englishes that it ceases to be Aboriginal English and becomes another language, called 'Kriol'.

Kriol is found in areas of northern Australia such as the Roper River in the Northern Territory and the Fitzroy region in the Kimberley, where the pidgin has developed into a distinct language. It has its own spelling system (although this is not uniform between different regions) and is the medium of education in these communities. The following example of written Kriol clearly illustrates the connections with and differences from non-Aboriginal Australian written English. *Wel mela bin start klaimapbat ontop la il en ai bin stat lukranabat langa that pokupain wen thei bin digimbat.* [Well we started climbing to the top of the hill and looking around for where the echidnas had been digging.] Walsh and Yallop (1993), p. 165.

Though there are many personal variations within the general linguistic pattern, there is a major language divide between northern Australia and southern Australia. Northern Australia includes the Northern Territory and central Australia, most of Western Australia except for the south-west, and northern and western Queensland. Southern Australia includes south-western WA, southern SA, Victoria, Tasmania, most of NSW, and south-east Queensland. The differences between the two are the result of the 'travelling frontier' of colonisation and the density of settlement by the occupying culture. In southern Australia, colonisation has been established longest and the proportion of Aboriginal people to non-Aboriginal people is very low. It is the area where there has been the greatest displacement of peoples and the greatest loss of languages and other traditional aspects of life such as ceremony. In northern Australia Aboriginal people have been better able to retain language and traditional aspects of culture because European occupation is much more recent (in some areas within living memory), and the population densities of the two cultures and the patterns of European settlement are quite different. This has meant that the Aboriginal English spoken in northern Australia is in general more different from other Australian Englishes and more likely to be spoken as a second language than that spoken in southern Australia.

How Aboriginal English is used throughout Australia also differs. Some people speak it as a second language, to be used outside their community or where non-speakers of their language are present. For others it is their only form of language. Some speakers will vary the kind of English they speak, according to the social context. They might speak Aboriginal English in their home community or with other Aboriginal people, and use the majority form of Australian English at work or in conversation with non-Aboriginal people. In this they have much in common with speakers of other minority dialects of English, such as Scots and Irish.

The status of Aboriginal English

It is only recently that Aboriginal English has been recognised as a form of Australian English. Generally it has been called either pidgin or 'broken' English and has been viewed as a form of language that needed remedial attention. While there are Aboriginal people who are second language speakers of English, and may therefore need some second language assistance, the majority of speakers of Aboriginal English are using a dialect which functions as a fully sufficient language. Within the last few years, there has been a recognition of the existence and integrity of the dialect. Some Aboriginal English terms have appeared in major newspapers; people speaking Aboriginal English on television now have their language heard, with subtitles provided if the producers feel the dialect might make it difficult for non-Aboriginal people to understand. Publishers have begun to tackle the problem of presenting Aboriginal English to the reading public. If the form of Aboriginal English is not significantly different from non-Aboriginal English, footnotes or bracketed material can make the material accessible. Editors have tried to make the text of the Aboriginal English from northern Australia accessible to non-speakers: breaking up the text on the page to represent the patterns of speech or providing a parallel translation into general English, are two ways in which both comprehensibility and credibility can be retained.

Some of the problems of representing Aboriginal English in print have arisen because most of the material is a printed version of oral speech. Transcribed spoken English is different from written English and is not always easy to understand because it lacks the conventions that written language has developed to aid comprehension. Aboriginal English now is still primarily a spoken rather than a written language, but with the number of Aboriginal authors producing written work, it may evolve a distinctive printed form as other Englishes have done.

The purpose of this book

This book is a collection of words from Aboriginal English. It is not about grammatical structure for its own sake, or pronunciation, but is concerned with the meanings of words. Some are those found in other Englishes but which have extended or different senses in Aboriginal English as in **business**, **owner**, **clever**. Others, such as **gammon** or **humbug**, are no longer used in other Australian Englishes, but are part of the vocabulary inherited from nineteenth-century pidgin. Some are words from Aboriginal languages which are used in an Aboriginal English context, for example **moorditj** or **jarjum**, or words whose meanings mirror those words in Aboriginal languages, such as **hear** which means both 'to hear' and 'to understand'. The focus of the book is cultural rather than linguistic as it looks at contemporary Aboriginal Australia through the medium of one of its languages.

As with most studies of Aboriginal English it is not a study of the whole language but a study of differences between it and other Australian Englishes, differences which represent the alternative experiences of Aboriginal Australia.

The sources

The use of material written within one culture to record the use of spoken language in another culture is always problematic, and this work cannot escape this tension. Some of the examples in this book have been taken from material that was often not in the main written down by Aboriginal people (although it was sometimes originally spoken by them). In such a situation, words could be reproduced which represent the way non-Aboriginal people imagined Aboriginal people spoke, or the way Aboriginal people had once spoken but no longer do. Writers could record words spoken in one area of Australia and ascribe them to another. Many works, especially older works of fiction, use a form of Aboriginal English that is almost a literary cliché and one that is usually unlocalised and ahistorical. Because of the previous low status of Aboriginal English publishers and editors have seen it as a trivial or unimportant act to 'regularise' Aboriginal English material. However, the core works on which most of this book is based are edited transcripts of Aboriginal oral history, Aboriginal autobiographical or literary works, and others in which there has been a consciousness of the integrity of the dialect. Some of the major works used for northern Australia are land claim reports, which aim to reproduce language verbatim (though they are sometimes inaccurate), and P. and J. Read's *A View of the Past* and D. B. Rose's *Hidden Histories* which make a similar claim of accuracy. In the south, the work of Aboriginal writers such as Kevin Gilbert, Glenyse Ward and Phillip Pepper have provided much evidence, as have Aboriginal newsletters such as the Tasmanian *Puggana News*. This does not mean that the problem of the separation between the words in this book and the actual language of Aboriginal people has been removed, but it has, I hope, been reduced.

The evidence

This is not a complete dictionary of Aboriginal English. The nature of the sources and the limitations presented by the lack of a national study of the dialect using spoken rather than written material preclude this. It is, however, a collection of many of the significant words in the Aboriginal English vocabulary, and one which I believe is sufficiently wide to give some cultural insights into Aboriginal society.

The collection is primarily contemporary but, where possible, a history of each word is provided. In some cases there is recorded evidence back to the pidgin of the nineteenth century; sometimes it is not possible to say when the word was first used by Aboriginal people. More work of the calibre of Jaki Troy's study of early Sydney pidgin (Troy 1990) needs to be done in other areas of Australia to set all the words in their historical context.

With each word are some examples of its use in print. I have not reproduced all the material I have found for each word, but have selected a sample which gives an idea of where, how, and sometimes when this word is used. Words which figure largely in the evidence or are culturally significant generally have a larger number of citations. For some words I have very little evidence, but they are included because they add to a general understanding of the nature of Aboriginal English and of Aboriginal cultures. Some may prove to be idiosyncratic.

Each word is marked with a general geographical location unless it is used throughout Australia. In this way the geographical variations of Aboriginal

English have been recorded. Many words have the location marker *northern Aust.* for example. This covers the area that is predominantly the domain of traditional culture, of northern, central and north-western Australia. Each citation is then given an approximate geographical location where possible, from the place where the work was set or the speakers belong; this is sometimes a more precise location than that attached to the word at the head of the entry.

Because of the nature of the evidence, the recording of usage will favour areas where there is written material, such as the south-west of Western Australia in the work of Jack Davis, or north-western Northern Territory in the work of Deborah Bird Rose, or eastern New South Wales in that of Ruby Langford Ginibi. This means that with each word it is possible to say this word is used in a particular area, but it is not as clearly possible to say that this word is not used elsewhere.

Aboriginal English and Aboriginal languages

Aboriginal languages have different sound systems from English. There is generally no semantic distinction between voiced and unvoiced consonants, so that the English 'hard' *g, b* and *d* may not be distinguished from *k, p* and *t. S, sh, th, v* and *f*, and consonant clusters such as *st, str* and *spl* are not generally found in Aboriginal sound systems. There is also generally a narrower range of vowel sounds than in English, so that to an untrained ear *a, i* or *u* might appear to cover most of them. These differences have produced Aboriginal English ways of pronunciation which have sometimes led to a distinctive printed form. **Gubment**, **yepeyepe** (sheepy), **walypala**, **wadgula**, **bunjiman**, **tidda** are some of the words whose pronunciation and hence spelling have been influenced by Aboriginal language characteristics. Some spellings reflect nineteenth-century Aboriginal pronunciation rather than current ones, but have remained the Aboriginal way of saying it. For example, **gunjible** (now often abbreviated to **gunjy**) is a nineteenth-century pronunciation of 'constable', where the *c* sound has been rendered as *g*, and the *st* combination as *j*. **Poligman** and **bulliman** are both early pronunciations of 'policeman'.

Well-known Aboriginal words have a spelling convention, but others have not. **Kartiya, cardiah, cuddyair, cudeha, gardia, gadeja, gadia, gudeeah, kardiya** are all variant spellings of the same word for 'white person' in the Kimberley region of northern Australia. The *c, g* and *k* represent one sound, as do the *t* and *d*, and the *i, y, j* and *h*.

Some English words have a repetitive pattern imposed on them and have a *y* sound added at the end of the word, probably as a result of the influence of the underlying structures of Aboriginal languages: for example, **piggy piggy**. Some other English words have also begun to have a distinctive Aboriginal English spelling, such as **fulla**, for 'fellow', which more accurately represents Aboriginal pronunciation.

On the other hand, Aboriginal languages have sounds such as *ng* at the beginning of a word and a trilled *r* that English does not have, but in general they have not been represented in the text, as English does not have the conventions to represent them, nor often are the English-speaking listeners able to hear them.

Aboriginal English also reflects some of the structural characteristics of Aboriginal languages. Aboriginal languages do not have the equivalent of pre-positions, such as *of, on, to, for*, or the articles, *a* and *the*; the senses conveyed by the use of these terms are provided by other grammatical forms, such as suffixes attached to words. For example, in the Paakantji language of western New South Wales, *yaparra* is the word for 'camp', *yaparra-ri* 'to the camp', *yaparrandu* 'from the camp', and *yaparrana* 'in the camp'. Prepositions and articles tend then to be used differently in Aboriginal English than in non-Aboriginal English. Aboriginal languages sometimes duplicate the word, or extend the vowel to express an intensification of meaning. This is found in some Aboriginal English usage, such as **different-different**, 'very different', or **biiiig**, 'very big'. Conversely, when Aboriginal language words are taken into Aboriginal English they are usually given English grammatical endings, hence 'two little **jarjums**' for 'two little children'.

Aboriginal English is also influenced by the semantic structures of Aboriginal languages. In many Aboriginal languages, what a thing is made from is used for the thing itself, so that the same word can be used for 'fire' and 'firewood', as in *gadla* from the Kaurna language of the Adelaide region. In Aboriginal English, then, the word **calico** can be used for a 'tent', because that is the material from which tents were made. Similarly what something will be used for can be used to describe the thing, so that a food animal can be called **meat**. The intention of an action and the action itself are also sometimes represented by one word, so that 'to hit' and 'to kill', and 'to look' and 'to see', are frequently found as one word in Aboriginal languages.

The structure of the dictionary

Most dictionaries present the words in their collections in a continuous alphabetical list. Because the form of this dictionary is cultural rather than linguistic, it has been organised differently. It is constructed around the experiences which shaped this semantic domain and is presented as accumulations of words about these experiences. They are words which mark out a territory belonging to Aboriginal Australia alone, words that relate to understandings of the world and of human relationships, of cultural practices and historical events. They belong to that 'other' Australia which Aboriginal people inhabit by inheritance, by choice and by force of colonisation.

Chapters 1 to 4 contain words that belong to the continuing tradition of Aboriginality after 1788. The event of colonisation was a catastrophic fracture in Aboriginal history, but there was still some continuity of tradition, of values, of ways of looking at the world, and of personal histories giving the next generation the understanding of what it was to be Aboriginal. The words found in Chapter 1 belong to the experience of describing cultural activities and identifying values of Aboriginal society within the colonising situation and within a form of the colonisers' language. That is, it concerns words that are used to talk about (and practise) the **business** of Aboriginal society. Chapters 2 to 4 contain words to do with family, human relationships and feelings, country and spiritual beliefs. Terms such as **grow up**, which can be used in Aboriginal English to mean 'to raise a child', can also be used to describe the way a country **grows up**, that is, raises the people who live on it. Similarly **clever** means spiritually powerful, a **second mother** can be an aunt, while **dangerous** means spiritually hazardous. Chapters 5 and 6 deal with the experience of colonisation. Chapter 5 is a collection of words for the colonisers, their controlling agents and their legislative restrictions, as well as, more prosaically, the words for the material goods they brought with them. These include **gubba**, 'white person', **dog licence**, 'exemption certificate' and **bullocky**, 'cattle'. This chapter also contains words for the new categories of Aboriginal people that colonisation brought about: before **whitefellers** there were no **blackfellers**. Chapter 6 includes a particular collection of words which came about through the involvement of Aboriginal people in the pastoral industry, where Aboriginal people have transferred a range of English words they learnt in the pastoral station context and applied them to human situations. A term such as **quiet**, the word used to describe cattle that are easy to manage, is then taken over to describe a pacified people, while **run**, the term used to describe the grazing of cattle over a particular area is applied to the geographical extent of the use of a particular ceremony.

Chapter 7 considers the linguistic and cultural history as it is manifested in language itself. This chapter contains structures of Aboriginal English that refer to its pidgin heritage and to the legacies of the Aboriginal languages, documenting in the language itself the experience of its formation and history. For example, the use of words such as **to** and **for** owe their particular use in Aboriginal English to the structure of Aboriginal languages. This chapter also contains words whose function depends on the cultural and social traditions of Aboriginal societies. The use of narrative markers such as **alright** and **finish**, and the use of a tag such as **eh** at the end of a non-inverted question are two examples. The chapter also places Aboriginal English in the context of other post-colonial Englishes with which it shares some vocabulary.

Chapter 8 looks at the new cultural forms that have emerged through the experience of colonisation. The historical events of the last 200 years have meant that people have arrived at new ways of being Aboriginal. Aboriginal peoples' perception of themselves has changed; new group identities such as **Koori** and **Murri** have emerged. They have formed new cultural structures such as **keeping places**. There has also been a retelling by both sides of the history of Aboriginal and White interactions, and from this retelling have come expressions such as **concentration camp**, and **Day of Mourning**.

The arrangement of words in themes is intended to provide some general insights into Aboriginal society. For example, the number of new terms in Aboriginal English for family and kin, such as **cousin-brother**, indicates cultural differences from the idea of family in most of non-Aboriginal Australia. Words, such as **story**, which contain both an historical and a spiritual meaning, and the number of words for spiritual beings (of which the ones recorded here are only a fraction), testify to the spiritual dimension of Aboriginal Australia. Other terms such as **shame** mark alternative social behaviours to the dominant one.

The focus of this study is on the central themes of continuity of tradition, colonisation and cultural survival. There are other categories into which these words could have been organised that would have given insights into other aspects of Aboriginal Australia. This dictionary attempts to provide some understanding of the social organisation, the history, the value system, and the linguistic history of Aboriginal Australia through the ways in which Aboriginal people have extended, altered, and in other ways made a language of Europe their own.

Jay Arthur
Canberra, 1996

CHAPTER 1
Always was, always will be

Aboriginal people belong to a different Australia.

They live in a place where many of their ancestors have lived for at least 50,000 years. Since the British occupation, Aboriginal culture and society have undergone violent change, including the loss of many languages. Despite the changes, there remain concepts, behaviours and understandings of life that are in many ways continuous with pre-invasion Australia. They are not identical—all cultures are dynamic—but they continue out of this tradition. This collection of words tracks the survival of these traditions and the perceptions of life arising from them— understandings that are now expressed in the new language of Aboriginal Australia.

For many Aboriginal people, this new language was the one in which they expressed their continuing traditions. Others who spoke their own language still had to communicate these specific concerns to non-Aborigines. Concerns that did not belong in the European world still had to be spoken about in the European language. Aboriginal people who spoke English as their first language still had their own concerns to talk about.

The central words in this first chapter are the **law** (or the **rule**), the **dreaming** and the **culture**. These words provide a sense of the world being organised from a different starting point from that of the non-Aboriginal world. The **law** connects the spiritual and the physical, gives meaning to ritual and the organisation of life, connects the past to the present, and is the heritage of the Aboriginal people. It comprises an alternative reality to that of European Australia.

In this other reality, the spiritual and the physical are coterminous. The spiritual world is everywhere manifested in the physical. It is manifested in **clever** people, in **maban** men, in spiritual beings, the **dreamings**, which created and create the earth, and it is present in ritual, where to perform a ceremony such as to **sing** someone, has a physical effect carried out by spiritual powers. Rituals were an activity separated from the European world both physically and in terms of European knowledge and participation. They were seen as the particular **business** of Aboriginal people. This connectedness of the spiritual and physical is also found in words which relate to knowledge, so that the **story** of the place may contain both mythical and historical facts.

While most of these words are originally English words whose meanings have been transformed or extended to provide the Aboriginal sense, there are also many Aboriginal language words which are used for spiritual beings, such as **mamu** or **dulugal**, or **boolya** for spiritual power. There are undoubtedly many more used in Aboriginal conversation to refer to spiritual presences in different regions, but they are less likely to be found in print, partly because they may not be something people wish to talk about in public, and partly because of the concerns of writers and editors with cross-cultural comprehension.

ashes *noun* **in the ashes**, a traditional cooking method, using the heat of camp fire ashes.

1982 J. Davis *Kullark* p. 10 [south-west WA] We was at Moore River sittin' round the fire cooking *gilgies* **in the ashes**. **1982** R. Lindsay (ed.) *Bush Tucker* p. 6 [western NSW] English name: Red Kangaroo. Paakantji name: Tharlta . . . You can eat *tharlta* cooked **in the ashes**, cut up for skins, curried, steamed, minced, fried, grilled or potted. **1989** B. Morris *Domesticating Resistance* p. 84 [northern NSW] Mullet and eel were traditionally cooked '**in the ashes**' or on a *baral*. The latter consisted of three forked sticks placed in a triangle around the fire onto which a lot of little sticks [were] put in a grill-like fashion across [the top] where the fire was made! **1989** B. Morris *Domesticating Resistance* p. 83 [northern NSW] 'Cookin' **in the ashes** as it is called, was not a simple process.

Hence to **grow up in the ashes**, to have a traditional Aboriginal upbringing, centred around the family camp fire.

In some Aboriginal languages the word for 'camp' is the same as the word for **ashes** or ' fire'; for example in the Nyungar language of south-west WA, *karl*, 'fire, camp, homeland, country' and in the Bundjalung language of northern NSW, *diman*, 'ashes, camp'.

1980 T. Donaldson *Ngiyambaa* p. 13 [western NSW] But the affection which the last speakers of Ngiyambaa feel for the time when they '**grew up in the ashes**' is something they can sense and draw strength from.

ashes damper *noun* Damper cooked in ashes. Also **ashes bread**.

1978 K. Gilbert *People are Legends* p. 29 [NSW] Our fare is **ashes damper**, stew or mungulmay. They eat real flash all on our cash up there at D.A.A. **1989** D. Walker *Me and You* p. 22 [north coast, NSW] We always had syrup with **ashes bread** and fish. **1991** A. Jackomos & D. Fowell *Living Aboriginal Hist. of Vic.* p. 114 [Vic.] We would buy a 25-pound sack of flour and live on **ashes-damper** and Johnny-cakes. **1992** R.L. Ginibi *Real Deadly* p. 5 [north coast, NSW] He caught bush tucker for us, made **ashes damper**, and told us stories.

bakery grub *noun* [Tas.] A witchetty grub.

Origin unknown.

1985 *Aboriginal Health Worker* (Little Bay) Dec. Vol. 9 p. 8 Meats . . witchetty grubs (known to us as **bakery** and workery **grubs**).

bamboo *noun* [northern Aust.] A didgeridoo. Also **bamboo pipe**.

From the *bamboo* from which didgeridoos are sometimes made.

1969 A.A. Abbie *Original Australs* p. 173 The *didjeridu*, also known as 'drone pipe', 'bambo pipe' and '**bamboo pipe**', is a wooden tube varying from some two inches to four inches in diameter and ranging in length from about three feet six inches to over six feet. **1980** B. Sansom *The Camp at Wallaby Cross* p. 63 [Darwin, NT] The men who . . bring out '**bamboos**' to stage fun corroborees . . have style.

bamboo man, a didgeridoo player.

1980 B. Sansom *The Camp at Wallaby Cross* p. 252 [Darwin, NT] The Wallaby Cross mob was willing to draw on the pool of pension earnings to support . . an instrumentalist (a **Bamboo Man**).

bamboo puller, a didgeridoo player. See PULLER.

1957 W.E. Harney *Life Among Aborigines* p. 54 [NT] We slept on the beach to the chants of the Wargite tribesmen as their didgeridus roared and droned on the lips of the 'bamboo puller'.

baygal *noun* [northern NSW] An Aboriginal person, specifically one from the Bundjalung country of northern NSW and south-eastern Queensland. Also **bagal**.

From the Bundjalung language of northern NSW and south-eastern Queensland *baigal*, a 'man', a 'person'. This is a different use from that of 'Koori' or 'Murri' in that its primary user group has not changed—i.e. it is still used essentially by Bundjalung people and has not been utilised as a term by other non-Bundjalung people. The use of a term such as **baygal** is complex and still in a process of change. See KOORI.

1978 T. Crowley *Middle Clarence Dialects Bandjalang* p. 1 [north coast, NSW] I must admit that my ability to judge on this matter has been clouded somewhat by Aboriginal usage, where **baygal** 'Aborigine' and yirali 'whiteman' are clearly differentiated. **1988** M.C. Sharpe et al. *An Introduction to the Bundjalung Language and its Dialects* p. 7 [north coast, NSW] In Bundjalung the word **baygal**, which once meant 'man' is now only used for an Aboriginal man. White people looked so different . . that Aboriginal people gave them a completely different name, sometimes *dagay*, the word for 'ghost'. **1992** R.L. Ginibi *Real Deadly* p. 1 [north coast, NSW] No jobs around for **bagal** or dubays or jarjums too, now the place has been colonised and settled.

bird people *noun* People whose totem is a species of bird.

A totem is a way of connecting the natural and human world, and of giving people particular responsibilities for knowledge and ritual. In the 1993 citation, Evelyn Crawford says that her totem is an eaglehawk, which means that she is spiritually connected to the eaglehawk dreaming ancestor; the knowledge and ritual associated with that dreaming and the sites associated with that ancestor would belong to the eaglehawk people. See DREAMING, MEAT.

1987 B. Gammage & P. Spearitt (eds) *Australians 1938* p. 121 When you're born your grandfather or your father, he gives you a bird. Some are given a bird, some are given a fish. Generally, all the **bird people** can marry each other. **1993** E. Crawford *Over my Tracks* p. 2 [western NSW] My mum . . her totem was eagle hawk, so we're all **bird people**.

birrik *noun* [south-west NSW] A spirit; a floating ghost.

From an Aboriginal pronunciation of the English word 'spirit', among the Wiradjuri people of south-western NSW.

1975 R.J. Merritt *Cake Man* p. 19 [Erambie, south-west NSW] No, **birriks** might get me . . birriks get me I go out in the dark. **1995** *Koori Mail* Lismore 4 October p. 6/2 [south-west NSW] And he would talk. Talk about **birik**, (good) and the wandang (bad) spirits.

bone *verb* To gain psychic power over somebody through particular rituals, usually to cause illness or death. The ritual is centred upon an object, such as a bone, which is used to direct the malevolent energy towards the victim, by being ritually pointed, or burned or buried. See also CLEVER, DOCTOR, POINT, SING.

The act is carried out by a spiritually powerful person, a doctor or cleverman, although the actual identity of the sorcerer is usually not known to the victim.

Healing can only take place by the removal of the curse by the cleverman, or by the intervention of a more powerful spiritual healer. In Aboriginal society spiritual power can be a form of social control, as a final punishment for those who have transgressed, and as an expression of the power of Aboriginal law. In this ritual, the connectedness of the spiritual and physical world is confirmed and the ultimate power of the spiritual over the physical is shown in its control over human life itself. See LAW.

1928 W. Robertson *Coo-ee Talks* p. 78 When it was found that he refused to believe that he was being '**boned**', they arranged that he should behold the tribal doctor pointing the death-bones in the direction of his mia-mia. **1959** L. Rose *Country of Dead* p. 80 Old Unda had once '**boned**' a man for selling his tjuringa to a white man. **1941** K.S. Prichard *Moon of Desire* p. 175 [WA?] Gabriel asserted he had been '**boned**' by an old man of the tribe he had fallen in with; Mission boy though he was, and 'a good Christian', he had been powerless to avert the death willed on him. **1985** B. Rosser *Dreamtime Nightmares* p. 47 [northern Qld] They think the other tribes are out to kill them or **bone** them. **1993** E. Crawford *Over my Tracks* p. 60 [western NSW] You couldn't have an educated Aboriginal person on a Mission. You either starved him out, or **boned** him or shot him.

Hence **bone pointing**, the ritual associated with pointing the bone.

1977 J. Carter *All Things Wild* p. 58 They had heard nothing of '**bone pointing**', although they acknowledged this form of tribal justice is still practised.

boning *noun* The ritual act of using a bone to direct a malevolent psychic force against another person.

1925 M. Terry *Across Unknown Aust.* p. 147 [northern Australia] There is a custom, common to all Australian natives, whereby an enemy can be killed without violence. It is called '**boning**', or 'singing'. **1936** 'L. Kaye' *Black Wilderness* p. 158 An old man sitting in the dust with a long bleached bone pointing before him toward someone he could not see—that was all. But death went out from him. Someone would die . . . 'Who's the old devil **boning**'?' Lex wondered. **1984** H. McKellar *Matya-Mundu* p. 10 [south-west Qld] **Boning** was done in secret by a 'goobi' man who was especially appointed for that purpose. **1988** S. Dunlop *All that Rama Rama Mob* p. 127 [central Aust.] **Boning**, only person who bones can fix up. Never fixed up if person who bones dies.

boolyaduk *noun* [south-west WA] A spiritually powerful person. See also CLEVER.

From the Nyungar *bulyakarrak*, 'a spiritually powerful person'.

1986 J. Davis *No Sugar* p. 55 [south-west WA] Gran: Choo, you fellas want to dubakuny wahuginy. He might be **boolyaduk**.

boolyah-man *noun* [south-west WA] A spiritually powerful man. Also **bollia man**, **boolya man**, **boylea man**. See CLEVER, MABAN.

From the Nyungar *bulyakarrak* 'a spiritually powerful person'. In the west of Australia, 'boolya' and more particularly 'maban', are used where in the east and south 'clever' might be used.

1872 Mrs E. Millett *Australian Parsonage* p. 79 A faint type of priesthood may be found in the **Bollia men**, as those persons are called who pretend to know Jingy's manoeuvres on given occasions. **1889-1890** W.H. Timperley *Bush Luck* p. 258 So they have '**Boolyah-men**' or doctors who they believe can work a counter influence and drive away the magic that is making the patient ill. **1936** *W.A. Historical Society* (Perth) Vol. II, Part XIX, p. 32 The natives were intensely alarmed and decamped declaring that a '**Boyleaman**' had come from the North threatening death to those of them who were bold enough to remain near the spot. **1982** J. Davis *Kullark* p. 86 [south-west WA] An' them *moodgah, they* strong . . an' only **boolya man** can go there near the *moodgah*, 'cause the *boolya* man is strong too. **1987** S. Morgan *My Place* p. 176 [south-west WA] My uncle and grandfather were also **boolyah men** . . . I remember when my grandfather was dying, he called . . 'you know I can't use my power to heal myself. I will pass my powers into you and then I want you to heal me.'

borning *noun* [northern Aust.] The act of being born, and hence entering into complex spiritual and social relationships.

The form **borning** is also found in American English.

1987 *Aboriginal Health Worker* (Little Bay) Sept. Vol. 11 p. 9 [central Aust.] The consultations have redefined Aboriginal ways—**borning** is not equivalent to Western birthing, but refers to a much wider symbolic process. **1989** G. Knepfer *Nursing for Life* p. 33 The long-term plan for Alukura is the reassertion of the Grandmother's Law, and its incorporation into '**borning**' and obstetric services. **1991** D.B. Rose *Hidden Histories* p. 46 [north-west NT] 'Where you been **borning**?'

boss *noun* **1** A person accepted as a leader in an area of traditional activity (such as a ritual) or responsibility (for example the spiritual and physical care of country). See COUNTRY.

This is an extension into Aboriginal matters of the general use of the English word *boss*, 'a person in charge' but it would not generally be used in the following contexts in other Australian Englishes. This is really the opposite sense of the other Aboriginal English sense of the word *boss*, 'a European', who may or may not be a boss. See also BOSS in Chapter 5.

1965 F.G.G. Rose *Wind of Change* p. 153 [central Aust.] He is the '**boss**' of the corroboree associated with the area. **1975** I. Robertson *Sport and Play Aboriginal Culture* Pt I p. 3 When they all get together, the **boss** of the land gives them the time to begin burning. **1975** I. Robertson *Sport and Play Aboriginal Culture* Pt I p. 3 The yams have **bosses** to look after them. There is a man or woman who has to look after them . . . They have to wait until the boss says the time has come. **1978** *Alyawarra Land Claim* p. 484 [central Aust.] Do the Ukuruputinya mob own those places—are they **bosses** for those places? **1986** B. Shaw *Countrymen* p. 168 [Kimberley] We're just **bosses** for the *mamul.*

boss man, a male leader, **boss woman**, a female leader.

1978 K. Palmer *Somewhere Between Black and White* p. 11 [Pilbara, north-west WA] Then, before dawn, the few old **boss women** would go out, back to the creek. **1989** B. Neidjie *Story about Feeling* p. 99 [Arnhem Land] Nobody can change, no matter who! Headman or might be manager, top-man, might be **boss-man** e can't change it we say because that Law.

2 A non-human thing or concept regarded as a leader or authority.

1983 *Mankind* (Sydney) April p. 497 [northern Qld] '**Boss**' is also used in English today by Kuku-Nyungkul to refer to one's totem species. **1992** D.B. Rose *Dingo Makes Us Human* p. 45 This is established as fact through Dreaming Law: no species, group or country is '**boss**' for another, each adheres to its own Law.

brown jack *noun* [NSW] A small spirit being.

1988 K. Gilbert *Inside Black Australia* p. 86 [northern NSW] Just the same. The **brown jacks** our children cannot see. For they are only visible to adults like me. They don't mean harm to anyone. And only come to have some fun. **1993** J. Janson *Gunjies* p. 41 [NSW] **Brown jacks** we call 'em. He's was brown and 'airy about two an' a half feet tall. Little tiny feet, crossed teeth, red eyes.

bugeen *noun* [south-east Aust.] A clever person. See CLEVER.

From the Wiradjuri language of south-western NSW *bageeyn* or *bageenj* a 'cleverman', 'doctor'. The word *bugheen* in the 1980 citation could be a similar one from a Victorian language, or its use in a Victorian context could have resulted from the spread of a Wiradjuri word with the new contacts made between Aboriginal groups after colonisation.

1958 R. Robinson *Black-Feller White-Feller* p. 111 [southern NSW] Someone, a **bugeen** perhaps, is sneaking up on me to kill me with his *guneena*, his devils' stones. **1980** P. Pepper *You are what you make Yourself* p. 33 [Vic.] Their parents went to the **bugheen**, that's the clever bloke of the tribe and got him to sing the one who took the girls away. **1989** R. Robinson *The Nearest the White Man Gets* p. 33 [south coast NSW] The dark people would never go lookin' for whales. The killers would let them know if there were whales about. Ole Uncle would speak to them killers in the language. They must have been **bugeens**, clever blackfellers. **1995** *Koori Mail* Lismore 4 October p. 6/2 [south coast NSW] And he would talk. Talk about the birik (good) spirits and the wandang (bad) spirits. . . and the Wiradjuri **bageeyn** (clever man).

bunning *noun* [northern NSW] An echidna.

From the Bundjalung language of northern NSW and south-eastern Queensland *bunihyn* 'an echidna'. Aboriginal language names for common animals, especially those used for food, are found throughout Aboriginal Englishes. This use is not however widely recorded.

1988 R. Langford *Don't Take Your Love to Town* p. 89 [north coast, NSW] '**Bunning**', I said to the kids, 'look, its quills are up. Get me a waddy, quick.'. . I hit the porcupine hard on the head. **1988** R. Langford *Dont Take Your Love to Town* p. 4 [north coast, NSW] Old folk hunted for bandicoot and **bunning** in this grass.

bush *adjective* [Chiefly northern Aust.] **1** (Of things, events, or places) Aboriginal as opposed to European.

1978 J. & P. Read *View of the Past* p. 164 [north-west NT] I living on my own tucker. I living for my own tobacco. Him **bush** tobacco. I got bush tea. I got bush tucker. **1985** *Lang. in Central Aust.* iv. p. 22 [central Aust.] But one of the main ways of distinguishing between Aboriginal and European things is between '**bush**' things and non-bush things—'bush well, bush name, bush string, bush welder, bush tucker, bush banana, bush tomato, bush turkey, bush potato, bush onion, bush medicine.' **1988** H. Ross *Community Social Impact* p. 72 [east Kimberley] My mother born there, la [by] creek. **Bush** way you know.

bush boy, a novice undergoing religious instruction by the elders apart from the rest of the camp.

1983 N. Green *Desert School* p. 97 [Western Desert] Becoming a **Bush boy** is an important step in the life of the Ngaanyatjarra. **1983** N. Green *Desert School* p. 97 [Western Desert] Dennis, Bobby and James were three **Bush boys** or novices, who had been sent out of the camp by the elders.

bush name, a person's Aboriginal name.

1983 *Bunji* (Darwin) May p. 3 [Darwin, NT] My real name, **bush name**, is Guyprulawuy. **1984** E. Roughsey *An Aboriginal Mother Tells* p. 129 [Mornington Island, northern Qld] Father knows his grandparents, they both have **bush names**. **1985** *Nungalinya* (Darwin) no. 26, p. 7 [northern NT] Although new tribal names may be given to individuals the teacher should continue to use the school name and deal with the upsets that occur from children mentioning **bush names** inappropriately.

2 Wild, as opposed to domesticated.

This sense can also include things produced naturally as opposed to things made.

1983 *Balgo Newsletter* 25 Jul. p. 7 [northern WA] We all went hunting for to kill some **bush** animals for meat. **1985** *Lang. in Central Aust.* iv. p. 22 [central Aust.] Sometimes bush means 'wild' as opposed to 'tame'. For instance a **bush** pussycat is a wild cat, not an Aboriginal cat. **1987** J. Isaacs *Bush Food* p. 138 Young children look around for what desert people term 'bush lollies' and climb trees to pick off the gum to stave off their hunger. **1989** B. Neidjie *Story about Feeling* p. 44 [Arnhem Land] You got to go hunting for long-neck turtle. You got to go lily. You got to go hunting for **bush**-honey.

bush blood, the blood of wild animals.

1990 S. Watson *Kadaitcha Sung* p. 210 [south-east Qld] I only cook 'em a little bit. I love that **bush blood**!

3 (Of people) not competent in European matters, or not well acquainted with the European world.

1978 J. & P. Read *View of the Past* p. 15 [NT] And in the night time, **bush** blackfeller [come out] when my father was alive, because no [white] man bin go through that place. **1992** D.B. Rose *Dingo Makes Us Human* p. 199 [north-west NT] Some **bush** blackfellows been go longa business [doing ceremony].

bush tucker *noun* Traditional food. Here 'bush' means 'Aboriginal' but also with some of the sense of 'wild, not domesticated'.

This term is also used in the non-Aboriginal community, though not always with a cultural distinction between Aboriginal and non-Aboriginal food, so that 'damper' and 'billy tea' might be included in the non-Aboriginal sense of 'bush tucker'.

1938 *Walkabout* (Melbourne) 1 Apr. p. 16/1 [NT] Constable: 'You all about gotten plenty **bush tucker**?' Reply: 'No more plenty. Little bit.' **1948** A. Marshall *Ourselves Writ Strange* p. 166 [northern Aust.] The searching for food is a woman's daily task. . . . The food she collects is called '**bush tucker**', but the men often refer to it with some contempt as 'woman tucker'. **1954** *Coast to Coast 1953-4* p. 90 The blacks said that he had gone walkabout, that he was hungry for '**bush tucker**' and the life of his own people again. **1974** G. Higgins *Stockyard Gospel* p. 7 [western NSW] Often a bit of **bush tucker** is a welcome change from damper and salt beef . . . I've met white stockmen who like it just as much as the dark. **1977** J.K. Doolan *Cattle Stations* p. 112 [north-west NT] Dagaragu is referred to as a 'proper hungry place' and Yarralin praised as a good place for **bush tucker**, fish and hunting. **1985** S. Cane & O. Stanley *Land Use and Resources in Desert Homelands* p. 120 [Western Desert] We use white fella mirka (vegetable food). Don't get **bush tucker**. **1988** P. Taylor (ed.) *After 200 Years* p. 88 [south-east Qld] I've got a cultural officers' meeting here on Monday and I'm going to get some **bush tucker** to feed them. **1993** *Koori Mail* (Lismore) 13 Jan. p. 16/3 It is envisaged that many will be '**bush tucker**' trees.

bushman *noun* [northern Aust.] An Aboriginal person who lives a particularly traditional life. See TRADITIONAL.

This is a parallel use to the Australian English sense of 'bushman', but with an Aboriginal rather than a non-Aboriginal cultural context.

1963 C. Duguid *No Dying Race* p. 81 (caption) [Western Desert] An old **bushman** from the Pitjantjatjara tribe, Musgrave Ranges.

bushman tucker, traditional Aboriginal food.

1986 B. Shaw *Countrymen* p. 43 [Kimberley] We don't look about any more for **bushman tucker**.

bushy *noun* A person or group retaining more traditional ways than others, especially in relation to law and other cultural knowledge.

This is a parallel use to the Australian English use of 'bushy' to describe a white person who lives in the country as opposed to the city. The Australian English sense sometimes can have derogatory associations of ignorance or unsophistication; the Aboriginal sense generally has the opposite connotation of greater knowledge.

1969 J.E. Bern *Report on the N.T.* p. 3 [southern NT] Its people are regarded locally, by both Aborigines and Europeans, as being more 'bushy' than the rest. The term '**bushy**' does not apply to the retention of traditional livelihood or nomadism, they are semi-permanent at the bore and receive regular rations from the station. They are held in esteem by other Aljawarra people for their traditional knowledge. 1987 S. Morgan *My Place* p. 211 [WA] They seemed to go for the real dark ones . . . The real **bushies**, too. I heard a rumour that they were worried the Japanese would get hold of the bushies and the bushies would lead them through the interior.

bushy tuckout, traditional food.

1915 J.R.B. Love *Aborigines* p. 18 [central Aust.] The young men and women . . procure enough native food supplies ('**bushy tuckout**' in 'pidgin English') to satisfy them.

business *noun* **1** Aboriginal ceremony and ritual. Also used adjectivally in combinations.

1978 *Land Rights News* Jan. p. 3 [NT] That time before, long time before, you think how no one is lost, it is only when **business** is done, then only then you know, you are not lost. 1986 B. Shaw *Countrymen* p. 164 [Kimberley] They taught me one . . then a different one, then another . . I went through three different **Business**. 1987 *Junga Yimi (Yuendumu)* Sept. p. 17 [Western Desert] In the middle of the B. Grade final, all the people ran away frightened . . . Everyone thought that the **business** was coming but it was nothing.

business camp, a camp held specifically for ceremonial purposes.

1978 *Cent. Aust. Land Rights News* (Alice Springs) p. 12 [central Aust.] People had gone to Mission Creek because they were frightened after hearing about shooting which was going on down the Lander River of people, and where a particular mob had been in the high school **business camp**.

business ceremony, Aboriginal ceremony.

1978 J. & P. Read *View of Past* p. 308 [NT] A lot of these girls here are all, all educated when there are **business ceremonies**, ceremonial things, our custom way . . . They still join in.

business country, an area known for its ceremonies, or where ceremonies are held. Also **business ground**.

1991 J. Wright *Born of Conquerors* p. 48 (from *Habitat* June 1983) [Lake Nash, NT] This waterhole where we live was Aboriginal place long time before white man came. It was Aboriginal place for it became 'pastoral lease'. It is **business country** for us. Our law does not change. We are staying here. **1984** P. Harris *Teaching about Time* p. 6 [NT] 'I'm just going to work. I'm going down to the **business ground**.'

business time, the time ceremonies are held.

1980 *Mikurrunya* (Strelley) 7 Nov. p. 3 [Strelley, WA] The **Business Time** is part of the Aboriginal School. The Aboriginal School goes on all the time.

ceremony business, ceremony.

1991 R. Bardsley *Karramarra* p. 26 [northern Qld] You've been through all the **ceremony business**, Uncle.

man's business, ceremony open only to men.

1986 J. Davis *No Sugar* p. 68 [south-west WA] *Mary*: I bin watchin' youse. *Joe*: It's all right, it wasn't **man's business**.

sorry business, mourning ceremony. See also SORRY.

1989 G. Knepfer *Nursing for Life* p. 39 [NT] The families . . carry out their traditional burials and '**sorry business**' without interruption.

Sunday business, a particularly sacred ceremony.

1949 Harney & Elkin *Songs of Songman* p. 143 [NT] The women . . go off to 'dance', that is perform their secret corroboree, their '**Sunday business**'.

women's business, ceremony open only to women.

1983 D. Bell *Daughters of Dreaming* p. 10 [NT] She invited me to the '**women's business**' which was to be held that day.

Hence to **do business** or to be **in business**, 'to have a ceremony'.

1988 P. Taylor *After 200 Years* p. 90 We used ordinary paint but when we **do business** we use proper Aboriginal paint. **1989** B. Neidjie *Story about Feeling* p. 17 [Arnhem Land] When you **in** 'business' you can't touch flying fox.

2 The particular knowledge (including ritual) belonging to a group, concept or tradition.

1976 *Students Storybook* (Aboriginal Teacher Education College) p. 26 [NT] My parents never allowed us all to be promised from childhood. They had often told us that was some promising **business**, but to my parents it didn't mean a thing. **1986** B. Shaw *Countrymen* p. 82 [Arnhem Land] The skin **business** is given by God. **1988** S. Dunlop *All that Rama Rama Mob* p. 128 [central Aust.] Lot of people dying of Aboriginal **business**. **1989** B. Neidjie *Story about Feeling* p. 13 [Arnhem Land] Even water python, grey one. We never eat that. But all, each animal, got '**business**'. They got story each. **1990** D.B. Rose *Gulaga* p. 22 Conception, pregnancy, and childbirth are 'women's **business**' . . **1991** J. Reid & P. Trompf *Health Aboriginal Aust.* p. 316 In Aboriginal Society, women's **business** and men's **business** are discrete and segregated modes of discourse and activity upheld by strict social rules. **1993** D. Hodge *Did you meet any Malagas?* p. 116 [northern NT] I said: 'Look . . I'm going. It's time for me to move on.' And the women said: 'We understand. You've got to do your whitefella **business**.'

buthera *noun* [northern NSW] Spirit, traditional belief.

Related to *budheram*, 'myth, sacred story' in the Bundjalung language of northern NSW.

1991 G.R. Langford *Journey into Bundjalung Country* p. 3 [northern NSW] Aunty Millie Boyd Githabel woman and keeper of the **buthera** of Mt. Jubbungum . . says . . 'You see they take the land but they can't take our buthera (spirit).'

butherum *noun* [northern NSW] Sacred stories, creation stories. Also **bootheram (story)**.

From the Bundjalung language of northern NSW, *budheram*, 'myth, sacred story'. This word is sometimes pronounced 'boodtheray' or spelt 'budgerans'.

1981 M.J. Oakes *Aborigines of our Area* (Introduction) The Kyogle Daily Examiner . . first published many of the legends with information about the exact spots commemorated in the **bootheram stories**. **1989** R. Robinson *The Nearest the White Man Gets* [north coast, NSW] The remainder of the collection comes from the North Coast . . . The poems are loosely grouped with . . material with strong religious elements last. Of course, none of this final group are, in this form, '**butherum**', or sacred stories.

carry *verb* **1** [Chiefly northern Aust.] To know and be responsible (for religious and cultural knowledge). See also HOLD.

This is one of a number of words used to refer to the knowledge of religious or cultural matters which have a sense of physical holding.

1978 K. Palmer & C. McKenna *Somewhere Between Black and White* p. 20 [north-west WA] There was never any question that because his father had been a white man that he would not be allowed to know the secrets, make the law, one day **carry** it himself. **1982** M. Howard *Aboriginal Power* p. 83 [Western Desert] Thus the Pintupi speak of 'holding' a country (e.g. ceremonial rights and obligations associated with a place) or of '**carrying** the Law' (responsibility of sacred knowledge) typically with phrases denoting some sort of physical object and indicating a weight, burden, or responsibility for the 'holder'. **1986** B. Shaw *Countrymen* p. 77 [Kimberley] I **carry** my own word. You can tell that straight as a fucking line, an old line like a fishing line. You know, you take your word straight.

2 [Tas.] To collect or kill (a number of mutton birds in a season).

1986 D. Van Eckert *Muttonbirding on Trefoil* p. 29 [Bass Strait, Tas.] The talk gets round to what kind of season you've had and how your rookeries were working. One would say he **carried** sixty birds and another says he carried seventy.

carry bark *noun* [Groote Eylandt] A piece of bark for carrying a baby.

1981 D. Levitt *Plants and People* p. 15 [Groote Eylandt, NT] Very young babies were carried on pieces of bark called '**carry-barks**' . . the baby was carried lying along the woman's forearm, with its legs tucked under the arm and the head protected by the mother's fingers. A little sand was placed on the bark to absorb moisture.

catch *verb* **1** To cast a spell over (someone). See SING.

Inanimate objects as well as living beings can **catch** a person.

1904 A.W. Howitt *Native Tribes S.-E. Aust.* p. 347 [south-east NSW] The next day the man fell sick, and told his friends that Bunbra had '**caught** him', that is, that he had placed some magical spell on him. **1926** L.C.E. Gee *Bush Tracks & Gold Fields* p. 36 [NT] That fire, that mud, that star **catch** him. Next morning him feel all right. By and bye him say 'Mee too much cold, want um big feller fire' him lay down there—too hot. Him go way longa bush, lay down; and then came back again longa fire. **1980** N. Mitchell & J.C. Anderson *Kubara* p. 12 [northern Qld] But *Bama* musta **catched** him (i.e. sorcerised him). **1993** J. Janson *Gunjies* p. 61 [western NSW] You reckon I've **caught** you? Sung you like the old fellas?

2 To influence (someone).

198- *Bush Stories no. 9* n.p. [Qld] Sometimes Christians stop in dangerous places . . . Maybe we sit down to watch a card game . . . But these places are not good for us. The card game or the beer or dirty thoughts might **catch** us. **1986** B. Shaw *Countrymen* p. 285 [Kimberley] We gotta interest that man because we might get **caught** on some *gadia* one day, ain't it?

ceremony *noun* Aboriginal ceremony and ritual. Also used adjectivally in combination. See BUSINESS.

Ceremony now appears to be the preferred term to 'business'.

1978 J. & P. Read *View of the Past* p. 47 [Elcho Is, NT] It was for **ceremony**, traditional string. **1986** S. Wild *Rom: Aboriginal Ritual of Diplomacy* p. 25 [Arnhem Land] A big mob of balanda (white people) can come to see the **ceremony**; a big mob of an-gigaliya (Aboriginal people) can come too. **1989** *Aboriginal Children* p. 4 [Arnhem Land] They listen to stories by adults: About old times when old people were little, about wars etc. About . . creation stories . . **ceremony**—what they should do. **1995** M. Brady *Giving away the Grog* p. 173 [NT] I bin doing things the right way even in men's **ceremony** side of it got very, very big responsibility.

camp ceremony, a ceremony that is public.

1986 S. Wild (ed.) *Rom: Aboriginal Ritual of Diplomacy* p. 26 [Arnhem Land] Rom is a **camp ceremony**. Everyone—old women, children can look.

ceremony ground, a place where a ceremony or ritual occurs.

1975 *Bunji* (Darwin) July p. 1 [Darwin, NT] In the old days Goondal used to be the **ceremony ground** for initiations.

ceremony man, a person significant in ceremony.

1992 *Canberra Times* 9 Nov. 11/2 The slogan. 'Put a **ceremony man** into government'—referring to a role in Aboriginal culture.

ceremony site, a place where a ceremony or ritual occurs.

1975 *Bunji* (Darwin) July p. 3 [Darwin, NT] One way to avoid paying rates on this **ceremony site** was to call it public parkland!

ceremony time, the time when a significant ceremony is being held.

1978 K. Palmer & C. McKenna *Somewhere Between Black and White* p. 37 [north-west WA] It was **ceremony time**, too, when the young men must finish with being boys.

clear *adjective* [northern Aust.] (Of a person or object) free of any negative or undesirable spiritual associations.

1950 I. Tonnies (ed.) *Beitrage* p. 71 [Daly River, northern NT] After Nym and Mosec had become 'clear', a child was born, whose mother could not find a name for it. **1980** B. Sansom *The Camp at Wallaby Cross* p. 219 [northern NT] Dinghy and outboard together . . would have to be ritually purified, smoked and daubed with ochre to make the objects '**clear**'.

clever *adjective* **1** (Of a person) spiritually powerful. See BOOLYAH-MAN, MABAN.

The powers referred to encompass those of healing, sorcery (including the power over life and death), being able to communicate with non-human living things, being able to fly from one place to another while in a spiritual state, and interacting with the physical world (especially regarding rainmaking). The knowledge **clever** people have of the spiritual world makes them very significant in the serious business of dying, when the spirit must leave the body and the transition must be peaceful both for the dying and for the community left behind. Not all **clever** people will have all these powers; some may have a particular power, such as healing. They have special powers but are not a specialist class of people and remain within the kin structure of the society. Both women and men can be **clever**, but the most powerful sorcerers are male, often called a 'cleverman'.

1897 R. Brothers *Travelling Teeth* p. 9 [south coast, NSW] Berriman Joe, of Ulladulla, tells that his father who was a **clever** doctor (and so is Joe) went to heaven while he was in a trance. **1904** *Journal & Proceedings Royal Society N.S.W.* Vol. XXXVIII p. 255 [NSW] When a **clever** man is out hunting .. he .. talks to the footprints all the time for the purpose of injecting magic into the animal which made them. **1935** *Oceania* Vol. VI. p. 33 [NSW] Several men had the reputation of being '**clever**' men. **1947** *Oceania* Vol. XVII. p. 330 [NSW?] The two women, who were '**clever**', and possessed a certain amount of magical 'power', had used .. a decoy. **1949** *Oceania* (Sydney) Vol. XX (2) Dec. p. 102 [north-west NSW] Besides the medicine man himself there are other aborigines in north-western N.S.W. who are believed to be 'a bit **clever**'. They do not possess the same extraordinary powers as the medicine man, but they are believed to be skilled in malevolent magic. **1983** P. Roe *Gularabulu* p. 8 [north-west WA] That man must be *maban* man he very **clever** man .. **1986** B. Shaw *Countrymen* p. 182 [Kimberley] If you get real magic you go **clever**. **1988** *We have Survived* Poster/n.p. [Arnhem Land] Satan said, 'Have you got power' (magic)? If you want to fight me you have to be a **clever** man. 'No, I haven't got power.' Captain only had a stone axe. **1988** D. Tunbridge *Flinders Ranges Dreaming* p.xliv [Flinders Ranges, SA] Urugi: doctor or **clever** man. He was a man with special powers. (There are none today.) **1990** P. Austin et al. *Lang. & Hist.* p. 250 [Oodnadatta, northern SA] I learned to be a clever man in Kalgoorlie country. That's a doctor place. An old man taught me to be a doctor and everything. My father was a proper **clever** man, very clever [mara muku]. **1990** A. Gaddes *Red Cedar* p. 151 [north coast NSW] The last two elder-doctors (**clever** men) on the Nambucca River .. died about the turn of the century. **1991** J. & S. Erbacher *Aborigines of the Rainforest* p. 30 [northern Qld] Fred is the **clever** fellow or tribal doctor who practises with the Kuku-Yalanji people. The tribal doctor's work includes curing sickness, finding out the causes of death, predicting the future and making and stopping rain. **1994** R. & J. Huggins *Auntie Rita* p. 62 [south-east Qld] Granny Liza Lampton .. was a kind and well-respected lady who was born on the banks of the Burdekin River and was a **clever** woman.

2 (Of animate or inanimate things) possessing spiritual powers.

1901 K.L. Parker in M.Muir *My Bush Book* (1982) p. 97 [NSW?] Old Bootha has what she calls a wi-mouyan, **clever**-stick. It is about six feet long, great lumps of beefwood gum making knobs on it at intervals, between each knob it is painted. Armed with this stick, a piece of crystal, some green twigs, and sometimes a stick with a bunch of feathers on top, and a large flat stone, she goes out to make rain. **1904** *Journal & Proceedings Royal Society N.S.W.* Vol. XXXVIII p. 348 [south-west NSW] On the Upper Lachlan River, flying foxes were supposed to be **clever** fellows who .. used to travel about spying out the location of their enemies. **1972** M.J. Oakes *Richmond Royal Historical Society* p. 2 [north coast, NSW]

A Rainbow Snake on a cliff at Paddy's Flat is a '**clever**'. . spot. **1992** D.B. Rose *Dingo Makes Us Human* p. 228 [Victoria River, NT] Similarly when Hobbles' turkeys would not be shot it became clear that they must have been '**clever**'. **1994** *Encyclop. of Aboriginal Aust.* p. 641 [northern Vic.] This huge Murray cod was also **clever**, and he made the River [Murray] (starting at the top end).

culture *noun* Aboriginal beliefs, values, attitudes and rituals. See also LAW.

Culture when used by Aboriginal people is generally closer to the anthropological or sociological sense of the word than to its popular meaning. It is also used more widely and more frequently by Aboriginal people because of the problems associated with being a minority population. The people of such a culture are more often called upon to justify themselves, to claim or demarcate boundaries, even to fight for cultural survival, than is the dominant population. For example, Aboriginal culture in Australia is often defined by non-Aboriginal people, who sometimes then go on to measure the 'Aboriginality' of particular Aboriginal people or situations. Non-Aboriginal Australians have been slow to accept that Aboriginal culture (like all cultures) is dynamic, and is not fixed as it was in 1788. Older Aboriginal people are also conscious of the pressures on younger people to adopt the pervasive Western culture.

1975 R.J. Merritt *Cake Man* p. 58 [south-west WA] Forget all that shit about giving me back my **culture**. **1978** J. & P. Read *View of the Past* p. 231 [Ngukurr, north-east NT] Now . . I find this better way: not to take your culture into another man's **culture**, in another man's door. **1980s** *North Coast Health Team* Poster/n.p. [NSW] 'Wanna hit' 'No way bud—that's not Koorie **culture**.' **1981** *Cent. Aust. Land Rights News* (Alice Springs) Dec. p. 13 [central Aust.] A lot of people put their head down poor bugger, shamed. I say, yeah, I got my **culture**, I been through initiation. That's why people here got more power. **1981** *Puggana News* (Launceston) Mar. p. 4 [Tas.] Our **culture** and dreaming our very being, Must go to the future forever appearing. **1988** J. Harkins *English as 'Two-way' Language* p. 260 [central Aust.] That is the convergence of the English word **culture** with the Arrernte *Kaltye* 'knowledge, learning, wisdom'. **1988** A. Moffatt (ed.) *Aboriginal Deaths in Custody* (Transcript) p. 241 [south-east Vic.] The elders is our main link to our **culture** and we just look after them. **1988** *La Perouse* p. 13 [La Perouse, central coast, NSW] One family was still making the artefacts. They kept the **culture** going. **1989** B. Neidjie *Story about Feeling* p. 119 [Arnhem Land] Oh, we got **culture**, we got story, we got 'business', we got oh! So you stay there, I stay here. **1991** J. Reid & P. Trompf *Health Aboriginal Aust.* p. 118 **Culture** is not people's song and dance and speech, it is an attitude and way of doing things. You can't kill culture until you kill Aboriginal people. **1992** D.B. Rose *Dingo Makes Us Human* p. 69 [north-west NT] To be different . . is to have a different shape . . . Out of that shape emerge other differences—animals of one shape, one species, share a language, a set of ceremonies, certain kinds of food, a way of life. In Kriol this specific way of life is termed '**culture**'. **1993** E. Crawford *Over my Tracks* p. 68 [western NSW] No one from the Aboriginal Protection Board didn't give one damn for our **culture** or laws.

cut out tree *noun* [SA] A tree from which a boomerang is made.

1990 A. Pring (ed.) *Women of the Centre* p. 80 [Ooldea, northern SA] He's got rifle too and he could see big tree—**cut out tree**—you know they cutting boomerangs and all.

dance *noun* Aboriginal ceremonial dance.

In Aboriginal society, ceremonial dance is a spiritual, educational and social experience. Body decorations, music (mostly percussive) and singing are the accompaniments of dance. Dance presents understandings of life and religion, retells for the community significant social happenings, and enacts particular spiritual events. For example, at a northern cattle station, the incompetence of a new station hand might be reproduced in dance form for the amusement of the camp. The crash of an aeroplane in the Gulf country and the ultimate rescue of one of its crew, led to the creation of a long song and dance cycle, in which the reproduction of an aeroplane form was a central part. Dances are also performed for initiation rituals, for the increase of plants and animals, and for reconciliation of communities. Dance can be part of the interaction of the physical and spiritual worlds which characterises Aboriginal ritual. Contemporary culture now also includes dance festivals, where different groups perform for each other and for non-Aboriginal audiences, often with modern adaptations of traditional materials.

1971 K. Gilbert *End of Dreamtime* p. 9 [NSW] They called me, Kalari, a 'Pommy' and 'Gub', laughed at my speaking, laughed when I tried to join in their song and **dance**. **1978** R. Tonkinson *Mardudjera Aborigines* p. 100 [Western Desert] The 'big' **dances** that come at the end of each day's performance may not be witnessed by the newest initiates. **1988** J. Davis *Barungin—Smell the Wind* p. 44 [south-west WA] **Dances** are gone, laws gone, lingos just about gone. **1988** M.C. Sharpe et al, *An Introduction to the Bundjalung Language and its Dialects* p. 27 [northern NSW] *To dream* (a song or a **dance**) means to get the idea or inspiration for it from *the dreaming*, not necessarily while sleeping. You lie down quietly in the grass and *catch* it. **1989** J. Thomson *Reaching Back* p. 15 [northern Qld] They know part of our **dance**. We know part of their dance. **1989** R.M. Baker *Land is Life* p. 244 [Borroloola, north-east NT] He recalls how they could have 'one day, or two day off, they have the **dance**, go back to work'. **1991** *Aboriginal History* (Canberra) XV. i. p. 8 [northern Qld] Our lot Kubbi, they'll have their own **dance** too. A lovely dance. **1993** E. Crawford *Over my Tracks* p. 37 [western NSW] Kids who chose to concentrate on the **dances** for corroborees had a different teacher.

dance man a leading figure in a dance or a person in charge of a ceremony. Also **dancing man**.

1980 B. Sansom *The Camp at Wallaby Cross* p. 222 [Darwin, NT] From [that] day . . Tommy Atkins became that **Dancing Man** from the day of his public declaration of intent. **1986** J. Davis *No Sugar* p. 66 [south-west WA] You song man, you fella **dance man**.

dance *verb* To perform an Aboriginal dance.

To **dance** can mean not only to participate in an entertaining or aesthetic activity, but to participate in a spiritual activity which can affect the physical world. Part of a ritual may involve particular relatives dancing 'for' the person to whom it is so directed, the act of dancing effecting change in the person.

1978 J. & P. Read *View of the Past* p. 226 [central NT] 'You got to **dance** now. You got to have your proper mark, you know, proper culture.' **1983** G. Gleave *Battling for Basics* p. 3 The two ladies had been **dancing** the whole night for a relative. **1985** B. Rosser *Dreamtime Nightmares* p. 63 [northern Qld] My mother and father would **dance**. They all got their own tribal mark. **1987** D. Bate *Language Education Course*, Deakin University p. 12 [central Aust.] Sasha: And what they gotta **dance** for na? Antronese: For our brother, they gotta make-em strong man na. **1989** B. Morris *Domesticating Resistance* p. 141 [northern NSW] She didn't **dance** for me while I was out in the bush. **1993** G. Koch *Kaytetye Country* p. 115 [central NT] Ivy knew that awelye [women's corroboree] and **danced**!

dangerous *adjective* [Chiefly recorded in north and central areas but probably also common in the south and south-west] **1** Hazardous because of the possible effect of spiritual powers.

In the Aboriginal landscape, the spiritual world is manifested in physical space, and in certain places in this landscape such forces are particularly powerful. Such a place might be a waterhole where an ancestral spirit, a 'dreaming' is present, or a ceremonial ground where secret ceremonies are held, or a cave containing sacred rock paintings. Some of these places may be approached by the whole community if people are aware of the possible dangers, and how to circumvent them—for instance, by asking permission of the spiritual owner of the waterhole. Other places are open only to those who have the right to be there—for example, members of a particular clan, senior initiated men at a men's site, senior initiated women at a site closed to all but women. For those who trespass on a **dangerous** place, the spiritual forces present there can bring about sickness and even death.

1972 M.J. Oakes *Richmond Royal Historical Society* p. 2 [northern NSW] A Rainbow Snake on a cliff at Paddy's Flat is a 'clever' or '**dangerous**' spot. **1978** L.R. Hiatt *Aust. Aboriginal Concepts* p. 98 [Arnhem Land] **Dangerous** places exist wherever life spirit is concentrated. They will always threaten the life and health of the living who approach without sufficient preparation and protection. **1981** D. Levitt *Plants and People* p. 52 [Groote Eylandt] Certain areas were known as '**dangerous** places'. These were ceremonial grounds where magic rites could be performed to hurt people . . . People doing this had to be very careful, as, if not done properly, the magic could rebound back on them, with disastrous results. This is why these areas were called 'dangerous places'. **1985** S. Cane & O. Stanley *Land Use and Resources in Desert Homelands* p. 89 [Western Desert] Kesteven . . recorded that Mt Theo was thought of as a '**dangerous**' place for women and children. **1988** P. Taylor *After 200 Years* p. 165 [Arnhem Land] That place belongs to two Rainbow Snakes, that place is too **dangerous** for kids. **1994** *Encyclop. of Aboriginal Aust.* p. 257 The source of human life is a place, created in the Dreamtime, from which the spirits go out to enter women, and to which, after death, those spirits return. Such places are usually extremely **dangerous**.

2 Having hazardous consequences, physical or spiritual.

In the first citation, 'blackfeller Law' is seen as **dangerous** because breaking the Law could result in injury or death; in the second the dance is seen as **dangerous** because it was intended to bring harm to another.

1986 B. Shaw *Countrymen* p. 187 [Kimberley] That blackfeller Law is a bit **dangerous**, a bit hard, and the church is a bit easier. **1987** N. Williams *Two Laws* p. 105 [Arnhem Land] In a similar vein a woman observing her brother perform a '**dangerous** dance', a ritual that signified the continuation of his hostility towards another man, said 'I don't like to see that brother'.

Darling River talk *noun* [western NSW] The Paakantji language.

The ancestral country of the Paakantji people is along the southern Darling River in western NSW.

1984 *Aboriginal History* (Canberra) Vol. 8 Pt 1–2 p. 38 The language called *paawantkay* in *Ngiyampaa* is referred to in English as Paakantji, or as '**Darling River talk**'.

death bird *noun* A bird that tells of a death.

> **1988** A. Gray *The 'Death Bird'* p. 3 For many Aboriginal people . . fatalism takes the form of beliefs concerning portents of death. The most ominous . . is the '**death bird**': it is known by that name to Aboriginal people in the study and we talked to no-one who knew any other European name for it. **1991** L.M. Wilkinson *Aboriginality* p. 241 [south-west Vic] The Gunditjmara made a banner depicting . . a picture of an owl with the words the '**death bird**' inscribed on the banner. **1994** R. & J. Huggins *Auntie Rita* p. 113 [south-east Queensland] When someone dies in our Aboriginal community, we believe we get a sign. There is a strong belief that the messages come through an animal or bird. We call it the **death bird**. . . I got up early one morning and . . I saw a black crow. . . His arms were outstretched and the rest of his body was straight. It was the sign of the cross and suddenly his beak raised up and he looked right at me. I knew Mama had left us.

djubal *noun* [northern NSW] Witchetty grub(s).

From the Bundjalung language of northern NSW *jubal*, a witchetty grub that lives in acacia trees.

> **1989** D. Walker *Me and You* p. 54 [north coast, NSW] We call them **djubal**, white people call them witchetty grubs.

doc doc *noun* See DOCTOR.

doctor *noun* A spiritually powerful person whose powers include healing; a 'clever person'. See CLEVER.

The recorded use of **doctor** by Europeans to refer to Aboriginal 'clever' people dates from 1834 (see below for the first recorded example). It was also applied in British English to persons of similar spiritual and social significance in other non-European cultures—sometimes in the form 'witchdoctor'. It is interesting to note that the sense of 'doctor' as a 'learned person' is older in general use than the narrower contemporary sense of 'doctor' as 'medical doctor'.

> **1834** G. Bennett *Wanderings N.S.W.* Vol. 1 p. 190 [NSW] Kradgee Kibba, or **Doctor** Stone. **1893** *Transactions Royal Society S.A.* (Adelaide) Vol. XVII p. 260 [Daly River, NT] 'No! . . him no more want im hole, that one **doctor**, him too much savey no more hole.' **1914** F.A. Fitzpatrick *Peeps into the Past* p. 30 [Manning River, northern NSW] Johnny Martin the '**doctor**' had far more influence. **1978** K. Palmer *Somewhere Between Black and White* p. 8 [Pilbara, WA] The old **doctor** fellows, the *mubans* they could tell you when it would rain and when it would stay fine. **1989** E. Jones *The Story of the Falling Star* n.p. [western NSW] Well, Leah, a miikika is a **doctor**. They have powers of healing people. They're also like pastors . . people go to them with their problems and ask their advice. **1992** R.L. Ginibi *Real Deadly* p. 5 [north coast, NSW] While he worked, we were looked after by Uncle Ernie Ord, tribal **doctor** and clever man.

doc-doc, a spiritually powerful person.

> **1859** J.D. Mereweather *Diary Working Clergyman* p. 109 Each tribe has an individual who is set apart to perform the functions of medicinal man and magician. Him they call '**Doc-doc**'.

doctor bloke, a spiritually powerful person.

> **1979** M. Heppell *A Black Reality* p. 84 [Arnhem Land] The actual and purported ministrations of '**doctor blokes**' vary widely, but they generally have in common a magical control over a person, the possession of a personal trace of the victim and various internal 'operations' on the person which eventuate in his death.

doctor bloke business, the activities of a spiritually powerful person.

1979 M. Heppell *A Black Reality* p. 84 [Arnhem Land] The fear of '**doctor bloke business**' has been the single most often expressed fear given as justification for various defensive behaviours, such as securing one's house at night.

doctor country, an area that is known for its number of learned people.

1990 P. Austin et al. *Lang. & Hist.* p. 251 [Oodnadatta, northern SA] *Mundulu* and Turkey Creek, the same one. A lot of blackfellers are there. That's the **doctor country**. They have a different language. I can't catch it. Warramala, they're desert people. And a different lingo again, Warramanga. They're the fellers who gave me that.

doctor man, a spiritually powerful man.

1978 *Yura Aboriginal* (Kent Town) Jan. p. 4 [SA] We recorded the site where the '**doctor man**' buried some wild men on the bank of Chambers creek. **1978** J. & P. Read *View of the Past* p. 85 [Western Desert] And they, they picked two old blokes up here longa Mt. Doreen, .. **doctor man** you know.

doctor place, an area where there is a strong tradition of spiritual knowledge and teaching.

1990 P. Austin et al. *Lang. & Hist.* p. 250 [Oodnadatta, northern SA] I learned to be a clever man in Kalgoorlie country. That's a **doctor place**. An old man taught me to be a doctor and everything. My father was a proper clever man, very clever [mara muku].

doctor power, spiritual power.

1990 P. Austin et al. *Lang. & Hist.* p. 251 [Oodnadatta, northern SA] I still have the **doctor Power** a long way yet.

doctor woman, a spiritually powerful woman.

1990 P. Austin et al. *Lang. & Hist.* p. 252 [Oodnadatta, northern SA] All the dead fellers were long time ago when I was a young feller. They wanted to be doctors. Some blackfeller doctors pull out the bone. There was a **doctor woman**. She pulled them out like nothing.

doctor *verb* [Recorded in SA but used elsewhere] To exert spiritual powers over somebody, particularly to heal.

1990 P. Austin et al. *Lang. & Hist.* p. 250 [Oodnadatta, northern SA] A long time a doctor wanted me to **doctor** another man in Adelaide. He was proper sick. He was a white man. I felt him. I went through and made him all right—pulled it out. That was the Thing now. He might have been lost or cut. I pulled it out there. I gave it to him, 'Ah, a'right, finish. Ow you feel this morning?' 'Oh just gotta the cold'. That was a whitefeller. I doctored him in the morning outside the hospital.

dog man *noun* A person knowledgable in the spiritual and material world of dingoes and dogs.

Knowledge here connects the spiritual and material world, so that knowledge of dog 'dreamings' carries into the knowledge of ordinary dogs.

1992 D.B. Rose *Dingo Makes Us Human* p. 29 Old Tim is an owner of country rich with Dingo Dreamings; he is a '**dog man**' *par excellence*, with an intimate concern for, and understanding of, dingoes and dogs.

dream *noun* **1** A collection of events beyond living memory which shaped the physical, spiritual and moral world and which is still manifested in and sustains the present. See DREAMING.

1986 B. Shaw *Countrymen* p. 33 [Kimberley] My other, blackfeller, name was Munnai (Munniim). My father put that, from the **Dream** now. **1989** B. Neidjie *Story about Feeling* p. 114 [Arnhem Land] You got to put im on yellow clay because all that **dream**, all that story is there . . . That painting you say . . 'That lovely painting'. **1990** O. Noonuccal *Aust. Legends and Landscapes* p. 128 [Tas.] 'What's a Neaggara Pe-na Granpop?' asks Rosie. 'It's a dream spear of the spirits my girl,' Granpop gives the answer. 'Yuh see, this Neaggara Pe-na, when it kills Mayworick, it brings his **dream** to life'. **1991** D.B. Rose *Hidden Histories* p. 108 [Victoria River, north-west NT] Only by *puwarraja* [Dreaming]. They followed by **Dream** . . by Dream they followed now that one.

2 A state of trance or sleep in which one can come to an awareness of some spiritual event or understanding.

1933 *Oceania* (Sydney) Vol. IV (III) June p. 444 [Kimberley] In all three tribes, a father 'finds' in a **dream** a spirit-child. **1978** C. Coulhard *Mt Chambers* p. 14 [Flinders Ranges, SA] There might be a witch-doctor man, 'yura-wungi', he goes into a **dream** to follow the eagle who has left a red mark along his trail.

dream *verb* **1** To be in a heightened state of perception in which one is able to apprehend spiritual matters.

1988 M.C. Sharpe et al. *An Introduction to the Bundjalung Language and its Dialects* p. 27 [northern NSW] To **dream** (a song or a dance) means to get the idea or inspiration for it from *the dreaming*, not necessarily while sleeping. You lie down quietly in the grass and *catch* it. **1989** B. Neidjie *Story about Feeling* p. 19 [Arnhem Land] And when you sleep you might **dream** something. You might dream moon, or you might dream water, storm. You might dream tree, wind . . . That dream e's true.

2 To give (something) psychic power. See SING.

1986 B. Shaw *Countrymen* p. 200 [Kimberley, WA] I'd say, 'I **dream** you, that tin tobbaca, you givim to me, got something.' [that is, he'd sung the tobacco to give it the power of a love-potion.]

dreaming *noun* **1** A collection of events beyond living memory which shaped the physical, spiritual and moral world and which is still manifested in and sustains the present.

From the word 'dreamtime', first used by Frank Gillen as a translation of the Arrernte *altyerre*. The English word 'dreaming' lacks the associations of power, significance and creative force that this concept holds in Aboriginal culture, but it is now established in Aboriginal and Australian English. It is also sometimes used in Australian English in a trivialised form to refer to non-Aboriginal history and cultural matters.

1948 C.P. Mountford *Brown Men & Red Sand* p. 23 [northern Aust.] In the beginning, or the '**Dreaming** Times' as old Nantawana poetically described the creation period. **1951** E. Hill *Territory* p. 346 [northern NT] Laws, legends, languages, the corybantic corroborees, every tribal rite and belief belong to 'blackfella **dreamin**'. **1961** M. Kiddle *Men of Yesterday* p. 9 At all times he was close to the time of **dreaming**, because the rocks and trees, the creeks and waterholes had all played their parts in the legends. **1979** W.E.H. Stanner *White Man* *got no Dreaming* p. 24 I can recall one intelligent old man who said to me, with a cadence almost as though he had been speaking verse: White man got no **dreaming**, Him go 'nother way. White man, him go different. Him got road belong himself. **1981** *Puggana News* (Launceston) Mar. p. 4 [Tas.] Our culture and **dreaming** our very being, Must go to the future forever appearing. **1985** I. & T. Donaldson *Seeing First Australs.* p. 207 Discussing the history of [Canberra] and being shown archaeological sites and nineteenth-century pictures of old Aborigines .. Gurrmanamana said that once, long ago, Aborigines had lived here and that they would have known these attributes of the land which still existed somewhere, but that now, in his own words, 'This country bin lose 'im **Dreaming**.' **1989** B. Neidjie *Story about Feeling* p. 78 [Arnhem Land] This time White-European must come to Aborigine, listen Aborigine and understand it. Understand that culture, secret, what **dreaming**. **1990** *North West Tel.* (Port Hedland) 26 Sept. p. 3/3 [north-west WA] During the four day walk, guardian and law-keeper Paddy Roe taught ancient laws, bush food collection, bush medicine and the **Dreaming**—an ongoing state which draws together past, present and future.

2 (As adjective) having **dreaming** significance.

1976 *Identity* (Sydney) Jan. p. 14 [Arnhem Land] We did not want to cross a **dreaming** river in case we were drowned. **1988** *La Perouse* p. 3 [La Perouse, NSW] The other Moreton Bay fig trees are .. called '**Dreaming** Trees'. **1989** B. Neidjie *Story about Feeling* p. 80 [Arnhem Land] Can't break Law. The Ring-place must stay way e started because that Ring-place is important, just about like Djang .. **dreaming** place. **1991** D.B. Rose *Hidden Histories* p. 251 [Victoria River, north-west NT] Allan, just going on to something different now—forget about that **dreaming** talk.

3 A dreaming being, one who shaped the landscape; a totemic ancestor, hence the totem itself and the particular sacred knowledge associated with it.

1937 *Mankind* (Sydney) Jan. p. 51 Indeed, in many parts the totem is also called the '**dreaming**'. **1950** I. Tonnies (ed.) *Beitrage* p. 68 [Darwin, NT] That is, a person's cult-totem, '**dreaming**' (or *dorlk*) is the 'dreaming' of the locality in which his (or her) conception totem or *maroi* .. is 'found' .. As one informant put the matter with three of his children: 'Got no other *dorlk* and *maroi* (cult and conception totems) for these, because sit down here'. **1955** M. Durack *Keep him my Country* (1966) p. 75 [Kimberley] The goanna would be his '**dreaming**', and this his spirit place. **1983** D. Bell *Daughters of Dreaming* p. 22 [NT] At other points we would drive quietly so as not to disturb the **dreamings** who had passed through this area. **1984** M. Gumbert *Neither Justice nor Reason* p. 159 [NT] A travelling **dreaming** may pass through estates of several clans . . . These clans are said in Pidgin to be 'company' for Rain, and may run the dreaming together in ritual. **1986** *Austral. Aboriginal Studies* no. 1 p. 24 [NT] In one community an old man asked a friend of mine, 'Do you think that **Dreamings** go to heaven? You can see that they are all dying, and do you think they will go to heaven?' **1992** R.L. Ginibi *Real Deadly* p. 71 [north coast, NSW] What had happened to the people; had they all moved away to find their **dreaming**? Did some of the old elders still live there? **1994** *Encyclop. of Aboriginal Aust.* Vol. 1 p. 305 [central Aust.] My dreaming is the kangaroo Dreaming, the eagle Dreaming and budgerigar Dreaming so I have three kinds of **Dreamings** in my jukurrpa and I have to hang on to it.

dreaming track, the path followed by a dreaming being travelling through the landscape.

The dreaming track exists as much as an event, the travelling of the dreaming being, as it does as a place.

1978 *Transcript of Proc. Alyawarra Land Claim* Oct. Pt 2 p. 45 [south-east NT] It will be the transparency showing **Dreaming tracks** in the claim area. **1979** *N.S.W. Parl. Papers* (1980-81) 3rd Session, IV. 756/2 [NSW] That is a line where the old people go and the young fellows are in the middle . . . The line goes up in the mountain and that track is sacred, that is a **dreaming track**. **1991** *North West Tel.* (Port Hedland) 15 May p. 1/6 [north-west WA] Parngurr is an important sacred site on the **Dreaming Track** from Roebourne, through Karunjini, the Hamersley Range, Marble Bar, Nullagine, Pangu, Well 33 and Kiwi Kurra toward Alice Springs. **1993** D. Hodge *Did you meet any Malagas?* p. 48 [northern NT] Traditionally, Larrakia society is linked with Gagadju people and our **Dreaming tracks** travel from Kakadu, come up through Darwin, and go down to Port Keats and onwards.

4 A site of dreaming significance.

1943 W.E. Harney *Taboo* p. 199 [northern Aust.] Their religion, wherever it came from in the past, is now bound up in those '**dreamings**', the traditional sites and memorials of the great deeds of the culture heroes of the past. **1948** A. Marshall *Ourselves Writ Strange* p. 198 My dreaming different. It near old camp, long time ago. Near running water. White people, he call it '**Dreaming**'. We call it 'Maraiin'. When I die, I go longa my Maraiin, long running water. **1950** I. Tonnies (ed.) *Beitrage* p. 68 [Daly River, NT] It is associated with '**dreamings**', that is, places sanctified by mythical events. **1952** Miller & Rutter *Child Artists* p. 22 Every member of the tribe was allotted at birth by a process of divination, not only a section of his country that was his spirit home—his '**dreaming**'—but his particular relatives in the plant and animal world. **1964** D. Lockwood *Lizard Eaters* p. 66 [Western Desert] The place was now a sacred **Dreaming**, a totemic centre of great significance in the tribal culture.

dreamtime *noun* See DREAMING.

The term was first used as a translation by Frank Gillen of the Arrernte language of central Australia *altyerre*. It is used by both Aboriginal and non-Aboriginal people but is included here because of its significance to Aboriginal society. The use of the word *dreamtime*, which lacks in its English language associations the power of the original concept, underlines the limited understanding of Europeans of this aspect of Aboriginal culture. **Dreamtime** is now sometimes used in other Australian English in a trivialised sense to mean 'before recorded history' or 'unreal time'.

1896 B. Spencer *Report Horn Scientific Exped. Central Aust.* Pt 1 p. 50 [NT] They say that what they call the Alchèringa or as Mr Gillen appropriately renders it the '**dream times**' a certain noted warrior journeyed to the east. **1958** R. Robinson *Black-Feller White-Feller* p. 42 This was a song of the '**dreamtime**' when Narait screamed down from the paperbarks and told the blacks how they could live in the desert. **1963** D. Attenborough *Quest under Capricorn* p. 159 [northern Aust.] Although the **Dreamtime** was in the past, it is also co-existent with the present, and a man, by performing the rituals, can become one with his 'dreaming' and experience eternity. It is to seek this mystical union that the men enact the ceremonies. **1977** P. Popescu *Last Wave* p. 50 The earth, the sky and all living beings had been created by spirits during the so-called **Dreamtime**, which incorporated all their major myths and miraculous happenings. The Dreamtime was bygone and prehistoric, and yet it was present still, because it had a flow of its own, separated from the time of normal daily activities. **1978** *Cent. Aust. Land Rights News* (Alice Springs) Jan. p. 2 [central Aust.] My **dreamtime** country, my dreaming is a Storm Bird (Karrakurr) and Brown Snake, the quiet one, blackfellows call 'em Coonatjewi. **1984** *Puggana News* (Launceston) Feb. p. 10 [Tas.] Aboriginal Spirit, **Dreamtime** is what is real. **1991** *North West Tel.* (Port Hedland) 21 Aug.

p. 1/1 [north-west WA] Lesley Salt ponds already covered **dreamtime** land and the people were not consulted years ago when the ponds were first established.

dreamtime story, a narrative of the dreamtime. See DREAMING.

1981 *Kimberley Land Council* (Derby) Mar. p. 21 [Kimberley, WA] When they first came to this land they saw Aborigine painted up in his **dreamtime story** and they shot him in his dreamtime. **1990** *Koori News* Vol. II no. 1 p. 21 [Sydney, NSW] **Dreamtime story**—the creation of the shark and the stingray. **1991** *Amanbidji Land Claim* 21 Aug. [northern NT] Is this country important for you? . . . Why is it important for you? . . . Well, just because it got my **dreamtime story** and everything I know all that, you know, so I can use it. Any time I go for ceremony, I use it.

dreamtime story place, a place significant in a dreamtime story.

1978 L.R. Hiatt *Aust. Aboriginal Concepts* p. 97 [Arnhem Land] Some **dreamtime story places** are thought to be extremely dangerous, others are only relatively so.

dreamtime track, the path followed by a totemic ancestor.

1934 *Oceania* (Sydney) Vol. V (2) Dec. p. 173 [NT] The importance of the '**dreamtime**' **tracks** is seen in the custom of approaching sacred totemic and heroic sites by the actual path believed to have been followed by the hero or ancestor.

dulugal *noun* [south-east Aust.] A hairy man, a monstrous spirit figure. Also **doolagarl, dooliga, dulagal, thooligal**. See HAIRY MAN 1.

1910 *Bulletin* (Sydney) 1 Sept. p. 44/2 A **thooligal** . . can only be driven away by incantations, which none but a bangal (a blackfellow doctor) knows how to say. **1969** L. Hercus *Language of Vict.* p. 392 [Vic.] **dulugal** = wild man, killer. **1970** R. Robinson *Altjeringa* p. 12 [south coast, NSW] He is called the **Doolagarl**. He seizes men, tears them apart, and eats them raw. **1990** D.B. Rose *Gulaga* p. 64 [south coast, NSW] I am authorised to discuss only the type called **Dulagal**. Yuin people say that this type of being is also called Yowie. **1993** J. Janson *Gunjies* p. 41 [NSW] He says he seen **Dooliga**, you know yowie, the hairy man.

dzundzedi *noun* [south-east Qld] A small spirit being. Also **jonjardi, junjidis**.

Probably from a south-eastern Queensland Aboriginal language.

1984 C. Allridge *Aboriginal Eng.* p. 105 [south-east Qld] **Dzundzedi** and njundzi. These refer to little mythical beings who haunt the area around Woorabinda. **1984** L. Fogarty *Ngutji* Dedication page [south-east Qld] Under the stones live little hairy people with shiny eyes, called the 'net-nets'. You told me that you have them up your way too, called '**junjidis**'. **1985** *Nelen Yubu* (Melville Island) Spring no. 24 p. 15 The belief in the **jonjardi** is very widespread. He is described as a little hairy man, only knee high. A friend of children, he is frequently seen by them and plays with them when they are ill. Adults don't interfere with the play because while they know that the children are safe with the *jonjardi*, if they did approach the *jonjardi* may disappear and carry the children away.

elder *noun* A person of recognised authority within the community, normally an older person. See COMMUNITY.

In all societies with an oral culture, such as Aboriginal society was before the invasion and is still to a great extent, knowledge is not separated from human relationships. The history, beliefs, and knowledge belonging to that society are held in the living memory of its members. In this circumstance it is the older members who have the greatest knowledge and the greatest understanding. The term **elder** has been used similarly in Australian English since 1879.

1973 M. Fennel & A. Grey *Nucoorilma* p. 98 [northern NSW] The **elder** used the term 'hatred' to describe those who had married outside the kinship pattern . . for the hurt to their elders was too great. **1980** P. Pepper *You Are What You Make Yourself* p. 33 [south-west Vic.] Well, this lakes tribesman told the **elders** he wanted one of these girls. **1986** *Messagestick* (Cairns) Oct. p. 16 [south-west Qld] Also when someone died in a particular family the **elders** would smoke all of the family members. **1988** C. Mattingley & K. Hampton (eds.) *Survival in Our Own Land* p. 220 [Flinders Ranges, SA] Each home had its hedge of grey bush and we used to hide in them and play tricks on the **elders** going past. We used to make pea shooters out of reeds. **1988** A. Moffatt (ed.) *Aboriginal Deaths in Custody* (Transcript) p. 133 [south-east Vic.] He was an **elder** of the Kernai people. **1992** R.L. Ginibi *Real Deadly* p. 1 [north coast, NSW] Gone are all our tribal ways, only three **elders** left; all dubays, no old nugthungs, to tell our stories and legends or give us our laws. **1991** L.M. Wilkinson *Aboriginality* p. 187 [south-west Vic.] To be regarded as an **elder** it is necessary to be associated closely with Framlingham and to be descended from one of the original Framlingham families. **1991** *Dugite* i. p. 7 [south-west WA] **Elders** of clan groups have given Yothu Yindi permission to perform traditional songs and dances outside of their communities. **1992** *Puggana News* (Launceston) Dec. p. 19 [Tas.] A group of **Elders** from around Hobart enjoyed a trip to Oyster Cove. **1993** J. Janson *Gunjies* p. 51 [western NSW] **Elders** wanted to pull out the nulla nullas and clout em.

elder doctor, a spiritually powerful person.

1990 A. Gaddes *Red Cedar* p. 151 [northern NSW] The last two **elder-doctors** (clever men) on the Nambucca River . . died about the turn of the century.

fat *noun* Kidney fat, ritually removed to obtain destructive power over another person, to kill the victim, or to use the victim's kidney fat for sorcery over another. See KIDNEY FAT.

Most of these references are historical rather than current, but the nature of the ritual means that it is something less likely to be discussed or to occur now.

1845 *Sentinel* (Sydney) 5 Feb. 3/3 [Melbourne, Vic.] Gendin, alias Jack Weatherly, (a black well known in Melbourne) was bit by a snake and died; before death he described the distance and the country to the north, saying, 'that a black of that country had got into the snake and taken his **fat**'. **1880** (Mrs) J. Smith *Booandik Tribe* p. 9 [south-east SA] He came running towards me . . rushed into the house. The young woman said, 'Him cranky'. The fellow came out with a gun in his hand, and pointing it towards Woakwyne . . said 'If I could I would kill him and have his **fat**'. **1904** A.W. Howitt *Native Tribes S.-E. Aust.* p. 376 [south-east Vic.] When a spear was rubbed over with such **fat** it became, as the Yuin say, 'poisoned', that is, infected with evil. **1986** B. Shaw *Countrymen* pp. 45-6 [NT] 'Singing' was done by getting the boots, trousers or shirts belonging to the white man, rubbing in bullock fat mixed with blackfeller **fat** taken from the kidney of a live man while he sleeps—he dies later—and burning the clothes. The white man's body swelled up.

feather foot *noun* A person with 'clever' powers used on a mission of revenge. Also **feather footer**. See CLEVER.

The name comes from the 'shoes' made from feathers which it is said such people wear in order to disguise their tracks.

1966 M. Brown *Jimberi Track* p. 78 Ralph was thinking: Might be **featherfoots** watchin' me that side! **1980** *N.S.W. Parl. Papers* (1980-81) 3rd Sess. IV. p. 1666 [NSW] At Kinchela we had a **feather foot**, a Kadachi man, and he came to do the programme . . . Normally Aborigines are frightened of these people. **1982** J. Davis *The Dreamers* p. 129 [south-west WA] Aw Mum, he's talkin' about **feather foots**. **1987** S. Morgan *My Place* p. 177 [WA] We were going through a gorge when the **feather foots** . . began to whistle . . the whistling means they want you to talk. **1991** L.M. Wilkinson *Aboriginality* p. 240 [south-west Vic.] The people from South Australia were sometimes described as 'feather-footers'.

fingertalk *noun* [northern Aust.] A system of sign language using the fingers.

Sign languages are used in many parts of Aboriginal Australia, except in the southeast and south-west. They are complete if simplified languages, based on the spoken language of the user, and are used whenever spoken language is inappropriate. This can be while hunting, in ceremonies, and in societies such as that of the Warlpiri and other peoples of central western NT, which place a ban of silence upon bereaved relatives. Warlpiri women may have a ban of silence placed upon them for more than a year; consequently **fingertalk** has been developed among them to a greater degree than elsewhere.

1936 'L. Kaye' *Black Wilderness* p. 166 Talk to him, Kombi . . . He might have a word or two of your lingo. Anyway you've both got hands for **finger-talk**. **1947** V.C. Hall *Bad Medicine* p. 147 [northern NT] Menikman glanced back and shot up a hand in a 'finger-talk' question. **1962** D. Lockwood *I, Aboriginal* p. 121 [northern NT] **Finger-talk** is also constant among men who speak the same tongue. It not only saves unnecessary speech but has the added advantage that evil spirits cannot hear it. **1976** C.D. Mills *Hobble Chains and Greenhide* p. 173 He waved to me in 'finger-talk' that he was set. **1976** J. Mirritji *My People's Life* p. 63 [Arnhem Land] I tried to say a few more words with my hands. I don't know if the driver understood my **fingertalk**.

fingertalk *verb* To communicate using a system of sign language.

1956 T. Ronan *Moleskin Midas* p. 48 [northern Aust.] I was **finger talking** with one old King and he is bringing two singers, one for me and one for you, up to the top end of the waterhole. I hear the Boss sayin' we'll be shiftin' camp tomorrow, and you and me will be able to sneak up and sleep with them every night.

firestick way *adverb* In the traditional manner. From the firestick, carried by Aboriginal people from one campsite to another. See TRADITIONAL.

The fire, the hearth, is the centre of an Aboriginal campsite. In some Aboriginal languages, the word for 'camp' is the same as the word for 'fire' and 'firewood'— for example the Nyungar language of south-west WA, *karl*, 'fire, firewood'.

Firestick was first recorded in 1804 and used by the colonists to describe the smouldering sticks carried by Aboriginal people from campsite to campsite.

1990 A. Pring (ed.) *Women of the Centre* p. 135 [northern SA] I got married **firestick way**, not the Christian way.

follow *verb* [Aust. but more common in northern and central areas.] To be associated with the beliefs, rules and conditions of life belonging to a particular direction, sometimes of choice, as in **follow** the Mission, and sometimes by inheritance, as in **follow** the father. Also **follow up**.

This is used in non-Aboriginal English as 'follow' the rules, but Aboriginal English has extended the sense to include the sense of inheritance. This is also an example of the Aboriginal English use of spatial language for conceptual matters. See CARRY, HOLD, RUN.

1880 L. Fison & A.W. Howitt *Kamilaroi & Kurnai* p. 73 [south-east Vic.] But there can be no possibility of mistake as to maternity, and therefore it seems natural enough that children should '**follow** the mother', as several of our correspondents phrased it; in other words, that they should be of the mother's class . . not of the father's. **1958** J. Becket *A Study of a Mixed Blood Aboriginal Minority* p. 136 [western NSW] The majority of those living in each centre seem content—'We **follow** the Mission' to remain where they are. **1964** P. Dalton *Broome* p. 135 [north-west WA] The system is kept going by the practice of making the children in the Aborigine's words, '**follow** the father'. **1971** *New Dawn* (Sydney) Jan. p. 2 [western NSW] Nowadays . . the young people of the reserve are not healthy enough. They marry relations. They don't **follow** the rules. They marry with whites . . agh! **1978** J. & P. Read *View of the Past* p. 200 [Ali Curung, NT] Ah, don't go to rubbish place . . and don't **follow** your mother and father . . . Got to learn this way. Follow this one. **1980** K. Liberman *Decline of Kuwarra People* p. 131 [north-west? WA] We got to **follow** it, *tjukurpa* . . otherwise they'll let go like Europeans. They've got no *tjurkurpa*, nothing. **1982** M. Howard *Aboriginal Power* p. 81 [Western Desert] The Pintupi appear to have interpreted their society as the continuation into the present of . . the Dreaming . . which it has been men's duty to '**follow up**'. **1989** R.M. Baker *Land is life* p. 338 [Borroloola, NT] Some people '**follow**' their father and adopt the skin that follows the father's skin, other people 'follow' their mother by assuming the marriage is right way and adopting the skin they would have got from such a right way father. **1990** R. Bardsley *Kingfisher Bay* p. 12 [Cape York, northern Qld] Hey! . . . Are you **following up** God or somethin'. **1991** *Amanbidji Land Claim* 21 Aug. [Amanbidji, north-west NT] What country they **follow**? . . . They got to follow grandmother. **1995** M. Brady *Giving away the Grog* p. 118 [northern NT] I identify with the Larrakia people because my mother is Larrakia. And as with most Aboriginal people, you can **follow** your father or your mother's side. We follow our mother's side because she's the one who nurtured us and instilled Aboriginal awareness into us.

foot *noun* This term is used in combination with other words to refer to activities carried out on foot. See also FOOTWALK.

With the advent of the British and their wheeled and mounted forms of transport, what had been the only form of land transport, i.e. the foot, became one form, and hence needed to be distinguished from non-traditional forms.

by foot-bucket, carrying (water) in a bucket while walking.

1983 A.H. Ross *Austral. Abor. Perceptions Dwellings & Living Environments* p. 203 [Kimberley] It was still necessary for them to carry water **by** '**foot-bucket**' over distances which were difficult for pensioners to manage.

foot-Falcon, travelling by foot.

This ironic reference to the Ford Falcon car works in the same way as does the general expression 'shank's pony'.

1987 A. McGrath *Born in the Cattle* p. 152 [NT] The responsibility of maintaining the horse was considered a liability, and Aborigines were pleased to have the change from stockwork and enjoy their old ways of 'foot-walking', or '**foot-Falcon**', as the modern expression has it.

foot muster, to muster on foot.

1991 D.B. Rose *Hidden Histories* p. 180 It was known the boys made it their business to **foot muster** small mobs.

on footback, while walking.

1945 *Hist. Soc. of Queensland* (Brisbane) Feb. p. 316 Camp equipment and the rest of my gear had to be carried **on 'footback'** to the camp site six miles away.

footwalk *verb* [northern Aust.] To travel by foot.

1952 *Bulletin* (Sydney) 17 Dec. p. 12/1 [northern NT] Rosie, our housegirl, recently received a filial visit from her son. He '**footwalked**' direct overland from the Daly River to Darwin. 1946 W.E. Harney *North of 23 Degrees* p. 172 [north-east NT] Natives went **footwalk** to Borroloola for assistance through the mud of the rainy season. 1963 F. Flynn *Northern Gateway* p. 138 [northern Aust.] He is known to have '**footwalked**' far to the south and way over into West Australia during his younger, more adventurous days. 1984 K. Benterrak et al. *Reading Country* p. 109 [north-west WA] So we went down the beach .. all the way, **footwalk.** 1991 *Amanbidji Land Claim* 21 Aug. [north-west NT] Yes, my father used to bring me **foot walking.**

Hence **footwalker,** a person who travels on foot.

1937 M. Terry *Sand & Sun* p. 22 A **footwalker** appeared over a sandhill ... After the footwalker a string of camels. 1951 E. Hill *Territory* p. 301 For ten years there were only occasional horsemen and '**foot-walkers**' along the Murran-ji.

gibberish *noun* [south-east Aust.] Aboriginal language. See LINGO.

This does not have the pejorative associations that the word has in non-Aboriginal English.

1985 *Aboriginal History* (Canberra) Vol. IX Pt 1-2 p. 134 [northern NSW] 'Dagos learn their own kids their own yabber' (or 'gibberish') 'so why are we shamed?' ['Yabber' and '**gibberish**' here are not pejorative so much as relaxedly Aboriginal. That they may seem pejorative to non-Aborigines is a reflection on the kind of English vocabulary which was used in the pidgin of early contact, and so survived in the English that Aboriginal people made their own.] 1990 A. Schmidt *Loss of Australia's Aboriginal language heritage* p. 39 For many Aboriginal individuals and groups, it was no longer a stigma to claim Aboriginal identity or to publicly speak the Aboriginal language ... Hence the notion of 'rubbish language' or '**gibberish**' was gradually replaced by a strong pride and consciousness of the political and social value of Aboriginal language and identity.

gin talk *noun* Aboriginal language.

As with 'gibberish' the origin of the term was probably in pejorative non-Aboriginal use, but it has been taken over into Aboriginal English use without pejorative associations.

1988 I. Keen *Being Black* p. 68 [southern NSW] People of the town acknowledge the use of language as a code when they refer to '**gin talk**' or 'blackfella talk'.

give *verb* To bestow (on someone) access to (a form of) knowledge (such as a 'dreaming' story).

In Aboriginal culture, knowledge is 'owned' in a form of personal copyright, which carries with it responsibility for its correct memorisation and proper use. As it 'belongs' to someone, that person thus has the right to **give** it to someone else, in the sense of access rather than possession.

1979 G. Bardon *Aboriginal Art of Western Desert* p. 6 [Western Desert] I later had occasion to ask him for a special painting. To paint the picture Mick told me he had to see his brother about it to get his permission. After a while Mick told me that his brother had said it was alright to '**give**' me their father's Dreaming. So we then drove to the painting room. **1985** B. Neidjie *Kakadu Man* p. 33 [Arnhem Land] I **give** you this story. This proper, true story. People can listen. I'm telling you this while you've got time .. time for you to make something, you know, .. history .. book.

go through *verb* To undergo the rituals that make one an adult in traditional society. Also **go (went) with.**

1958 *Oceania* (Sydney) Vol. XXIX (1) p. 98 [NSW] You ought to **go through** the rules. I've been through. **1975** *Bunji* (Darwin) July p. 1 [Darwin, northern NT] All the women agreed they wanted their children to **go through** the ceremonies. **1983** S. Butters *God's Law and God's Power* p. 8 [Kimberley] I was put through my tribal law and being a half-caste I had a choice . . . Because I wanted to make people proud of me I **went through** it. **1984** E. Roughsey *An Aboriginal Mother Tells* p. 190 [Mornington Island, northern Qld] It's so sad to think they were not regarded as one of the men who **went through** the law. **1988** *Mosa* (Clayton) no. 2 p. 18 [north-west WA] Well because you **went through** another law, you've got to finish your law on that side, and when everything's finished you come back home. **1990** P. Austin et al. *Lang. & Hist.* p 24 [Oodnadatta, northern SA] I **went with** the blackfeller Law in the Walbiri language, dog and everything: chased to another mob again, boxed up with another mob again, and go and boxed up again with another different-different tribe.

grass *noun* **1** [central Aust.] Any soft-stemmed plant.

1988 J. Harkins *English as 'Two-way' Language* p. 232 [central Aust.] **Grass** is extended to cover all soft-stemmed plants, including herbs and wildflowers as well as what non-Aboriginal speakers regard as grasses.

2 [Vic.] As **basket grass**, particular grasses used to make a traditional basket.

1991 A. Jackomos & D. Fowell *Living Aboriginal Hist. of Vic.* p. 72 [Vic.] All around here there used to be **basket grass** but now we've got to go a long way for them.

grass basket, a traditional basket.

1991 L.M. Wilkinson *Aboriginality* p. 263 Connie Hart .. today makes **grass baskets** like her mother did last century.

gurrnki *noun* [western NSW] A ghost. Also **gunki.**

Origin unknown, probably from a western NSW Aboriginal language.

1978 P. Hanigan & R. Lindsay *No Tracks on the River* p. 51 Budgie said 'I don't want no **gungki** getting at me.' **1993** E. Crawford *Over my Tracks* p. 53 [western NSW] I tell you what, the first time we saw the nuns with their habits, we thought they were **gurrnkis** (ghosts).

hairy man *noun* [south-east Aust.] **1** A spirit being taking the form of a large hairy ape-like man. Also **hairyman.** See DULUGAL.

1876 *Town & Country Jrnl* (Sydney) 4 Nov. p. 729/2 [NSW] It has been believed by the settlers of that wild part of the country, that the Walla Walla scrub was inhabited by a monster commonly called 'the **hairy man** of the wood'. **1963** D. E. Barwick *Little More than Kin* p. 291 [south-east Vic.] In Gippsland these spirits have several native names, but young people generally call them 'the **hairy men** of Suggen Buggen'. **1980** P. Pepper *You Are What You Make Yourself* p. 57 [south-east Vic.] There was a story about the **Hairy Man**; it could be a man or a woman, but the Aborigines called it a man. **1982** R. Hall *Just Relations* p. 24 [NSW] It was uninhabited and commonly believed to be dangerous with the forces of Aboriginal spirit: little mountain men, the **hairy men**, gunjes and the like. **1993** J. Janson *Gunjies* p. 41 [western NSW] He says he seen Dooliga, you know yowie, the **hairy man**.

2 A smaller spirit being.

1978 *The Hairyman* (Western Reader Committee, Brewarrina Central School) p. 21 [western NSW] As they ran through the weeds and grasses, each boy recalled in his own mind with a growing amount of fear, some of the legends and stories they had heard by the campfire of **hairymen**. These small brownish creatures, no bigger than a year-old baby, were known to coax people away from their camp . . . In fact they sometimes killed people by frightening them and scaring them to death. **1991** L.M. Wilkinson *Aboriginality* p. 238 [south-west Vic.] During a children's camp in the Framlingham forest, the children saw a little **hairy man**—a 'doolagar'. *Doolagars* are not totally malevolent, but merely lure people away into the bush till they are lost. They are hairy, small and have pointed ears.

history *noun* [Recorded in northern SA, central Aust., and WA but probably used elsewhere.] The history of a people where the history in the non-Aboriginal sense is not separated from what non-Aboriginal people would describe as mythology or creation stories. See STORY.

1978 L.R. Hiatt *Aust. Aboriginal Concepts* p. 69 [central Aust.] The most important songs of the Central Australian and northern South Australian people with whom we have worked are the '**history**' songs; songs retelling the events when the ancestral beings populated the known world and created the landscape. **1980** K. Liberman *Decline of Kuwarra People* p. 172 [WA] That's the song. That's a big **history**, from this mark. **1980** K. Liberman *Decline of Kuwarra People* p. 131 [WA] It'll still be in the **History** (*tjukurpa* or Dreaming). **1988** D. Tunbridge *Flinders Ranges Dreaming* p.xxii [Flinders Ranges, SA] Occasionally we have used . . the term 'mythology' . . . Older Adnyamathanha people use the English word 'history'— a translation of *muda*.

hold *verb* [northern Aust.] To spiritually own, look after and be responsible for (something). Also **holding**, **hold up**.

The **holding** is often expressed and confirmed in ritual. It can also apply in reverse—the culture holds up the people, see the 1989 citation.

1964 P. Dalton *Broome* p. 145 [north-west WA] We **hold** our own law. **1979** *Cent. Aust. Land Rights News* (Alice Springs) Dec. n.p. [central Aust.] We **hold** the land in a stronger way than white fellers. We hold it from our fathers and grandfathers. We hold it as Kurtingurlu. **1982** M. Howard *Aboriginal Power* p. 83 [central Aust.] The concept *kanyininpa*, translated as 'having', '**holding**' or 'looking after' articulates and unifies several aspects of Pintupi life. **1987** *Yeperenye Yeye* (Alice Springs) Dec. p. 20 [central Aust.] Some people said, 'Keeps the language going very strong. Aboriginal schools should be in Aboriginal language for us to **hold**'. **1988** C. Dunne *People Under the Skin* p. 169 [central Aust.] The dancing **holds** up the country . . . His mother, as a leading woman in the Lander Warlpiri Community holds the ceremonies for the Warlpiri area. **1989** B. Neidjie *Story about Feeling* p. 102 [Arnhem Land] Law e said 'Never change!' So we can't. Something **holding** you, you see. You can't do it.

holder *noun* [northern Aust.] A person who 'holds' cultural knowledge.

1980 B. Sansom *The Camp at Wallaby Cross* p. 24 [northern NT] And just as the word can be given or stolen, its **holder** can stint it: 'No. Leave him. He not gonna get that word.' **1989** *Canberra Times* 4 Dec. p. 12/3 [Darwin, NT] Claimants have died, many of them the knowledge-**holders** of the Larrakia.

inside *adjective* [northern and central Aust.] (Of a secret or sacred version of a 'dreaming' story) accessible only to those Aboriginal men or women entitled to the knowledge. See OUTSIDE.

1989 B. Neidjie *Story about Feeling* p. 101 [Arnhem Land] This 'outside' story. Anyone can listen, kid, no matter who, but that '**inside**' story you can't say . . you not supposed to tell im anybody.

janak *noun* [south-west WA] An evil spirit. Also **janark, jannock**.

From the eastern dialect of the Nyungar language of south-west WA *djanak*, 'spirit, ghost, devil'.

1910 (1975) E. Hassell *My Dusky Friends* p. 32 [south-west WA] First, the two fires were to protect their master from the **jannocks** or evil spirits that he would meet at Twertip. **1970** J. Davis *First-Born* p. 43 (appendix) [south-west WA] **Janark**, evil spirit. **1988** I. Keen *Being Black* p. 245 [south-west WA] The old grandmother had joined in the joke by asserting that she was indeed a **janak** (a devil/ghost).

jingy *noun* [WA] An evil spirit. Also **jinggi, jinghi, jingie**.

From the northern dialect of the Nyungar language of south-west WA *djanka*, 'spirit, ghost, devil'.

1872 Mrs E. Millett *Australian Parsonage* p. 197 [WA] A queer little old native, who, from having lost his heels in a fire, and being in consequence obliged to walk on tiptoes, was commonly called **Jingy**—I suppose because the tracks he left were nothing human, just as the prints of bullocks and of men wearing boots were pronounced by the natives . . '**Jingy**', i.e. 'devil' tracks. **1909** H.G.B. Mason *Darkest West Australia* (1980) p. 48 [WA] Deep pools . . are supposed to be the night habitations of the '**Jinghi**' or 'Devil-Devil'. **(1933)** J.E. Hammond *Winjan's People* p. 60 [south-west WA] The '**jingie**' (or evil spirit) was blamed for all sickness and accidents. **1984** W.W. Ammon et al. *Working Lives* p. 166 If a dead body passes close to the Aboriginal quarters it is '**jingy jingy**' and they will have bad luck and sickness to follow. **1988** I. Keen *Being Black* p. 240 [south-west WA] 'I seen him there, **jinggi, jinggi**', as he thought it was a ghost.

keeper *noun* [south-east Aust.] A person with responsibility for some aspect of Aboriginal culture. See HOLDER, OWNER.

Recorded in south-east Australia, but used more widely elsewhere. These terms emphasise the responsibilities of the 'keeping' rather than any sense of the right of one who is a **keeper** to give away that which is kept.

1986 Invasion Diary Collective *White Invasion Diary* 20 Jan. [southern SA] Our society was guided by the land and by the cycles of the circle songs. The circle songs are maintained by the elders who are **keepers** of the components of the song. **1988** R. Langford *Don't Take Your Love to Town* p. 242 [northern NSW] I heard there was a cleverwoman, Aunt Millie Boyd, who had become **Keeper** of the Rock. **1991** G.R. Langford *Journey into Bundjalung Country* p. 3 [northern NSW] Aunty Millie Boyd Githabel woman and **keeper** of the buthera of Mt. Jubbungum . . says . . 'You see they take the land but they cant take our buthera (spirit)'.

kidney fat *noun* The fat surrounding the kidneys, secretly removed by ritual killers to cause a delayed death in their victim. See FAT.

1991 J. McGinness *Son of Alyandu* p. 3 [NT] We were also often reminded to be on the lookout for chingarucks 'Doctor Blackfellas' who were often accused of removing the **kidney fat** of their victims.

kidney-fat man, a person who removes the kidney fat of another in ritual killing.

1985 *Nelen Yubu* (Melville Island) Autumn no. 22 p. 4 [northern NT] My father was a bad man. He was a **kidney-fat man,** always cutting out the kidney fat from people.

kidney fat *verb* To remove the kidney fat of a person in a ritual killing.

The fat is removed when the victim is asleep.

1949 *Oceania* (Melbourne) Vol. XX no. 1 p. 101 [NSW] If one of their number dies or becomes seriously ill they still say: 'Someone might have **kidney-fatted** him,' although they do not seriously believe that this practice is still continued. **1977** *Ink no. 2* p. 86 The two hunters came on stealthily, 'singing' their intended victim, but the victim . . began to 'counter sing' the opposition, first one and then the other. When they were helpless in a deep sleep from the 'singing', he quietly **kidney-fatted** them both and upstaked his camp and moved on.

Hence **kidney fatter,** a person who removes the kidney fat of another in ritual killing.

1991 L.M. Wilkinson *Aboriginality* p. 239 [south-west Vic.] A story of a man who seven years ago had been afraid of '**kidney fatters**' was related by a Framlingham man.

kupamari *noun* [northern Qld] A method of cooking in the ground; an earth oven. Also **copper Maori, covermarie hole, cup-mari, cup murray, kup-murri.**

Probably from a Pacific island language.

1912 *Mod. Dict. Eng. Lang.* MacMillan n.p. **Copper Maori** . . a native oven, consisting of a hole dug in the flat ground. **1984** E. Roughsey *An Aboriginal Mother Tells* p. 51 [Mornington Island, northern Qld] How to cook a wallaby . . we dig a long deep **covermarie hole** . . . When the old tribes think its cooked enough they undo the cover marie. **1986** *Kowanyama News* Dec. p. 18 [northern Qld] They would come back with their kill and have a big **kup-murri,** and eat all day or sleep in under shady trees. **1987** J. Isaacs *Bush Food* p. 53 [northern Queensland] Thancoupie supervises the removal of hot food wrapped in foil from a **cup-mari,** the Cape York ground oven. **1987** B. Gammage & P. Spearitt (eds) *Australians 1938* p. 100 [Palm Island, northern Qld] We used to have bullock riding . . foot races, big **cup murray** (earth oven cooked food). **1993** *Koori Mail* (Lismore) 24 Feb. 11/4 [northern Qld] The Aussie **Kupamari** held its own.

covermarie ground, a place where there is an earth oven.

1984 E. Roughsey *An Aboriginal Mother Tells* p. 221 [Mornington Island, northern Qld] So here you see where the **covermarie** ground is highly kept all together and where customs are kept still.

kup mari damper, a damper made in an earth oven.

1988 P. Taylor *After 200 Years* p. 261 We made **kup mari damper.**

kup-mari *verb* To cook something in the ground.

1988 P. Taylor *After 200 Years* p. 259 [northern Qld] Before, our ancestors used to **kup mari** it in the earth ovens, but now we boil it sometimes.

language *noun* An Aboriginal language; Aboriginal language. Also **langwige.**

The sense is both of a particular Aboriginal language and Aboriginal language in general, so that the query, 'Can she speak **language**?' can mean either 'Is she able to speak a particular Aboriginal language?' or, 'Does she have the knowledge of Aboriginal languages generally?'

1936 M. & E. Durack *Chunuma* p. 42 [Kimberley] Me got plenty **langwige. 1949** *Oceania* (Melbourne) Dec. p. 91 [north-west NSW] All aboriginal dialects are known locally either as 'the **language**' or 'the lingo'. **1972** M.J. Oakes *The Aborigines of Richmond Area* Pamphlet no. 2 n.p. [north coast, NSW] The porpoises . . had been dark people so of course they could understand 'the **language**'. **1978** *Yura Aboriginal* (Kent Town) Jan. p. 7 [southern SA] It makes me sad to hear people say, 'I often used to talk **language** to Dad, but since he's died I seem to be forgetting more and more'. **1978** J. & P. Read *View of the Past* p. 94 [NT] 'Where you gonna camp?' You know, not English, but **language**, you know. **1986** B. Shaw *Countrymen* p. 102 [Kimberley, WA] If you switch that thing now (the tape recorder), I got not much **language** to talk, but I can talk to you in English. **1990** A. Schmidt *Loss of Australia's Aboriginal Language Heritage* p. 12 [Hope Valley, northern Qld] We used to get cane if we talked language there . . . No **language**. It was all English then.

language belt, an area where a particular language is or was used by the people of that region.

1981 *N.S.W. Parl. Papers (1980-1981)* 3rd Sess. IV p. 884 [NSW] Is the term **language belts** Aboriginal terminology? . . . It is a term used by Aboriginal people to me as an Aborigine. **1981** *N.S.W. Parl. Papers (1980-1981)* 3rd Sess. IV p. 879 [NSW] People in the North Coast and the Wiradjuri group; and people in the south east corner, the Muttie-Daddie, the Balranald area, speak of the Aboriginal **language belts** . . . Some call them regions or areas . . . As Aborigines we want to be able to show our major **language belts** in the area in the state.

language group, a group of people having a common language or formerly having a common language.

1978 *Tracks* (Nelen Yubu) Nov. p. 8 [NT] My people belong to the Murinbata **language group. 1979** M. Wilson *Original Culture* p. 34 [NSW] I have lived all my life in the inner city area of Sydney. However, this is not my **language group**. Wiradjeri is the area where I belong and identify.

language name, a person's Aboriginal name.

1989 J. Thomson *Reaching Back* p. 15 My father's name was Albert Myowe. His **language name** is Myowe which means soothing, calming, soothing.

language song, a song in an Aboriginal language.

1988 P. Taylor *After 200 Years* p. 264 I was in Sydney . . teaching the students how to make spears and artefacts and **language songs**.

law *noun* **1** The body of religious and cultural knowledge that informs and directs Aboriginal society. See DREAMING, DREAMTIME. Also used as an adjective in compounds.

The use of the English word 'law' both illuminates and obscures the Aboriginal sense of the word. Both Aboriginal and non-Aboriginal law provide a structure for the harmonious ordering of society, but the Aboriginal sense is grounded in an order derived from spiritual understandings of life with an emphasis on this order having been there 'from the beginning'. Non-Aboriginal law in Australia, on the other hand, is consciously separated from religious life and endeavours to present itself as responsive to changing contemporary conditions. It does not, nor would it seek to recognise, the spiritual dimensions of society and life. In most Aboriginal languages there is not one word equivalent to 'law'; Aboriginal people will sometimes use the Aboriginal English word **law** while speaking an Aboriginal language, because it so usefully encapsulates a range of meanings.

1950 I. Tonnies (ed.) *Beitrage* p.x [Daly River, NT] Informants say that they would be 'ashamed' and that it is against the '**law**' to call a man by his name, unless he were one's 'mate'. **1951** R. & C. Berndt *From Black to White in SA* p. 137 [Ooldea, northern SA] '**Law**' ... This word is sometimes used, in 'pidgin' English, in a general sense, to refer to religion and ceremonial tradition in all its forms; and it includes all the customs, sanctions and laws handed down from the first Spirit-ancestors who in the Beginning shaped the earth and the creatures that live on it. **1974** J. Bern *Blackfella Business* p. 26 [Ngukurr, northern NT] Blackfella **law** is the framework—the code of proper conduct—which subsumes the content and consciousness of Ngukurr society. **1976** J. Mirritji *My People's Life* p. 10 [Arnhem Land] For all of the time in the bush we lived by the **law** of the Mardayin (old time Aboriginal law). **1978** J. & P. Read *View of the Past* p. 353 [NT] Tribe **law** was very hard law. That's why they think .. they gotta keep everything true, straight. **1978** K. Palmer & C. McKenna *Somewhere Between Black and White* p. 20 [north-west WA] There was never any question that because his father had been a white man that he would not be allowed to know the secrets, make the **law**, one day carry it himself. **1979** C. Johnson *Long Live Sandawara* p. 18 [WA] The **Law** is one, unchangeable—the protection of the people. **1983** A.H. Ross *Austral. Abor. Perceptions* p. 264 [Kimberley, WA] We never been in school, we been schooling our **law**. **1984** P. Toyne & D. Vachon *Growing up the Country* p. 8 [central Aust.] Aboriginal people throughout Australia, from the deserts to coastal rainforests, symbolise people and its places by *tjukerpa*, although they may call it 'the dreaming' or some other name. *Anangu* say it is 'the **law**', the rational and moral order to their existence. **1987** J. Davis *Honey Spot* p. 5 [south-west WA] Now I am brother to the plura. Peggy: What's the plura? Tim: The bees. That's our **law**, Nyoongah way. **1988** J. Downing & A. Smith *Ngurra Walytja, Country of my Spirit* p. x For the Aboriginal person '**law**' embodies his creation stories, his religion, his social relationships and behaviour, his identity. It corresponds more to the fullness of the Biblical concept 'Word' ... European law on the other hand is a code of conduct. **1988** P. Marshall *Raparapa* p. 213 [Kimberley, WA] They have the **law** to that country, they have the culture to that country. **1989** B. Neidjie *Story about Feeling* p. 80 [Arnhem Land] I can't make any camping area there because no good for anybody .. no matter my Aborigine, no matter White-European because **Law** .. 'got to be stay out!' ... Can't break Law. **1989** M. Edmunds *They Get Heaps* p. 143 [Roebourne, WA] How are they going to run the **law** after we are finished? **1991** L.M. Wilkinson *Aboriginality* p. 215 [south-west Vic.] There is some evidence that the 'old **law**' is still used with regard to marriage. **1992** R.L. Ginibi *Real Deadly* p. 1 [northern NSW] Gone are all our tribal ways, only three elders left; all dubays, no old nugthungs, to tell our stories and legends or give us our **laws**. **1993** E. Crawford *Over my Tracks* p. 68 [western NSW] No one from the Aboriginal Protection Board didn't give one damn for our culture or **laws**.

law business, ceremony connected with the law.

1978 K. Palmer *Somewhere between Black and White* p. 38 [Pilbara, WA] He knew that the flour must be for some **Law business**, but then there were all sorts of different things going on at that time of year.

law camp, a camp where aspects of law are taught.

1984 B. Swanton *Aborigines and Criminal Justice* p. 104 [NT] This was attributed to . . the Aboriginal community extending the '**law camps**' to involve more juveniles for longer periods of time.

law carrier, a person knowledgable in the law.

1964 P. Dalton *Broome* p. 130 [north-west WA?] Some of the men . . say (he) is not really a '**law-carrier**'.

law centre, a place known for knowledge of the law.

1977 L. Sackett *Liquor and the Law* p. 97 [Western Desert] People from neighbouring **Law centres** travel to Wiluna . . to have Law business and to get drunk in a relaxed atmosphere. **1981** W.J.K. Christensen *The Wangkayi* p. 283 [Kalgoorlie, WA] Some young men come to Kalgoorlie precisely because it is a weak **Law centre** where they can evade their traditional responsibilities.

law ground, a place for holding ceremony.

1978 H. Dagmar *Aborigines and Poverty* p. 71 [Gascoyne, WA] They're trying to put the **Law ground** in the Ingganda country.

law-making, a ceremony where the law is enacted in ritual.

1991 *Dugite* i p. 8 He often sings at initiations and **law-making** ceremonies.

law meeting, a ceremony.

1981 *Kimberley Land Council* (Derby) Mar. p. 26 [Kimberley, WA] He met up with all the blackfellows there. They were having a big **law meeting** for man-making.

law place, a ceremonial ground.

1978 K. Palmer & C. McKenna *Somewhere between Black and White* p. 50 [Pilbara, WA] 'Well, can you go and get him for me?' Sammy knew it wasn't the thing to do to go over to the **Law place** himself.

Words associated with the **law** are often ones that are associated with living things or with physical objects, so that a person can 'hold', 'carry' or 'run' the **law**.

1964 P. Dalton *Broome* p. 145 [north-west WA] We hold our own **law**. **1978** K. Palmer & C. McKenna *Somewhere between Black and White* p. 20 [north-west WA] There was never any question that because his father had been a white man that he would not be allowed to know the secrets, make the **law**, one day carry it himself. **1989** M. Edmunds *They get Heaps* p. 143 [Roebourne, WA] How are they going to run the **law** after we are finished?

2 The law as embodied in a particular ceremony.

1984 S. Cane *Desert Camps* p. 81 [Western Desert] Can't cook him. He got no fire, no **law**, no law, just eating. **1986** B. Shaw *Countrymen* p. 66 [Kimberley, WA] I had been through the first **Law** . . I had the second Law . . [subincision] later. They dont do that now, no. **1987** C. Glass & A. Weller *Us Fellas* p. 25 [south-west WA] Then eventually I grew up and had my own children and I put my older son through the **law**. 1988 *Sydney Morning Herald* 4 Jan. 11/2 [Derby, north-west WA] He has connections with One Arm Point Community and has been through the **law**.

3 [Chiefly northern Aust.] The law as embodied in song, or in physical objects. This is often a secret and sacred object of wood or stone, often decorated with significant **law** patterns; it should not be seen except by those who have the right to do so. The object might be buried, or hidden in a cave. The third citation refers to such an object, which was covered by the waters of the Argyle Dam.

1986 B. Shaw *Countrymen* p. 139 [Kimberley, WA] One .. has the **Law** on a string which goes wrrrr when you swing it. 1986 B. Shaw *Countrymen* p. 148 [Kimberley, WA] Father .. came and said play that **Law**, and we took him to a *nanguru* place .. and we played for him. 1986 B. Shaw *Countrymen* p. 171 [Kimberley, WA] I didn't know they were going to put this backwater right up to Argyle [the Argyle Dam and Lake] .. My private **Law** is under water now.

lawstick, a ceremonial object. In the following citation it is a carved object which records a person's relationship to the law.

1977 F.B. Vickers *Stranger No Longer* p. 166 [north-west WA] This led to me being accepted as a friend of the Pindan people, and .. Peter Coffin presented me with his own personal **lawstick**. It is a sliver of wood shaped like a long, thin gum-leaf. It is bevelled on one side and flat on the other, some two inches wide and about sixteen inches long. On the flat side the Law by which Peter has to live as a man of the tribe is carved in an arched snake pattern.

4 Any other cultural or legal power, especially European law. This use of **law** is a wider use than is found in most Englishes, in that it implies a wider cultural attitude or content behind the legal system. The meaning is closer to the first sense of **law** in that it includes a cultural context.

1983 *Conference of Abor. Communities* (Darwin) p. 27 [central Aust.] Why is the NT Government putting its **law** on Aboriginal people, like poking Aboriginal people with a stick at Barret Drive in Alice Springs. 1983 *W.A. Historical Society* (Perth) 1 Mar. p. 27 [NT] 'Papulanyi **Law** (White Australian)' said another claimant, 'is a paper law. It can be torn up, it can be changed. Our law comes from the land.' 1984 B. Swanton *Aborigines and Criminal Justice* p. 141 [north-west WA] La Grange has now moved towards a synthesis of the customary **law** and by-laws referring to them as the 'Bidyadanga Law.' 1986 B. Shaw *Countrymen* p. 224 [Kimberley, WA] Well, this is another **Law** that's come along. That's the Law in the town.

lawman *noun* [Chiefly northern Aust.] A person very knowledgable in the law; a ceremonial leader. Also **law man**.

1980 *Visions of Mowanjum* p. 109 [Mowanjum, north-west WA] The spear became Yaada's sacred object and he became a **lawman**. 1981 *Kimberley Land Council* (Derby) Mar. p. 3 [Kimberley, WA] **Lawmen** from many communities spoke on how the Law is always respected by Aboriginal people. 1981 *Kimberley Land Council* (Derby) Mar. p. 17 [north-west WA] We tribal **lawmen** like to see sacred sites left alone. We can't give it to him, gardia (white man). 1986 R. Moncrieff *Nigger Nigger* p. 51 [WA] They be killin' (him) when I teachin' him to be **lawman**. Blackfeller law. 1986 B. Shaw *Countrymen* p. 188 [Kimberley, WA] They reckon for the Law a bloke is fixed like that, he knows he'll make the girl happy, but I don't know about it. You have to ask a **Law man**. 1986 *Koori Mail* Lismore 28 June p. 2/1 [central Aust.] Senior Arrernte **law man** Wenten Rubuntja .. was made a member of the Order of Australia.

leaf *noun* [south-east Aust.] **1** A gum leaf played as a musical instrument. See GUM LEAF.

1980 P. Pepper *You Are What You Make Yourself* p. 103 [Vic.] The Gum Leaf Band was still popular . . . A lot of Aborigines played the **leaf**.

leaf band, a band which creates music using gum leaves as instruments.
1980 P. Pepper *You Are What You Make Yourself* p. 103 [Vic.] They had a **leaf band** amongst themselves and they used to play at the AIF recruiting centres.

2 A leaf used in traditional cooking.
Some foods were wrapped in the leaves of particular plants before cooking.
1982 *Puggana News* (Launceston) p. 14 No more 'sugarbag' and 'cooking with **leaf**' but butcherman selling beef.

leg cutter *noun* [Tas.] A person responsible for part of the processing of the muttonbird.

1984 Tas. Educ. Dept. *Return to Islands* p. 38 The last Season we kept hearing, Uncle Keith singing out, '**Leg-cutter**!' Leanne would be out on the rocks . . instead of in her place.

line *noun* The correct sequence of kinship relationships, and the behaviour appropriate to this sequence, especially in relation to marriage. See also STRAIGHT.

1949 *Oceania* (Sydney) Vol. XX no. 1 p. 116 [north-west NSW] It kept the blood straight, kept the **line** straight and clean. **1957** W.E. Harney *Life Among Aborigines* p. 18 [northern Aust.] Marriage in the Karamalah tribe was 'wrong side'—an aboriginal saying that means 'not in **line**' or not correct by tribal law . . **1978** H. Dagmar *Aborigines and Poverty* p. 67 [Gascoyne, WA] They didn't teach me what **line** I belong to. Nowadays they don't teach young fellas anything at all. **1988** P. Marshall *Raparapa* p. 77 [Kimberley, WA] When they drink that heavily, they don't call that one 'sister' or this one 'cousin', they forget about their skin **line**.

lingo *noun* Aboriginal language.

The *Oxford English Dictionary* defines 'lingo' as a 'contemptuous designation' for a foreign language. As with 'gibberish', Aboriginal English uses a word once used derogatorily about an aspect of Aboriginal society and gives it a purely descriptive sense. It should be noted here that the modern Australian English sense of lingo as defined by the *Australian Concise Oxford Dictionary* is 'a foreign language' and has no pejorative sense. See GIBBERISH.

1905 A.A. Davidson *Journal of Explorations* p. 48 [north-west NT] These natives spoke the same language as the tribe west of Barrow Creek, and it was the same '**lingo**' as that spoken on Hooker's Creek. **1957** *Oceania* (Melbourne) Mar. p. 206 [north coast, NSW] Shhh! don't talk in the **lingo**, the white people might hear you. **1976** *Black Liberation* (Brisbane) Oct. p. 2 [south-east Qld] Then there's the English lessons—where does that leave the black child who speaks **lingo** (Aboriginal language) at home and then is forced to speak English at school. **1982** *Aboriginal History* (Canberra) Vol. 6 Pt 1-2 (I) p. 5 [western NSW] She grew up speaking Ngiyampaa, 'the **lingo**'. **1985** B. Rosser *Dreamtime Nightmares* p. 118 [northern Qld] Its the Warluwara tribe that you and Ruby belong to, isn't it . . do you still speak the **lingo**? **1988** J. Davis *Barungin—Smell the Wind* p. 44 [south-west WA] Dances are gone, laws gone, **lingos** just about gone.

maban *noun* [WA] A spiritually powerful person. Also **maban man, mabarn, moppan, moppin**. See CLEVER.

Probably from a language of the Pilbara region. This term is also used to describe spiritual power.

1929 K.S. Prichard *Coonardoo* p. 105 [WA] When the boy was found alive he was brought up by the old women who said he was **moppin**, knew the things other moppins knew. **1966** M. Brown *Jimberi Track* p. 24 [WA] Lallili, who was a four-eyes—a **moppan** who could see twice as much as other man. **1978** R. Tonkinson *Mardudjera Aborigines* p. 107 [Western Desert] Men who most often use their special powers for socially approved ends are termed **Mabarn** throughout the Western Desert; the same term refers to the magical stones or shell objects they are said to carry in their stomach. **1984** B. Swanton *Aborigines and Criminal Justice* p. 333 [WA] **Mabarn** or 'witchdoctors' are the closest equivalent to psychologists in Aboriginal culture. **1986** B. Shaw *Countrymen* p. 154 [Kimberley] They reckoned she was a **maban** girl, a devil with a bullock foot. **1987** C. Glass & A. Weller *Us Fellas* p. 83 [southwest WA] My grandfather is gifted, we don't know whether he got the **Mobrun** first . . I think that it really is a Mobrun that he got from tribal people or whatever. **1989** A. Haebich *For their own Good* p. 219 [WA] **Maban men** were accorded considerable respect and many southwest people . . followed the policy of 'be nice to them and they'd be nice to you'.

magic *noun* **1** Spiritual power. See CLEVER, POWER.

As *magic* in general English has a weakened or trivial sense, words such as *power* or *clever* are closer to the real meaning and are more often used in this context by Aboriginal people.

1981 D. Levitt *Plants and People* p. 52 [Groote Eylandt] Certain areas were known as 'dangerous places'. These were ceremonial grounds where magic rites could be performed to hurt people . . . People doing this had to be very careful, as, if not done properly, the **magic** could rebound back on them, with disastrous results. This is why these areas were called 'dangerous places'. **1986** B. Shaw *Countrymen* p. 182 [Kimberley, WA] If you get real **magic** you go clever. **1990** S. Watson *Kadaitcha Sung* p. 42 [south-east Qld] Their **magic** is nothing to do with that . . . Their special sort of poorie comes from deep within them.

love magic (love making magic), psychic power directed at erotic love relationships.

1983 A.H. Ross *Austral. Abor. Perceptions* p. 28 [East Kimberley, WA] In the East Kimberley, the women concentrated on djarada and ilbindji . . both types of **love-making magic**, whereby partners were sought, retained, or won back. **1987** N. Williams *Two Laws* p. 60 [Arnhem Land] You are always singing the girls' song into your face, your body and your clothing using '**love magic**'. **1989** R.M. Baker *Land is Life* p. 339 The recent introduction of powerful *jarada* '**love magic**' is usually held responsible.

2 (As adjective) having spiritual power.

1958 D.E. Perez *Kalumburu* p. 35 [north-west WA] Such was the case of the mysterious . . **magic** 'roaring-stick' . . a thin elongated wooden slab, broad in the middle, thinner and narrower towards the ends . . . A hole in one end allowed the use of a string. **1977** J. Barker *Two Worlds* p. 9 [western NSW] He owned a *wilida*, which is a stone axe with **magic** properties . . . With the *wilida* a man must use only one blow when killing.

mailman *noun* [Now chiefly northern Aust.] A person in the community whose business it is to carry news and messages.

1880 L. Fison & A.W. Howitt *Kamilaroi & Kurnai* p. 103 [south-east Vic.] The lewin may be described very sufficiently by the English term now adopted by the Kurnai, namely, '**mailman**', that is, one whose business it is to convey messages and carry news. This custom of 'mailman' is probably universal throughout Australia. **1989** R.M. Baker *Land is life* p. 342 [Borroloola, north-east NT] Girls too young to be the subject of advances were still used by Europeans as '**Mailmen**' to deliver requests to older women. **1990** *Ethos* (Washington) p. 231 [south-east Arnhem Land] Friends act as go-betweens . . . It is from amongst the peer group that a '**mailman**' is recruited to carry the verbal messages or letters that announce desire and fix assignations.

The synonym **postman** is found in earlier records.

1881 A.C. Grant *Bush Life in Qld* Vol. 1 p. 240 [Qld] He himself is a '**postman**' . . travelling on a special mission from one tribe to another. **1883** *Jrnl. & Proc. Royal Soc. NSW* Vol. 17 p. 19 [south-west NSW] Each tribe possesses a *Ngalla watlow* or **postman** who can speak and understand the dialects of all the tribes within a radius of 150 miles.

make *verb* To initiate a child into adulthood through ritual; usually as **make a man**.

1947 W.E. Harney *Brimming Billabongs* p. 60 [northern NT] It was at the trading time that my uncle gave the sign that I was ready to be **made a** young **man**. **1961** *Oceania* (Sydney) Vol. XXXII p. 82 When a boy reached puberty . . the initiative to '**make** him **a man**' might be taken by one or more of several classes of men. **1977** *Black News Service* July p. 10 [Qld] This ceremony is held every year when Aboriginals **make** young boys into **men**. **1985** I. White et al. *Fighters & Singers* p. 5 [central Aust.] We were following the business . . . We were **making** young **men**. **1989** P. Lyon & M. Parsons *We are Staying* p. 13 [central NT] Tommy Turner was **made a man** near Ilperrelhelame. **1991** *Amanbidji Land Claim* 21 Aug. [Amanbidji, north-west NT] My father . . **make me man**, young man.

Hence **man making**, the initiation of young men or women into adulthood through special ceremonies. Also **making a man (woman)**.

There were (and are) ceremonies of initiation for girls into adulthood (see the 1904 citation), although generally they were less spectacular than those for boys, and the references in the literature are much rarer. This is partly because many writers are male and thus would have limited access to information about women's ritual and partly because the holding of such ceremonies seems to have been more affected by colonisation than were the ceremonies for males.

1856 J. Bonwick *W. Buckley* p. 77 [Vic.] **Man making** is attended with several mysterious and often torturing ceremonies. **1904** A.W. Howitt *Native Tribes S.-E. Aust.* p. 237 [south-east Qld] The Wide Bay, Burnet, and Brisbane tribes met for the purpose of '**making young men**'. **1904** *Jrnl. & Proc. Royal Soc. NSW* Vol. XXXVIII p. 336 [northern Vic.] Among the Yota-yota and adjoining tribes on the Murray River the ceremony of '**making young women**' is called *dhuddiwai*. **1982** *Aboriginal History* Canberra Vol. IX Pt 1 p. 10 [western NSW] The most intense period of contact with other Ngiyampaa groups . . came at the end of Eliza's childhood when the last . . 'school for **making men**' was held in bull oak country in 1914.

mamu *noun* [northern SA and central WA] An evil spirit, especially one associated with the dead.

Probably from the word for 'evil spirit' in the Wangkathaa and nearby languages of this region.

1981 W.J.K. Christensen *The Wangkayi* p. 321 [Kalgoorlie, WA] **Mamu** are most likely to be found near a gravesite but may wander far and wide. **1985** P. Muir & Pukunga *Ngalia Family*

p. 64 [Wiluna, central WA] A **mamu** has the general appearance of a human, speaks the same language but differs physically in that the feet are bigger and the toes longer and spread out, with large prominent ears of a reddish colour contrasting with the similar brown skin of the aborigines. A special feature being long sharp prominent front teeth. **1985** P. Skrzynecki (ed.) *Joseph's Coat* p. 177 [NT] We all heard about these cats and possums that had changed into **mamu**. **1989** M. Lennon *That's How it Was* p. 1 [Oodnadatta, northern SA] Each night she must darken the baby's hair so that it doesn't show up in the darkness. Otherwise a **mamu** might find it. Maybe then it would get sick or even taken away. **1995** M. Brady *Giving away the Grog* p. 126 [northern SA] Daisy Bates saw I was one of the half castes and she said 'ugh that's a **mamu** [devil] chuckem away that's a mamu'.

mamu country, an area where there are many ghosts.

1990 A. Pring (ed.) *Women of the Centre* p. 101 [Oodnadatta, northern SA] You know **mamu country**? . . lot o' dead people around here.

man *noun* An initiated man.

1988 C. Mattingley & K. Hampton (eds) *Survival in Our Own Land* p. 73 [SA] And after that . . we set off,—just **men**, no uninitiated people—we went off to have a look, and we took a few whitefellas with us, so they'd understand. **1988** J. Harkins *English as 'Two-way' Language* p. 241 [central Aust.] **Man** usually refers to initiated men, or to non-Aboriginal men mature enough to be treated for everyday purposes as initiated.

half a man, one not fully initiated.

1978 K. Palmer & C. McKenna *Somewhere Between Black and White* p. 46 [Pilbara, WA] You . . only **half a man** now.

mark *noun* A traditional mark on the body, made either as a scar or a painted area or line, which is worn by right of one's ritual place in society. Also **tribal mark**.

Permanent body marking in the form of ritual scarring was once very important throughout Aboriginal Australia, but is now restricted to the Arnhem Land region. The scars are made by cutting or burning and are arranged in patterns that encode information about that person and about his or her relationship to the society (for example, which clan a person belongs to). Temporary body decoration, in the form of ritual patterns traditionally made with ochres and clays, together with string, feathers, fur, shells, etc., is still an essential part of ritual throughout Aboriginal Australia. See also PAINT.

1978 J. & P. Read *View of the Past* p. 226 [north-east NT] You got to dance now. You got to have your proper **mark**, you know, proper culture. **1985** B. Rosser *Dreamtime Nightmares* p. 69 [Qld] They all got their own **tribal mark**. My father has a different mark. I can use his mark but nobody else can paint up with my father's mark. **1987** B. Gammage & P. Spearitt (eds) *Australians 1938* p. 118 [south-west NSW] You got your Aboriginal **mark** put on you. **1989** J. Thomson *Reaching Back* p. 15 [northern Qld] The **marks** on our bodies? They're something like our water, cave and our fighting ground.

Hence **marking**, the process of putting such marks on a person.

1920 *Bulletin* (Sydney) 1 Jan. 20/4 [northern Aust.] The aboriginal custom of '**marking**' the males seems to be dying out in the North. Years ago the belief among the blacks was that if a male got married without being first marked he would not last till the next moon after the ceremony. Marking consisted of cutting deep gashes across the breast and stomach with a sharp knife or piece of broken glass.

meat *noun* **1** A totem.

The word *totem* is from a North American native peoples' language and was first used in Australia by anthropologists, and later by Aboriginal people to refer in English to the association between people and the natural world, particularly animals and birds. To belong to a totemic group gives a person a relationship to other people, to particular places, to the past, and to certain areas of knowledge. People normally receive their totem through laws of inheritance. The first citation makes the connection between the Aboriginal language word and the Aboriginal English word which in this case is a 'translation' of the language word. This is probably also true in some of the other citations. The relation between **meat** and a totem is possibly the connection between 'animal' and 'meat', in that an animal is (potentially) 'meat'. For a fuller discussion see the Introduction.

1945 *Mankind* (Sydney) Apr. p. 209 [Walgett, north-west NSW] Most people, probably all, have totems or 'dinga, **meat**'. **1949** *Oceania* (Sydney) Vol. XX (I) p. 106 [north-west NSW] When a stranger comes to an aboriginal camp or settlement in north-western NSW, he is asked by one of the older aborigines: 'What **meat** (clan) are you?'. **1973** M. Fennel & A. Grey *Nucoorilma* p. 93a [northern NSW] Granny Sullivan was 'dead against' the match at first because they did not know 'what my **meat** was and because I was a bit on the fair side.' **1977** A.K. Eckermann *Group Organisation and Identity* p. 302 [south-east Qld] Some people maintained that she was 'sung' because her family had killed or eaten the '**meat**' (totem) of another group. **1992** P. Taylor *Tell it Like it Is* p. 108 [western Qld] Our family . . usually married the red kangaroo '**meat**'. **1993** J. Janson *Gunjies* p. 42 [western NSW] That's a beautiful goanna. . . He's my **meat**, can't eat him.

The synonym **flesh** is found in earlier records.

1904 A.W. Howitt *Native Tribes S.-E. Aust.* p. 145 [south-east Aust.] In this tribe the group totem is called by the terms *Mir, Ngirabul,* and *Yauruk,* the latter word meaning **flesh**. **1935** *Oceania* (Sydney) Vol. VI. no. 2 Dec. p. 135 [Flinders Ranges, SA] The social totem or *balu* is a person's '**flesh**', the symbol of his membership of an exogamous matrilineal clan, and therefore is not killed or eaten. **1937** *Mankind* (Sydney) Jan. p. 51 The totem as a man's '**flesh**', appears and warns him against danger.

2 An edible animal.

In many Aboriginal languages there is a linguistic relationship between what something is used for and the thing itself.

1986 J. Davis *No Sugar* p. 29 [south-west WA] Eh, you remember Streak. Kill and show dog, used to catch **meat** for every blackfella in Northam. **1988** J. Harkins *English as 'Two-way' Language* p. 234 [central Aust.] This **meat** includes live game; people often speak of going hunting as *going for meat* . . and edible native animals are often referred to collectively as *bush meats,* whether alive or dead.

medicine *noun* **1** Spiritual and psychic power. See CLEVER.

1980 B. Sansom *The Camp at Wallaby Cross* p. 63 [Darwin, NT] Doses of sorcery **medicine** are both task-specific and person-specific. That they can strike a 'wrongfella' is not anomalous. **1984** E. Roughsey *An Aboriginal Mother Tells* p. 69 [Mornington Island, northern Qld] They known to be **medicine** chant alright, and it does work . . other songs again for Mulgree when a person gets sick. **1986** B. Shaw *Countrymen* p. 123 [Kimberley, WA] Tomorrow you sick, next day you die. E give you that sick **medicine**, in the back near the kidneys.

medicine grass, grass used as medicine.

1984 E. Roughsey *An Aboriginal Mother Tells* p. 77 [Mornington Island, northern Qld] These **medicine grass** are used for any illnesses . . colds, headaches, for sores.

medicine man, a person with psychic powers.

1949 *Oceania* (Melbourne) Dec. p. 102 Besides the **medicine man** himself there are other aborigines in north-western N.S.W. who are believed to be 'a bit clever'. They do not possess the same extraordinary powers as the medicine man, but they are believed to be skilled in malevolent magic. **1991** G. Ward *Unna you fullas* p. 67 [south-west WA] Get Uncle Jack too, he's the **medicine man.**

open medicine, a treatment applied to an open wound.

1988 *Social Alternatives* (Brisbane) Vol. I no. 23 p. 7 [south-east Qld] Yea, they used the bush medicine, Penny Royal, they used to use that for **open medicine,** and they used to boil it down and have a bath in it. It was good medicine for drying up sores, and they'd drink the water.

2 [northern Aust.] Non-Aboriginal medicine reflected in a range of terms used by Aboriginal people to describe non-Aboriginal medical treatments as in **bang bang medicine,** physiotherapy for chest infections, **rub medicine** (also **rubbing medicine**), externally applied medications, and **stick medicine,** medication given by injection.

1987 *Tjakulpa Kuwarritja* (Papunya) Dec. n.p. [central Aust.] The physiotherapist from Alice Springs hospital came to talk about **bang bang medicine** with all the ladies with young kids. She taught all the ladies how to do bang bang properly so that they could help their kids to stay healthy. **1965** F.G.G. Rose *Wind of Change* p. 166 [central Aust.] The Aborigines are at present continually asking for '**rub medicine**' for coughs and chest complaints, but unfortunately I do not have any. **1989** B. Neidjie *Story about Feeling* p. 67 [northern NT] All that string . . that's like **rubbing medicine.** You doing it rubbing medicine. That paint e take what you got sick inside. **1981** G. McKenzie *Aurukun Diary* p. 29 [Aurukun, northern Qld] This was before the days of speedy, spectacular cures with '**stick medicine**' as the bush-folks later called injections.

merrigan *noun* [south-east Aust.] A dog or dingo. Also **merrigarn.**

From Wiradjuri *mirrigan,* a 'dog'.

1980 P. Pepper *You Are What You Make Yourself* p. 101 [Vic?] 'Course, they had their **merrigarn** with them—that's their dingo. **1993** J. Janson *Gunjies* p. 87 [western NSW] **Merrigans** barkin'.

messenger bird *noun* [south-east Aust.] A bird that gives warning to a person or a group.

1934 P. Leason *Last of Vict. Aborigines* p. 6 [Gippsland, Vic.] The behaviour of the '**messenger**' **bird** always advises the Lakes people that an aborigine is coming through Gippsland from New South Wales. **1992** R.L. Ginibi *Real Deadly* p. 5 [north coast, NSW] He gave me my totem because I was the eldest: willy wagtail. He said it would tell me good news, or bad; it was my **messenger bird** and would watch and warn me.

moigoi *noun* [south-east Qld] A ghost. Also **moggi, moikoi, muggae.**

From the Bundjalung language of northern NSW and SE Queensland, *maguy,* 'ghost'.

1977 A.K. Eckermann *Group Organisation and Identity* p. 18 [south-east Qld] A number of Aboriginal words . . are still used by the whole community . . **muggai** = ghost. 1979 M. Heppell *A Black Reality* p. 84 Personal observations include seeing an elderly couple bathed in perspiration after just meeting a **moikoi** (the spirit of a deceased Aboriginal). 1983 J. McKenzie *Fingal Tiger* p. 24 [Qld] 'You want to go fishing but there's a '**Moigoi**' down there.' 'Moigoi' is Aboriginal for 'ghost'. 1988 R. Langford *Dont Take Your Love to Town* p. 16 [northern NSW] He . . came back with the guts of the bullock . . . He washed the innards thoroughly then cut it into small rings like washers, rolled them in flour and fried them . . . He call them **moggi**, meaning ghost in the Bundjalung language.

mook mook *noun* [NSW] A ghost. Also **mok mok, muk muk**.

Origin unknown.

1971 *New Dawn* (Sydney) May p. 3 [NSW] To quieten naughty, noisy children, Aboriginal parents used to say something like 'Behave yourselves now, or the **mook-mooks** will get you'. 1977 M. Tucker *If Everyone Cared* p. 51 [south-west NSW] It was difficult to find her because the old **mok mok**, whenever they came near, would stand so still she looked like a black stump. 1977 *Meanjin* (Melbourne) no. 4 p. 541 We find that some Aboriginal words . . are often used . . **muk muk**—spirit, ghost.

moonbird *noun* [Tas.] The muttonbird, the focus of the muttonbirding industry of the islands of Bass Strait.

1981 M. Small & R. Ingpen *Night of Muttonbirds* p. 57 To start with, you people have a far better name for them in **moonbird**.

moonbird gales, the winds associated with the coming of the muttonbirds.

1981 M. Small & R. Ingpen *Night of Muttonbirds* p. 16 They're real spiteful, those **moonbird gales** though I thought they was finished.

mulba *noun* [WA] An Aboriginal person, particularly from the Pilbara region of WA.

From the Panyjima language of the Pilbara area, *marlba*, 'a person'.

1929 K.S. Prichard *Coonardoo* p. 15 [north-west WA] You are **mulba**, strong fellow. 1987 S. Morgan *My Place* p. 221 [WA] There's **mulbas** here know their language and won't speak it . . . I speak it anywhere, even in front of white people. 1989 S. Morgan *Wanamurraganya* p. 136 [north-west WA] It seemed that you had to choose one way or the other, no one would let you be both. The problem was, if you chose to be a **Mulba** you and your family never had any rights at all and you could kiss any hopes of getting on goodbye. Yet if you chose to be a whiteman, you had rights, but you couldn't mix with everyone. It was very hard, very hard.

muttonbird dance *noun* [Tas.] A dance to celebrate the muttonbird, the source of the culturally significant muttonbirding industry of the Bass Strait Islands.

1983 *Community* (Tas. Educ. Dept.) p. 8 The Weilangta Dancers from Launceston perform the **Muttonbird dance** during lunch time.

net net *noun* [eastern Vic.] A small spirit being which lives in the Lake Condah region of eastern Victoria.

1984 *Lake Condah Mission* (Aboriginal Hist. Program) n.p. [Gippsland, Vic.] The mission is surrounded on one side by stones . . . The old people would tell us the **net-nets** would catch us, they are little hairy men . . we often saw small foot prints . . the size of a baby's foot. 1984 L. Fogarty *Ngutji* Dedication page [Gippsland, Vic.] Down in the western district of Victoria, there's a place called Lake Conda . . . At Conda there's a large area covered by volcanic rocks, called the 'stones'. Under the stones live little hairy people with shiny eyes, called the '**net-nets**'.

old *adjective* (Of a person) having recognised wisdom and authority (usually a chronologically older person). See ELDER.

As with 'elder', the use of the word **old** to refer to important and significant people (and also things), reflects the cultural patterns that prevailed in Aboriginal society, and to a great extent still do, where learning is lifelong and knowledge held in personal memory. Thus an older person will have greater access to knowledge about society. In other Englishes, the word *old* is generally associated with loss and weakness rather than power and significance, though in fact, the **old men** who are significant in Aboriginal society are much the same age as the men who control most other societies. In Aboriginal society too, older women, through the gender separation of ritual knowledge and activity, can have a more powerful position within their own culture than do women in the wider Australian society.

1855 W. Howitt *Land, Labour and Gold* p. 129 [south-east Aust.] Allan took no notice . . of their calling him **old** man, though he was a much younger man than either of them, for he had already heard that phrase used. **1976** *Students Storybook* (Aboriginal Teacher Education College) p. 26 [NT] I used to love going hunting with the **old** ladies. **1981** G. McKenzie *Aurukun Diary* p. 30 [Aurukun, northern Qld] But one meets noble men here and there and old Sambo . . was one of them . . . He was not old, just middleaged, the term '**old**' amongst Aborigines being a term of respect, and so was applied to him. **1984** P. Read *Down There with Me on Cowra Mission* p. 12 [south-east NSW] 'What does the **old** feller want?' 'Oh, they're trying to take you out and get you initiated.' **1986** B. Shaw *Countrymen* p. 144 [Kimberley, WA] The barra blackfellers come and look at his hair and they might say 'Oh, you're not really **old**, young feller yet'. **1990** *Aboriginal History* (Canberra) Vol. XXIV p. 44 [Borroloola, NT] '**Old**' is a term of respect many people, including many older than him, use for Steve Johnson (junior).

old fellow, a person of recognised authority within the community, normally an older person. Sometimes used adjectivally. See ELDER.

1976 *Black Liberation* (Brisbane) Apr. p. 3 That's where they've got a big mining field now . . . That's in the **old-fellows** territory, and what's he getting out of it? **1978** J. & P. Read *View of the Past* p. 209 [north-east NT] Oh, this is what the **old feller** trying to teach me. **1983** *Yeperenye Yeye* (Alice Springs) Mar. p. 5 [central Aust.] It's the **old fellas**, they can see it, they can see what's happening. **1984** P. Read *Down There with Me on Cowra Mission* p. 12 [south-west NSW] 'What does the **old feller** want?' 'Oh, they're trying to take you out and get you initiated'. **1986** B. Shaw *Countrymen* p. 161 [Kimberley] When you've been through the last time like we **old fellers** now, you can go through any way. **1987** G. Francis *God's Best Country* p. 66 Those **old fellas** still singing us? **1988** A. Moffatt (ed.) *Aboriginal Deaths in Custody* (Transcript) p. 379 [south-east Vic.] And was that among your friends pretty much the same age when they started drinking? . . . Yes, and few of the **old fellows** and that. What, did you start drinking with the old fellows when you were about 15 or 16? **1991** A. Jackomos & D. Fowell *Living Aboriginal Hist. of Vic.* p. 84 [Vic.] I'm not in the league of the **old fellows** yet.

old man, a figure of authority. Sometimes used adjectivally.

1848 T.L. Mitchell *Jrnl. Exped. Tropical Aust.* p. 269 Each of them carried . . three or four missile clubs . . . They said, by signs, that the whole country belonged to the **old man**. **1854**

W. Howitt *Boy's Adventures* p. 306 The **Old Man**, as they call Pungil their god, not unlike the Hebrew term, Ancient of Days, now held out his hand to 'Gerer', the sun, and made him warm. **1960** *N.T. News* (Darwin) 26 Jan. 1/1 [NT] The '**Old Men**' of Windi's tribe had tried to take Windi's sick brother Wimmarty and initiate him. **1977** *National Times* (Sydney) 4 July 18/5 [Arnhem Land] Juvenile males on Groote Eylandt paid no attention to the will of the elders and dismissed their instruction as 'silly, **old man** stuff'. **1978** R. Tonkinson *Mardudjera Aborigines* p. 122 [Western Desert] The men shout back, '**Old man**! (a term of respect, since Didi is in fact middle-aged) Don't be that way; come back here'.

old old, very old, very learned.

1986 B. Shaw *Countrymen* p. 124 That was the Law, those old blackfellers knew, the **old-old** father, but I can't do it. **1990** P. Austin et al. *Lang. & Hist.* p. 250 A long time ago I was taught by an **old-old** feller in Alice Springs country—only just for nothing.

old man *noun* A plant, animal or other thing which is particularly large, important, or old. Often used adjectivally to refer to a thing, etc. of exceptional size, importance, age, etc.

In the 1989 citation, the English word 'man' is replaced by the equivalent in the Western Desert language. The term 'old man' has now been taken into general Australian English.

1830 R. Dawson *Present State Aust.* p. 139 [NSW] The kangaroos were called by my natives, **old man**, 'woolman'; and the females, young ladies, 'young liddy'. **1886** R. Henty *Australian* p. 244 [northern Aust.] There were very few red kangaroos of the **old man** species. **1889** C. Lumholtz *Among Cannibals* p.x [northern Aust.] In almost every hive some old honey is to be found which has fermented and become sour . . this old honey, which the bees do not eat themselves, looks like soft yellow cheese, and the civilised blacks call it **old-man**-sugar-bag. **1928** B. Spencer *Wanderings in Wild Aust.* p. 163 [central Aust.] The largest . . is known as '**old man**' porcupine, or *Trioda Mitchell*. **1948** J. Fairfax *Run o'Waters* p. 103 [south-west NSW] There were three tribes, and they received blankets and clothes from a paternal Government. They were particularly fond of sour milk in a thickened state, for which they used to beg, referring to it as '**old man's** milk'. **1977** M. Tucker *If Everyone Cared* p. 147 [NSW] When we got sick we would gather '**old man** weed' and make a brew. Amongst our peoples, it is known as a cure for a wide range of ailments. **1984** P. Read *Down There with Me on Cowra Mission* p. 33 [south-west NSW] They'd incorporate a bit of the old Aboriginal medicine, the **Old Man** Weed, it's a native cure-all. **1989** M. Lennon *That's How it Was* p. 63 [Oodnadatta, northern SA] According to Clancy the Perentie is called **Old Tjilpi** meaning a senior grey haired man.

paint *noun* Material, traditionally ochres and clays, used in ceremonial body decoration.

1979 M.C. Sharpe *Alice Springs Aboriginal English* p. 738 [central Aust.] They got **paints** on their faces. **1987** J. Davis *Honey Spot* p. 38 [south-west WA] I haven't got me **paint**. . . *Mother*: He needs paint to put on his skin. **1989** D. Walker *Me and You* p. 56 [north coast, NSW] Collected ochre **paint** from the rocks on the river bank. There were four different kinds that gave us red, yellow, cream and black . . . We'd paint our lips and faces. You mix the dust up with a little bit of water then rub it on the lips with your finger. **1989** B. Neidjie *Story about Feeling* p. 67 [Arnhem Land] They used to paint themselves alright . . . Aborigine . . . They used to paint themselves because it wasn't ordinary **paint**. **1993** E. Crawford *Over my Tracks* p. 106 [western NSW] You'd see the dancers comin' from way down the end of the creek, all done up in their **paint** and feathers and leaves.

painting *noun* An Aboriginal rock painting.

1993 E. Crawford *Over my Tracks* p. 111 [western NSW] In the caves [at Mootwingee] where whole families lived there are **paintings** on the walls.

paint up *verb* To wear or apply ritual designs using 'paint' for ceremonial purposes.

The decoration of the body using clay and ochres is a significant element in ceremonies. The traditional language of the designs expresses the social and ritual position of the person. A design might denote the clan the wearer belongs to, or represent an ancestral being. In some ceremonies, ornaments of feathers, shells, leaves etc. are added to the body decoration. The application of the designs, sometimes by a traditionally designated person to the accompaniment of singing, is part of the ceremonial process.

1985 B. Rosser *Dreamtime Nightmares* p. 69 [northern Qld] I can use his mark but nobody else can **paint up** with my father's mark. **1985** H. Koch *Non-standard English in Aboriginal* p. 19 [NT] Colin Heywood: **Paint up**. Kurtungurlu word . . . *Paint up* was used by these Aboriginals in the intransitive sense of 'be **painted (up)**' 'wear painted designs on one's body' . . the corresponding transitive verb would be *paintem (up)*. **1987** B. Cohen *To My Delight* p. 6 [north-east NSW] I didn't know my own Dad. Why? because he was **painted up** with pipe clay. **1988** *La Perouse* p. 51 [La Perouse, NSW] He would **paint** himself **up** and entertain at parties. **1989** R. Allan *Tennis with Jack at Warren's* p. 104 [northern NT] I **painted up** with ant bed mixed with ochres and white clay.

Hence **painted up**, decorated with ochre paint, and the **paint up**, the process of decoration.

1976 *Students Storybook* Aboriginal Teacher Education College p. 29 [NT] Then she said the kurdaji is all **painted up** and he is the most deadly person alive. **1979** *Tjaru* (Alice Springs) Aug. n.p. [central Aust.] Girls from all different tribes were **painted up**—some Pitj, Aranda and Walpiri girls. **1995** *Koori Mail* Lismore 29 November p. 32/1 The earth is part of the spiritual ceremonies of many clans; using ochres of different colours such as yellow, black, red and white. Ochre is applied in designs according to your totem, so that your totem spirituality is awakened during the **paint up**.

pay-back *noun* An act of retribution.

The 1930 citation is possibly the first written evidence of the word **pay-back**, although here used as a verb. Within the sound systems of most Aboriginal languages, the words *pay* and *buy* could easily be conflated, leading to transcription errors.

1930 *Amer. Anthrop.* (Wisconsin) p. 214 Warlumbopo wailed for his dead brother. He refused to allow the wives of the dead man to bury him. 'I'll cry no more for you. I'll not show my sorrow now. I'll **buy** you **back** first.' He went down to the country where the brother had been mortally wounded; through cunning and skill he killed the slayer of his wawa and escaped. **1935** D. Thomson *In Arnhem Land* (1983) p. 67 [Arnhem Land] Many remembered feuds of long standing—for blood feuds among these people are carried on for many generations. The '**pay back**' as they call it, may be delayed for years in order to catch a man, or a group, off guard. **1962** D. Lockwood *I, Aboriginal* p. 22 [NT] Aborigines never forget. All wrongs must be set right by a system known as **Pay-Back**. **1970** M. Kelly *Spinifex* p. 63 'I can remember him taking part in a big pay-back raid a few years later.' '**Pay-back**?' 'Pidgin for vendetta.' **1985** B. Rosser *Dreamtime Nightmares* p. 54 [Qld] Yes, that's what they call their **pay-back**. **1994** *Encyclop. of Aboriginal Aust* p. 607 A second [characteristic] is, or was, the endemic cycle of injury and revenge—of '**payback**'. There are checks, however, on arbitrary power and endless cycles of revenge . . procedures to settle differences, such as the buluwandi ceremony of the Warlpiri or the makarrata ceremony of northeast Arnhem Land.

people *noun* (With a qualifying word such as **bailer-shell, fish, forest** or **tree**) the people belonging to an area characterised by particular environmental features.

> 1979 L. Andrews *Kinship & Community at Wreck Bay* p. 7 Another division . . was between the 'fish people' and the 'tree **people**' . . . The first group utilised predominantly marine resources and spent most of their time in close proximity to the ocean and estuaries. **1988** K. Gilbert *Inside Black Australia* p. 66 [north-west WA] The children play like Yukana . . like happy bailer-shell **people** from times of long ago. **1992** *Canberra Times* 19 Mar. 13/6 We are the tree people, the forest **people**.

photo *noun* [north-west NT] A rock painting.

> 1992 D.B. Rose *Dingo Makes Us Human* p. 107 [north-west NT] **Photo** [rock art] there all around Daguragu.

point *verb* To direct a malevolent force against another by the use of a spiritually charged piece of bone. See BONE.

The term **point** comes from the action of pointing the spiritually charged bone in the direction of the person who is to be affected.

> 1933 C.W. Peck *Austral. Legends* 2nd ed. p. 159 Some people who have been on most intimate terms with the blacks aver that 'boning' is more than simply pointing. They say that the expression 'to **point**' is the only one the natives had when they wished to convey something like 'to shoot'. They did not mean that the bone was only 'pointed'. They actually pierced. **1978** 'B. Wongar' *Track to Bralgu* p. 4 [NT] Some of your Riratjingu mob had **pointed** bones at you or finished you off with a spear. **1980** P. Pepper *You Are What You Make Yourself* p. 44 [Vic.] Those fellas had this special power and they could *nur-ritch* a person; that means they could sit down in the bush and **point** the bone, or sing you. **1984** H. McKellar *Matya-Mundu* p. 7 [Qld] A girl was chosen as a wife for someone . . she had to be from the right totem or meat (for example emu or possum) . . I was told once of a Kooma man who married into the wrong meat . . the bone was **pointed** at him and he died.

poison *noun* Malevolent power conveyed supernaturally.

There is a similar word *poisin* in Tok Pisin from Papua New Guinea, meaning 'sorcery, a sorcerer'. The word is not as common in contemporary material.

> 1886 *Journal Anthrop. Inst.* (London) 9 Feb. p. 44 'They can also find out who it is that has put poison into a person.' The word '**poison**' is very generally used by the aborigines as we should use the word 'magic' . . . Perhaps the best equivalent is the North American term 'medicine'. **1904** A.W. Howitt *Native Tribes S.-E. Aust.* p. 362 [south-east Aust.] His friends had made a very strong stick to point at him with, singing his name over it, and spitting strong **poison** over it. He used the word 'poison' for 'magic'. **1924** R.S. Newall *Stone Implements from Millstream Station, WA* p. 304 [WA] On showing her another, a yellow coloured scraper, she said, 'He bad fella, he **poison**.' **1980** B. Sansom *The Camp at Wallaby Cross* p. 59 [Darwin, NT] That blackfella **poison** bin for onefella really. Them other dead body bin got accident. **1992** B. Attwood & J. Arnold *Power, Knowledge & Aborigines* p. 116 [northern SA] Malevolent spiritual forces were active in the south and that the poison of the bombs was linked to the traditional '**poison**' of *mamu*.

Hence **poisoned**, conveying malevolent power supernaturally.

1904 A.W. Howitt *Native Tribes S.-E. Aust.* p. 376 [south coast, NSW] When a spear was rubbed over with such fat it became, as the Yuin say, '**poisoned**', that is, infected with evil.

poison bone, a bone used in directing malevolent power.

1928 B. Spencer *Wanderings in Wild Aust.* p. 566 [Borroloola, north-east NT] The younger spirit . . told him that he was now a medicine man and showed him how to make '**poison bones**' out of dead men's bones.

poison song, a song used in directing malevolent power.

1976 J. Mirritji *My People's Life* p. 42 [Arnhem Land] People learned in the beginning, to use their own thoughts to kill anybody using some **poison songs**, with their mouths full of the power of animal languages, to hypnotise the people of the other tribes.

porcupine *noun* An echidna. Also **porky, porky pine**.

This is also used by non-Aboriginal people in rural areas. It was the common term in nineteenth-century Australian English, when Aboriginal communities learned the word.

1966 M. Boney *Bigga-Billa Porcupine* p. 1 [western NSW] This old grandfather, he'd kill a **porcupine**. He'd send the two poor little fellers out to get some leaves, coolibah leaves, to cook in a ground oven with the porcupine. 1980 P. Pepper *You Are What You Make Yourself* p. 85 [Vic.] The old **porcupines** love eating bull-dog ants. 1982 L. Fogarty *Yoogum Yoogum* p. 26 [south-east Qld] Most times we like eating **porky**, too. Goanna meat. 1986 *Austral. Abor. Studies* no. 2 p. 60 [NT] The Aboriginal people supplemented the ration store diet with . . the 'wild meat' of goanna, emu, kangaroo, **porcupine** (echidna) all of which abounded. 1989 J. Thomson *Reaching Back* p. 98 [northern Qld] He . . used to track **porcupines** (echidnas). 1989 D. Walker *Me and You* p. 7 [north coast, NSW] We used to go hunting every day—honey, **porcupine**. 1992 *Puggana News* (Launceston) Dec. p. 21 [Tas.] We can remember from when he was a youngster his father got a **porky pine**.

power *noun* **1** Psychic or supernatural strength, especially such as that possessed by a CLEVER person.

1958 J. Becket *A Study of a Mixed Blood Aboriginal Minority* p. 59 [western NSW] 'We haven't the **power**' was how one old Wongaibon explained their failure to carry the *borba* on. 1987 C. Glass & A. Weller *Us Fellas* p. 49 [north-west WA] And I lost my Mobbin . . Mobbin, that's supposed to be some sort of **power**, where Aboriginal people . . you could protect yourself . . it'll help you. 1988 *We have Survived* Poster/n.p. Satan said, 'Have you got **power**' (magic)? If you want to fight me you have to be a clever man. 'No, I haven't got power.' Captain only had a stone axe. 1990 P. Austin et al. *Lang. & Hist.* p. 250 [Oodnadatta, northern SA] I doctored him in the morning learned about that **power**. I showed him. I pulled it out and gave it to him. I could look at the bones and everything with my forehead—guts, what sort of guts.

2 See DREAMING.

1980 M. Etienne & E.F. Leacock *Women and Colonisation* p. 243 [central Aust.] All aspects of Warlpiri society . . derive form and meaning from the sustained and complex notion of the dreaming (*jukurpa*)—now sometimes translated as '**power**' by literate Aborigines.

puller *noun* [northern Aust.] A didgeridoo player.

Origin unknown.

1943 W.E. Harney *Taboo* p. 80 [northern NT] From the river bank came the droning of the didgeredoo. The player—or **puller** as he is called—was playing a walika. **1947** W.E. Harney *Brimming Billabongs* p. 65 [northern NT] The **puller** of the didgeridoo waved it about as he beat out the dance. **1953** J.K. Ewers *With Sun on my Back* p. 25 Each group had its own '**puller**', as they call the didjeridoo player.

put through *verb* To initiate (a person). Often as **put** a person **through the rules**. See GO THROUGH.

1928 W. Robertson *Coo-ee Talks* p. 139 'I'll have to marry them.' They **put** these two young people **through** the *bunian* ceremony. The old men give the young man his *moodjingarl*, his totems, birds or animals. The women do the same for the girl. **1958** *Oceania* (Melbourne) p. 97 [NSW] 'What's happening', I said. 'They're going to **put** me **through**'. **1978** *Yura Aboriginal* (Kent Town) Feb. p. 3 [Flinders Ranges, SA] The first Malkara I can remember, is when they **put** Maurice Johnson **through the rule** and also when they put him through the last rule to become Wilyaru. **1979** J. Byno & D. Wright *Mundagudda and Warwai* p. 7 [western NSW] He went over to the Bogan, where the old people **put** him **through the rules** and made a young man out of him. **1981** S.A. Dept of Environment (Minerawuta) *Ram Paddock Gate* p. 4 [Flinders Ranges, SA] As many as six initiation ceremonies were conducted for twelve men to be **put through the rules** of the first stage and eighteen *vadnappa* were fully initiated.

rear *verb* [northern Aust.] To care for a promised wife when she is a child.

1981 G. McKenzie *Aurukun Diary* p. 193 [Aurukun, northern Qld] But this was dangerous, especially if her husband had '**reared**' her, as it was said. This meant that her husband had known from her birth that she was destined to be his when she matured, and gave his future mother-in-law presents of food for her.

right through *adverb* (Of a language) fully, fluently.

1980 T. Donaldson *Ngiyambaa* p.xvii [western NSW] And you would have to travel hundreds of miles north from Wangaaybunan country into Queensland .. before encountering a language with younger or more numerous speakers who are confident that they speak it '**right through**'. **1981** *AIAS Newsletter* (Canberra) Mar. p. 26 Flattering rumours .. surround some of us who have been active in the field that we speak this or that language '**right through**'.

rubbish *noun* Something or somebody that is taboo.

Rubbish here denotes something that cannot be said. Restrictions on speaking to someone, of someone, or something, arise for several reasons. Traditionally, in many areas, certain relatives such as brother and sister, mother-in-law and son-in-law, are forbidden to speak to each other. In many places, mentioning names associated with the recently dead is forbiddden.

1986 P. Duncan *Shame in Australia* p. 35 [Arnhem Land] A man should never speak directly to his sister . . . He . . may refer to her formally as '**rubbish**' or 'thing'.

rubbish place, a substitute name for a place which cannot be mentioned because of a recent death.

1988 Downing & Smith *Ngurra Walytja, Country of my Spirit* p. 27 [central Aust.] The death of a child . . caused them to go into the Mission. He said in interview, 'We went to the Mission because we had no food, and we didn't know what to think. This is our place . . . So we went to buy food with dingo scalps . . . We . . stayed a long time in that **rubbish place**.' [The term 'rubbish place'—'ngurra rapitji' came to mean a house or place, the name of which had become taboo because of a death there.]

rule *noun* The belief system governing Aboriginal society. See LAW 1.

> 1945 *Mankind* (Sydney) Apr. p. 208 [western NSW] The majority are influenced by Aboriginal 'rules' and express Aboriginal values and attitudes. 1971 *New Dawn* (Sydney) Jan. p. 2 [western NSW] Nowadays . . the young people of the reserve are not healthy enough. They marry relations. They don't follow the **rules**. They marry with whites . . agh! 1989 G. Knepfer *Nursing for Life* p. 52 [northern Aust.] It would not be right for Margaret, the health care worker, to take blood from an 'outside' man, because she could be 'sung' for breaking the **rule**. 1990 P. Austin et al. *Lang. & Hist.* p. 250 [Oodnadatta, northern SA] Lots of men used to come up here pretty crook. I'd have a look at their Thing and tell them too and get it without cutting them. That's the **Rule** for the Aborigine. I had to just feel him, put my hand like that and pull it out. 1993 E. Crawford *Over my Tracks* p. 154 [western NSW] 'I'll be breakin' a **rule**.' What those grannies told you stuck for life!

senior man *noun* A person of recognised authority within the community, normally an older person. See ELDER.

> 1991 *Amanbidji Land Claim* 21 Aug. n.p. Mulligan is a **senior man** . . who's very ill, and quite old.

shake a leg *noun* A traditional dance.

In traditional **shake-a-leg** dancing, the participants stand in a ring, and one at a time come forward and perform a dance, which involves a rapid in-and-out movement of the knees. The emphasis in the dance is on the virtuoso performance of this action. The dance is usually accompanied by particular music.

> 1982 L. Fogarty *Yoogum Yoogum* p. 3 [south-east Qld] He is spirit cause dancing well put **shake-a-leg** you can do. 1983 *Aboriginal History* (Canberra) Vol. 7 Pt 2 p. 161 '**Shake-a-leg**' is performed solo or as part of a small group with the dancers using an extreme spread leg movement. 1988 A. Moffat (ed.) *Aboriginal Deaths in Custody* (Transcript) p. 225 [south-east Vic.] What sort of dance do you do? . . .. There's Kangaroo dance, emu dance, crocodile dance, **shake a leg**. 1988 P. Taylor *After 200 Years* p. 263 [Cape York, northern Qld] On National Aboriginal Day we . . danced '**Shake-a-leg**', the old traditional dancing.

Hence **shaking the leg**, dancing of this kind.

> 1949 *Oceania* (Sydney) Vol. XX (I) p. 111 [north-west NSW] You got no shame, **shaking the leg** like that.

Shake a leg song, a song sung at such a dance.

> 1983 *Aboriginal History* (Canberra) Vol. 7 Pt 2 p. 160 [north Qld] A '**shake-a-leg**' **song** . . about the 'cattle station manager' is pointed social commentary. 1984 *Austral. Abor. Studies* no. 2 p. 70 Other songs sung by Dick Donnelly in the collection are . . a lullaby and a **shake-a-leg song**.

sing *verb* To make a ritual incantation, sometimes over an object or a person, usually for malevolent intent, but also for reasons of 'love magic'. See also BONE, BONING, POINT.

This ritual is a powerful expression of the action of the spiritual on the physical world and the participation of the human in this action. The spiritual world is invoked to affect the human world, either by causing injury or by affecting emotions.

1896 B. Spencer *Rep. Horn Sci. Exped. Central Aust.* Vol. IV p. 130 The man, on being told that the spear which had caused the injury had been '**sung**', that is, had undergone an incantation which bewitched it, proceeded to pine away, and he eventually died without the supervention of any surgical complications which could be detected. **1978** J. & P. Read *View of the Past* p. 314 [NT] They **sing** the nose (i.e. they sickened from sorcery) sing the two eyes, that's all. **1987** G. Francis *God's Best Country* p. 66 Those old fellas still **singing** us? **1987** N. Williams *Two Laws* p. 60 [Arnhem Land] You are always **singing** the girls' song into your face, your body and your clothing (using love magic). **1991** J. & S. Erbacher *Aborigines of the Rainforest* p. 23 [northern Qld] A girl was given over to her promised partner when she was about fifteen years of age. A ritual was performed in which the girl was '**sung**' to put a spell on her so that her affections could be caught by the promised man. **1995** *Koori Mail* Lismore 19 April p. 4/2 Not singing of that sort, Opera or country, church or pop . . . Singing the land, singing the spirits, singing the women. To **sing** up their lands, That singing—I mean.

singer *noun* A person who has a significant role in performing songs at a ceremony. See SONGMAN.

1978 K. Palmer *Somewhere Between Black and White* p. 39 [Pilbara, WA] Several of the women were acknowledged as being 'big' **singers** and took off where the men left off. **1978** *Yura Aboriginal* (Kent Town) Aug. p. 4 [SA] We stayed at Nepabunna during all the malkara times, because my father was one of the two ceremony **singers** left. **1989** A. Haebich *For their own Good* p. 218 [south-west WA] And some of the men and women were really solid **singers**.

singing *noun* A ritual incantation intended to affect another, usually with malevolent intent. See SING.

1905 R.H. Mathews *Ethnological Notes* p. 75 [south-east Aust.] If this '**singing**' has not the desired effect . . one of the invading muyulus takes off his belt and tears it down the middle. **1925** M. Terry *Across Unknown Aust.* p. 147 There is a custom, common to all Australian natives, whereby an enemy can be killed without violence. It is called 'boning', or '**singing**'. **1977** *Ink no. 2* p. 86 The two hunters came on stealthily, 'singing' their intended victim, but the victim . . began to 'counter sing' the opposition, first one and then the other. When they were helpless in a deep sleep from the '**singing**', he quietly kidney-fatted them both and upstaked his camp and moved on. **1984** *N.T. News* (Darwin) 20 Sept. p. 6/5 [northern NT] 'I like to think the black man sang them,' he says. 'They did a lot of **singing** the white man. They're sort of having their revenge.' **1986** B. Shaw *Countrymen* p. 45 [Kimberley, WA] '**Singing**' was done by getting the boots, trousers or shirts belonging to the white man, rubbing in bullock fat mixed with blackfeller fat taken from the kidney of a live man while he sleeps—he dies later—and burning the clothes. The white man's body swelled up.

smoke *noun* Smoke used for ritual purposes, particularly for cleansing rituals.

A person involved in a such a ritual may be required to walk through the smoke of a fire, or smoking branches may be carried by appropriate members of the community through a place that is to be cleansed. These practices are most often carried out after a death, to dissuade the spirit of the recently dead from disturbing the living.

1980 *Visions of Mowanjum* p. 110 [north-west WA] The women too put **smoke** on the men. This smoking ceremony is called dilni. **1986** B. Shaw *Countrymen* p. 183 [Kimberley] When he makes her bogey and gives her **smoke** she stops and forgets about it . . . They all jump over the fire and it's done. **1993** E. Crawford *Over my Tracks* p. 41 [western NSW] Kids older than us went and got the . . bush to make a **smoke**.

smoke *verb* To use smoke for ritual reasons, often in cleansing rituals after a death. People, places or things may be smoked.

> **1904** *Jrnl. & Proc. of the Royal Soc. NSW* Vol. XXXVIII p. 337 [northern Vic.] After a married woman has a child, she and her babe must be **smoked** by her old women friends, before she can appear in the main camp. **1949** *Oceania* (Sydney) Vol. XX (I) p. 104 [north-west NSW] A 'white' woman at Coonamble **smoked** her house after her husband died, and the local mixed-bloods did not really know till then that she was of aboriginal descent. **1977** A.K. Eckermann *Group Organisation and Identity* p. 304 [south-east Qld] 'Pop' was able to drive away ghosts, and to 'smoke' out houses after a death. **1980** B. Sansom *The Camp at Wallaby Cross* p. 219 [Darwin, NT] Dinghy and outboard together . . would have to be ritually purified, **smoked** and daubed with ochre. **1991** J. & S. Erbacher *Aborigines of the Rainforest* p. 21 [northern Qld] If the person dies in his house, someone is appointed to **smoke** the house . . . The people believe that the spirit of the dead person wants to continue on its journey to his place of birth, but that the familiar smell of his body draws him back to his beloved surroundings. The smoke removes his smell and releases his spirit so that it can continue on its journey. **1991** L.M. Wilkinson *Aboriginality* p. 242 [south-west Vic.] It was suggested that the house should be **smoked** with burning branches from the native cherry tree, in order to remove the spirit from the house. **1993** E. Crawford *Over my Tracks* p. 44 [western NSW] Dad, you ought to go and **smoke** yourself . . stay there all day.

smoking *noun* The act of using smoke for ritual purposes.

> **1977** A.K. Eckermann *Group Organisation and Identity* p. 304 [south-east Qld] The 'smoking' was directed equally towards the brothers, who were so frightened by the ghost that they were unable to sleep. **1980** *Visions of Mowanjum* p. 45 [north-west WA] 'Smoking' plays an important part in ceremonies. sometimes it is done with the hand which is held in the smoke of the fire, then placed on various parts of the body. Sometimes it is done with the branch of a special tree. The branch is placed in the smoke, then waved over particular persons involved in the ceremony. **1984** H. McKellar *Matya-Mundu* p. 30 [southern Qld] Granny McKellar practised **smoking** of children in time of death or when the children were playing up.

song *noun* A traditional Aboriginal song.

Songs are used within Aboriginal culture to hold the knowledge of the 'law' or the 'dreaming'. Through the singing of songs this knowledge and the ritual power of that knowledge are manifested to those in the community entitled to it. Sometimes songs are performed in a special language, different from everyday speech. Songs also have a secular, socialising role recounting events for the whole community. See DREAMING, LAW.

> **1971** K. Gilbert *End of Dreamtime* p. 9 [NSW] They (Aboriginal people) called me, Kalari, a 'Pommy' and 'Gub', laughed at my speaking, laughed when I tried to join in their **song** and dance. **1978** K. Palmer *Somewhere Between Black and White* p. 10 [Pilbara, WA] In their heads the **songs** of the old people . . in their stomachs *wibela* beer . . more bitter than the native tobacco that was chewed into a bolus ball with cadjeput bark ash. **1978** L.R. Hiatt *Austral. Aboriginal Concepts* p. 69 [central Aust.] In some areas there remain **songs** to be sung at difficult births, but these are never performed for us because they are 'too strong.' **1980** K. Liberman *Decline of Kuwarra People* p. 172 [Western Desert] That's the **song**. That's a big history, from this mark. **1988** J. Harkins *English as 'Two-way' Language* p. 137 [central Aust.] We still got the **song** for it, and we not gonna lose it, nothing. **1988** *We have Survived* Poster/n.p. [Arnhem Land] You've got to have a lot of learning to know Captain Cook. More culture. I can sing it now for this bark painting. This is the way his **song** goes. **1993** E.

Crawford *Over my Tracks* p. 164 [western NSW] He had a very, very loud voice, this Aboriginal feller, 'cos since he was a little boy he was trained to be a singer of **songs** for Corroborees.

circle song, a song consisting of a series of short songs which together tell a dreaming story.

1986 *White Invasion Diary* Invasion Diary Collective 20 Jan. n.p. [SA] Our society was guided by the land and by the cycles of the **circle songs**. The circle songs are maintained by the elders who are keepers of the components of the song.

dead song, a song associated with mourning ceremonies.

1976 J. Mirritji *My People's Life* p. 33 [Arnhem Land] I didn't understand either why so many people were coming to the camp and why they were all singing. They sang **dead songs** while the kids were playing around.

songman *noun* [Chiefly northern Aust.] A person who has a significant part in the singing at a ceremony.

In traditional Aboriginal music, the human voice is the central musical instrument, with the other instruments such as clapsticks or didgeridoo providing accompaniment. Consequently, to be a renowned singer is to be a person of importance within the community. This is further reinforced by the significance of the material being sung. Also **song man** and **song-woman**. See SONG.

1943 W.E. Harney *Taboo* p. 19 [northern NT] He is considered a great '**song man**' in the tribe. 1949 W.E. Harney *Songs of Songmen* p. 7 [northern NT] I heard the **Songman** chanting and tapping his 'time-sticks'. 1959 D. Lockwood *Crocodiles & Other People* p. 186 [northern NT] The deep bass of the didgeredoo already filled the air with rhythmic beat and a **songman** was chanting the overture to the Wonga. 1969 A.A. Abbie *Original Australs.* p. 125 Jolly, a talented Njalkpon **songman** in south-western Arnhem Land, exercised considerable individual judgement in staging publicly dances the old men considered sacred and secret. 1980 M. Dugan *Early Dreaming* p. 34 [Arnhem Land] There was the night in Arnhem Land by the banks of the Koolatong river when I talked to a **songman** who told me how he explained to his people why rivers ran. 1985 B. Neidjie *Kakadu Man* p. 26 [Arnhem Land] [He] was a prominent ceremonial leader throughout the entire region. 'He was a big **song man**'. 1986 J. Davis *No Sugar* p. 66 [south-west WA] You **song man**, you fella dance man. 1994 *Encyclop. of Aboriginal Aust.* p. 639 [SA] Pinkie was a **song-woman** and her clear sweet voice was enchanting . . . One [song] the Piltindjeri lament, relates to Pinkie's own clan: Where are those Piltindjeri now? All gone. . .

story *noun* **1** The belief system of a person and the society, especially as manifested in accounts of the dreaming. See DREAMING, LAW.

The general English use of the word is almost in direct opposition to the Aboriginal sense, in that it most often contains the idea of fiction as opposed to fact. However, the alternative meaning of the *story*, that is 'the truth', the real account of an event or situation, is closer to the Aboriginal sense.

1981 *Kimberley Land Council* (Derby) Mar. p. 21 [Kimberley] When they first came to this land they saw Aborigine painted up in his dreamtime **story** and they shot him in his dreamtime. 1985 B. Neidjie *Kakadu Man* p. 32 [Kakadu, northern NT] I hang onto this **story** all my life. My father tell me this story. My children can't lose it. 1989 R. Robinson *The Nearest the White Man Gets* p. 86 [northern NSW] This **story** is a *budgeram*. When the old people said *budgeram*, they meant 'Away back from the beginning'. 1989 B. Neidjie *Story about*

Feeling p. 123 [Arnhem Land] They can go school but this **story**, spirit, dream, e got to keep im. E got to keep it this story because this the one. **1993** E. Crawford *Over my Tracks* p. 13 [western NSW] They were dressed as all sorts of animals and birds, dressed to dance **stories**.

story place, a place associated with an important religious event, such as the activities of one of the 'dreamings'.

1978 L.R. Hiatt *Austral. Aboriginal Concepts* p. 97 [Arnhem Land] Some dreamtime **story places** are thought to be extremely dangerous, others are only relatively so. **1985** D. Eades *You Gotta Know How to Talk* p. 104 [south-east Qld] Several children had travelled with William and myself to a **story place**. **1988** P. Taylor *After 200 Years* p. 255 [Cape York, northern Qld] It's my responsibility to look after the country and the **story places**. **1991** J. & S. Erbacher *Aborigines of the Rainforest* p. 39 [northern Qld] The China Camp area contains the Kuku-Yalanji's most important religious site and is the **story place** for the beginning of their people.

story wire, a piece of wire used to trace marks on the ground to aid the telling of a story.

1983 N. Green *Desert School* p. 68 [Western Desert] They . . spent much of their leisure time in the playground playing knuckle jacks in the dust or hitting the ground with a **story wire** as they had seen the older girls doing.

2 A true account, which may include spiritual truth, of a thing, event or place.

1986 L. Hercus & P. Sutton *This is what Happened* p. 276 [NT] This is the **story** of Guns, the card game . . . That Guns is the game for which we are always sitting around. **1991** *Amanbidji Land Claim* 21 Aug. [Amanbidji, north-west NT] I'm the Land commissioner who is going to be listening to your evidence, your **stories**. **1991** D.B. Rose *Hidden Histories* p. 47 [Victoria River, NT] They reckon it's one story, every way. . . . Walman, they know. Because whitefellow never do only one place this way. Every way [they were] shooting . . . They try it in the Territory every way. That's the **story** we know from Top End—old people were losing all the people every way. Aboriginal never got away.

straight *adjective* According to the 'law', especially in relation to marriage. See RIGHT.

1938 D. Bates *Passing of Aborigines* p. 107 [Ooldea, northern SA] Irregularity crept over until there was not one **straight** marriage among the thousands I encountered. **1949** *Oceania* (Sydney) Vol. XX (I) p. 116 [north-west NSW] It kept the blood straight, kept the line **straight** and clean. **1978** K. Palmer *Somewhere Between Black and White* p. 16 [Pilbara, WA] That *nuba* **straight** one to me, you got to leave that one. **1978** J. & P. Read *View of the Past* p. 353 [NT] Tribe law was very hard law. That's why they think, gotta be, you know, they gotta keep everything true, **straight**. **1978** R. Tonkinson *Mardudjera Aborigines* p. 123 [Western Desert] No! Don't hold back; you're alright. That's a **straight** word you're giving us. **1986** P. Duncan *Shame in Australia* p. 50 They feel 'shame' until they can make the relationship '**straight**' by passing on a gift of some kind to the person they have wronged.

strong *adjective* **1** Spiritually powerful. See CLEVER.

1904 A.W. Howitt *Native Tribes S.-E. Aust.* p. 362 [south-east Vic.] His friends had made a very **strong** stick to point at him with, singing his name over it, and spitting strong poison over it. He used the word 'poison' for 'magic' . . . **1980** *Mikurrunya* (Strelley) 6 June p. 14 [Pilbara, WA] The Law at Roebourne is one of the best Laws. It is one of the **strongest** Laws there is. We cannot let that go. **1986** B. Shaw *Countrymen* p. 150 [Kimberley, WA] It's a very **strong** corroboree but we make fun at the same time. **1987** *Tjakulpa Kuwarritja* (Papunya) June n.p. [Western Desert] He said people here had to look after it . . that this place should be a **strong** place because it was our grandmothers and grandfathers' place. **1984** E. Roughsey

An Aboriginal Mother Tells p. 111 [Mornington Island, northern Qld] Well, the Dunga fish went into his belly and poked him in the eye. That fish has a **strong** legend too. **1989** D. Graham *Dying Inside* p. 75 He kept seeing things that were not there, '**strong** Aboriginal things'.

2 Powerful in Aboriginal ways. (Sometimes used adverbially.)

1978 K. Palmer & C. McKenna *Somewhere Between Black and White* p. 94 [Pilbara, WA] They were fortunate in having Tommy Sampy from Beagle Bay Mission, who knew enough to teach school, and he began to make the children **strong**. **1984** *Yeperenye Yeye* (Alice Springs) Oct. p. 7 [central Aust.] Because we want to stay **strong**, we have to speak strong. **1987** *Yeperenye Yeye* (Alice Springs) Dec. p. 20 [central Aust.] Some people said, 'Keeps the language going very **strong**. Aboriginal schools should be in Aboriginal language for us to hold'.

strong talk, angry speech.

1987 M. Christie et al. (eds) *Teaching Aboriginal Children* p. 19 '**Strong Talk**' in *yolngu* culture is associated with animosity or anger. . .

talking strong, speaking angrily.

1988 J. Harkins *English as 'Two-way' Language* p. 279 [central Aust.] **Talking strong** was used to describe speech acts . . where speakers lost their cool.

sugar bag *noun* **1** Honey, particularly that of the Australian native bee; the hive containing the honey; the bee itself.

Before the advent of European food, **sugarbag** would have been the food with the highest calorific content. Methods of finding the hive include fastening a piece of white down upon the back of a bee and following its flight home. The term probably came from the Australian English term *sugarbag*, a bag of fine sacking used to contain sugar. Aboriginal people in the nineteenth century used old sugarbags, shredded and boiled in water, to make a sweetened drink called 'bull'. This was based on a traditional drink, which was made by steeping flowers such as the banksia in water. In the last citation the term **tree sugar bag** is used to describe the honey to distinguish it from 'ground sugar bag'.

1830 R. Dawson *Present State Aust.* p. 136 [northern Aust.] The strange native pointed with his tomahawk to the tree and . . repeated the words, 'Choogar-bag Choogar-bag, Choogar-bag!' (**sugar-bag**) their English expression for honey or anything sweet. **1870** E.B. Kennedy *Four Yrs. in Qld.* p. 78 The Aboriginals . . cut out possums from a tree or **sugar bag** (wild honey) by means of a tomahawk of green stone. **1902** E.B. Kennedy *Black Police Qld.* p. 83 Ever and anon would he cast his eyes aloft and scan the spouts of the gumtrees within view looking for '**sugar bag**'—wild bees' nests. **1935** T. Rayment *Cluster of Bees* p. 513 With the advent of the white man, the more comprehensive term, '**Sugar-bag**' was used by the blacks for all species of social bees. **1947** W.E. Harney *Brimming Billabongs* p. 136 [NT] They found a '**sugar bag**' in one of the stunted gums that grew along the stony ridges of the pocket; and when it was cut out of the log, what a feast, as they sat down to scoop out the honey with their fingers. **1978** *Cent. Aust. Land Rights News* (Alice Springs) Aug. p. 8 [central Aust.] We used to go hunting for **sugar bag**, long yam, water yam, water lillie. **1982** *Puggana News* (Launceston) p. 14 [Tas.] No more '**sugarbag**' and 'cooking with leaf' but butcherman selling beef. **1986** B. Shaw *Countrymen* p. 130 [Kimberley, WA] I still go out after kangaroo and **sugar bag**. Some forget about it but I'm still after that turnout. **1986** B. Shaw *Countrymen* p. 51 [Kimberley, WA] That's the ground sugar bag, you know, not the **tree sugar bag**.

sugarbag dreaming, dreaming sites and stories associated with bees.

1994 *Encyclop. of Aboriginal Aust.* p. 475 Beeswax was used in artefacts such as mouthpieces in didjeridus and in rock art in some areas, and hives are portrayed in paintings. There are important **sugar bag** Dreamings in Northern Australia.

sugarbag fly, native bee.

1988 J. Harkins *English as 'Two-way' Language* p. 242 [central Aust.] The honey of native bees is usually called *sugarbag*, and the bees themselves are usually called *flies* or **sugarbag flies**, while the introduced bees are always called *honeybee*, never just *bee*, and their honey is called *honeybee sugar*, or just *honeybee*.

sugarbag wax, wax made by native bees.

1988 P. Taylor *After 200 Years* p. 264 [Weipa, northern Qld] They . . have to hunt around for **sugarbag wax** to fit the shells on the end of the woomera.

2 Honey produced by a honey ant; the honey ant itself.

In the second citation the honey is also called **ground sugar bag** to distinguish it from the honey of the native bee.

1985 B. Rosser *Dreamtime Nightmares* p. 63 [Qld] 'She went out and hunt rabbit, goanna. She used to get **sugarbags**.' 'Sugarbags?' 'Honeyants!'. 1986 B. Shaw *Countrymen* p. 51 [Kimberley, WA] Ground sugar bag is made by little ants. It can be covered by the tide, the saltwater everyway right round. And when the tide goes back and the men go down there, oh, you see that **sugar bag** everywhere. That's the **ground sugar bag**, you know, not the tree sugar bag.

Sunday *noun* [northern Aust.] A major ceremony (especially as **Big Sunday**).

Probably from associations with the Christian observance of Sunday as an important day of worship. Aboriginal people would have observed the significance given to Sunday by missionaries and some others, and the adoption of the term probably arose from Aboriginal (and non-Aboriginal) people attempting to convey the seriousness of Aboriginal ceremonies to non-Aboriginal people.

1947 *Oceania* (Sydney) Vol. XVIII (2) p. 266 [NT] Major ceremonies, related to what is known in the Territory as '**Big Sunday**' . . were . . discouraged. 1950 I. Tonnies (ed.) *Beitrage* p. 77 [NT] But there used to be an annual ceremony (Inawana '**Big Sunday**' that is, important secret ceremony) held at a special place. 1956 *Oceania* (Sydney) Vol. XXVI (3) p. 214 [Arnhem Land] His country, the Djaru, had three '**Sundays**' or big ceremonies. 1966 *Oceania* (Melbourne) Vol. XXXVI (1) p. 175 [central NT] Walbiri men know the Territory-wide terms '**Big Sunday**' . . and employ them especially when discussing ritual matters with Europeans. 1986 B. Shaw *Countrymen* p. 161 [Kimberley, WA] That's the **Sunday** we'd finish with, the full Sunday now taught for that young feller. 1986 B. Shaw *Countrymen* p. 145 [Kimberley, WA] Then we learnt the **Big Sunday**. You could see the sacred sticks hanging up. 1991 D.B. Rose *Hidden Histories* p. 6 [north-west NT] Stanner also found that the ceremonial complex known as '**Big Sunday**' had been taught to people of the Daly River by those of the Victoria River. 1994 *Encyclop. of Aboriginal Aust.* p. 486 [north-west NT] He spent much of his life in the bush where young men joined him to learn about the country, Dreamings, religious ritual, bushcraft and fighting. . . He was also involved at the time in organising **Big Sunday** (or Gunabibi). . .

second Sunday, a ceremony which marks another stage in acquiring sacred knowledge.

1986 B. Shaw *Countrymen* p. 161 [Kimberley, WA] When he'd finished that operation the young man stopped till he grew and nearly had a moustache . . then he was taken to the **second Sunday**.

Sunday business, a particularly sacred ceremony. See BUSINESS.

1980 T. Donaldson *Ngiyambaa* p. 79 [Daly River, NT] These were the days of poonj or '**Sunday business**'.

take *verb* [northern Aust.] To spiritually own, look after and be responsible for (something). See CARRY, FOLLOW, HOLD.

1988 J. Harkins *English as 'Two-way' Language* p. 19 [central Aust.] E gonna be **take** e's grandfather's, mother's, mother's, father's, father's, father's lingo. Gotta take four corners. 1991 *Amanbidji Land Claim* 21 Aug. [north-east NT] What country do those children **take**?

thing *noun* [northern Aust.] A euphemism for a sacred or secret object or concept or for a person with whom one has an 'avoidance relationship' (someone with whom one should have minimal social contact). For a fuller discussion on avoidance relationships see Chapter 2.

1980 B. Sansom *The Camp at Wallaby Cross* p. 62 [Darwin, NT] That fella bin singin that **thing** (the spell) and gibin that thing (the substance) bin make mistake! 1986 P. Duncan *Shame in Australia* p. 35 [Arnhem Land] A man should never speak directly to his sister . . . He . . may refer to her formally as 'rubbish' or '**thing**'. 1986 B. Shaw *Countrymen* p. 125 And if the mother is found, gets that **thing** he'll (the ghost) go away properly the next year, not today. We watch that woman who has the right Thing, that dead body come back to her, and we have to call the baby the same name as the feller who died. 1988 P. Taylor *After 200 Years* p. 277 [Western Desert] All the old men's **things** are kept in this one place now . . . They should not be seen by women and children.

time *noun* [Chiefly northern Aust.] A specific period.

Traditional Aboriginal society did not use numerical ways of measuring time, or of registering the chronological relationships between one event and another. In contemporary society, to locate an event in the same time period as another, or to fix it in relation to the present, different referential systems are used alongside the non-Aboriginal ones. One may categorise a **time**: by reference to seasons or natural occurrences, such as **hot time, married turtle time**; by reference to the name of a significant person such as **Father Gribble Time** or **Gough Whitlam time**; by reference to a set of events and experiences associated with particular social circumstances, such as **police time, welfare time**; by reference to significant cultural happenings, such as **corroboree time**. Non-Aboriginal speakers of Australian English have a similar use in expressions such as **Christmas time, springtime** but the Aboriginal use is far more extensive.

1 With reference to seasons and weather.

1965 F.G.G. Rose *Wind of Change* p. 179 [central Aust.] A large number of Aborigines are on their way here from Ernabella for corroborees and man-making ceremonies during the coming '**hot-time**'. 1978 J. & P. Read *View of the Past* p. 171 [central Aust.] 'We have clothes for you-feller, and blanket too.' Like this time, now **cold weather time**, you know. 1983 *Upper Daly Land Claim* p. 48 [north-west NT] The Wagiman people divide the annual cycle into five seasonal periods: . . 'little bit warm, hot time' . . '**rain time**, main rain'. 1984 K. Benterrak & S. Muecke & P. Roe *Reading Country* p. 109 That was south-east time too, **cold time**. 1995

M. Brady *Giving away the Grog* p. 93 Next morning he went walking from there to Kildurk, but he couldn't make it, **hot weather time.**

2 With reference to the activities of plants and animals.

1984 S. Cane *Desert Camps* p. 33 [central Aust.] Summer rains stimulated plant growth . . this growing season was called the '**green grass time**' (*yugari*) by the Aborigines and extended from about March until May. **1984** S. Cane *Desert Camps* p. 34 [central Aust.] The end of the cold season was heralded by the sudden appearance of warm westerly winds and the movement of reptiles from hibernation. The Aborigines called this season the '**goanna get up time**' or *Djintubalya* (sun good). This season lasted from August until October. **1984** E. Roughsey *An Aboriginal Mother Tells* p. 54 [Mornington Island, northern Qld] My people never knew to call our weathers by their seasons . . . It was by certain food . . 'water lily time, we dig for and eat them', or '**Palm nut time** is on'. **1987** E. Paddy & M. Smith *Boonja Bardak Korn* p. 6 [north-west WA] Inland bloodwood is good firewood during July, the cold season, and for '**married turtle time**' in November–December. **1990** Davis et al. *Paperbark* p. 70 [Western Desert] It was spring time, **quondong ripe time.**

3 With reference to particular events or occasions.

1978 *Yura Aboriginal* (Kent Town) Aug. p. 4 [Flinders Ranges, SA] We stayed at Nepabunna during all the malkara [**ceremony**] **times**, because my father was one of the two ceremony singers left. **1980** *Puggana News* May p. 7 [Tas.] Old coves, I s'pose that's what we'll be, just like Truganinni. They'll talk about us, **birdin' time** Old coves that used to be. **1980** *Mikurrunya* (Strelley) 7 Nov. p. 3 [Strelley, north-west WA] The **Business Time** is part of the Aboriginal School. The Aboriginal School goes on all the time. **1980** *Visions of Mowanjum* p. 80 [Kimberley, WA] **Corroboree time**—the 'balga', or 'cobba cobba'—was, and still is, a time of deep joy. **1985** H. Koch *Non-standard English in Aboriginal* p. 183 The time of the initiation ceremony may be called **making young man time** . . or simply *young man*: (42) Mr Howie: When do they do it? Archie Long: We do it for *young man* . . Yes, we do it at *young man*, every Christmas.

4 With reference to a collection of events and experiences. Most **times** are self-evident, except possibly **police times**, the period up till about the Second World War in the Northern Territory when police were the official 'protectors' (controllers) of Aboriginal people; **welfare times** the period following this when there was an Aboriginal welfare department run by the Commonwealth Government; **mission times** the period in Queensland when church missions were a major influence in some Aboriginal communities, as opposed to the **government times** when the government took over the management of Aboriginal affairs.

1978 J. & P. Read *View of the Past* p. 71 [Victoria River, NT] Keep him there for, I dont know, might be nearly twelve years. From **young time** to old. **1981** A. Cavadini et al. *Two Laws* p. 70 [Borroloola, north-east NT] They talk about the attempted destruction of their Aboriginal law, about **police times** and **welfare times**, about what has happened, how and why. **1981** *Social Alternatives* (Brisbane) Vol. II no. 2 p. 25 They have a firmly established history . . later through **mission times** and finally in '**government' times**. **1984** S. Cane *Desert Camps* p. 126 [central Aust.] As the hot time progressed the supplies of food . . ran out . . . The only food left to collect within the foraging radius of the rockhole were goannas . . . The Aborigines aptly called this the '**hard time**', '**hungry time**' or '**meat time**'. **1988** J. Harkins *English as 'Two-way' Language* p. 245 [central Aust.] Aboriginal and non-Aboriginal speakers share a set of terms specific to, or with specialised meanings in, the contact situation, which can only be briefly mentioned here. These include terms such as **welfare-time** (the protectionist era), **army-time** (World War II). **1990** A. Pring (ed.) *Women of the Centre* p. 12

[central Aust.] The rhythms of Areyonga residents lives were partly structured by the alternation of '**buyin' time**' (pension week) and 'nothing-a-week'. **1990** *Aboriginal History* (Canberra) p. 38 [north-east NT] In some cases such alignment was an important survival tactic during the '**wild times**' when Aboriginal people not associated with a European boss were often indiscriminately killed. **1991** L.M. Wilkinson *Aboriginality* p. 216 [Vic.] This may have been the influence of both parents who were raised during the **mission times**.

5 With reference to significant people or places.

Father Gribble was a well-known missionary in North Queenland; Barambah was the name of a mission in North Queensland; **Macassan times** refers to the period ending early this century when Indonesian fishermen came to the coast of northern Australia in search of trepang.

1988 *Social Alternatives* (Brisbane) p. 24 [south-east Qld] And I remember the time when our people only had humpies to live in, at **Barambah time**, when it was Barambah mission. **1989** J. Thomson *Reaching Back* p. 57 [northern Qld] In **Father Gribble time**, we just go down to the flat where the men play football. **1989** R.M. Baker *Land is Life* p. 195 (caption) [Borroloola, north-east NT] **Macassan times** . . **Gough Whitlam times**, This (**tourist time**) . . Yanyuwa recognised historical phases.

traditional *adjective* Of or relating to Aboriginal people, events or other matters that are directly connected to or very like Aboriginal life before the British invasion.

This term was first used by non-Aboriginal people but is now used by Aboriginal people to describe aspects of their heritage; it is also applied to some of the cultures and people making up contemporary Aboriginal Australia.

1973 *Durrung* (Northcote) July p. 15 [Vic.] *Aborigines Demand Land Rights Now!!!* i.e. all reserves, sacred sites, areas of **traditional** or cultural significance. **1978** J. & P. Read *View of the Past* p. 47 [Arnhem Land] It was for ceremony, **traditional** string. **1983** *Community* Tas. Education Department p. 8 [Tas.] As well as modern foods, **traditional** foods like periwinkles, abalone and wallaby are prepared. **1985** *Aboriginal Health Worker* (Little Bay) Dec. Vol. IX p. 44 We keep our **traditional** view of our land as something not only belonging to us, but something to which we belong. **1985** *Aboriginal Health Worker* (Little Bay) Dec. Vol. IX p. 17 [Tas.] In May this year we held a **traditional** ceremony cremating our ancestors' remains and setting their spirits free in their homeland. **1988** P. Taylor *After 200 Years* p. 263 [Cape York, northern Qld] On National Aboriginal Day we . . danced 'Shake-a-leg', the old **traditional** dancing. **1988** C. Mattingley & K. Hampton (eds) *Survival in Our Own Land* p. 76 [SA] He . . was seeking half an acre for a hut in Meningie, his **traditional** country, to make it easier to send his children to school. **1989** J. Thomson *Reaching Back* p. 128 [Yarrabah, northern Qld] I have **traditional** land, way up the beach. **1995** *Koori Mail* Lismore 4 Oct. p. 40/2 From the opening ceremony . . aspects of all the cultures present were performed in song, dance and **traditional** language.

tribal *adjective* (Of people or societies) relating to Aboriginal life before the British invasion.

This term is used in the same way as 'traditional'.

1957 *Sydney Morning Herald* 4 Jan. p. 11/2 [WA] I was in B-wing which contained all the old **tribal** people. Some were very homesick for their country so far away. **1978** J. & P. Read *View of the Past* p. 234 [Lajamanu, north-west NT] They're broken up in culture and they're broken up in **tribal** law. **1979** M. Wilson *Original Culture* p. 34 [NSW] Even though I don't come from the Northern Territory or Queensland, and I'm not **tribal**, still I can assure you that's what I am, an Aborigine. **1979** L. Andrews *Kinship & Community at Wreck Bay* p. 35

[south coast, NSW] Not all the '**tribal**' names, as they are called by the people, died out. **1979** *Puggana News* (Launceston) Dec. p. 5 [Tas.] Less than two centuries ago our **tribal** ancestry possessed and used the land that is Tasmania. **198**- S.M. Kelly *Long Road Back* p. 71 [north-west WA] They do not have stock on 'Strelley'. It is **Tribal** Law country. **1981** W.J.K. Christensen *The Wangkayi* p. 223 [Kalgoorlie, WA] Elements of this traditional pattern survive in what is now recognised in Kalgoorlie as '**tribal**' . . marriage. **1982** C. Russell (comp.) *People in a Community* p. 2 [Qld] They would . . teach them to forget about their Aboriginal **tribal** teaching, laws and language. **1983** P. Roe *Gularabulu* p. 21 [north-west WA] He had his wife too—married **tribal** way you know. **1984** B. Swanton *Aborigines and Criminal Justice* p. 92 [central Aust.] They said they needed an Aboriginal person who was tribal, who understood their . . **tribal** responsibilities. **1985** *Black Voices* (Townsville) Oct. p. 22 [northern Qld] He stayed with Graham because he was his **tribal** brother. **1987** C. Glass & A. Weller *Us Fellas* p. 45 [northern WA] I look quite fair and that but I'm really **tribal**. Got tribal ways. **1989** J. Moore *Aboriginal Deaths in Custody* (Transcript) p. 76 [Swan Hill, northern Vic.] Any Aboriginal from these areas that don't fight with one another, I don't want to know them because right back from **tribal** days it's always happened. **1992** R.L. Ginibi *Real Deadly* p. 43 [NSW] James asked me to look after the girls until he could send them back to their **tribal** granny in Coonamble.

war *noun* [Chiefly northern Aust.] A conflict between Aboriginal groups.

Non-Aboriginal people generally use the terms 'fight' or 'battle' to describe conflict between Aboriginal groups, possibly because they lack an understanding of the nature of Aboriginal political structures, and hence estimate serious conflict as 'only' a 'fight'. An Aboriginal group from a different country is likely to describe conflict with another as **war** which might be made up of different 'battles'. See COUNTRY.

1987 N. Williams *Two Laws* p. 151 Yolngu often referred to the suppression of revenge killing, which they sometimes called 'Yolngu **war**' that followed the imposition of Australian law in terms that implied they were grateful. **1989** *Aboriginal Children* p. 4 [Arnhem Land] They listen to stories by adults: About old times when old people were little, about **wars** etc. About . . creation stories . . ceremony—what they should do. **1991** *Hidden Histories* p. 103 [north-west NT] Every way they were fighting, blackfellow. That **war** fight . . Yanyuru, Wardaman, Nungali, Ngarinman, Jaminjung, everywhere they fought now. War fight. **1991** *Hidden Histories* p. 103 [north-west NT] Big Mick also spoke back to the time of his father, before European invasion, saying that conflict was both present and manageable: 'That was good country, then. They used to knock it off, that **war**.'

whiskers *noun plural* [Formerly widespread but now chiefly northern Aust.] Facial hair; the beard. Also **whisker**.

The term is used to locate an event in a man's life time by reference to whether it was before or after he had **whiskers**. See also TIME. This is another example of the use of a term no longer current in general Australian English, where the singular **whisker** is not used in this sense and the plural **whiskers**, meaning the 'beard', is generally associated with historical references as in 'mutton chop whiskers' or used in joking reference.

1904 A.W. Howitt *Native Tribes S.-E. Aust.* p. 256 Berak . . added that at that time he was a boy without **whiskers**. **1978** J. & P. Read *View of the Past* p. 89 [central Aust.] I bin see him (when I was) little bit young feller. Havem **whisker** today. I bin little young feller. **1981** *Aboriginal History* (Canberra) Vol. V Pt 1 p. 13 [northern Qld] I was only a good sized boy no **whiskers** yet. My father and I lived . . on top, in the hills . . not sandbeach. **1990** P. Austin et al. *Lang. & Hist.* p. 244 [Oodnadatta, northern SA] I was a big boy then, a little bit **whiskers**. **1995** M. Brady *Giving away the Grog* p. 142 [northern SA] **Whiskers**, *tjuta* lot of whiskers, i.e., young adult drinking then, fighting round.

word *noun* **1** An understanding; a statement of an idea or truth.

1980 B. Sansom *The Camp at Wallaby Cross* p. 24 [Darwin, northern NT] And just as the **word** can be given or stolen, its holder can stint it: 'No. Leave him. He not gonna get that word.' **1986** B. Shaw *Countrymen* p. 215 [Kimberley, WA] The young boys had to take all those ideas from the old people, those who could stand and listen to you and catch that **word**. **1986** B. Shaw *Countrymen* p. 77 [Kimberley, WA] I carry my own **word**. You can run that straight as a fucking line, an old line like a fishing line. You know, you take your word straight. **1987** T.S. Dixon *The Wizard of Alice* p. 348 [central Aust.] I 'eard this word when they read . . it out to me. All that **word** true . . the English word 'statement' is translated by 'angukatja' which is the basic idea of anything spoken. **1991** D.B. Rose *Hidden Histories* p. 202 [Victoria River, NT] I'm talking for the girls' **words** now.

2 Aboriginal language.

1985 B. Neidjie *Kakadu Man* p. 47 [Arnhem Land] I speak English for you, so you can lis . . so you can know . . you will understand. If I put my **words** [language] in same place, you won't understand. **1990** P. Austin et al. *Lang. & Hist.* p. 246 [Oodnadatta, northern SA] I came back to Kununurra when I was a big man. I was there a long time one year. They were Warramanga blackfellers, a different lingo. I can catch different **words**. That Kimberley word's too quick. I can't catch it.

3 The Aboriginal belief system. See LAW.

1986 B. Shaw *Countrymen* p. 83 [Kimberley, WA] They put me through the **word**, and they taught me.

wrong *adjective & adverb* Outside the 'law', especially in relation to marriage.

A person or relationship can be said to be **wrong** for somebody or a person can be said to have married **wrong**. See also RIGHT. **Wrong** marriages are those outside the structure of Aboriginal marriage patterns, which were based on a kinship group structure and the limitation of the choice of marriage partners from among different groups. A **wrong** marriage can cause great social distress, because it disrupts the social alliances made through marriage. Colonisation has greatly altered marriage patterns in the south, although people are in general aware of inappropriate relationships, but in northern Australia the traditional structure is still apparent among some groups of people.

1928 B. Spencer *Wanderings in Wild Aust.* p. 169 [central Aust.] All I found was that some women belonged to what our boy called the right side of the tribe whom he could marry, and others belonged to the **wrong** side, and these he could not marry. **1935** *Aborigines Protector* (Asscn for Protection of Native Races) June p. 8 No one should be given a permit to employ natives who allow 'wrong' marriages, the great cause of tribal demoralisation. **1943** W.E. Harney *Taboo* p. 183 [northern Aust.] I accused him of being 'wrong side' as he, being a Jumbijinya, would call a Numbunya, sister. **1949** *Oceania* (Melbourne) Vol XIX p. 108 [north-west NSW] Marrying **wrong** is the ruination of the aboriginal race. **1950** I. Tonnies (ed.) *Beitrage* p. 74 [Daly River, north-west NT] Names are not normally exchanged in *Warabatj*; there are cases of such exchanges, but it is regarded as going 'wrong' way' or 'short cut'. **1957** W.E. Harney *Life Among Aborigines* p. 18 [northern Aust.] Marriage in the Karamalah tribe was 'wrong' side'—an aboriginal saying that means 'not in line' or not correct by tribal law. **1958** J. Becket *A Study of a Mixed Blood Aboriginal Minority* p. 55 [western NSW] At Carowra Tank, people began marrying '**wrong**' after the first world war. **1980** *Yorky Billy* (Film Transcript) AIAS Canberra p. 4 [NT] Yes, her father and mother .. she was promised .. these Aborigines they say sometimes **wrong**-side, for your half mother, half sister, and all this. But my wife, they said 'You're *straight* for her'. **1989** R.M. Baker *Land is Life* p. 253 [Borroloola, NT] Until about 1960 couples who had left Borroloola to marry **wrong** way would expect a fight on their return. **1991** L.M. Wilkinson *Aboriginality* p. 215 [south-west Vic.] One older man (aged 74) has never married. He described his reasons, as fear of marrying someone of the '**wrong** skin'.

yorga *noun* [south-west WA] A woman. Also **yok**, **yoka**, **york**.

From the Nyungar language of south-western WA *yok*, 'a woman'. Although an Aboriginal language word, it is used with English plural endings.

1910 (1975) E. Hassell *My Dusky Friends* p. 132 [south-west WA] At last he took a third **york**. She was a foolish young thing, but very fond of him .. he paid her more attention than the generality of husbands. **1968** W.H. Douglas *Aboriginal Language of south-west Aus.* p. 23 [south-west WA] '**Yokas**' is 'girls' (Note the English plural suffix on yoka). **1981** Archie Weller *Day of Dog* p. 135 [south-west WA] 'Not much work going 'ere, orright, drinkin' gabba and smokin'. Where's all the **yorgas**?' Pretty Boy grins. **1982** J. Davis *Kullark* p. 16 [south-west WA] I'll tell you what 'e'll do, e'll finish up marryin' some Wetjala **yok**, 'ave blue-eyed kids and 'e won't want nothing to do with us. **1986** A. Weller *Going Home* p. 141 [south-west WA] 'Yeah. Us blokes are fuckin' muritch,' said Morry lazily .. 'Ssh, youse mob. Couple **yorgas** comin' in.' **1991** G. Ward *Unna you fullas* [south-west WA] Their mother had told them he met a **yorga**, whom he was mardong for.

young *adjective* (Of a person) newly initiated through ceremony into adulthood.

As with 'old', the emphasis is on someone who is young in knowledge rather than age, although in fact it almost always refers to chronologically young people. The citations almost all refer to **young** men; records of ceremonies for 'making' **young** women are less often found in the literature because the gender basis of knowledge in Aboriginal society meant that male anthropologists had only a partial understanding of ceremony. Also, these particular ceremonies seem to have been more adversely affected by colonisation than those for men.

1976 *Identity* (Sydney) Jan. p. 18 No .. you are too young to have a lubra. I could not let you have one. You are not a **young** man yet. **1979** J. Byno & D. Wright *Mundagudda and Warwai* p. 7 [western NSW] He went over to the Bogan, where the old people put him through the rules and made a **young** man out of him. **1985** H. Koch *Non-standard English in Aboriginal* p. 183 [NT] The term **young** man .. is more restricted in its meaning in Aboriginal usage than in SE; it refers specifically to an initiated male youth. **1986** B. Shaw *Countrymen* p. 143 [Kimberley, WA] All the way I did the Law, in every place I came through, the Law for the **young** men. **1993** D. Hodge *Did you meet any Malagas?* p. 51 [northern NT] And in Larrakia eyes, I'm only considered a **young** boy at the moment. I haven't had my final cut, as they say.

young man corroboree, a ceremony of initiation. Also **young man ceremony**.

1937 E. Hill *Great Australian Loneliness* p. 33 [NT] Its only navigators were the native tribes, travelling up and down for feasts and fights and '**young man corroborees**'. **1970** J. Makin *The Big Run* p. 13 [Victoria River, north-west NT] The most important aspect of initiation was his preparation to be a man of the tribe—hence the operation was (and is) known as the '**young-man ceremony**'.

young man time, the period when initiation occurs.

1985 H. Koch *Non-standard English in Aboriginal* p. 183 [NT] The time of the initiation ceremony may be called making **young man time** . . or simply *young man*: (42) Mr Howie: When do they do it? Archie Long: We do it for *young man* . . Yes, we do it at *young man*, every Christmas.

young woman, a woman newly initiated through ceremony into adulthood.

1904 *Jrnl. & Proc. of the Royal Soc. NSW* Vol. XXXVIII p. 336 [Vic.] Among the Yota-yota and adjoining tribes on the Murray River the ceremony of 'making **young women**' is called *dhuddiwai*.

CHAPTER 2

Kin

One of the characteristics of contemporary Aboriginal life is a continuing importance of family in the structure of society. Aboriginal society before Europeans arrived functioned to a great degree through kinship. The sharing of food, participation in ritual, and responsibility to land were all understood in kinship terms. The way one person behaved towards another was governed to a great extent by his or her kin relation to that person. For example, an uncle might have certain ritual responsibilities in his nephew's initiation ritual, a woman in labour might be helped by certain relatives, a person might become responsible for the ritual associated with a part of country because it was that person's grandmother's country, and a hunter might be obliged to share particular parts of his kill with particular relatives.

In the traditional kinship terminology of Aboriginal languages, two processes were at work. One was the use of a more detailed kinship vocabulary than is found in languages such as English. This made it possible to distinguish for instance between elder brother and younger brother, mother's sister and father's sister, cross cousin (the children of mother's brother or father's sister) and parallel cousin (the children of mother's sister or father's brother). The other process was to apply kinship terms such as **father** or **mother** to people biologically distantly related but who had parental obligations to those whom they would then call **son** or **daughter**. The effect of this terminology was that the term 'mother' was applied to a person who was not necessarily a parent but who functioned socially as a mother and hence owed and was owed the social and economic obligations that went with being a 'mother'.

Colonisation brought great changes to the Aboriginal kinship systems, especially in the south, but there are still differences in the way Aboriginal kinship works from the way it does among most non-Aboriginal Australians. Aboriginal people recognise and claim as kin, people who have long dropped out of recognition in many non-Aboriginal families. The Aboriginal English sense of 'family' is different from that of the majority of other Australian communities. The word 'family' as posed in the question commonly heard among Aboriginal people in Southern Australia 'What's your **family**?' includes a far greater range of relatives than would be understood in standard English except in the context of a family reunion. The answer is not a nuclear family or even an extended family but a grouping of extended families. People are called by their kin names as once was common in British English, because the mutual obligations of kinship are still significant within Aboriginal society, and addressing someone by their kin name is a recognition of this.

Kin categories found in Aboriginal languages now need to be expressed in Aboriginal English. Sometimes new combinations of terms have been formed such as **cousin sister** for a parallel cousin, to cover the sense not found in either the English terms 'cousin' or 'sister', or the terms have been qualified, as in **second mother** meaning 'aunt'. Generally, however, Aboriginal society has taken English kin terms and expanded the meaning, so that **mother**, **father** and **sister** are all applied to people who in general English use might be called 'aunt', 'uncle' and 'cousin'. Aboriginal English has also retained archaic kin terms once commonly used in English such as **cuz** or **granny**. LANGUAGE words are sometimes used for kin terms, such as **jarjum** for 'child'. Also included in this chapter are words that describe other human relationships, such as **jarmbie**, 'mate'.

aunty *noun* [Chiefly recorded in southern Australia but probably becoming more widespread] An older woman, often wise in traditional knowledge, having status within her community. It is also used as a term of address to such a person. Also **aunt**.

'Aunty' is used in other Englishes to refer to non-relatives, usually by children of a close family friend. It does not have the sense of a recognised social status of the Aboriginal English use.

1949 *Oceania* Vol. XIX Dec. p. 94 [western NSW] The commonest of these terms is '**aunty**' which is used for any female who is approached for money or food. **1973** M. Fennel & A. Grey *Nucoorilma* p. 98 [N. Ucumbal, NSW] Those in the aunt/uncle relation are called by their Christian names; those not in this direct relation are addressed as '**Aunt**' or 'Uncle' as a term of respect. **1985** *Puggana News* (Launceston) July p. 5 [Tas.] WWPS next trip down was with **Auntie** Ida, Auntie Girlie and Verna. **1988** I. Keen *Being Black* p. 80 [Adelaide, SA] The majority of younger people addressed . . Mary as . . '**Aunty**', 'Nana' . . . Most of these were genealogically related to Max and Mary . . but the few who were not addressed them as kin nonetheless. **1991** A. Jackomos & D. Fowell *Living Aboriginal Hist. of Vict.* p. 166 I was . . brought into the world by an old Aboriginal midwife, **Aunty** Florrie Walker. **1993** E. Crawford *Over My Tracks* p. 14 [western NSW] All of us had to call all grownups Mister, Missus, Uncle, **Aunty**, Granny, Grandfather, whatever was respectful, even if they weren't our real Uncle or Granny.

blood *adjective* Of relatives, close. See also CLOSE, NEAR, TRUE.

Blood relatives are usually those who are too close to be eligible for marriage. Traditionally, Aboriginal people had a limited range of people considered appropriate marriage partners. See RIGHT and WRONG.

1949 *Oceania* (Melbourne) Vol. XIX Dec. p. 107 [north-west NSW] If there is a medicine-man in the community, or an elderly initiated man, he acts as the conscience of the group in heightening their awareness of irregularities in marriage, voicing his disapproval of those who have chosen partners who should be classified as '**blood**' relatives. **1949** *Oceania* (Melbourne) Vol. XIX Dec. p. 106 [north-west NSW] What would the old people think? There's — living with — and he's her **blood** uncle. **1963** D.E. Barwick *Little More than Kin* (PhD thesis) p. 263 [Vic.] People feared that 'soon the whole group will be **blood** relations'. **1974** *Aborigines in the 70's* Monash University; Centre for Research into Aboriginal Affairs p. 66 [Vic.] I got into close contact with Bill Onus who was a **blood** uncle, my mother's brother. **1978** *Working Together* Qld. Aboriginal and Islander Teacher Aide Dev. p. 32 [northern Qld] Your mother's brother's son is your **blood** cousin. **1984** E. Roughsey *An Aboriginal Mother Tells* p. 107 [Mornington Island, northern Qld] As I grew up to understand my people, I soon found out that most of the people weren't real full **blood** relation but . . they were countrymen. **1990** S. Watson *Kadaitcha Sung* p. 99 [south-east Qld]

No, mate, me and the lad here are **blood**. **1991** L.M. Wilkinson *Aboriginality* p. 203 [western Vic.] Up to fourth cousin is regarded as '**blood**' and from then on regarded as 'kin'.

blooded *adjective* Eligible for marriage.

1980 R.M.W. Dixon *The Languages of Australia* p. 39 [northern Qld] I asked on what grounds Gambilbarra and Jabunbarra were regarded as two parts of a single tribe, and Dulgubarra as belonging to a different tribe. The answer was that the Jirrbalgnan were 'all **blooded**'; that is, . . a Gambilbarra would normally acquire a spouse from within either Gambilbarra or Jabunbarra local groups—from within the Jirrbalgnan tribe.

boori *noun* A child. Also **boorie, boorai**.

From the Wiradjuri language of south-western NSW *buurraay* 'a child'. For the plural form, the English plural ending *s* is used.

c.**1900** R.H. Mathews (Field Notebk.) iii p. 51 **Boorai**, a child of either sex. **1906** J.F.H. Mitchell *Aboriginal Dict.* p. 9 **Bouri** . . . A boy. **1971** *New Dawn* (Haymarket) Apr. p. 9 [NSW] Send them to **Booris** Corner c.o. The Editor NEW DAWN. 'Bye for now kids, see you next month. **1977** M. Tucker *If Everyone Cared* p. 50 [south-west NSW] The people in a cluster of mia-mias were a peaceful-living lot, their children happy and well-cared for little **boories**. **1991** *Sydney Morning Herald* 16 Dec. 1/5 [south-west NSW] The Aboriginal children are of the Wiradjuri tribe, and although none can speak the entire language, some words survive, and are used by all the pupils. In their own playground kidspeak, *narrabung* is silly, a *yamble* is a tall story, a **boori** is a child, a *warjin* is a girl, and so on.

brother *noun* **1** A close relative of the same generation, often a parallel cousin.

1884 *Jrnl. Royal Anthrop. Inst. Great Brit. & Ireland* (1971) Vol. XIII p. 301 [Qld] Hundreds of times a black boy has said 'Such and such a one is my **brother**', when I knew he was not a brother as we call such a relationship . . . A blackfellow will say . . . 'So many are my fathers', or 'So many mothers I have', he should call them uncles or aunts. **1903** *Folklore* (London) p. 14/4 [WA] Josepha . . calls boys and girls her **brothers** and sisters, whose parents are neither of them hers. **1931** *Understanding Austral. Aborigine* (Morpeth Booklet no. 2) p. 14 [NSW] Thus, when a blackfellow says that such and such a native is his **brother**, the white person, knowing that they are not blood brothers, thinks his informant is untruthful. But the white man errs. **1991** Reid & Trompf *Health Aboriginal Aust.* p. 82 The most outstanding aspect of Aboriginal kinship systems was, and in many places still is, the existence of whole classes of people identified by an Aboriginal person as his, or her '**brothers**', 'fathers', 'sisters', 'mothers', 'husbands', 'wives' or the various other classes of affines.

2 A form of address for a sibling, as once was common in English, or a gesture of solidarity with another Aboriginal person of the same generation.

1990 R. Bowden & B. Bunbury *Being Aboriginal* p. 16 Even if you don't know them . . in a restaurant or a pub . . It's . . 'Sis' or '**Brother**'. **1993** E. Crawford *Over my Tracks* p. 41 [western NSW] My Uncles and Aunties called each other Sister and **Brother**, and so that's the way we grew up. My kids do it sometimes too.

budda *noun* [south-east and south-west Aust.] A term of address for an Aboriginal man of the same generation as the speaker, used as a term of some degree of kinship, and/or affection and solidarity. Also **budder**.

Probably from an Aboriginal pronunciation of 'brother'.

1982 YACS *Mt. Penang's Young Men go West* n.p. [NSW] Each calls the other brother, or as they say '**budder**'. **1986** A. Weller *Going Home* p. 1 'Now, Dougie would of been in the New division.' 'Ow'd they treat ya, **budda**?' **1991** L.M. Wilkinson *Aboriginality* p. 204 'Sis' and '**budda**' may refer to siblings, but this term may equally apply to those kin who are not siblings, but are within the same age group.

bunji *noun* A mate, a close friend. Also **bunjie**.

Origin unknown.

1972 *Bunji* (Darwin) Feb. p. 1 [Darwin, NT] But the day is coming, and its not far. When you must decide, **bunji**, who you are. 1982 L. Fogarty *Yoogum Yoogum* p. 47 [south-east Qld] Fill it up **bunji** I'll have another. 1988 K. Gilbert *Inside Black Australia* p. 54 Aboriginals collectively believe that no 'honour' can come from one as dishonourable as the thieving British Empire, believing instead that our 'Good on you, **Bunji**' . . is the greatest accolade we . . can bestow on one another. 1990 S. Watson *Kadaitcha Sung* p. 134 [south-east Qld] He always big-noting himself, but he your **bunjie** so I'd better not rubbish him too much. 1993 C. Mackinolty (Private Letter to W.S. Ramson) n.p. Over much of the Northern Territory and into the eastern Kimberleys, the word **bunji** has a quite different meaning! Over this way bunji is a kinship term, loosely a brother-in-law, or someone you are in a marriageable relationship with, and as such is a term of respect. In recent years, the meaning especially in towns where there is less knowledge of strict kinship systems, the term has a broader meaning, perhaps, of mate (and indeed sometimes in Kriol and Aboriginal English, the term mate is used interchangeably with bunji).

close *adjective* (Of a relative) having a very close familial relationship—as distinct from a person who may be addressed as mother, sister, etc., but whose relationship is actually more distant. See also NEAR, TRUE.

This is also used in non-Aboriginal English, as in 'close family', but is applied to a greater range of kin situations in Aboriginal English.

1962 M.J. Meggitt *Desert People* p. 44 [central NT] Eventually Judy became such a nuisance that she was leg-roped to a shady tree for some days, and her **close** daughter Polly kept her supplied with food, water and words of comfort. 1977 *Black News Service* Dec. p. 1 'Is it right?' His **close** relations will cry, But share lots of money when he's die. 1981 *AIAS Newsletter* (Canberra) 15 Mar. p. 14 But we not family. We not **close**-to relations. 1981 W.J.K. Christensen *The Wangkayi* p. 203 [Kalgoorlie, WA] He nodded towards a **close** 'brother' who had joined him, in Perth, adding simply 'my mob's here.' 1983 M. Sharpe *Traeger Kid* p. 69 [northern NSW] The **close** family were crying and wailing. 1987 S. Morgan *My Place* p. 231 [WA] My children would be your relations. Tommy, he's **close**, and others, too, then there's some that you're related to but not close, if you get what I mean. 1988 V.K. Burbank *Aboriginal Adolescence* p. 70 [northern Aust.] Lyle and Margot did not succeed in marrying until 1970 . . . This couple is regarded as incorrect because Lyle married his '**close**' 'mother's brother's daughter'.

coe *noun* [Tas.] A person from the islands of Bass Strait. Also **co**, **cove**.

From 'cove', originally sixteenth-century criminal slang for 'bloke'. There is also a sixteenth-century slang form 'co'. This is used by both Aboriginal and non-Aboriginal people on the Bass Strait islands. It is included here because of its significance in Tasmanian Aboriginal life.

1980 *Puggana News* (Launceston) May p. 7 Old **coves**, I 'spose that's what we'll be, just like Truganinni. They'll talk about us, birdin' time. Old coves that used to be. 1985 *Puggana News* (Launceston) July p. 10 [Tas.] Who was the grizzly **co** . . who greeted the Nuclear Disarmament Party. 1990 O. Noonuccal *Aust. Legends and Landscapes* p. 115 They were yarning away about all sorts of things, the old **coes*** on the islands, where family is now, all that kind of talk. [*Old coes is an island slang meaning 'old coves', coming from seamen's slang meaning 'mate'. Used mainly by Cape Barren Islanders and the people on Flinders Island, the non-Aboriginal islanders use it also]. 1990 *Puggana News* (Launceston) Dec p. 35 [Tas.] Well this old **coe** jumped to his feet.

cousin *noun* A relative of either sex, not necessarily close, but of one's own generation; it is also used as a form of address.

The wide use of the word **cousin**, which can refer to quite distant relatives, marks the significance of the extended family in Aboriginal society.

1964 F. Gale *Study of Assimilation* p. 140 [Adelaide, SA] Even distant relations, all of whom are loosely termed **cousins**, demand help. 1981 W.J.K. Christensen *The Wangkayi* p. 241 [Kalgoorlie, WA] '**Cousin**' or 'brother' and 'sister' are now used interchangeably and without any obvious friction. 1986 R. Moncrieff *Nigger Nigger* p. 24 Christ, **cousin**, I gotta be gettin' outa here. Whiteman's justice comin' to kick me into Dreamtime. 1988 J. Davis *Barungin—Smell the Wind* p. 57 [south-west WA] Shane, wake up, **cousin**. Wake up. 1988 I. Keen *Being Black* p. 182 [south-west NSW] In fact, the fighters themselves are not genealogically close, although they refer to each other as **cousins**. 1991 L.M. Wilkinson *Aboriginality* p. 203 [Vic.] 'He is my **cousin**' . . may indicate that he is in fact the mother's sister's son. Alternatively, it may indicate that the relationship is far distant. It may be mother's mother's sister's daughter's daughter's son. 1993 E. Crawford *Over my Tracks* p. 119 [western NSW] What're you doin' up there on that horse, **Cousin**?

cousin brother *noun* A close relative of the same generation, usually a mother's sister's or father's brother's child. Also **cousin sister**.

This phrase is used for a person who is biologically a cousin but has the same status as a brother or sister. Similar terms, *kazenbrada* and *kazensista*, meaning 'male or female relative, male or female cousin', are found in Torres Strait Creole.

1984 E. Roughsey *An Aboriginal Mother Tells* p. 149 [Mornington Island, northern Qld] **Cousin brothers** and sisters take their part. 1986 B. Shaw *Countrymen* p. 47 [Kimberley, WA] Molly Pierce is my cousin and her brother calls me cousin again, and so I call him **cousin-brother**. 1987 H. Ross *Just for Living* p. 44 [Kimberley] Her mother's '**cousin-sister**' (parallel cousin) had looked after her as a child . . 1988 J. Harkins *English as 'Two-way' Language* p. 242 [central Aust.] In the area of kin terms, where the English terms are not specific enough to satisfy Aboriginal speakers' communicative needs, agnate and non-agnate cousins may be distinguished by the terms **cousin-brother** and *posing cousin* as well as by the extension of *brother* to cover the former. 1989 M. Lennon *That's How it Was* p. 3 [Oodnadatta, northern SA] I remember . . . My old **cousin-brother** who lives at Hamilton Station now.

cuz *noun* A familiar form of address for a 'cousin'; also used as a term of solidarity. Also **cous, cus**. See BROTHER, SISTER.

This was once more common in the non-Aboriginal community as a form of address for a biological cousin; it did not however include the sense of social solidarity, a sense also found in Maori English.

1981 M. Brusnaham *Gateway* n.p. [SA] Wish I'd told you I love you **cuz**. 1983 *Dark Side of the News* p. 146 [NT] Hey, hey I'm no superman. Numore, **cus**, I'm nobody's hero. 1987 B. Cohen *To My Delight* p. 121 [northern NSW] Let me deal with him, **cous**. I am his height. 1988 J. Davis *Barungin—Smell the Wind* p. 27 [south-west WA] Good on you, **cuz**, put it there. 1988 I. Keen *Being Black* p. 102 [south-east Qld] Thus the use of the term of address 'cuz' in a meeting or a tutorial in a tertiary institution . . both maintains and reminds Aboriginal participants of a speaker's relationship to another participant and the accompanying rights and responsibilities. **1990** P. Read *Charles Perkins* p. 169 [NSW] **Cuz**, let me in. **1991** L.M. Wilkinson *Aboriginality* p. 203 [Vic.] The term '**cuz**' is used loosely to refer to relationships that may not be able to be reckoned or recounted through all genealogical links, and may include those people (generally of the same age group) who are known to be related in some way.

daughter *noun* [south-east Qld] A term of address for a woman of the great-grandparents' generation, as addressed by her great-grandchildren.

In some Aboriginal societies the kinship terms are used cyclically, so that the same terms might be used three or four generations later.

1988 I. Keen *Being Black* p. 102 [south-east Qld] The following examples . . are English translations of traditional labels: '**Daughter**' is used to address an old woman by her great-grandchildren.

dubay *noun* [northern NSW] A woman. Also **dubai**.

From the Bundjalung language of northern NSW and south-eastern Queensland *dubay* 'a woman'.

1988 R. Langford *Dont Take Your Love to Town* p. 200 [northern NSW] All he talks to me is about **dubays**. **1992** *Koori Mail* (Lismore) 18 Nov. 14/4 [northern NSW] Wandarrah Koori-**Dubais** Touch Football Presentation. **1992** R.L. Ginibi *Real Deadly* p. 25 [Sydney, NSW] Then they'd take off to the pub to play pool, or ogle some **dubays** . . . I scolded the two of them huntin' them home.

family *noun* All one's blood relatives.

This is far more inclusive than the sense of the term in most other Englishes, where it generally is taken to mean the nuclear family or possibly the extended family. It is only in such phrases as 'family reunion' and 'family tree' that a similar group of relatives would be included by the term in general English use.

1973 M. Fennel & A. Grey *Nucoorilma* p. 95 [northern NSW] It was one 'miramar' day that several members of the Munro **family** took their visitor to their camp at Bassendean. **1983** J.G. Steele *Aboriginal Pathways* p. 29 North-east of Kyogle . . is an unusual ceremonial ground. It has been described as a 'place of judgement' according to a member of the Roberts **family** (Lismore Aboriginal) resident in Kyogle. **1987** *Junga Yimi* (Yuendumu) Sept. p. 2 [central Aust.] Other people in the **family**, children, nieces, nephews, other uncles will sit down for a short time, depending how close they were to that person. **1988** I. Keen *Being Black* p. 141 The members of the Kin group, the all one **family**, only use the surname to refer to themselves when they are explaining to a complete outsider who they are and what kin group they are affiliated with, or as the Nyunger people would put it, who they are 'in with'. . . . All one family is divided into a number of sections of approximately forty to 150 people. These sections have no specific name but are variously and interchangeably referred to as 'lots', 'mobs'. **1992** P. Taylor *Tell it Like it Is* p. 108 [western Qld] Our **family** . . usually married the red kangaroo 'meat'.

father *noun* [Aust., predominantly in traditional areas] A man of the generation above who stands in the relation of a parent, usually a biological father, a stepfather, or close uncle. Also **second father**.

Torres Strait Creole has a similar term *dadi*, which means both 'father' and 'father's brother'.

1832 R.E. Ball *Aboriginal Situation in Newcastle* (1982) p. 108 [Tas.] The people at the Settlement call their chiefs by the appellation of **Father**, and speak of the members of their own tribes as Brothers and Sisters. **1884** *Jrnl. Royal Anthrop. Inst. Great Brit. & Ireland* (1971) Vol. XIII p.xx [Qld] A blackfellow will say . . . 'So many are my **fathers**', or 'So many mothers I have', he should call them uncles or aunts. **1956** *Oceania* (Melbourne) Mar. p. 213 [NSW] He feels just as much 'at home' in the home of a female or male relative whom he calls 'mother' or **'father'** and who call him 'son' as he does in his own home. **1976** J. Mirritji *My People's Life* p. 9 [Arnhem Land] I did not know where I was born until my **second father** (father's brother) had explained it to me. **1980** M. Etienne & E.F. Leacock *Women and Colonisation* p. 264 [central Aust.] The girls' . . **'fathers'** and male kin will not support them. **1984** E. Roughsey *An Aboriginal Mother Tells* p. 112 [Mornington Island, northern Qld] My youngest **father** Gully and his wife Cora took me out one night in a dugout. **1988** P. Marshall *Raparapa* p. 267 [Kimberley, WA] Jinayikon (old Billy Barnes) adopted me; he married my mother . . . That **father** started me working in the cattle jobs. **1988** *Royal Comm. Aboriginal Deaths in Custody:* (H. B. Day) p. 616 [Vic.] If you had no mum you had so many mothers and **fathers** anyway. **1995** M. Brady *Giving away the Grog* p. 99 [north-west NT] . . my father he died . . . And I got an old **father** that dragged me up from the very start, that old Paddy lives at Gilwil now. And I classed him as my father, full father.

friend up *verb* [northern Aust.] To become friends, or to become a girlfriend or boyfriend.

1986 B. Shaw *Countrymen* p. 160 [Kimberley, WA] When they finished they're sort of settled then and all **friended up**. **1990** Chi & Kuckles *Bran Nue Dae* p. 53 [Broome, north-west WA] Come on my boy, you gotta **friend** him **up** and try grab'em. **1991** D.B. Rose *Hidden Histories* p. 161 [Victoria River, north-west NT] Well, she was **friend up** with my uncle (took Jack's uncle as her boyfriend) see.

full *adjective* [Chiefly northern Aust.] (Of a relative) pertaining to the closest biological relation that is covered by that term, as in **full** sister as opposed to 'half' sister. See CLOSE, NEAR, TRUE.

This is similar to the standard use of *full* in reference to a relative but is much more significant and is applied to a much wider set of relatives in Aboriginal English than in general English usage, because of the different use of English kin terms. Because Aboriginal people have extended the sense of kin terms such as 'sister' to include people not usually covered by the term, it then needs to be qualified by a word such as **full** to cover the original sense of the word.

1965 F.G.G. Rose *Wind of Change* p. 145 [central Aust.] Ronnie is (his) **full** cousin. **1978** K. Palmer *Somewhere Between Black and White* p. 38 [Pilbara, WA] Fortunately, Murphy's **full** brother, Jenkin, had been staying at Limestone for several weeks following the death of his wife. **1978** J. & P. Read *View of the Past* p. 90 [northern NT] Half-brother or even brother . . might be **full** uncle even. **1983** A.H. Ross *Austral. Abor. Perceptions* p. 29 [Kimberley, WA] Genealogical kinship, through shared descent, is designated by Gidja and Djaru people by prefixing a kinship term with 'full', such as 'full father', who may be distinguished from paternal uncles and other classificatory fathers. **1986** B. Shaw *Countrymen* p. 76 [Kimberley, WA] My mother had eight brothers and I had to call them uncle, **full** uncle. **1991** *Amanbidji Land Claim* 21 Aug. [northern NT] Is it **full** brother and sister, or cousin brother and sister, or what?

full blood, having a close biological relationship. Also **full blooded**.

1984 E. Roughsey *An Aboriginal Mother Tells* p. 89 [Mornington Island, northern Qld] Everyone had to live alike, as they were really in **full blood** relation line. Those who were born not too far away, also were treated as full blood to each other. **1986** B. Shaw *Countrymen*

p. 81 [Kimberley, WA] Well, he's the **full-blooded** cousin to me. **1995** M. Brady *Giving away the Grog* p. 93 [north-west NT] See my nephew . . . I remember him from small, my **full blood** nephew.

grand *adjective* (Of a close relative) of the grandparents' generations.

This is a parallel use to that of MOTHER or FATHER for 'aunt' or 'uncle' in that it refers to a more distant relative as if he or she were a closer one. **1981** M. William *Traditionally My Country* p. 39 [south-east Qld] My paternal grand-mother's brother is remembered as **Grand** Jim . . . The reference to Grand Jim indicated a lateral extension of the status of grandparent. **1985** *Special People* p. 8 [Vic.] I can remember my **grand** aunt . . and other ladies going out looking for basket grass. The grass is a special grass and it has to be pulled out a certain way otherwise you could cut your hands.

grandfather *noun* [Aust., predominantly in traditional areas.] **1** A man of one's parents' parents' generation, who stands in the relation of a grandparent, usually a biological grandfather or a great-uncle.

1978 J. & P. Read *View of the Past* p. 49 [Elcho Island, Arnhem Land] So my grandfather and two my **grandfathers** (i.e. great uncles) they were hiding along . . at the side of the creek. **1993** D. Hodge *Did you meet any Malagas?* p. 75 [northern NT] And I'm also a **grandfather**. One of my nephews has recently become a father. I know that's a great uncle in European law but Aboriginally, I'm a grandfather.

2 An elderly respected member of a community.

1966 M. Boney *Bigga-Billa Porcupine* p. 1 [western NSW] This old **grandfather**, he'd kill a porcupine. He'd send the two poor little fellers out to get some leaves, coolibah leaves, to cook in a ground oven with the porcupine. **1992** R.L. Ginibi *Real Deadly* p. 63 [northern NSW] 'Do you know that granny Wilson and another old full blood are still on the mission there at Box Ridge?' 'Oh gosh, granny Wilson nursed me when I was little; I've got a photo of her and old **grandfather** Breckenridge'. **1992** P. Taylor *Tell it Like it Is* p. 30 [SA] There was no blood link but . . he was affectionately known as **Grandfather** Dennison to all who were descendants of Florence. **1993** E. Crawford *Over my Tracks* p. 54 [western NSW] We all loved Father Tracey and claimed him as a '**grandfather**.'

grandmother *noun* [Aust., predominantly in traditional areas] A woman of one's parent's parent's generation, who stands in the relation of a grandparent, usually a biological grandmother or great-aunt.

1988 C. Mattingley & K. Hampton (eds) *Survival in Our Own Land* p. 113 [SA] I never knew I had so many **grandmothers**. **1989** D. Walker *Me and You* p. 92 [north coast, NSW] There are lots of other kiddies who look on me as a **grandmother** . . . I suppose its just the aboriginal way.

grandmother's law, women's traditions, in this case in respect of childbirth. The Alukura referred to in the citations is a women's health and birthing centre in Alice Springs which incorporates traditional Aboriginal attitudes to pregnancy and birth into its approach.

1987 *Aboriginal Health Worker* (Little Bay) Vol. 11 Sept p. 9 [central Aust.] Aboriginal way by the **Grandmother's law** is directed and carried out by Aboriginal women in the security and ancestral traditional and the warmth of the Alukura. **1989** G. Knepfer *Nursing for Life* p. 33 [central Aust.] The long-term plan for Alukura is the reassertion of the **Grandmother's Law**, and its incorporation into 'borning' and obstetric services.

grandpa *noun* A respectful term of address for an older male member of the community.

As a term of address in general English use, it is often used to convey contempt, as in a call 'Hey grandpa' from a group of younger people to an older man.

1989 J. Moore *Royal Commission into Aboriginal Deaths in Custody:* (Transcript) p. 185 You had always to call everybody auntie or uncle. You know, disregard whether they were your auntie or uncle. The older people you always had to call them grannie and **grandpa**.

granma mother *noun* [northern Qld] A maternal grandmother.

Most Englishes do not distinguish between such kinship categories as mother's sister and father's sister, mother's mother and father's mother. In Aboriginal communities, however, such differences can have social consequences.

1984 C. Allridge *Aboriginal Eng.* p. 108 [Palm Island, northern Qld] No, I'm gonna tell my **granma mother**.

granny *noun* 1 A term of respect for an older woman, who need not be a relative. Also **grannie**.

Granny was used as a term of address for an older woman in British English but this is no longer current in non-Aboriginal Australian English. It only exists now in reference to a non-relative as a mild insult, as in 'You're just a bunch of old grannies'. In any case, the original sense lacked the sense of respect found in Aboriginal English.

1984 B. Borey *Myora Aboriginal Cemetery* p. 19 [south-east Qld] I can remember the **Grannies** collecting reeds from the swamp and drying them out to be used to make baskets. The Aboriginal name for the reeds that they used is called noongies. **1988** D. Tunbridge *Flinders Ranges Dreaming* p. xxv [Flinders Ranges, SA] Then at the beginning of 1980 with the two '**grannies**' of Nepabunna, Annie Coulthard and Gertie Johnson, we began to . . translate the stories which Annie Coulthard knew. **1989** J. Moore *Royal Commission into Aboriginal Deaths in Custody:* (Transcript) p. 185 [Vic.] You had always to call everybody auntie or uncle. You know, disregard whether they were your auntie or uncle. The older people you always had to call them **grannie** and grandpa. **1991** G.R. Langford *Journey into Bundjalung Country* p. 1 [north coast, NSW] We pulled up in front of **Granny** Marj and Granny Wilson's place. **1993** E. Crawford *Over my Tracks* p. 26 [western NSW] All those old **grannies** smoked pipes.

2 [south-west WA] A relative of either sex of one's grandchildren's generation or of one's grandparents' generation.

This is a transference to English of the cyclical nature of Aboriginal generational naming patterns, where the same kinship categories could occur in alternate generations. In this case it is the Nyungar term *murran* which can mean either a grandparent or a son or daughter, which is being 'translated' as **granny**. See DAUGHTER.

1981 J. Davis *The Dreamers* p. 134 [south-west WA] Oh, Uncle, that's Robert, he's one a' your **grannies**. He's one of Elaine's boys. **1985** S. & M. Kaldor & I.G. Kaldor *Aboriginal Children* p. 234 [south-west WA] Nyungar . . Aboriginal children use the term **granny** to cover all male and female relatives of their grandparents' generation, viz. FM (father's mother), MF (mother's father), MM (mother's mother), FF (father's father), MMB (mother's mother's brother), MMS (mother's mother's sister), FMB (father's mother's brother, FMS (father's mother's sister), MFB (mother's father's brother), MFS (mother's father's sister), FFB (father's father's brother), FFS (father's father's sister). **1988** I. Keen *Being Black* p. 231 [south-west WA] Now the birth and lives of her descendants, the 'little **grannies**', her children's children and their children, had been set in meaningful conjunction.

grow up *verb* [Chiefly Northern Aust.] To bring up, to rear (a child).

1938 V.E. Turner *Good Fella Missus* p. 91 You won't . . leave me?. . . You **growed** me **up**. **1961** W.E. Harney *Grief, Gaiety and Aborigines* p. 16 [northern NT] He recounted in his soft drawl how the manager had '**grown up**' a copper-skinned native girl. **1962** D. Lockwood *I, Aboriginal* p. 35 [northern NT] If I thought my testing time was now ended I was soon disillusioned. Marbunggu, tribally appointed to '**grow** me **up**' like a Christian Godfather, laid down the law. **1963** W.E. Harney & D. Lockwood *Shady Tree* p. 95 [northern NT] More than sixty years ago at Charters Towers, while my mother toiled to keep the family going, it was Beattie who became responsible for me and, as the natives say, '**grew** me **up**.' **1975** J.P. Roberts *Mapoon Story* i p. 7 [north Qld] My father reared Jerry's father . . . my father **grew** him **up**. **1977** J. & P. Read *A View of the Past* p. 249 [northern NT] That's all, my old boss. He **grow** me **up**. Poor feller, my old boss. **1986** B. Shaw *Countrymen* p. 123 [Kimberley, WA] Whenim **grow up** this girl you can takim, I'll give you. **1993** D. Hodge *Did you meet any Malagas?* p. 74 [northern NT] And soon after giving birth to Daddy, she passed away. I don't know, it was a difficult birth. So after that his father **grew** him **up** as far as he could. . .

gudjahgah *noun* [south coast, NSW] A child.

Probably from a NSW south coast language word. Wiradjuri, an adjacent language, has a similar word *guudha* for 'child'. See BOORI, JARJUM.

1990 *Wreck Bay Koori Newsletter* Aug. p. 4 [south coast, NSW] Goodbye to all my little **gudjahgah's** . . I know I leave my kids in good hands.

half *adjective* (Of a kinship relationship) not of the biological closest kind.

The term is used to distinguish between closely and more distantly related people of the same generation who have the same relationship with a person; for instance, two women named as 'mother' and 'half mother' both have the social relationship of a mother, but one is biologically more closely related than the other.

1980 *Yorky Billy* (Film Transcript) AIAS Canberra p. 4 [NT] Yes, her father and mother . . she was promised . . these Aborigines they say sometimes *wrong-side*, for your **half** mother, half sister, and all this. But my wife, they said 'You're *straight* for her'. **1990** P. Austin et al. *Lang. & Hist.* p. 244 [Oodnadatta, northern SA] That feller was a **half** father to me.

half half, (of people) not closely related.

The reduplication of the word **half** intensifies the sense of 'reduced belonging' of the word **half**. See also BOSS BOSS (Chapter 5), DIFFERENT DIFFERENT (Chapter 7).

1965 *Oceania* (Melbourne) Sept. p. 12 [NT] Local groups on tribal borders might occupy indeterminate positions, being regarded as belonging to no tribe in particular; or, as the aborigines expressed it in English, '**half-half** people'.

in with *prepositional phrase* [south-west WA] Used to indicate with which family a person identifies.

1988 I. Keen *Being Black* p. 141 [south-west WA] The members of the Kin group, the all one family, only use the surname to refer to themselves when they are explaining to a complete outsider who they are and what kin group they are affiliated with, or as the Nyunger people would put it, who they are '**in with**'. **1988** I. Keen *Being Black* p. 129 [south-west WA] 'That's Arnold Halfpenny.' 'Who's he **in with**?' 'He's one o' them Calleys.'

jarjum *noun* [northern NSW] A baby, a young child. Also **tcharjoom**.

From Bundjalung *jahdham* 'child'.

1935 *Hist. Soc. of Queensland* (Brisbane) Nov. p. 231 [southern Qld] She informed me that when I was a 'little pfeller **tcharjoom**' (baby) she nursed me. **1984** B. Borey *Myora Aboriginal Cemetery* p. 13 [south-east Qld] When it came time to go home our Grandmother would say to us 'Come on you **jarjums**, better get ready to go home, Biggyjabba going down'. **1992** R.L. Ginibi *Real Deadly* p. 31 [north coast, NSW] I'd have chooks, ducks and geese, grow my own vegies and have a couple of milking cows for milk for the **jarjums**. **1993** J. Janson *Gunjies* p. 16 [western NSW] You're just a **jarjum**, you listen!

jarjum centre, a child care facility.

1986 *Abor. Inform. Directory* (Dept of Aboriginal Affairs) n.p. [northern NSW] **Jarjum Centre**, 71 Phyllis St, South Lismore 2480.

jarmbie *noun* [south-east Aust] A mate.

Origin unknown.

1969 *Koorier* (Melbourne) p. 28 [Vic.] It is a pity our old **jarmbie** (mate) Harry Hayes doesn't take the fight game more seriously . . all he managed to do was scrape home on points.

jungin *noun* [Tas.] A young person, a youngster.

1990 O. Noonuccal *Aust. Legends and Landscapes* p. 121 'Hoy! You **jungins***, come away from there or Kuti Kina will come and get yuh!' . . . *The spelling of the word *jungins* is correct. It represents the English slang of Tasmanian Aborigines on the islands, especially Cape Barren Island, second largest . . of the Furneaux Group. *Jungins* means 'youngsters'.

just livin *verbal phrase* Living together in a sexual relationship.

Equivalent to a de facto relationship in the European sense; in Aboriginal society the relationship could have an Aboriginal validity.

1964 E.G. Docker *Simply Human Beings* p. 9 Not many aboriginal couples are married in the Christian sense. In aboriginal language, they are '**just livin**'.

kangaroo marriage *noun* [Chiefly northern Aust.] A sexual relationship not bound by Aboriginal or European law. Also **kangaroo relationship**.

It has been described as 'Hop on, hop off and hop away'. The term **kangaroo court**, an illegal court, is a parallel but probably unrelated use of the word 'kangaroo'.

1954 T. Ronan *Vision Splendid* p. 252 [NT] Had Steve Blake not decided that there was nothing among the Milderi lubras worth riding fifty miles after, taken Topsy to himself, by **kangaroo marriage**, and built a hut alongside the saddle-shed . . the homestead would have needed enlarging. **1981** G. Ngabidj *Country of the Pelican Dreaming* p. 140 [northern NT] Oh you not proper married. You only just a **kangaroo marriage**. **1988** J. Collman *Fringe-dwellers and Welfare* p. 123 [central Aust.] Her sons have each made proper marriages . . her one daughter has established only **Kangaroo relationships**. **1988** P. Marshall *Raparapa* p. 58 [Kimberley, WA] As long as you had the woman walking with you, you were married. That's what we call a **kangaroo marriage**. **1995** M. Brady *Giving away the Grog* p. 68 [northern NT] I found another girl . . . And then, got married—not married in church, bush marriage, they called '**kangaroo marriage**'.

Hence **kangaroo marry**, to live with someone in such a relationship.

1986 B. Shaw *Countrymen* p. 44 [Kimberley, WA] On Ivanhoe I was first **kangaroo married**, in my Law.

kin *noun* Family.

> **1988** H.B. Day *Royal Commission into Aboriginal Deaths in Custody* (Transcript) p. 533 After the death of his grandmother Harrison continued to live with his **kin**. **1991** L.M. Wilkinson *Aboriginality* p. 203 [Vic.] Up to fourth cousin is regarded as 'blood' and from then on regarded as '**kin**'. **1994** R. & J. Huggins *Auntie Rita* p. 151 [south-east Qld] **Kin** came from Adelaide, Rockhampton, Woorabinda, to attend the event.

lady *noun* A woman.

It is widely used in Aboriginal Australia, especially in reference to older women, where the standard use would be 'old *woman*'. A possible language origin of the Aboriginal English use is seen in the 1981 citation.

> **1971** *Hope Vale Hotline* Aug. p. 5/2 [northern Qld] Some of our **ladies** get milkadindal for news from home. **1978** J. & P. Read *View of the Past* p. 66 [NT] And when the shooting started, they start to follow them people . . . All the old **ladies** couldn't run fast enough. **1979** *Tjaru* (Alice Springs) Aug. n.p. [central Aust.] Then on the next day the **ladies** took some girls to show them dancing. **1981** G. McKenzie *Aurukun Diary* p. 72 It was not derogatory to address . . a woman as Wunjintha, old woman. But perhaps a translation nearer to the respectful polite feeling of the Aborigines would be . . . 'Elder **Lady**' for the old woman. **1984** P. Read *Down There with Me on Cowra Mission* p. 95 [south-west NSW] She didn't drink at home, she used to go out with other **ladies**, have a few beers, that way. **1985** *Special People* (Melbourne) Aboriginal History Programme p. 8 [Vic.] I can remember my grand aunt . . and other **ladies** going out looking for basket grass. The grass is a special grass and it has to be pulled out a certain way otherwise you could cut your hands. **1987** C. Glass & A. Weller *Us Fellas* p. 46 [south-west WA] They used to see Yamajee ladies coming back . . black **ladies** coming back after having a night out with a white guy and that was really a shame. **1988** P. Taylor *After 200 Years* p. 149 [north-west WA] In this picture we are all Wangkajunga and Walmajarri **ladies**.

lady one, belonging to women.

> **1984** S. Cane *Desert Camps* p. 74 [Western Desert] Hard work, **lady one**, all the ladies. Man come and eat.

lation *noun* A relation.

> **1969** *Koorier* (Melbourne) Vol. 1. no. 8 p. 21 [Vic.] So now the battles over, And serenity reigns at last, For our '**lations** from the Ministry, Regard Johnny in the past. **1980** B. Sansom *The Camp at Wallaby Cross* p. 253 [Darwin, NT] These women accept those they call their ''**lations**' into cooking-pot dependency. **1988** J. Davis *Barungin—Smell the Wind* p. 8 [south-west WA] Yeah, there was '**lations** I haven't seen for years.

little bit *adjective* [northern Aust.] (Of a relative) distant but with kinship obligations, and called by the same term as a closer one. See also HALF, SECOND.

> **1935** M. & E. Durack *All-About* p. 101 [Kimberley, WA] His death will be put down to the magical powers of Macha's '**little bit** father-in-law' or some other such extraordinary relation. **1944** W. Hatfield *Australia Reclaimed* p. 60 Those men within the totem group who *might* have married his mother are his '**little-bit** fathers'. Similarly women his father *might* have wedded become his 'little-bit mothers'.

lot *noun* A section of a family.

> **1988** I. Keen *Being Black* p. 141 [south-west WA] The all one family is divided into a number of sections of approximately forty to 150 people. These sections have no specific term but are variously and interchangeably referred to as '**lots**', 'mobs'. **1989** J. Thomson *Reaching*

Back p. 77 [northern Qld] He belong to Midge's **lot** Midge Colston. **1989** M. Lennon *That's How it Was* p. 4 [Oodnadatta, northern SA] Ngaanatjara like Antakarinja, Aluritja and Yungkutatjara, they are all one **lot**.

married *adjective* Having sexual relations (as a married person).

1978 J. & P. Read *View of the Past* p. 83 [central Aust.] Freddie was in bed, yeah, **married** man, with that old lady. **1987** E. Paddy & M. Smith *Boonja Bardak Korn* p. 6 [northern WA] Inland bloodwood is good firewood during July, the cold season, and for '**married** turtle time' in November-December. **1988** P. Marshall *Raparapa* p. 58 [Kimberley. WA] Our people just used to live together '**married** up' and that was it. **1991** D.B. Rose *Hidden Histories* p. 39 [north-west NT] He was **married** with that girl.

mix blankets *verb* To live in a de facto relationship. See also **kangaroo marry**.

1974 G. Higgins *On Right Track* p. 4 We are not married . . . We are just living together; just **mixing blankets**.

mother *noun* A female relative of the same generation as the speaker's biological mother, usually a mother's sister.

In traditional Aboriginal society, a range of female relatives may have the obligations and responsibilities of a 'mother'. Torres Strait Creole has a similar usage, with *mama* meaning 'mother', 'mother's sister' and 'husband's mother'.

1956 *Oceania* (Melbourne) Mar. p. 213 [south-west NSW] He feels just as much 'at home' in the home of a female or male relative whom he calls '**mother**' or 'father' and who call him 'son' as he does in his own home. **1980** M. Etienne & E.F. Leacock *Women and Colonisation* p. 264 [central Australia] The girls '**mothers**' and some female kin may give them support. **1988** H.B. Day *Royal Commission into Aboriginal Deaths in Custody* (Transcript) p. 616 [Vic.] If you had no mum you had so many **mothers** and fathers anyway. **1993** E. Crawford *Over my Tracks* p. 26 [western NSW] Our teachers were our grandparents and our oldest aunty—in our customs she's our second **mother**.

mum *noun* [NSW] A term of respect and affection for an older woman. See also AUNTY, GRANNY.

1992 R.L. Ginibi *Real Deadly* p. 35 [Sydney, NSW] 'Thanks **mum** Ruby, thanks', he called out.

mum mum *noun* [WA] A person's maternal grandmother. See GRANMA MOTHER.

In Aboriginal society, just as the distinction between mother's sister and father's sister is significant, so is that between father's mother and mother's mother.

1980 S. & M. Kaldor & I. G. Kaldor *Language of School* p. 421 My **mum mum** (maternal grandmother) tole me.

near *adjective* [Aust., chiefly in traditional areas] (Of a relative) having a very close familial relationship—as distinct from a person who may be addressed as mother, sister, etc., but whose relationship is actually more distant. See CLOSE.

1904 A.W. Howitt *Native Tribes S.-E. Aust.* p. 257 [Vic.] It was forbidden to the children of a brother on the one side, and a sister on the other, to marry . . . It was held that they were 'too **near**'. **1950** I. Tonnies (ed.) *Beitrage* p. 67 [Daly River, NT] A man may also marry his '**near**' sister's (parallel cousin's) daughter's or son's daughter. **1965** F.G.G. Rose *Wind of Change* p. 141 [central Aust.] A **near** 'mother' of the boy makes the fire and prepares red ochre. **1984** E. Roughsey *An Aboriginal Mother Tells* p. 182 [Mornington Island, northern Qld] You could not tell who was your **near** relation to our parents, because everyone was my uncle, . . cousin, brother.

ol' gooman *noun* [northern Aust.] **1** An old woman. Also **olgumin, ol' goomun, wuluguman.**

From an Aboriginal pronunciation of 'old woman' and influenced by the word for 'woman' in Marra and other Northern Territory languages, *gaminy* (together with 'old').

1978 J. & P. Read *View of the Past* p. 60 [northern NT] You know that white man pickem up that **ol' gooman** when he bin longa that coolamon. **1980** M. Brandl *Wuluguman and Wulman* n.p. The archetypal image of an old Aboriginal, *wulman* or **wuluguman** (old man or old woman) is a tranquil grey-haired person seated in the shade of a tree. . . **1993** G. Koch *Kaytetye Country* p. 102 [central NT] But that old—two **olgumin** bin take me now, Nellie— Jackie's wife and old Ruby.

2 (In Aboriginal cosmology) the sun.

1977 X. Herbert *Dream Road* p. ix [NT] The **Ol' Goomun** and Igulgul, the sun and the moon.

poison *adjective* [northern Aust.] Pertaining to a person with whom one has an 'avoidance relationship' i.e. a person one is traditionally forbidden to associate with, particularly to speak to.

In traditional Aboriginal society, certain categories of kin have particular rules controlling their association, which means that in general they have to minimise social interaction. This might mean only speaking through intermediaries, not looking at one another, or even avoiding being in close physical proximity. In different Aboriginal cultures these rules apply to different kinds of kin, but brother and sister, father-in-law and son-in-law, and particularly mother-in-law and son-in-law, are the relationships most commonly affected. Obligations of respect and care still operate in avoidance relationships and avoidance does not imply a lack of affection.

1946 *Bulletin* (Sydney) 2 Jan. 12/3 [Cape York, northern Qld] Among native tribes in Cape York Peninsula a '**poison**-uncle' is a common relationship, though its meaning is shrouded in the mysteries of tribal law. In our mustering camp Dodger was 'poison uncle' to Jimmy, and in the two years they worked and ate together I never heard them exchange a word. **1978** *Working Together* Qld. Aboriginal and Islander Teacher Aide Dev. p. 32 [northern Qld] The cousin is **poison** to the man or woman. You can't even speak to the Uncle's son or daughter. **1986** P.D. Black (ed.) *Growing in Language* p. 15 We use different registers to different relations, for instance, like when I want to talk to my **poison** cousin or poison auntie. But I don't just go up and talk to them face to face. I usually talk to my uncle and he talks to my poison auntie or my poison cousin.

promise *noun* [Chiefly northern Aust.] An arranged husband or wife; an arranged partner.

1978 J. & P. Read *View of the Past* p. 336 [NT] They used to marry full tribe, full **promise**, promise wife, wife, yes. **1978** J. & P. Read *View of the Past* p. 137 And my promise girl, there my uncle there **promise**. **1980** B. Sansom *The Camp at Wallaby Cross* p. 84 Yesterday ol Luke bin miss that **promise** (wife). **1993** G. Koch *Kaytetye Country* p. 15 He's—he's my daughter. I bin give him **promise** to that old man there. He's my lamparra [son-in-law].

Hence **promise-married**, married in accordance with the system of arranged marriages. See SKIN.

1988 P. Marshall *Raparapa* p. 16 [Kimberley, WA] Those women that they are with were already married in the blackfella sense; they were **promise-married**.

skin promise, the system of arranged marriage, working within the 'skin' system, which provides a system of social classification.

1982 *Nelen Yubu* (Melville Island) Dec. p. 33 [Groote Eylandt] The Christian leaders are very strong that the **skin promise** must continue and not be twisted but kept honest.

promise *verb* [Chiefly northern Aust.] To arrange a marriage, one which would take place when the (generally much younger) woman is of age.

Arranged marriage was one way in which Aboriginal society contracted alliances between individuals and groups, through the obligations that the society put upon people associated with the marriage. Girls were often promised to their husbands as babies, which meant that the contractual obligations inherent in the 'in-law' relationship could begin to operate. Both the *Australian Concise Oxford Dictionary* and the *Oxford English Dictionary* record *promise*, meaning 'to betroth, to arrange the marriage of one's daughter' as not being current in general English use. Here, as in other cases such as GAMMON, Aboriginal English has retained a sense that probably came into Aboriginal use in the nineteenth century.

1936 M. & E. Durack *Chunuma* p. 61 [Kimberley, WA] 'Well 'im little bit father bin **promis'm** me', Dicky persisted. **1976** *Students Storybook* (Aboriginal Teacher Education College) p. 26 [NT] My parents never allowed us all to be **promised** from childhood. They had often told us that was some promising business, but to my parents it didn't mean a thing. **1910** (1975) E. Hassell *My Dusky Friends* p. 31 [south-west WA] I solemnly said I thought Guablich was too young whereupon Guablich smiled . . saying 'Me **promise** um a long time'. **1986** B. Shaw *Countrymen* p. 208 [Kimberley, WA] Well in the old people's day we still **promised** young girls and I had one here in the camp. **1991** J. & S. Erbacher *Aborigines of the Rainforest* p. 23 [northern Qld] Often the girl was **promised** to her partner when a young child. The uncles, and sometimes the grandparents arranged the marriage.

promising *adjective* [Chiefly northern Aust.] Pertaining to an arranged marriage. In the last citation, the use of 'very' is close to that of 'strongly'.

1976 *Students Storybook* (Aboriginal Teacher Education College) p. 26 [NT] My parents never allowed us all to be promised from childhood. They had often told us that was some **promising** business, but to my parents it didn't mean a thing. **1987** B. Gammage & P. Spearitt (eds) *Australians 1938* p. 59 [north-west WA] Aboriginal law was a good law in them days, very **promising** law.

relation *noun* A relation.

The word is invested with greater significance because of the importance of the ties of kinship within Aboriginal society. The 1990 citation encapsulates this sense of the pervasive significance of kin. There is an Aboriginal rock music group called 'Just Relations'.

1971 *New Dawn* (Sydney) Jan. p. 2 [western NSW] Nowadays . . the young people of the reserve are not healthy enough. They marry **relations**. They don't follow the rules. They marry with whites . . agh! **1978** J. & P. Read *View of the Past* p. 185 [central Aust.] Come up and get a feed. Tea and sugar and tobacco, something, for his **relations**, you know. **1981**

AIAS Newsletter (Canberra) 15 Mar. p. 14 But we not family. We not close-to **relations**. 1986 *White Invasion Diary* (Invasion Diary Collective) 19 May n.p. [northern SA] I saw my **relations** taken away and sent down to Adelaide. 1988 A. Moffatt (ed.) *Aboriginal Deaths in Custody* (Transcript) p. 387 [south-east Vic.] Can you tell us who the other fellows were who were drinking in the sheds that day? . . . There was me, my other two brothers, and the rest—just **relations**. 1990 P. Read *Charles Perkins* p. 168 [NSW] 'No, I dont want you.' 'But I'm your **relation**.' 1991 D.B. Rose *Hidden Histories* p. 155 [Victoria River, north-west NT] Pensioner blokes, all the pensioner rations, because all their **relations** were working. 1994 R. & J. Huggins *Auntie Rita* p. 140 [south-east Qld] I asked him if he was rich now he replied, 'Hell no. You know how it is Mum. I got too many **relations** for that!' 1995 M. Brady *Giving away the Grog* p. 111 [north-west NT] Like these days now you see people in the alcohol they don't even respect their own culture, because alcohol make them gone silly, they don't even respect their own **relation**!

right *adjective* (Of a marriage) following traditional rules. Also **right sort**, **right way**.

Traditional Aboriginal society is divided up into kinship groups, often called SKINS. Marriage partners for one skin should only be selected from other particular skins. Marriages traditionally were arranged (PROMISED); these arrangements cemented social alliances through the obligations operating between groups related by marriage. A WRONG marriage, that was however between appropriate groups, might find social sanction, but one between people considered too CLOSE caused, and can still cause, great social tensions. In the past such behaviour might have resulted in the death or exile of one or both parties. Colonisation has greatly affected marriage patterns in southern Australia, but in northern Australia the persistence of traditional marriage has meant the recognition of tribal marriage in non-Aboriginal law. See also PROMISE, SKIN, WRONG.

1928 B. Spencer *Wanderings in Wild Aust.* p. 169 [central Aust.] All I found was that some women belonged to what our boy called the **right** side of the tribe whom he could marry, and others belonged to the wrong side, and these he could not marry. 1973 M. Fennel & A. Grey *Nucoorilma* p. 181 [northern NSW] She spoke . . about '**right**' and 'wrong' marriages. 1989 B. Morris *Domesticating Resistance* p. 64 [northern NSW] The emphasis on avoiding 'close' marriages rather than '**right sort**' marriages can be seen. 1989 R.M. Baker *Land is life* p. 338 [Borroloola, north-east NT] Some people 'follow' their father and adopt the skin that follows the father's skin, other people 'follow' their mother by assuming the marriage is **right way** and adopting the skin they would have got from such a right way father.

second *adjective* (Of a relative) having similar kinship obligations to another person called by the same kinship term, but without being as closely related. See OTHER.

1913 *Science of Man* (Sydney) 2 June p. 51 [south-west WA] Daddel's own mother and his '**second**' mother . . caught the infection. 1976 J. Mirritji *My People's Life* p. 9 [Arnhem Land] I did not know where I was born until my **second** father (father's brother) had explained it to me. 1988 S. Dunlop *All that Rama Rama Mob* p. 102 [central Aust.] For example, children may refer to their mother and her sisters by the one term, often translated into Aboriginal English, as 'my mother' and 'my **second** mothers'. 1993 E. Crawford *Over my Tracks* p. 39 [western NSW] Your father's brother was your **second** dad. 1993 E. Crawford *Over my Tracks* p. 26 [western NSW] Our teachers were our grandparents and our oldest aunty—in our customs she's our **second** mother.

sis *noun* Abbreviation of 'sister', used as a form of address indicating affection and solidarity.

This is also used in the non-Aboriginal community, but generally only as a term of address for a speaker's 'biological' sister; it is occasionally used as a term of solidarity in political movements.

1957 *Oceania* (Melbourne) Dec. p. 105 [western NSW] The women are furious when their Mission cousins get drunk and come up to them in the street and say 'Hello, **sis**'. **1963** D. E. Barwick *Little More than Kin* p. 287 [Vic.] **Sis** and coz are the passwords among the dark people. **1990** R. Bowden & B. Bunbury *Being Aboriginal* p. 16 There's a natural bond that I feel towards Aboriginal people . . . It's 'Cous' or '**Sis**' or 'Brother'. **1991** L.M. Wilkinson *Aboriginality* p. 203 [Vic.] The use of terms such as 'cuz', '**sis**', 'budda', 'aunty', or 'unc' does not always indicate the true 'blood' relationship between individuals. **1991** L.M. Wilkinson *Aboriginality* p. 203 [Vic.] '**Sis**' and 'budda' may refer to siblings, but this term may equally apply to those kin who are not siblings, but are within the same age group. **1992** R.L. Ginibi *Real Deadly* p. 80 [north coast, NSW] 'We'd better take cardigans, we won't be back till late **sis**', I said. **1993** J. Janson *Gunjies* p. 29 Why's that **sis**? **1991** L.M. Wilkinson *Aboriginality* p. 205 [Vic.] I was occasionally referred to as '**sis**' as a term of inclusion and affection.

sister *noun* A female of the same generation, either a biological sister or a close cousin, or a person classified as such. It can also be used, as with 'sis', to express solidarity.

Generally it is used to refer to a cousin who is the child of a sibling of the mother rather than the father. As with 'sis' **sister** is also used in the non-Aboriginal community as a term of solidarity in some political movements.

1950 I. Tonnies (ed.) *Beitrage* p. 68 [Daly River, NT] To us this latter is a second cousin marriage, though to the Aborigines it is marriage with the daughter of mother's 'brother' or of mother's '**sister**'. **1988** I. Keen *Being Black* p. 143 [south-west WA] The child's cousin wants a share, he or she will be instructed to share in the following terms: 'Give some to **sister** now, good girl'. **1992** R.L. Ginibi *Real Deadly* p. 92 [north coast, NSW] 'I love yas, **sisters**' she called and tears misted up our eyes. **1993** E. Crawford *Over my Tracks* p. 41 [western NSW] My Uncles and Aunties called each other **Sister** and Brother and so that's the way we grew up. My kids do it sometimes too.

sister girl, an affectionate variant on **sister**.

1991 G. Ward *Unna you fullas* p. 141 [south-west WA] Gimmie some apple, **sister girl**, give us a bite.

skin *noun* [Chiefly northern Aust.] A division of society into which one is born by a law of inheritance. Also used adjectivally.

Under a skin system, society is divided into a number of groups, usually four or eight. 'Skins' summarise the rules of marriage; one does not marry someone of one's own skin, and usually marries somebody from a specific other skin. The system also decides the **skin** to which one's children will belong. For example, in the Warlpiri society of Central Australia, a *Napaljarri* woman should marry a *Jakamarra* man; their female children will be called *Napurrula* and their male children *Jupurrula*. *Jupurrula* marries *Napanangka* and their children are *Jakamarra* and *Nakamarra*. This system is in effect another way of organising society by kin relationships. It has spread widely in recent years through traditional areas and is a useful mechanism for providing a relationship system for people from different communities. Non-Aboriginal people can also be temporarily brought in to the system by allotting them **skin names**. In societies where this system is used, people are often addressed as, or referred to by, their skin name as in 'there's that Nangala'. Skin names are also used with a European name as a form of 'public name', as in 'Johnny Japaljarri'.

1926 *Votes & Proceedings* (W.A.) (1927) I. no. 3 p. 83 [WA] The hurt, or the injury that I might do to one A, a native, is a hurt done not primarily to him, but done to the — group or **skin**, as they call it, of which he is a member. **1933** *Oceania* Vol. III. p. 401 The common pidgin term for sub-section is 'skin'. . . Individual Nangiomeri were told . . that their '**skins**' were so-and-so, and that such-and-such a natural species, or object, 'belonged' to them. **1949** H.E. Thonemann *Tell White Man* p. 61 As well as dividing the tribes into eight sub-sections which we call 'skins' (social groups), we also have 'dreamings', which are the names of animals or other things, such as lilies or whirlwinds, to which our spirit belongs. The 'skin' groups are what you call 'social', the 'dreamings' are cult totemic (spiritual) groups. **1982** *Nelen Yubu* (Melville Island) Dec. p. 33 [Melville Island, NT] The christian leaders are very strong that the **skin** promise must continue and not be twisted but kept honest. **1985** O. Stanley *The Mission and Peppimenarti* p. 72 [Daly River, north-west NT] Strict adherence to **skin** group laws is required . . . Many Europeans believe that **skins** were introduced since the 1930's from Western Australia. **1986** B. Shaw *Countrymen* p. 82 [Kimberley, WA] The **skin** business is given by God. **1988** P. Marshall *Raparapa* p. 77 [Kimberley, WA] When they drink that heavily, they don't call that one 'sister' or this one 'cousin' they forget about their **skin** line. **1987** N. Williams *Two Laws* p. 23 [Arnhem Land] I told the people there, my **skin** relation, bone relation, language, tribe, Dreaming. **1989** *Aboriginal Children* p. 4 [Arnhem Land] Children talk about . . things in the community . . names, **skins**, family, country, animals, plants etc. **1993** D. Hodge *Did you meet any Malagas?* p. 166 [northern NT] So right from that age the promises are still made, and people can still tell you 'That girl's my promise' or a woman will say 'That guy is my right **skin**.'

skin name, the name of one of the subsections.

1976 *Students Storybook* (Aboriginal Teacher Education College) p. 12 [NT] My name is Mangiwa, my **skin name** is Ngalnamut. **1986** T. Scanlon *Arafura* p. 103 They both had the **skin-name** of Jangala. **1989** R. Allan *Tennis with Jack at Warren's* [northern NT] I was 'claimed' by the Wanguri clan, one of the more powerful groups. My tribal father was the chairman of the town council. My **skin name** became 'Bunany'.

son *noun* A male of the next generation who is in the relationship of a son, but who may be more distantly related than a biological son, particularly a nephew.

1956 *Oceania* (Melbourne) Mar. p. 213 [western NSW] He feels just as much 'at home' in the home of a female or male relative whom he calls 'mother' or 'father' and who call him 'son' as he does in his own home. **1978** J. & P. Read *View of the Past* p. 331 [NT] That two my **son** from my brother, my brother bin finish. They call me uncle.

tidda *noun* [south-east Aust.] Sister. Also **tita**, **titi**.

From an Aboriginal pronunciation of 'sister'. The *s* sound is not one that is found in Aboriginal languages, and *d* and *t* are not generally distinguished in Aboriginal language sound systems.

1982 L. Fogarty *Yoogum Yoogum* p. 78 [south-east Qld] Calling memory back, jammin jammin no gammin gammin Yubba, **tidda**, Moondi up. **1988** R. Langford *Dont Take Your Love to Town* p. 133 [northern NSW] Yes, it was Short Stuff . . my old **titi** from home . . **1991** G.R. Langford *Journey into Bundjalung Country* p. 8 (caption) [north coast, NSW] **Tita** Gertie Williams. **1993** *Sydney Morning Herald* 22 Jan. 3/3 (suppl.) Women feature strongly in this year's festival. The Victorian Women's band, **Tiddas** (Aboriginal for 'sisters'), caused a minor sensation with their CD *Inside My Kitchen*.

true *adjective* (Of a relative) related in the closest biological way. See FULL.

There is a similar use in Tok Pisin, from Papua New Guinea, with *papa true* 'biological father'.

1978 K. Palmer *Somewhere Between Black and White* p. 40 [Pilbara, WA] The 'workers', as they were known, were those of the same section as Clancy, or his **true** sisters. These girls were responsible for much of the early dancing. **1989** J. Hamilton *Just Lovely* p. 16 [northwest NSW] One of Dad's sisters—. . Alice, ended up with Mum's old grandfather, Harry Yates, so my Great Grandfather was also my **true** uncle.

uncle *noun* A respectful term of address for an older man. See also AUNTY, GRANDFATHER.

1964 P. Dalton *Broome* p. 150 [north-west WA] Terms like 'uncle' and 'aunt' are used widely to include quite distant classificatory kin and affines. **1973** *Durrung* (Melbourne) July p. 3 (suppl.) [Vic.] **Uncle** Alick Jackomos 'killed them' with his boomerang displays. **1981** J. Davis *The Dreamers* p. 105 [south-west WA] There they was: 'Give me fifty cents, brother', 'Give me a dollar, nephew', 'Give me fifty cents **Uncle**'; and you know none of them black bastards are related to me. **1988** A. Moffatt (ed.) *Aboriginal Deaths in Custody* (Transcript) p. 405 [south-east Vic.] Did he tell you before you went to see **uncle** that they had planned to put him off the train at Warragul? **1988** I. Keen *Being Black* p. 80 [Adelaide, SA] The majority of younger people addressed Max . . as '**Uncle**' . . . Most of these were genealogically related to Max . . in some way, but the few who were not addressed them as kin nonetheless. **1990** R. Bowden & B. Bunbury *Being Aboriginal* p. 27 [western NSW] I learned from men, some of them in their sixties and seventies, to make these particular weapons . . they'd teach you what to do . . . We weren't allowed to call them by their first names. It always had to be '**Uncle**'. **1995** *Koori Mail* Lismore 17 May p. 1/3 [NSW] **Uncle** Fletcher is pictured holding the 1994/5 NAIDOC Award which was won by the *Koori Mail.*

us mob *noun* A connected group. Also **us people**.

The term can apply to a whole 'family' or just part of one, or a group connected in some other way.

1980 B. Sansom *The Camp at Wallaby Cross* p. 11 [Darwin, NT] 'All **us mob**?' asked Johnson. 'He got room?' **1986** A. Weller *Going Home* p. 47 [south-west WA] **Us mob** are really rich now. **1988** *Us Mob* (Aboriginal and Islanders Studies Unit) Sept. n.p. (title) [Qld] **Us Mob**. Aboriginal and Islander Studies Unit. **1991** C. Pybus *Community of Thieves* p. 188 [Tas.] 'Governments come and go', he says with a laconic shrug, 'but **us mob**, we're still here.' **1995** *Koori Mail* Lismore 22 March 7/2 Cuz's keep'n an eye on those tourist eh? Yeah, makin sure there's enough fish for **us mob**. **1990** J. Chi & Kuckles *Bran Nue Dae* p. 84 [north-west WA] **Us people** bin waiting for dijwun for 200 years now.

CHAPTER 3

Us Mob

This chapter contains words about states of feeling and social interactions which are used in Aboriginal English differently from the way they are used in non-Aboriginal Australian English, and words that are not found in non-Aboriginal English. They are not the only words used by Aboriginal communities concerning human relationships but they are distinctive ones.

Certain words flag the cultural differences between Aboriginal and non-Aboriginal Australia. For example, **shame** is a very important word used throughout Aboriginal Australia for a kind of emotion related to social misbehaviour which has no exact equivalent in other Australian Englishes (but is found in a similar form in Tok Pisin from Papua New Guinea). It covers a range of meanings including embarrassment, fear and ridicule. Aboriginal Australian society is more community orientated and less individualistic than most non-Aboriginal Australian communities. Public opinion as a form of social control is more significant and individual actions are expected to show respect for the values and traditions of the society. Members of Aboriginal society generally place less value on the individual who makes his or her own way or departs from moral traditions. A person who does so is likely to be made to feel **shame** and those associated with such a person might feel **shamed**.

Some of the words are an historic legacy of the nineteenth-century English that the Aboriginal people learned from the British. *Jar*, 'to bicker', from which Aboriginal English has formed **jar**, 'to scold', is no longer generally current in non-Aboriginal English, nor is **gammon**, 'pretence or deception', or **to gammon**, 'to pretend or lie'. However, **gammon** is used by non-Aboriginal Northern Territorians, for the larger Aboriginal population has meant that some Aboriginal English words have become part of everybody's language. **Deadly**, meaning 'great, terrific', is another example of a word that is elsewhere found only in the Aboriginal community but is used widely in Darwin in the Northern Territory. **Humbug** appears somewhat old-fashioned in non-Aboriginal Australian English but is used widely in the Aboriginal community; it has also gained an extra meaning in some parts of Australia, where it includes the sexual harassment of Aboriginal women by white men.

Other words, such as **finish** and **growl** come from the pidgin that was an ancestor of Aboriginal English. Others are probably words that Aboriginal people learnt from the nineteenth-century British colonisers and have taken into their speech. **Cheeky** is a word used widely throughout Aboriginal Australia to mean not just insolence but behaviour that is dangerous, or violent. Anything that offers harm, be it person, animal, plant or inanimate object, can be called **cheeky**. It is possible that this sense of 'dangerous insolence' came about because any violent resistance to the British by Aboriginal people was characterised as 'cheeky' behaviour by the colonists. (In South African English, *cheeky* is applied to Africans who are seen by Whites as being 'uppity', 'not knowing their place'.) To resist is to upset what is seen by the colonists as the moral order of society. (It is also characteristic of colonial societies that they diminish powerful qualities of the colonised, so that resistance becomes 'cheekiness'.) Some pidgin words such as **rubbish**, meaning 'worthless', and **big** (as **bigpela**) meaning 'serious, important', are also found in Tok Pisin. **Big** has also been taken into general Australian English as *big smoke*, 'the city'.

Aboriginal language words from the original language of the area where they are used are sometimes retained by local communities. Often they are words for particularly personal aspects of life, such as **goona** for 'faeces', **doori** for 'sexual intercourse', or **kwon** or **bunti** for 'backside'. Sometimes they refer to states of being such as **mooritj**, 'good', or **gwangi**, 'stupid'. Because these language words are not understood by non-Aborigines, or are about particularly personal things, they are found less often in print and are under-represented here.

bad *adjective* Dangerous.

The term could be related to *bad* meaning 'dangerous, hostile', used by non-Aborigines of Aboriginal people who resisted the occupation of their country, so that to travel there was dangerous, although the term is not recorded in this sense in the *Australian National Dictionary* until 1910. *Bad* was also used in American English of resisting Native Americans.

1861 J.D. Lang *Qld. Aust.* p. 342 [NSW] Daggar weng. The stranger is a **bad** fellow. Dagga bumma. Beat the stranger. **1898** G.M. Fenn *Dingo Boys* p. 23 [northern Qld] No drinkum rum. Bah! ugh! **Bad**, bad, bad. **1914** R.S. Newall *Stone Implements from Millstream Stn, WA* p. 304 [WA] On showing her another, a yellow coloured scraper, she said, 'He **bad** fella, he poison.' **1962** J.H. Bell *Aboriginal Education in NSW* p. 122 [Sydney, NSW] Those . . in the Riverina, are described disparagingly as 'wild blackfellers', 'bush natives' and as '**bad** mobs'. **1978** L.R. Hiatt *Aust. Aboriginal Concepts* p. 95 [Arnhem Land] It is not at all uncommon for specific localities to be identified as dangerous places . . ('that's a **bad** place', we can't go there.). **1985** *Nelen Yubu* (Melville Island) Autumn no. 22, p. 4 [Melville Island, northern NT] My father was a **bad** man. He was a kidney-fat man, always cutting out the kidney fat from people.

bad friend, an enemy.

1986 G. Koch *Kaytetye Country* p. 45 [central NT] That old fella bin fight because twofella bin **bad friend**.

big *adjective* Large, important, powerful, especially spiritually powerful. Also **big fellow, big one**.

The term is also used in other Englishes with a similar meaning, although it appears to be a more recent sense of *big*, and comes mostly from American English. Tok Pisin of Papua New Guinea has the term *bikpela*, meaning 'large, big, important, huge'. The pidgin use from which the Aboriginal English comes may be an independent or related usage.

1840 J.P. Johnson *Plain Truths* p. 17 The natives appeared equally afraid of the horses and bullocks, which they called **big** dogs. **1887** 'Overlander' *Austral. Sketches* p. 37 He told me that Jim had a **big**-fellow growl at him. **1930** A.E. Yarra *Vanishing Horsemen* p. 17 The boss was a **big** feller medicine man, able to smell out the sleeping-places of lazy scrub choppers. **1951** R. & C. Berndt *From Black to White in SA* p. 43 [Ooldea, northern SA] In some cases . . aboriginal women have '**big**' ceremonies of their own, to which men may not come. **1980** B. Sansom *The Camp at Wallaby Cross* p. 225 [Darwin, northern NT] In its financial aspect, the '**big** thing' Tommy Atkins mooted could not be contained in the ordinary . . arrangements of mob and company. **1984** P. Harris *Teaching about Time* p. 11 [north Qld] In Wik-Munkun (Queensland) the English terms are usually used, but brown coins may also be referred to as '**big**' and 'small', and the silver (white) coins may be distinguished as 'small', 'bit big' and 'big'. **1988** J. Harkins *English as 'Two-way' Language* p. 244 [central Aust.] *Big* often means important; non-Aboriginal speakers use it this way too in expressions like *a big man around town*, but only Aboriginal speakers would call a tiny but very sacred cave a **big** place. **1995** *Koori Mail* (Lismore) 5 April p. 17/4 [Vic.] I can't express what it meant to us. It has a '**big** meaning'. Coranderrk is our home, our history.

big sick, leprosy.

Until recently, leprosy was particularly feared by Aboriginal communities as the sufferers were removed to isolated leprosariums, often never to be seen again by their community.

1949 I.L. Idriess *One Wet Season* p. 267 The '**Big Sick**'—the actively virulent form of leprosy. **1955** F. Lane *Patrol to Kimberleys* p. 13 [Kimberley, WA] Additionally, there were cases of the '**big sick**'—leprosy—to investigate.

Big Sunday, a major ceremony. See SUNDAY (Chapter 1).

1957 W.E. Harney *Life Among Aborigines* p. 49 [NT] It was given a new title of '**Big Sunday**', meaning, of course, 'Very sacred'. **1966** *Oceania* (Melbourne) Mar. p. 175 [central NT] Walbiri men know the Territory-wide terms '**Big Sunday**' . . and employ them especially when discussing ritual matters with Europeans . . **1986** B. Shaw *Countrymen* p. 145 [Kimberley] Then we learnt the **Big Sunday**. You could see the sacred sticks hanging up. . .

The Australian English expression **Big Smoke**, for town or city, was originally an Aboriginal expression.

1848 H.W. Haygarth *Recoll. Bush Life* p. 6 He gradually leaves behind him the '**big smoke**' (as the aborigines picturesquely call the town).

Extremely large, serious or important is registered by reduplication of the word or extension of the vowel.

1924 G. Horne & G. Aiston *Savage Life in Central Aust.* p. 120 [central Aust.] Make 'em **big big** rain, you wash away, no go home. **1984** C. Allridge *Aboriginal Eng.* p. 32 He run—**big, big, big** crocodile nearly opens his mouth. **1983** M. Sharpe *Traeger Kid* p. 41 [central Aust.] 'It's a **bi-ig** town,' said Trish, looking out. **1988** J. Davis *Barungin—Smell the Wind* p. 34 [south-west WA] They was **bi-i-ig** strong men, and they both had beautiful whi-i-ite feather.

booki *adjective.* [NSW] Tired.

Origin unknown.

1993 J. Janson *Gunjies* p. 12 [western NSW] Bit **booki** are ya darls? . . Yeah. God, I'm tired.

bunti *noun* [south-east Qld] Bottom, bum. Also **bunthie** and **buntey**.

From the Gubbi Gubbi language of south-eastern Queensland *bunthi* meaning 'buttocks'.

1977 *Meanjin* (Melbourne) no. 4 p. 541 We find that some Aboriginal words . . are often used . . **bunti**—posterior, bottom. **1977** A.K. Eckermann *Group Organisation and Identity*

p. 308 [south-east Qld] A number of Aboriginal words .. are still used by the whole community .. Word **bunthi**, Meaning *buttocks*, Origin *Kabi*, Source: similar to *bundhur*, meaning back—Mathew 1919:226. **1990** S. Watson *Kadaitcha Sung* p. 101 A little migloo [white] **buntey** is just as good as a gin [Aboriginal], mate. **1994** R. & J. Huggins *Auntie Rita* p. 37 [south-east Qld] But sometimes out of sight of the mistress and master I would take my revenge and quietly smak my spoilt charges on the **bunthie**.

catch *verb* [northern Aust.] To understand.

This is an extension of the expression *to catch* (what someone has said) i.e. to hear. In Aboriginal languages, *to hear* and *to understand* are often related terms. See HEAR.

1986 B. Shaw *Countrymen* p. 210 [Kimberley] And me and Banggaldun are trying to teach those people to **catch** it. We want to give work to those boys who are broke down or sitting in the camp .. **1986** B. Shaw *Countrymen* p. 215 [Kimberley] The young boys had to take all those ideas from the Old people, those who could stand and listen to you and **catch** that word. **1990** P. Austin et al. *Lang. & Hist.* p. 246 [Oodnadatta, SA] I came back to Kununurra when I was a big man. I was there a long time one year. They were Warramanga blackfellers, a different lingo. I can **catch** different words. That Kimberley word's too quick. I can't catch it.

cheeky *adjective*

The various senses of this word (indicated below) could possibly have entered Aboriginal English by non-Aboriginal people labelling violent or insolent actions against them by Aboriginal people as *cheeky*, the use of the word implying that resistance is itself 'insolence' against an appropriate order. There is a South African use of *cheeky* which was applied to non-European people, especially Africans, who were perceived by the whites 'not to know their place'. Alternatively, it could have been an extension of the sense by the Aboriginal speakers, rendering what is generally a verbal insolence into a physical one, with a **cheeky** yam, dog, etc. being something that doesn't respond appropriately to some social or cosmic order. The *Australian National Dictonary* records *saucy* as a probably obsolete pidgin word with the same meaning as **cheeky**. There is also a nineteenth-century recording of *jolly* being used by an Aboriginal person to describe behaviour a non-Aboriginal person had called *insolent*.

1 Causing pain.

1925 P. Bridges *Walkabout in Aust.* p. 196 [central Aust.] .. a half-caste boy .. tossed a bit of wire over the line, which broke the current and gave him an electric shock in the arm 'He **cheeky** fellah. He bite,' said the half-caste. **1984** S. Cane *Desert Camps* p. 74 [Western Desert] **Cheeky** one spinifex (prickley).

2 Dangerous, violent.

1934 C. Warburton & W.K. Robertson *Buffaloes* p. 92 [NT?] They had been worried over our long absence, and thought we had fallen among '**cheeky** fellas.' **1976** J. Mirritji *My People's Life* p. 39 [Arnhem Land] The policemen said to them 'You **cheeky** buggers, you two guys are killers.' **1978** J. & P. Read *View of the Past* p. 70 [Victoria River, north-west NT] 'He too cheeky?' 'Yeah, I think he's too **cheeky** by the way he's firing'. **1985** I. White & D. Barwick & B. Meehan *Fighters & Singers* p. 81 [central NT] The mob .. at Gordon Downs were **cheeky**. They used to spear the whites .. **1990** P. Austin et al *Lang. & Hist.* p. 250 [Oodnadatta, northern SA] I was a young feller then. All the young fellers double-banked me all the time.

They were **cheeky**. They attacked me. Their spears never caught me. Only I caught them properly altogether.

3 Poisonous.

1927 M.H. Ellis *The Long Lead* p. 91 'I tink he **cheeky** (poisonous) beggar, too.' 1937 G.H. Sunter *Adventures Trepang Fisher* pp. 278-9 [northern NT] There was an abundance of '**cheeky** yams'. The name is well chosen; for these earth-fruits are so impregnated with a biting acid that they have to be roasted for twelve hours, cut into thin slices, and then subjected to a long boiling. 1977 R.M. Berndt & C.H. Berndt *World of First Australians* p. 113 Among them are various tubers, sometimes called in English '**cheeky** yam', which are poisonous if not treated. 1987 I. West *Pride Against Prejudice* p. 15 [Tas.] We had the copper head snakes . . . They were thin, long snakes and very **cheeky**. 1989 B. Neidjie *Story about feeling* p. 48 [Arnhem Land] Any sort of yam . . little one buried. This one '**cheeky** yam'.

4 Mischievous, but possibly also dangerous.

1972 *Identity (Sydney)* Jan. p. 30 The grass stood straight, not a stem unbroken, as if a **cheeky** spirit had stolen her footprints while she slept, leaving not a single imprint to read. 1988 J. Harkins *English as 'Two-way' Language* p. 244 [central Aust.] *Cheeky* can refer, as in non-Aboriginal usage, to insolence or mischievousness, but it can also mean strong or dangerous or unpredictable . . . **Cheeky** is used to describe poisonous snakes and plants, dangerous animals and people, medicines and liquor.

choo *noun* [south-west WA] An exclamation of disapproval, embarrassment or surprise. See SHAME.

From the Nyungar language of south-western WA *tju*, such an exclamation.

1982 J. Davis *The Dreamers* p. 88 [south-west WA] *Eli*: You got any *boondah* . . *Peter*: **Choo** *kynya*, you got no shame, Eli. Poor old fella. 1986 J. Davis *No Sugar* p. 42 [south-west WA] *Milly*: **Choo** Choo. Mum, don't shout. 1987 G. Ward *Wandering Girl* p. 93 [south-west WA] '**Choo**, I am *winyarn*, big shame!' 1991 G. Ward *Unna you fullas* p. 115 [south-west WA] 'And another thing. What does this "**choo**" mean? Last week when I held up one of my paintings, during our art lesson, all I could see were these grinning, silly faces all saying, "Choo, choo!" You don't know how stupid you all look and sound.'

cold sick *noun* [northern Aust.] A cold.

1935 in 1983 D. Thomson *Donald Thomson* p. 32 Joshua lay prostrate with a heavy '**cold sick**'—a condition which affects these people frequently at this season . . . It comes upon them quite suddenly . . He was quite unfit to work and too morose to speak. 1978 K. Palmer & C. McKenna *Somewhere Between Black and White* p. 69 [Pilbara, north-west WA] The . . **cold sick** no longer ran unabated through the camp. 1982 R.D. Eagleson & S. Kaldor & I.G. Malcolm *English and the Aboriginal Child* p. 98 [northern WA] There are a number of compounds found in WAACE in northern areas which are not commonly used by SAE speakers . . . camping-out . . **cold-sick** (a 'cold').

cruel *adjective* **1** [south-west WA] Great, terrific, very good.

This is similar to the slang use of *wicked*, meaning 'terrific'.

1968 W.H. Douglas *Aboriginal Language of south-west Aus.* p. 21 [south-west WA] '**Cruel**' 'good' as in 'that was a cruel kick (in football) for our side'. 1982 J. Davis *Kullark* p. 61 [south-west WA] An' I'll get some bacon, make a damper and we'll have a **cruel** feed. 1988 J. Davis *Barungin—Smell the Wind* p. 17 [south-west WA] Who's Lionel Rose? . . . Boxer, solid, real **cruel** fighter.

2 (As adverb) very.

The *Oxford English Dictionary* marks this use of *cruel* as obsolete except in some dialect use, such as Somerset English. The *Dictionary of American Regional English* records *cruel* meaning *very* but marks it as 'old fashioned'.

1981 J. Davis *The Dreamers* p. 94 [south-west WA] He got **cruel** drunk an' 'e rolled in the fire . . . **1986** J. Davis *No Sugar* p. 45 [south-west WA] Old skinny might be bony but his sheep are **cruel** fat. **1989** A. Haebich *For their own Good* p. 207 [south-west WA] They was terrible frightened . . . They was **cruel** frightened. **1991** G. Ward *Unna you fullas* p. 21 [south-west WA] She picked up a stick . . . 'Hurry up, girl!' I started shaking **cruel**.

3 [northern Aust.] (As noun) a cruel thing.

1984 *Aust. Ab. Stud.* no. 2 p. 39 [NT] You know, before, Captain Cook been making a lot of **cruel**, you know. **1991** D.B. Rose *Hidden Histories* p. 61 [Victoria River, north-west NT] Cruel, he done cruel . . . Buried alive. He done a **cruel**, I tell you.

cry *verb* [northern Aust.] To lament, to call out in need (for).

This use is no longer generally current in general Australian English, where the sense is usually restricted to 'weep (tears)', or appears in the form of *to cry out* (for).

1978 J. & P. Read *View of the Past* p. 178 [NT] I bin losem my father, friendly, and old woman go back. Right, find another people, you know, **crying** everything. We bin sorry you know. **1980** B. Sansom *The Camp at Wallaby Cross* p. 87 [Darwin, northern NT] I tell you that mob . . they gonna be **crying** for tucker. **1981** *Kimberley Land Council* (Derby) Mar. p. 17 [Kimberley] We're **crying** here for our laws. **1989** R.M. Baker *Land is life* p. 274 [Borroloola, north-east NT] They used to **cry** for tobacco to smoke.

deadly *adjective* Great, fantastic, terrific.

Possibly an extension of *deadly* meaning 'excessive, awful'. See also CRUEL and the general slang use of *wicked*. This has come into non-Aboriginal Australian English use in the Northern Territory, particularly in Darwin.

1984 *Black Voices* (Townsville) Apr. p. 30 [north Qld] The next day, Tuesday, was painting day and the nice new coat of green paint looked **deadly**, real deadly. **1986** *Why Wanda Said 'No' in Broome* Kimberley Aboriginal Medical Services Council n.p. [Kimberley] I've really got the hots for you! I think you're **deadly** too Phantom. . . **1986** *Koori News* no. 3 Sept 6 p. 1 [Sydney, NSW] *Joe*: Try it on *Gunga*: It fits perfectly *Joe*: Wow! That's **deadly** (!!) **1987** J. Davis *Honey Spot* p. 21 [south-west WA] Solid eh, Peggy? . . **Deadly** eh, Peggy? **1990** Chi & Kuckles *Bran Nue Dae* p. 2 [north-west WA] *Lucy*: Willie. *Rosie*: He stalebait. *Sally Anne*: He **deadly** boy. He come from Lombadine. **1990** S. Watson *Kadaitcha Sung* p. 42 [south-east Qld] But them fullah got **deadly** womenfolk, that's for sure. **1992** *Action Rev.* Oct. p. 6 [Murray River, SA] Kerry, an Aborigine whose people are the Ngarrindjeri from the Riverland, says art can be a great educator . . . People said, 'I really like your Mum, she's a **deadly** artist'. **1993** J. Janson *Gunjies* p. 11 [western NSW] There were some **deadly** speakers at the rally, mostly women, they were cranky about them plain clothesmen firin' shots on the sports day.

doori *noun* [south-east Aust.] **1** Sexual intercourse, a 'screw', a 'fuck'.

From the Wiradjuri language of south-western NSW *dhuurri* or *dharri*, 'sexual intercourse'. The recorded uses show **doori** for the noun and **doorie** for the verb, but this is probably an accident of orthography. Both the noun and the verb are used with English grammatical endings.

1982 E.A. Young & E.K. Fisk *Town Populations* p. 76 [NSW] **Doori** = Sexual intercourse.
1993 J. Janson *Gunjies* p. 26 [western NSW] Be a smart Koori when you're having a **doori**.

2 (As verb) to have sex (with someone).

1988 R. Langford *Dont Take Your Love to Town* p. 119 [NSW] I . . (was) stunned at the close-ups of giant bodies and their sexual desire, **doorieing** everywhere. 1990 S. Watson *Kadaitcha Sung* p. 197 [south-east Qld] That fullah trying to **doorie** you.

find *verb* [northern Aust.] **1** To spiritually conceive (a child).

1933 *Oceania* (Melbourne) June p. 445 [Kimberley] In all three tribes, a father '**finds**' in a dream a spirit-child . . 1989 R.M. Baker *Land is life* p. 189 [Borroloola, north-east NT] 'I been **find** all my boy long Borroloola . . me fella and Banjo find big mob girl too and boy.' . . . Tim uses 'find' here in terms of spiritual conception.

2 To give birth to, to have (a child).

1984 E. Roughsey *An Aboriginal Mother Tells* p. 6 [Mornington Island, north Qld] When I was born, my mother and her friends made a rough circle of windbreaks for my arrival, and so my mother could be kept warm and **find** her baby without harm. 1986 B. Shaw *Countrymen* p. 47 [Kimberley] All right, *nangari* **finds** (gives birth to) *djangala*. 1987 C. Glass & A. Weller *Us Fellas* p. 22 [south-west WA] I said to my sister 'I can't go out this morning. I'm going to **find** my baby so we can't go.' 1987 C. Glass & A. Weller *Us Fellas* p. 22 [south-west WA] We went to this woman who used to have very bad turns in **finding** her babies. 1991 D.B. Rose *Hidden Histories* p. 78 [north-west NT] Did that Nawurla **find** any kids? *Brumby*: Dead now. *Debbie*: Dead? Whole lot? *Brumby*: Whole lot. Mother and piccaninny, all died. 1995 M. Brady *Giving away the Grog* p. 67 [northern NT] After a while, I had a girl friend after a while. We run out together, then I **found** three kid.

finish *noun* [northern Aust.] **1** The end, an end.

1933? H.P. Smith *First Ten Years* p. 52 [north-central WA] They ask, 'Are there any emus, kangaroos and houses in heaven?' . . . 'What happens to those with Satan? Do they burn to a **finish** in a lake of fire?'

2 The end of life, death.

1984 K. Benterrak & S. Muecke & P. Roe *Reading Country* p. 166 [northern NT] He leave-im all dead, **finish**, people. 1985 B. Rosser *Dreamtime Nightmares* p. 68 [north Qld] 'Your tribe doesn't bother with that sort of thing, eh?' 'No, we kill em straight out, **finish**.'

finish *verb* [Chiefly northern Aust.] **1** To destroy; to kill.

1830 *Monitor* (Sydney) p. 15 S4pt 3/1 [NSW?] They believed that fall **finished** him; using their own language, and that the deceased never moved afterwards. 1978 J. & P. Read *View of the Past* p. 30 [northern NT] Want to try shootem whole lot, **finishem** up, finish all blackfellers. 1983 P. Nathan and D.L. Japanangka *Settle Down Country* p. 22 [central Aust.] All the whitefellows want to **finish** up all the Aboriginal places . . .

2 To end; to die. Also **finish up**.

1924 A.G. Bolam *Trans-Aust. Wonderland* p. 100 [Ooldea, northern SA] 'Lindy all finish' . . ' . . (yes) all **finish up**.' 1937 E. Morrow *Law Provides* p. 272 I think he close up **finishem**. 1977 *Black News Service* Sept p. 5 But isn't it better having a needle that hurts for a little while than go silly in the head or maybe even **finish up**. 1980 B. Sansom *The Camp at Wallaby Cross* p. 120 When the business is '**finished up**', the company dissolves. 1982 J. Davis *The Dreamers* p. 94 [south-west WA] Yeah, lotta fellas **finish** there, Mogumber. 1991 D.B. Rose *Hidden Histories* p. 229 [north-west NT] You reckon we should go back! We've been branding, everything—and they got that money and nothing for Aborigines. We're not going to go back. We're **finished** right **up**.

game *adjective* Brave, confident.

This is the same sense as in general English use but is used more widely in the Aboriginal community; in other Australian Englishes it may seem somewhat 'old-fashioned'. For example, the wording on the poster in the 1991 citation would probably not be one intended in the general community for a young age group—although the widespread recognition of that particular poster may have altered this.

1970 *Northern Times* (Gascoyne) 12 Mar. p. 10/5 [Gascoyne, northern WA] 'Go on Heather, I dare you. Gudah (white) children never are **game**'. 'Oh aren't they' said Heather, and took off her thongs and bit her lip. **1984** C. Allridge *Aboriginal Eng.* p. 17 [south-east Qld] I'm **game**. **1989** *Koori English* (Vic. State Board Educ.) p. 9 [Vic.] She's getting **game** = She's becoming more confident. **1991** Dept. Community Services & Health, *Aboriginal Health Workers of Aust.* Poster/n.p. [south-east Aust.] Condoman says *Don't be shame, be* **game**. **1992** *Dugite* ii. p. 14 [south-west WA] If you are **game** enough to tell us your story, you could win . . . **1993** E. Crawford *Over my Tracks* p. 130 [western NSW] This time I was pretty **game** on the train.

gammon *noun* Nonsense, pretence, rubbish. Also used as adjective.

The word originates in *gammon,* 'guile, deceit', from English criminal slang of the nineteenth century. The word, as both a noun and a verb, was used in nineteenth-century Australia, but has become obsolete in most Australian Englishes while being retained in Aboriginal English. In areas with a high Aboriginal population such as Darwin, it has re-entered the speech of the whole community.

1837 *Colonist* (Sydney) 22 p. 205/1 [Sydney, central coast, NSW] He replied, that he thought it was all **gammon** that master had told him about the Creation, for who was there who saw God create man! **1861** J.D. Lang *Qld., Aust.* p. 394 [Qld] They threatened without executing their threatenings, and the black fellows knew well that it was only **gammon**. **1889** S. Denton *Incidents of a Collectors Ramble* p. 136 'Ah, buncumb, **gammon**, English man all same liar.' **1922** R.L. Jack *Northmost Aust.* II. p. 590 [northern Aust.] Billy protested his sincerity in the words, 'No **gammon**—gammon no good.' **1980** B. Sansom *The Camp at Wallaby Cross* p. 33 [northern NT] My investigation was subverted by the fun of what people call 'gammon' and 'humbugging'. **1987** *Campfire Stories no. 1* p. 2 Perhaps you could call them '**gammon**' Christians. **1994** *Australian Author* (Sydney) Vol. 26, no. 3 p. 12 [northern Qld] You should never expect Aboriginal people to do all the education because its unfair and a personal drain—and we never get paid for it (**gammon**).

gammon *verb* To pretend or lie. Also used as an adverb.

See GAMMON in the previous entry.

1981 B.J. Blake *Australian Aboriginal Languages* p. 70 Words that are obsolescent in Australian English are common among Aborigines. For example, one hears 'plant' for 'hide' or 'hide oneself', 'shake' for 'steal', 'sticky' for 'nosey' and '**gammon**' for 'pretend' or 'feign'. **1984** C. Allridge *Aboriginal Eng.* p. 107 [north Qld] PRETEND: (H)e **gammon** think what my second card was . . . **1985** B. Rosser *Dreamtime Nightmares* p. 62 We used to **gammon** hunt. **1984** C. Allridge *Aboriginal Eng.* p. 107 [north Qld] *Gammon* means 'to lie' or 'to pretend' . . . LIE: he **gammon** say 'No'. **1989** *Koori English* (Vic. State Board Educ.) p. 9 [Vic.] She properly **gammon**. **1995** *Koori Mail* Lismore 9 August p. 4/2 [south-east Qld] The last time I saw Jimmy I'd been up to visit him [in gaol] he **gammon** said he'd be out here soon. **1995**

M. Brady *Giving away the Grog* p. 28 [northern NT] I don't really think they believed that I could do it. I done it and they can't believe it. 'Oh, you're **gammon**.' I said 'no, I'm not gammon.'

goona *noun* Excrement, shit. Also used as adjective. Also **guna**, **gunai**, **gunang**, **gunna**.

This word is found in many forms in almost all Australian languages. As GOONYA it is also used as the name for white people in southern South Australia; see Chapter 5.

1889 *Jrnl. & Proc. of the Royal Soc. NSW* Vol. XXXIII p. 360 Excrement . . gunang, **gunna** or gudna (Australia generally). **1904** *Jrnl. & Proc. of the Royal Soc. NSW* Vol. XXXVIII p. 236 [north coast, NSW] Excrement, **gunang**. [Thangetti vocabulary list] **1977** A.K. Eckermann *Group Organisation and Identity* p. 308 [south-east Qld] A number of Aboriginal words . . are still used by the whole community . . Word—**gunang**; Meaning—excrement; Origin—*Kabi*; Source—*gu'nang* meaning bowels. Mathew 1910:227. **1978** K. Palmer & C. McKenna *Somewhere Between Black and White* p. 90 [Pilbara, north-west WA] 'Well', replied Billy from Bungalow, looking at the mob, 'You remember the **gunai** we been eating all these years on the station?' **1982** E.A. Young & E.K. Fisk *Town Populations* p. 76 [southern NSW] **Gunan** Excrement Ngiyambaa. **1984** S. Cane *Desert Camps* p. 35 [Western Desert] Prolonged intake was said to have resulted in 'guts ache' and '**guna** like brildji'—or faeces like red ochre. **1985** D. Russel *Dreamtime Nightmares* p. 167 [north Qld] The white blokes had to empty their own **goona** bucket. There were no septic systems those days. **1987** S. Morgan *My Place* p. 328 [WA] There was a big water trough on Corunna, it was used for the animals . . . It was slimy and there was a lot of **goona** in the water, but we didn't care. **1988** R. Langford *Dont Take Your Love to Town* p. 196 [south-east Qld] I heard him . . talking about Cherbourg . . . They called it **Gunna** Gully meaning shit gully. **1991** G. Ward *Unna you fullas* p. 21 [south-west WA] Every now and then I'd get a yell from the two of them and they'd race over with me to a fresh patch of dung . . . By this time I was plastered with **goona**.

goonawodli, toilet. This term possibly derives from a South Australian Aboriginal language word for a shelter.

1988 C. Mattingley & K. Hampton (eds) *Survival in Our Own Land* p. 138 [SA] A man's ambition must be small to lean against a **goonawodli** (toilet) wall.

goonamia, toilet, literally 'excrement shelter'. From the Nyungar language of southwestern WA *maya* 'a shelter', and **goona**.

1982 J. Davis *Kullark* p. 80 [south-west WA] Aw, he reckon I king hit that *Wetjala* bloke in the **goonamia** Friday night.

goona *verb* To defecate, to shit.

1957 F. Clune *Fortune Hunters* p. 55 [Western Desert] Mick told me how Lasseter was found by the tribe, south of Lake Amadeus, after his camel had bolted. 'We carry 'im,' said Mick; 'I carry 'im plenty on my back. He very sick, his eyes *oona* (inflamed) and *peeka-boolka* (properly sore). His belly *peeka-booka*. He **goona-goona** (dysentery) all day.' **1991** G. Ward *Unna you fullas* p. 111 [south-west WA] He thought one of us **goon'd** ourself, choo, talk about shame!

growl *verb* To complain; to be angry; to quarrel with (someone).

It is often used without *with* or *at*, as in the 1933 example, probably because of the different use of prepositions in Aboriginal languages. See the Introduction.

1856 J. Bonwick *W. Buckley* p. 84 [Vic.] 'Speak plenty low; you no say the like of that; Blackfellow plenty **growl**.' **1893** A.T. Magarey *Smoke Signals of Aust. Aborigines* p. 5 A messenger from another tribe 'come **growl**' (i.e. with a complaint or threat of war). **1895** *N.T. Times (& Gazette)* Darwin 22 Feb. p. 6 [northern NT] Maggie .. said she was staying at the Union and the prisoner came there and **growled** with her. **1914** B. Spencer *Native Tribes of NT* p. 499 [Arnhem Land] Tjiritjerru widjeru .. very cross or **growling** very much. Kakadu tribe. **1933** *Oceania* (Melbourne) June p. 444 [Kimberley, WA] There must not be any joking between men of one *bor* and the women of the other, while the men must not 'growl' one another. **1976** *Primers in English* Strelley Community School n.p. [north-west WA] After that Wigley **growled** those three girls. The three girls ran away from Wigley. **1987** N. Williams *Two Laws* p. 133 [Arnhem Land] He '**growled**' at white interference in general and at a number of whites in particular. **1989** D. Walker *Me and You* p. 51 [north coast, NSW] He used to **growl** at the eldest boy . . . 'Well stop this, stop doing that, stop doing this.' **1992** R.L. Ginibi *Real Deadly* p. 93 [north coast, NSW] I had fond memories of 'Tiger' Magee, my old class teacher . . . We called him that because he **growled** a lot. **1995** M. Brady *Giving away the Grog* p. 76 [northern NT] You know I used to talk with someone, **growling** at someone and swearing at them.

growling *noun* Complaint, criticism, angry behaviour. Also used as adjective. Also **growl**.

1898 G.W. Walker *Notes on Aborigines* (1832, Flinders Island) p. 160 [Tas.] The parties approach one another face to face, and folding their arms across their breasts, shake their heads . . uttering at the same time the most vociferous and angry expressions . . . This custom is called by them **growling**. **1983** H.C. Coombs & M.M. Brandl & W.E. Snowdon *A Certain Heritage* p. 67 [NT] '**Growls**' are often public assertions that one's dignity has been affronted. **1987** A. McGrath *Born in the Cattle* p. 45 [NT] A heated argument ensued, and the Aborigine stormed off. Later the offender returned with 34 fish; the prospect of a good catch meant he could not waste time explaining to his '**growling**' boss. **1987** *Today* (Lawson) 1 Apr. p. 23 In her mind she heard old Granny's **growls** as they played about in the rain. **1988** J. Harkins *English as 'Two-way' Language* p. 278 [central Aust.] **Growling** is well described by Sansome (1980:82) and Malcolm (1980:58-59), who terms it 'brief and gruffly . . articulated warning to one committing, or about to commit, a social transgression.' **1988** C. Mattingley & K. Hampton (eds) *Survival in Our Own Land* p. 206 [SA] The discipline was strict and unlike that of parents, who 'never hit you but doubled the **growlings**'.

gwangy *adjective* [NSW] Stupid, soft in the head. Also **guangi, gwaan-gwaan, gwarng gwarng, gwarnghi**.

From the Wiradjuri language of south-western NSW *gwaangi* and *gwaang-gwaang* 'mad, soft in the head', possibly from *giwang* 'the moon', that is, 'lunatic'. There is a similar association here as in general English use with words to do with the moon and sanity. People were said to be mentally affected by phases of the moon.

1949 *Oceania* (Melbourne) Dec. p. 95 [north-west NSW] 'I don't like that feller. He's too **gwaan-gwaan**' a half-caste woman said, referring to a white man of obviously subnormal intelligence. **1977** *Meanjin* (Melbourne) no. 4 p. 541 [Sydney, NSW] We find that some Aboriginal words . . are often used . . **gwangy**—stupid. **1984** P. Read *Down There with Me on Cowra Mission* p. 103 [south-west NSW] And mum used to reckon I was stupid, **guangi**. **1984** P. Read *Down There with Me on Cowra Mission* p. 105 [south-west NSW] They're real mental there, real **guangi**. **1988** K. Gilbert *Inside Black Australia* p. 14 [NSW] I'm too **gwarng gwarng** for marry. But *not* too gwarng gwarng for *that*. **1993** J. Janson *Gunjies* p. 61 [western NSW] It's like somethin is pullin me to you . . feel like going **gwarnghi**.

hear *verb* [northern Aust.] To understand.

In many Aboriginal languages there is a connection between 'hearing' and 'knowing'. For example in the Wemba Wemba language of the western Murray River area, *nyernda* is 'to understand' and *nyerna* is 'to hear'; in the Yindjibarndi language of north-west WA *wanyaarri* means 'to hear, listen, understand'. There also are related uses in other Englishes of the word *hear* for *understand*, such as the contemporary American *I am hearing you*, meaning 'I understand what you are really saying' and conversely, the use of 'deaf' to mean 'I can physically hear you but am taking no notice' as in *they were deaf to her pleas*. See also CATCH.

1933 *Oceania* (Melbourne) June p. 388 [Daly River, north-west NT] It is common to meet men who can converse fluently in two or three languages, '**hear**' (that is, understand) several others, as well as speak English intelligibly. 1981 B.J. Blake *Australian Aboriginal Languages* p. 70 '**Hear**' means both 'hear' and 'understand' as in 'hear a lingo' i.e. understand a language. 1984 J. Hudson & P. McConnell *Keeping Language Strong* p. 11 [Kimberley] Often they could '**hear**' or understand a few languages even though they could not speak them.

hollow *adjective* Lacking in food or water; hungry or thirsty. See also STARVE.

1925 P. Bridges *Walkabout in Aust.* p. 190 [central Aust.] Ladybone was ill. Enquiries elucidated that she was not 'sick' but '**hollow**', accompanied by that expressive upward jerk of the thumbs under the ribs, by which a native intimates short rations. 1981 Bill Lennon *Yarns around the firebucket* p. 23 [northern SA] And you should have seen the poor sheep! They were lying round perishing for water. They were really **hollow** for water, and some were even lying in the troughs trying to get a bit of moisture there. 1993 E. Crawford *Over my Tracks* p. 177 [western NSW] You could see too that they'd had no water because they were all **hollow** and tucked up.

humbug *noun* [northern Aust.] 1 A wide range of senses including nuisance, trouble, difficulty, nonsense, rubbish, dishonesty, flirting, playing up.

In other Englishes the sense is more of *sham* or *pretence*, but the Aboriginal English sense, while sometimes including this element, is more likely to refer to something that causes trouble or difficulty. *Humbug* is somewhat 'old-fashioned' in other Australian Englishes.

1938 X. Herbert *Capricornia* p. 205 'Do you like the job?' 'No-more!' she cried, wrinkling a pretty nose. 'All dem sister proper **humbug**.' 'How's that?' 'All time roustin'. All time tink we go out wid boys.' 1946 W.E. Harney *North of 23°* p. 158 [NT] The greatest problem on station, mission or government compound is the dogs . . . Should you become desperate and destroy a number of these dogs, the natives might be annoyed at first, but afterwards they would tell you that 'it more better, as dog too much **humbug**'. 1974 G. Higgins *Stockyard Gospel* p. 3 [western NSW] Are you fulfilling the purpose God created you for? Or . . have you become a **humbug** to God and others. 1978 J. & P. Read *View of the Past* p. 253 (5 April) [northern NT] **Humbug!** Too much humbug, bullock! 1981 *Kimberley Land Council* (Derby) March 1 [Kimberley, WA] Young people who go out learning on their own learn nothing but **humbug**. 1982 *Yulngu* (Katherine) p. 18 [northern NT] A lot of people are leaving a lot of the **humbug** at Kalkaringi and moving out to a new outstation. 1993 *Australian* (Sydney) 20 Feb. p. 17/4 [northern NT] We never change . . . That is sickness country. All this **humbug** got to stop.

2 (As adjective) relating to trouble caused by white men sexually harassing Aboriginal women. Also **humbugging**.

1984 B. Swanton *Aborigines and Criminal Justice* p. 140 Can we make our own laws? We want laws about grog, motor cars, vandalism, **humbug** offences, breaking up property. 1989 R.M. Baker *Land is life* p. 393 [Borroloola, north-east NT] The fact that welfare was largely successful in stopping **humbugging** men is a major reason for women generally considering welfare days in higher regard than men do.

humbug *verb* [northern Aust.] **1** To annoy, to fool around, to cause trouble. In Tok Pisin of Papua New Guinea, there is a word *hambak* with a similar range of meanings.

1925 E.J. Banfield *Last Leaves from Dunk Island* p. 101 Suppose you **humbug** me, I take you back alonga Cooktown. 1982 *Yulngu* (Katherine) Dec. p. 13 [northern NT] We should try to get away from booking down food at Baruwei because too often Baruwei get stuck for money and **humbug** to be paid. 1989 *Mankind* (Sydney) Aug. p. 99 [Arnhem Land] '**Humbugging**' is an Aboriginal English word in this part of Arnhem Land, and in its loosest sense it means 'to annoy' (a child . . will be said to be humbugging if it doesn't obey its mother).

2 To make difficult in a particular way, originally in relation to white men sexually harassing Aboriginal women; now used of sexual harassment of any kind.

1984 *Aboriginal History* p. 53 [Borroloola, north-east NT] When European men came across '**humbugging**' for women, young women could disappear into the scrub . . . [note p. 138] Aboriginal English term for sexual harassment. It is usually used in the form 'humbugging whitefellas'. Also used to describe the activities of other people who are making life difficult, for example, politicians, drunks. 1993 D. Hodge *Did you meet any Malagas?* p. 81 [northern NT] My sister . . feels threatened having to live with five cousins that are gay. . . She asks me things like 'Do you reckon they'll **humbug** my husband? . . . Well, they're humbugging every one else's husband.'

jar *verb* To scold. Also **jar off**, **jar up**.

The term is an extended sense of *to jar*, 'to bicker, or wrangle'. This term is no longer widely current in other Australian Englishes, but has been retained in Aboriginal English in this form.

1979 T. Le & M. McCausland (eds) *Working Papers Language and Linguistics* p. 49 [south-west WA] What is a synonym for scolding? . . . **Jarred** . . . Right . . jarred. 1985 S. & M. Kaldor & I.G. Kaldor *Aboriginal Children* p. 234 [south-west WA] 'You gonna marry me?' an' 'e said 'No . . I got one already' and den 'e bin **jar** 'im **off**. 1991 G. Ward *Unna you fullas* p. 34 [south-west WA] I put my head down . . . I hated being **jarred** in front of the other girls. Talk about shame. 1993 J. Janson *Gunjies* p. 10 [western NSW] Ya told them a thing or two, did ya? **Jarred** them **up**?

jealous *adjective* [Chiefly northern Aust.] Envious, possessive and angry.

1978 J. & P. Read *View of the Past* p. 75 [central Aust.] Well they bin walkin round everyway. Everyway. Not **jealous** business . . not jealous business. Not like white people'. . . Not allowed coming through fence (to) nother place. 1978 J. & P. Read *View of the Past* p. 26 [north-west NT] Well they (the Europeans) bin **jealous** from cattle. 1981 G. McKenzie *Aurukun Diary* p. 47 [north Qld] The Itti-speaking people were **jealous** for their languages, and we came to realise that if we had adopted Wikmunkun as the official language of the mission we would have split the people. 1984 *Aust. Ab. Stud.* no. 2 p. 32 [NT] Country for that every one of them people. Captain Cook been **jealous** (envious). 1991 D.B. Rose *Hidden Histories* p. 98 [Victoria River, north-west NT] He used to (be) **jealous** for women. 1995 M. Brady *Giving away the Grog* p. 75 [northern NT] And some people **jealous** you know, 'oh, we've seen Mr M drinking there!'

jealousy.

1979 G.K. Cowlishaw *Woman's Realm* p. 209 [Arnhem Land] Aborigines use the English term for several forms of emotional reaction . . 'jealousy' is an explanation for most forms of anger.

Hence **to jealous**, to inflict envious anger on someone.

1979 M. Heppell *A Black Reality* p. 90 [Arnhem Land] In one instance a new vehicle, purchased in Darwin and driven to Maningrida, was doused with petrol and completely burned by the owner. The reason given by the owner was that he was being 'j**ealoused**' and pushed too much for the vehicle.

jengwallah *noun* [northern NSW] A chatterbox. Also **jeng-waller**.

From the Bundjalung language of northern NSW, *jeyang*, 'mouth'.

1992 R.L. Ginibi *Real Deadly* p. 101 [northern NSW] Jessica was a real little **jengwallah**. **1992** R.L. Ginibi *Real Deadly* p. 62 [northern NSW] This is the one who is a real **Jeng-Waller**—which means 'mouth almighty' in my lingo.

kill *verb* [northern Aust.] **1** To affect someone, generally by hitting; to injure.

Many Aboriginal languages have a word that covers the sense of both *hit* and *kill*. For example, in the Gooniyandi language of the Kimberley, *gard* means 'to kill, to hit, to fell' and in Eastern Arrente of Central Australia *atweme* means 'to hit' and 'to kill'. This sense of *to kill* is also found in Melanesian post-colonial Englishes.

1848 G. Wilkinson *South Australia* p. 328 [SA] The expression **killed** with them means only the receipt of a severe blow; but crack-a-back is the actual quietus. **1925** P. Bridges *Walkabout in Aust.* p. 211 [NT] Topsy . . spent her time . . regaling me with gossip about . . the strenuous ordeal which a young boy was undergoing during his initiation—how every evening he was '**killed**' with a stick etc. **1935** M. & E. Durack *All-About* p. 69 [Kimberley] 'Where you bin **kill** him, Charlie?' the white man asks calmly. **1977** *Black News Service* Mar. n.p. [northern Qld] Yea, you been **kill** me well I'm going to hospital. **1981** A. Hamilton *Nature and Nurture* p. 151 [Arnhem Land] 'Look, he's going to **kill** his mother,' say the onlookers, laughing. (Kill is used by many Aboriginal English-speakers to mean the inflicting of any kind of wound.) **1986** J. Davis *No Sugar* p. 76 [WA] He bin **kill** 'em me here, here, and in the guts. Aw, he bad fella. **1991** D.B. Rose *Hidden Histories* p. 40 [north-west NT] Old Harry Reid did that . . watch them fellows when he's tied up. They couldn't run away . . . And they got a big stick and hit him in the fucking head, and cripple them old people. They **killed** (beat) him, gave him a hiding, let him go.

2 Sometimes the 'hitting' can be metaphorical.

1893 *Trans. R. Soc. S.A.* (Adelaide) Vol. XVII p. 255 [Daly River, north-west NT] 'Lubra bin **kill'm** me eye' which translated means that he was bewitched by the woman's eye. **1961** J. W. Bleakley *Aborigines of Aust.* p. 334 'No more dead fella. Me bin **kill** 'em long tongue.' The word '**kill**' could mean 'cut, hurt, scold' etc.

3 To injure or hurt, where the agent is non-human.

1983 F. Gale *We are Bosses Ourselves* p. 68 [Borroloola, north-east NT] And after that, that debil been come and **kill** that *bardibardi* (old lady) and make her sick. **1991** D.B. Rose *Hidden Histories* p. 164 [north-west NT] Oh, I was pretty tired I tell you. I didn't like the spinifex you know when it **kills** (hurts) you when you walk. Oooh, I was sore.

4 For *kill* meaning 'to cause death', the expresssions **kill dead** and **kill properly** are often used.

1915 E.R. Masson *Untamed Territory* p. 156 [northern NT] 'Ya-as, me bin **killem dead** fella orright,' answers the culprit . . **1927** M. Terry *Through Land of Promise* p. 201 [northern

NT] When a black says someone has 'bin kill 'em' he means someone has been knocked about or hurt; he says 'bin **kill 'em dead** fellow' when he refers to death. **1953** L. Rees & C. Rees *Spinifex Walkabout* p. 121 Yes, I . . **killem dead**. **1986** B. Shaw *Countrymen* p. 58 [Kimberley, WA] The two blokes chased him and they killed him in the back low down. They left him half dead, then **killed** him **dead**. **1986** B. Shaw *Countrymen* p. 164 [Kimberley, WA] In the early days they **killed** them **properly**.

5 The qualification can work the other way, to reduce the intensity of the meaning, as **kill little bit**, to wound.

1968 S. Gore *Holy Smoke* p. 104 Glossary **Kill-im a little bit**: Wounded in a fight, but not dead. (*Pidgin*).

kwon *noun* [south-west WA] Backside, arse.

From the Nyungar language of south-western WA, *kwona* or *kwan*, 'faeces'.

1982 J. Davis *Kullark* p. 16 [south-west WA] Just because she lent you a bed an' mattress you think the sun shines out of her **kwon**. **1986** A. Weller *Going Home* p. 141 [south-west WA] 'That was somphin' not to miss. Diana Grey's big pink **kwon**,' whooped Morry. **1986** J. Davis *No Sugar* p. 23 [south-west WA] Seein' you're drinkin down the Federal every night, Sergeant, you can tell old skinny Martin to stick his stag ram right up his skinny **kwon**! **1987** J. Davis *Honey Spot* p. 54 [south-west WA] Look, a long neck, knees in, and stick out your **kwon**!

kynya *noun* [south-west WA] Embarrassment. Also **kienya**. See SHAME.

From the Nyungar language of south-western WA, *kynya* or *karnyya*, 'shame'.

1982 J. Davis *Kullark* p. 24 [south-west WA] *Alec*: Better git me best suit out of mothballs. *Jimmie*: (under his breath) **Kynya**. **1986** J. Davis *No Sugar* p. 27 [south-west WA] Did you get married at New Norcia? . . *Jamie:* An' engaged under a Government blanket. *Choo*, **kienya**.

learn *verb* To teach.

This form is also found in the non-Aboriginal community.

1936 M. & E. Durack *Chunuma* p. 80 [Kimberley, WA] 'Peter . . what about you **learn'm** me whiteman song.' **1978** J. & P. Read *View of the Past* p. 236 [northern NT] The munanga (white man) bin **learnem** me, and I bin stop here. **1981** W.J.K. Christensen *The Wangkayi* p. 167 [Kalgoorlie, Goldfields, WA] ' . . My mother **learned** me up.' **1986** B. Shaw *Countrymen* p. 73 [Kimberley] He . . **learned** me how to do everything. **1989** J. Thomson *Reaching Back* p. 16 [northern Qld] And so he started giving them tobacco and telling, **learning** them about prayer. **1991** *Amanbidji Land Claim* 21 Aug. [north-west NT] Well, old white feller **learn** him ride a horse . . . And after that when he get a bit older and he would **learn** gardener. **1993** E. Crawford *Over my Tracks* p. 23 [western NSW] There'd be heaps of us kids . . **learnin'** each other, teachin' each other.

Hence **learner**, a teacher.

1989 J. Hamilton *Just Lovely* p. 47 [north-west NSW] Dad was a sort of **learner** and he learnt me things.

long *adjective* (Of a person) tall.

This is found in general Australian English but is not used as commonly as in Aboriginal English. The *Oxford English Dictionary* records the use of *long* meaning *tall* as rare, except in 'jocular' use. It is also found in Torres Strait Creole, and in Tok Pisin from Papua New Guinea as *longpela*.

1898 T.F. Bride *Letters from Vic. Pioneers* p. 164 [Vic.] The man who escaped was afterwards known as '**Long Yarra**'—a very fine looking man. **1955** *Oceania* (Melbourne) Dec. p. 123 [northern NT] **Long** David spoke in his language with Dr. A. Capell. **1976** E.G. Vaszolyi *Aboriginal Australians Speak* p. 50 Thus *high* and *tall* and **long** are likely to coincide in Aboriginal English, resulting in references like *longfella* for a *tall man*. **1978** J. & P. Read *View of the Past* p. 89 [central Aust.] Murray, ain't it? Oh, yeah. **Long** bugger, long. **1986** B. Shaw *Countrymen* p. 110 [Kimberley] Well I said to Jimmy 'Look, you longer [taller] than me. Take Lizzie.' Those two were the same size, a **long** girl and a long boy.

look *verb* [northern Aust.] To see. Also **look out**.

In Aboriginal languages, 'to look' and 'to see' are often covered by the same word, as in the Diyari language of northern SA, *nhayi-rna*, and Murrinh-Patha from north-west NT, *ngkardu*. Torres Strait Creole and Tok Pisin from Papua New Guinea also have similar terms.

1936 M. & E. Durack *Chunuma* p. 38 [Kimberley, WA] Me gotta more better eye **look out** crocodile. **1978** J. & P. Read *View of the Past* p. 286 [central NT] Oh, get paid. That's the . . time now everybody we bin **look** money. **1985** H. Koch *Non-standard English in Aboriginal* p. 182 [NT] Another word whose sense is more extensive than in SE is *look*, which was used of ability to see . . in connection with a blind man. When he been **look** Old Charcoal . . when he was *looking* 'When Old Charcoal could still see'. **1985** B. Neidjie *Kakadu Man* p.x [Arnhem Land] Some bird, I think owl, e looking for something to eat in the night, daytime you cant mostly **look** im.

lose *verb* [Chiefly in northern Aust.] **1** To lose someone from one's ken; to lose (someone's) company.

1925 P. Bridges *Walkabout in Aust.* p. 213 Topsy reiterated her little farewell. 'Goo'-bye, I **lose** you. I lonely.' **1991** D. Pilkington (Nugi Garimara) *Caprice – a stockman's daughter* p. 40 [Pilbara, WA] We don't want Peggy to go 'nother way . . and **lose** 'em for good (go away and not return).

2 To forget.

In this sense the term is often used in the context of cultural items such as language or sacred stories, so that the 'forgetting' is a significant cultural loss.

1893 *Trans. R. Soc. S.A.* (Adelaide) Vol. XVII p. 262 [Daly River, NT] 'Ah too much long time; me been **lose'im**'. i.e. I have forgotten. **1950** I. Tonnies (ed.) *Beitrage* p. 73 [Daly River, NT] 'Can't **lose'im** name'. So we see a man and his son with the same name, and a woman as her brother's daughter. **1985** B. Neidjie *Kakadu Man* p. 32 [Arnhem Land] I hang onto this story all my life. My father tell me this story. My children can't **lose** it. **1986** B. Shaw *Countrymen* p. 143 [Kimberley, WA] Sometimes I talk Miriwong, sometimes I don't understand. You know, in some places I **lose** the language. **1987** E. Kolig *Noonkanbah Story* p. 118 [Kimberley, WA] We **lose** ourselves as people. **1983** P. Roe *Gularabulu* p. 17 [north-west WA] They bin make-im drunk (laughs) and the poor bloke—They bin make-im drunk . . yeah, an' he **lose** himself.

mardong *adjective* [south-west WA] Attracted to (someone), in love (with).

Possibly connected with *mardung* 'woman, wife' in the Nyungar language of south-western WA.

1986 A. Weller *Going Home* p. 81 [south-west WA] Ya know I'm **mardong** for ya, unna? **1990** Davis et al *Paperbark* p. 228 [south-west WA] ' . . What's wrong with him Paul?' '**Mardong**' Paul laughed. **1991** G. Ward *Unna you fullas* p. 119 [south-west WA] The boys used to watch the teachers' attitude towards some girls . . saying how the teacher must be **mardong** for us, and we were jirruping for him.

moorditj *adjective* [south-west WA] Good. Also **murditj, muritch**.

From the Nyungar language of south-western WA, *murditj* or *murdat*, 'hard, strong, solid'.

1968 W.H. Douglas *Aboriginal Language of south-west Aus.* p. 19 [south-west WA] 'He's an expert at his job . . another expression . . is . . 'he's a **murditj**.' (from mutitj 'strong'). 1986 A. Weller *Going Home* p. 39 Struth, it looked good—real **muritch**, you know, all red and shiny and all. 1986 J. Davis *No Sugar* p. 28 [south-west WA] *Jimmy*: You try that, dip the damper, **moorditj**. *Frank*: Yeah, we used to live on 'em when we was on the farm. 1991 G. Ward *Unna you fullas* p. 65 [south-west WA] Cos he thought he was **Moorditj**, taking off to town on his bike.

moot *noun* [south-east Aust.] Vagina, backside.

Origin unknown. This is similar to the general Australian English use of *fanny* where the word means both 'vagina' and 'backside'.

1978 K. Gilbert *People are Legends* p. 11 [NSW] I'll sell me **moot** for half a note . . . . moot vagina. 1984 L. Fogarty *Ngutji* p. 119 (glossary) [south-east Qld] **Moot** . . woman's vagina. 1993 J. Janson *Gunjies* p. 43 [western NSW] You gonna wiggle your **moot**, or what?

(As adjective) **mooted**, exhausted, 'rooted'.

1993 J. Janson *Gunjies* p. 29 [western NSW] Come on Barn . . No, I'm **mooted**. And I'm not drinkin'.

no good *adjective* Not any good, worthless. See RUBBISH.

1846 *Portland Gazette* 5 May p. 3/2 [northern NT] At the big Pandanus Swamp, another tribe of blackfellows guided us over the swamp, and behaved very kind. They used the words peri good (very good) **no good**, Mankitterra (Malay). 1900 T. Major *Squatter's Note Bk* p. 113 [south-west NSW] What had been her crime? . . the executioner . . merely replied 'No good womanee.' 1922 (1989) A. Haebich *For their own Good* p. 198 No cart, no horse, go into bush . . carry wood on back, one piece at a time. **No good**. [In *Great Southern Herald* 7 July, 1922] 1936 M. & E. Durack *Chunuma* p. 47 [Kimberley, WA] Me only got a **no-good** father. Plenty time 'im bin kill'm me. 1963 D.E. Barwick *Little More than Kin* p.xx [Vic.] Charlie admits that he 'was properly **no-good**, on the metho all the time.' 1965 M. Patchett *Last Warrior* p. 13 [south-east Qld?] Over the years the tribe had added many words of pidgin, 'No good. Him bob-tail. No good eatum.' 1978 J. & P. Read *View of the Past* p. 290 [NT] Pow! **No good**. No good altogether. 1987 R.M. & C.H. Berndt *End of an Era* p. 121 [NT] Aborigines were repeatedly told that they were '**no-good**-bugga 'long head'. 1985 B. Neidjie *Kakadu Man* p. 9 [Arnhem Land] That Native-cat . . **no-good**, silly man! 1990 P. Austin et al *Lang. & Hist.* p. 249 [Oodnadatta, northern SA] I came straight back from New Guinea and came into Hong Kong, went straight there. **No good** to come this way. Two or three rivers were there. We got back in a little aeroplane. The whitefellers took me in a boat. The boat took me only halfway from Hong Kong to Adelaide.

Formerly the expression **no good damper** was used of the poisoned flour and foods sometimes given to Aboriginal people as part of the violence of the invasion. In the first example, the term is being used, with a cruel irony, by the British. See also MACKENZIE SIT DOWN under SIT DOWN.

1843 *Port Phillip Patriot* (Melbourne) 16 Jan. p. 3/4 Found straying in the neighbourhood of **No Good Damper**, a bay Timor mare pony. 1903 *Truth* (Sydney) 4 Jan. p. 8/2 Arsenic and poisonous drugs . . were mixed with flour and manufactured into damper, which . . came to be known amongst the blacks as 'no good damper'.

poor *adjective* **1** Of a person who has died; (a euphemism for) deceased, late.

This is also found in most other Englishes, but is significant in Aboriginal English because of cultural restraints concerning mentioning the names of those who have died in the recent past. In some communities, if a living person or any other entity bears the same name as such a person, the name is changed or a special word is used in its place.

1978 J. & P. Read *View of the Past* p. 249 [northern NT] That's all, my old boss. He grow me up. **Poor** feller, my old boss. **1980** T. Donaldson *Ngiyambaa* p. 107 [western NSW] Ngiyambaa speakers . . prefer to use the less explicit term 'poor' which they also use in reference to the living. The chances are that if someone mentions 'my **poor** mother' or 'my poor sister', they mean that the relative concerned is dead. **1982** E.A. Young & E.K. Fisk *Town Populations* p. 75 [southern NSW] In several homes in Robinvale lights are left burning all night because '**poor** so-and-so has been walking about'. **1984** S. Cane *Desert Camps* p. 56 [Western Desert] Aboriginal people in this area are loathe to mention individuals who have died (*warri narri*—**poor** bugger, leave him). **1990** P. Austin et al. *Lang. & Hist.* p. 244 [northern SA] That dead feller old Tom **poor** old bloke used to look after me properly when I was a young blackfeller.

2 As **poor bugger**, or **poor fellow**. Expressions used to refer to the condition of oneself or others, implying a recognition of the plight of the human condition, often said with a mixture of bitter humour and compassion.

1861 L.A. Meredith *Over the Straits* p. 93 [central NSW] 'Bal you got no gin (you have no Gin); **poor fellow** you—you no Gin.' . . A 'poor fellow' meaning a bachelor. **1880** (Mrs) J. Smith *Booandik Tribe* p. 107 [south-east SA] Me think 'em no more blackfellow grow, only soon die—no more brother—**poor fellow** me! **1900** T. Major *Squatter's Note Bk* p. 108 [western NSW?] Give it bacca, **poor fellow** me. **1923** J.C. Hamilton *Pioneering Days in W.Vict.* p. 101 The '**poor fellow** me' of the blackfellow, in answer to an inquiry, often indicated that he was doomed. **1971** *Bulletin* (Sydney) 24 July p. 24/1 Long time people talk to Lord Vestey All about land belong to me, **Poor bugger** me, Gurindji. **1978** J. & P. Read *View of the Past* p. 43 [NT] They bin just come up roundem up, **poor fellow**. **1978** J. & P. Read *View of the Past* p. 93 [NT] You know, **poor fellers**, you might go, you-feller perish. **1978** J. & P. Read *View of the Past* p. 112 [central NT] And they bin turnem round, and shootem . . All Warlpiri, you know, all Warlpiri. **Poor bugger**. **1981** *Cent. Aust. Land Rights News* (Alice Springs) Dec. p. 13 A lot of people put their head down **poor bugger**, shamed. I say, yeah, I got my culture, I been through initiation. That's why people here got more power. **1984** *Oceania* (Melbourne) p. 202 [north-west NSW] '**Poor** little **fella**' is a frequent comment by parents watching a child at play. **1991** D.B. Rose *Hidden Histories* p. 22 [north-west NT] 'Aaaaah.' Old men cried la him. . . And that old fella was crying, old women were crying: '**Poor bugger**, no matter you can go.'

In the following citation, 'poor fellow' has been rendered as **porbella**, to more accurately represent an Aboriginal pronunciation. The reduplication of the *h* in *hhhhome* is being used to convey intensity of feeling. For other uses of this, see LONG, BIG.

1990 Chi & Kuckles *Bran Nue Dae* p. 81 [north-west WA] Porbella, **porbella**. We hhhhome now.

rubbish *adjective* Of little or no value, inferior in quality; NO GOOD.

Tok Pisin from Papua New Guinea has a similar term *rabis*, meaning 'something of no value, poor or impoverished'.

1959 W.E. Harney *Tales from Aborigines* p.xvi [northern Aust.] In the early days the native girls travelled around with their white companions, and being excellent cattle and horsewomen they became the ones who helped the early settlers to open up the land. They [the white men] were classed as '**Rubbish**-one-whites'. **1976** M. Clyne *Australia Talks* p. 215 [Western Desert, central Aust.] 'Wangkayi is a **rubbish** language, isn't it?' **1978** J. & P. Read *View of the Past* p. 200 [Alekarenge, central NT] The missionary was keep telling us 'Ah, don't go to **rubbish** place, and don't follow your mother and father.' **1982** *Yulngu* (Katherine) Dec. p. 17 [Katherine, northern NT] Too many Europeans working on communities pay **rubbish** prices to artists. **1983** P. Nathan & D.L. Japanangka *Settle Down Country* p. 13 [central NT] Time was spent . . distinguishing '**rubbish**' flowers from bush medicines or fruits or seeds. **1985** Borowski *Juvenile Delinquency in Aust.* p. 119 An adult would refer to children who got into trouble as those '**rubbish**' children who belonged to 'that other mob'. **1985** *Stories from Yuendumu* S.A.L. Literary Workshop n.p. [Yuendumu, central Aust.] You never know, he might be very tricky and try to talk you into buying a **rubbish** car. **1992** *Action Rev.* Oct. p. 4 [Alekarenge, central NT] Their very spirit is depressed, and they feel, and are often looked upon, as '**rubbish** people'.

rubbish man, a person of little or no value.

1988 J. Collman *Fringe-dwellers and Welfare* p. 157 [central Aust.] There are always a certain number of people who 'come for the grog', people who, it is known, either cannot or probably will not ever reciprocate. They are the camp's '**rubbish men**'.

rubbish tucker, non-nutritious food, generally European food of little value.

1969 J. Dingwell *One String* p. 46 Don't be offended if all they can address you as is 'Missus'. and don't be offended, either, if they reject what you offer as '**rubbish tucker**'. **1985** S. Cane & O. Stanley *Land Use and Resources in Desert Homelands* p. 100 [NT] Weekend visitors often came to outstations specifically to go hunting and collect bush vegetables and get away from the '**rubbish tucker**' eaten at Yuendumu. **1991** D.B. Rose *Hidden Histories* p. 206 [northwest NT] Take the sheet (table cloth) and chuck out **rubbish tucker**.

rubbish *noun* Something of little or no value.

1979 *N.S.W. P.P. Assembly* 7 Feb. p. 19 [NSW] This is our country . . . We don't want this **rubbish**, a little bit here and a little bit there. We want the whole lot. **1984** P. Toyne & D. Vachon *Growing up the Country* p. 83 We do not want our children to have **rubbish** but to have land and care for it. **1984** P. Harris *Teaching about Time* p. 13 [Kimberley, WA] The 'black money' (1c and 2c coins) is considered **rubbish** and thrown away.

rubbish *verb* To be made to feel of no value; to reckon something or someone of no value.

It is possible the general Australian English term *to rubbish (someone)* originated in the Aboriginal English use.

1983 *Cent. Aust. Land Rights News* (Alice Springs) Autumn p. 3 [central Aust.] Old people been living there. Grandfather and father, we been in that country ever since sacred sites. Aborigines not **rubbish** it. **1988** *Aboriginal Health Worker* (Little Bay) Vol. XII p. 26 The Chinese call this depression 'loss of face' . . . Aborigines call it 'being **rubbished**'. **1990** S. Watson *Kadaitcha Sung* p. 135 [south-east Qld] He always big-noting himself, but he your bunjie so I'd better not **rubbish** him too much.

savvy *verb* To understand.

This term is widespread in post-colonial Englishes throughout the world. It came originally from the Spanish *sabe usted* meaning 'you know'. In Tok Pisin, from Papua New Guinea, it appears as *save* and in Torres Strait Creole as *sabe*, 'to know'. **1893** *Trans. R. Soc. S.A.* (Adelaide) Vol. XVII p. 260 [Daly River, north-west NT] 'No!. . him no more want im hole, that one doctor, him too much **savey** no more hole'. **1928** B. Spencer *Wanderings in Wild Aust.* p. 590 'You savee him track?' 'Yes, me plenty **savee**.' 'You been see 'em which way him dig up potato?' 'Yes, me been see 'em, then me been follow 'em up that one track longa garden.' **1985** B. Rosser *Dreamtime Nightmares* p. 19 [northern Qld] They laughed and said 'You **savvy** that one?' **1990** Chi & Kuckles *Bran Nue Dae* p. 46 [north-west WA] No Uncle I don't **savvy** this kind of thing.

scrape *noun* Sexual intercourse, a 'screw'.

This term is used in general Australian English but appears to be more common in Aboriginal English.

1865 C. Harris *Terror of the Law (1982)* p. 29 [Qld] The victim Mrs Mee, . . had made a 'dying declaration' that the prisoner had 'twice attempted to violate her person.' He had asked her if she would 'give him a **scrape**' and 'tried to have connection with me.' (From *Queen v Jackey* Maryborough Circuit Court 15 Sept 1865. In letter 2908 of 1865. COL/A72 Q.S.A. in Harris 1982) **1880s (1990)** *Aboriginal History* (Canberra) XV. ii. p. 148 Johnny Campbell pointed a pistol at Mrs Stewart, said 'I want a **scrape**', indicating her sister and chased her until she submitted. **1990** S. Watson *Kadaitcha Sung* p. 134 [south-east Qld] He's a man and he needs a **scrape** every now and then.

scrape *verb* To have sexual intercourse, to 'screw'.

1955 *Meanjin* p. 169 Larrian was ready to **scrape** with the whitefellers. **1969** O. White *Under Iron Rainbow* p. 64 She said she didn't mind lying down for white men at three dollars a time . . . All the girls got **scraped** by someone . . . She'd give the old sergeant a scrape for free and he'd make things easy for her while she was in the lock-up.

shame *noun* Embarrassment; fear; a sense of having transgressed the social and moral code of society, intentionally or unintentionally.

This is one of the central concepts in Aboriginal Australia and a difficult term to translate into non-Aboriginal English. It differs from the general use of the word *shame* in that shame can be felt where there is not personal guilt and it can be felt in situations where a person receives positive public attention, such as winning a prize. **Shame** functions as a form of social control, whereby the force of the emotion affects people's behaviour, such that they are less likely to transgress rules of social behaviour. Aboriginal society is one that values social cohesion, the highly socialised person above the individual achiever. Tok Pisin from Papua New Guinea has a term *sem*, with the similar sense of 'embarrassment, contrition, humility, loss of face'.

1951 R. & C. Berndt *From Black to White in SA* p. 178 [Oodnadatta, northern SA] She's got no **shame**, pushing herself forward. **1951** R. & C. Berndt *From Black to White in SA* p. 155 [Oodnadatta, northern SA] 'No, I won't go . . . They might knock me back; I'd feel too much **shame**.' **1972** *Newsletter Abl. (Vic.)* (Melbourne) p. 9 [Vic.] 'Nah, too **shame**' is too often heard among you people. **1978** M. Kamien *Dark People of Bourke* p. 40 [western NSW] My friends come in and they say '**shame**, shame', and we laugh. **1980** R. Bropho *Fringedweller* p. 9 [south-west WA] There were other bad times at school, such as when we had no dinner

. . . I used to feel real **shame** over it. **1981** R. Box *Christian Marriage* p. 6 [Arnhem Land] Marriage was for life. Separation and divorce did not happen very much. If it did, it was a big **shame. 1982** J. Davis *Kullark* p. 10 [south-west WA] Yeah; y'all had to come back here after the funeral and get drunk. You ain't got no **shame. 1983** M. Sharpe *Traeger Kid* p. 22 [central Aust.] I was **shame.** I said nothing. **1985** *Aboriginal History* (Canberra) Vol. IX no. 1 p. 135 [NSW] **'Shame'** or 'shyness' in Aboriginal people, for want of better equivalents, translate *kuyan* and corresponding terms in other languages, is the moral response, the traditional safeguard of propriety 'our pride what we live by and the principle of the country.' **1986** P. Duncan *Shame in Australia* p. 47 People should not be publicly humiliated—'make people **shame'. 1987** G. Ward *Wandering Girl* p. 84 [south-west WA] I would have felt very **shame** if I'd done something silly. **1988** J. Harkins *English as 'Two-way' Language* p. 249 [central Aust.] **Shame** does not depend on being seen, for one can feel it when passing near a ceremonial ground even when no-one else is around, or when one sees a photo of something forbidden in a book in a library in Canberra. **1990** *Australian Linguistics* Journal of the Australian Linguistic Society Dec. p. 295 [central Aust.] Aboriginal people in Alice Springs and other parts of Central Australia give examples of *getting* **SHAME** when meeting strangers (Aboriginal or non-Aboriginal), or when entering an unfamiliar place, such as a school or office building, or the land of a different Aboriginal group. They feel SHAME in the presence of a prospective spouse, but also in the presence of some of their closest relatives, if the relationship is defined in the kinship system as an 'avoidance' relationship. They feel it when certain categories of kinfolk or strangers see them swimming, however modestly attired, but not at all when seen by other categories of people. **1990** *Koori News* Vol. I p. 21 [Sydney, NSW] Yeah LA PA School that's the name. We're all real cool and we got no **shame. 1994** *Encyclop. Aboriginal Aust.* p. 979 After 1788, many things changed . . . However, throughout this period there has been a continuity of kinship and family affiliation, and the value system of mutual aid and cooperation has been preserved . . . **Shame** is the linchpin which holds all these components together and perpetuates them. It differs from the concept of shame found in white society because of its historical and cultural contexts, and is continuous with the Aboriginal past and remains a powerful regulating device.

shame day, the 26th of January, the day of the invasion of the British. See INVASION DAY.

1992 R.L. Ginibi *Real Deadly* p. 111 [NSW] This story is about my birthday. You see I was born on **'shame day'** in 1934 . . . Shame day cause it was the day our land was taken over by the colonists in 1788.

shame job, an event or situation which can cause a person to feel shame.

This is one of the Aboriginal English words that has been taken over into Australian English, in the adolescent expression *shame job*. Adolescents are particularly conscious of the opinion of their peers and value public opinion, at least that of their age-group.

1977 *Nat. Aboriginal Day Mag.* p. 23 [south-west WA] **Shame job** car. **1985** *Matto's Koori Writers* p. 14 [Sydney, NSW] Then we heard the bus horn. When we went out everyone was looking at us. We said to each other 'what a **shame job** huh!' **1986** *Centralian Advocate* (Alice Springs) 4 July p. 9/- [central Aust.] It's no **shame job** to produce tourist items, provided they are high quality. **1993** J. Janson *Gunjies* p. 57 [western NSW] Eh, ya missed that kick eh brud, big **shame job** eh? **1994** R. & J. Huggins *Auntie Rita* p. 68 [south-east Qld] Neither did we have any shoes and would walk to school barefoot . . . Can you imagine your grandsons doing that today? It would be a real **shame job,** eh?

shame *verb* To cause shame to.

> **1963** D. E. Barwick *Little More than Kin* p. 331 [Vic.] Well, I'll invite everyone to our party, I won't have bad feeling by **shaming** people.

shamed *adjective* Causing shame; feeling shame; made to feel shame; embarrassed.

> **1950** I. Tonnies (ed.) *Beitrage* p. 69 [Daly River, northern NT] Ngeki . . is sharing the *ngirawat* taboo, because she is '**shamed**' for her sister. **1951** R. & C. Berndt *From Black to White in SA* p. 179 [Oodnadatta, northern SA] She ought to feel properly '**shamed**. **1958** J. Becket *A Study of a Mixed Blood Aboriginal Minority* p. 60 [western NSW] Young people . . complain that to hear the old people speak makes them feel '**shamed**'. **1963** D. E. Barwick *Little More than Kin* p. 210 [Vic.] Sometimes parents who are anxious that their children shall not be '**shamed**' in school keep them at home until they can afford . . clothing or shoes. **1982** C. Russell *People in a Community* p. 7 [Qld] But we must learn to project ourselves and our abilities, and not be **shamed** or embarrassed. **1990** A. Pring (ed.) *Women of the Centre* p. 112 [central Aust.] He got **shamed**—went to church two-three times.

shaming *noun* An act of causing shame. Also used as adjective.

> **1984** B. Swanton *Aborigines and Criminal Justice* p. 151 [WA] Women, in particular, invoked the traditional '**shaming**' sanction by haranguing defendants upon their return to community campsites. **1991** L.M. Wilkinson *Aboriginality* p. 335 [south-west Vic.] Rubbishing or '**shaming**' is used as a disciplinary measure for children. **1994** *Encyclop. Aboriginal Aust.* Vol. II p. 979 After 1788 many things changed and there were different ways of **shaming** in the very altered circumstances of Aboriginal society.

short *adjective* [northern Aust.] The term is used in Aboriginal English where in other Englishes the word is more likely to be *little* or *small*.

For another example of a use where the choice of a particular synonym in Aboriginal English is different from the choice generally made in Australian English see LONG.

> **1880** (Mrs) J. Smith *Booandik Tribe* p. 120 [south-east SA] Yara-nar-amen or **Short** Billy, died on the 7th of December. **1978** J. & P. Read *View of the Past* p. 42 [northern NT] All the way, you alda (always) look that **short** wood, all about him, stand up coolibah. **1992** *Mikurrunya* (Strelley) Nov. p. 26 [north-west WA] Roger found a coconut in a **short** tree.

side *noun* [Chiefly northern Aust.] An area of allegiance; a way of doing things or a sphere of knowledge.

This term has both a geographical and a conceptual element; traditionally it would have often been possible to point out the **side** (place) where that **side** (way of doing things) occurred. See also WAY in Chapter 7.

> **1980** B. Sansom *The Camp at Wallaby Cross* p. 111 [Darwin, northern NT] Unrolling a swag 'one **side**' and spending the long day-time hours 'other side' are contrary allocations of time. **198-** S.M. Kelly *Long Road Back* p. 47 [northern WA] A number of people wanted me to get a job with whitemen because I can talk the Aboriginal languages but its no good to me because its the whitemen's **side** I can't manage. **1985** *Lang. in Central Aust.* iv. p. 13 [central Aust.] I found when checking words with Warumungu people that they were quick to say if they thought a word was Warlpiri or Alyawarra . . . They would often say 'that **side**', and point in the direction of the country of the language group concerned. **1988** C. Dunne *People Under the Skin* p. 165 [central Aust.] After a couple of years people started coming back from Anningie and from Mount Barkly **side**. **1988** J. Harkins *English as 'Two-way' Language* p. 243 [central Aust.] English words relating to space and time are often used in distinctively

Aboriginal ways, reflecting concepts that are different from non-Aboriginal ones. *Way* and **side** are used for the concept expressed by Arrernte *theke*, resulting in slightly non-standard English utterances such as *We lived Hermannsburg way* (i.e. 'in the direction of Hermannsburg from here'). The various components of Yeperenye School's curriculum are referred to as *Arrernte-side* or *Arrernte-way*, *Luritja-side/way*, *English-side/way*. **1988** P. Marshall *Raparapa* p. 210 [Kimberley, WA] I know alcohol has done a lot of damage to the whitefella **side**. **1989** A. Haebich *For their own Good* p. 303 [south-west WA] One . . woman later told the 1934 Mosely Royal Commission that she could not go back and live on the Aboriginal **side** because 'she was not wanted there'. **1989** R.M. Baker *Land is life* p. 326 [Borroloola, north-east NT] Big mob of Borroloola boy been go along Fanny Bay (jail) . . . Garawa **side** too. **1990** Chi & Kuckles *Bran Nue Dae* p. 46 [north-west WA] Uncle, what are those two doing there? . . Nah, you don't look that **side**. You mind your own business. **1991** D.B. Rose *Hidden Histories* p. 101 [Victoria River, north-west WA] They still talk about *waringari* **side**. **1995** M. Brady *Giving away the Grog* p. 74 [northern NT] Corroboree at the Springvale [Homestead]. See, we used to go there and have a dance and then more grog on the dancing **side** you know.

silly *adjective* **1** Incompetent, childish.

The connection between the three different senses of the word is that the **silly** behaviour is or leads to socially irresponsible action.

1911 A.L. Haydon *Trooper Police of Aust.* p. 399 One man whom the boy described as 'silly fellow' because he had gone in his socks . . and gone lame . . **1980** B. Sansom *The Camp at Wallaby Cross* p. 80 [northern NT] . . their action is denied the form of fight. 'Youfella caan fightin! Two brother caan fightin. Youfellas you jus **sillyfellas**. Siddown.' **1989** B. Morris *Domesticating Resistance* p. 47 [northern NSW] He 'was goin' to be a man not **silly** anymore'.

2 Insane, out of one's mind.

1982 L.Fogarty *Yoogum Yoogum* p. 127 [south-west WA] Hey, him **silly**, him talk to that tree. **1987** C. Glass & A. Weller *Us Fellas* p. 22 [south-west WA] And after she had her baby she went a bit **silly** and we had to look after them . . and we notified the police and they came and strapped her down to the bed and sent her away. **1988** S. Dunlop *All that Rama Rama Mob* p. 74 [central Aust.] Used to tell too much about sacred sites. Maybe that's why the old people made him **silly**. **1992** I. Moores *Where is Wungawurra?* p. 149 [western NSW] I've had the job of taking people out of Orange Mental Hospital an looking after them when they got **silly**.

3 Wild or violent as a result of being drunk.

1978 H. Dagmar *Aborigines and Poverty* p. 106 [Gascoyne, northern WA] Sometimes people would return home from hospital where they had been treated for injuries received in a fight with their partner the preceding night and be completely unable to remember why they had started quarrelling. A usual answer would be: I was just **silly** you know. **1980** N. Mitchell & J.C. Anderson *Kubara* p. 13 [northern Qld] (Opium) Its not like that *kamu-kamu* (grog) make you go **silly**. **1982** *Tjakulpa Kuwarritja* (Papunya) Dec. n.p. [central Aust.] Be careful—don't get drunk, don't get **silly** at Papunya this season. **1988** P. Marshall *Raparapa* p. 76 [Kimberley, WA] When our people start drinking they go **silly**. **1995** M. Brady *Giving away the Grog* p. 111 [north-west NT] Like these days now you see people that in the alcohol they don't even respect their own culture, because alcohol . . make them gone **silly**, they don't even respect their own relation!

silly drunk, a violent or wild drunk; wildly or violently drunk.

1979 M. Heppell *A Black Reality* p. 191 [NT] . . J upbraided her daughter for spending too much time in town and thereby exposing herself and her baby daughter to the dangers of the town and especially '**silly drunks**'. 1980 B. Sansom *The Camp at Wallaby Cross* p. 61 [Darwin, northern NT] These rules are . . not foolproof, especially if drinkers become 'really **silly drunk**'.

solid *adjective* **1** Terrific, fantastic.

This sense could be connected with the sense of *solid* meaning 'of real value or importance' or it could be an inverted sense of the general Australian English *solid* meaning 'severe', 'difficult'. See also DEADLY.

1983 *Awabakal* Sept. p. 7 [central coast, NSW] The two groups have performed in front of crowds as big as 1,000 people and their latest performances were at the Newcastle City Hall for the 'Carnival 83'. Only one word can describe these koorie kids . . '**solid**'. 1986 A. Weller *Going Home* p. 132 [south-west WA] He was a **solid** dancer; his legs were rubber and his body was elastic, so Mum said. 1986 *Why Wanda Said 'No' in Broome* Kimberley Aboriginal Medical Services Council n.p. [Kimberley, WA] You're **solid** Phantom . . better than before. 1988 J. Davis *Barungin—Smell the Wind* p. 17 [south-west WA] Who's Lionel Rose? . . . Boxer, **solid**, real cruel fighter. 1989 A. Haebich *For their own Good* p. 218 [south-west WA] And some of the men and women were really **solid** singers. 1991 G. Ward *Unna you fullas* p. 32 [south-west WA] ' . . I dont care about Sister, no-one's going to touch my cobber'. I stood there with my chest stuck out, feeling **solid**.

2 (In reference to a romantic relationship) exhibiting serious interest; intimate.

1968 W.H. Douglas *Aboriginal Language of south-west Aus.* p. 21 [south-west WA] 'Solid' 'going steady' 'courting'; as in 'they're **solid**'. 1990 S. Watson *Kadaitcha Sung* p. 142 [south-east Qld] How **solid** you and that white girl? 1990 Davis et al *Paperbark* p. 237 [south-west WA] Paul had told him that she was **solid** for him.

sorry *adjective* [Now chiefly northern Aust.] Sorrowful; full of grief, grieving.

The term is used particularly in association with matters to do with death or with associations with COUNTRY. It is closer to the general sense of *sorrowful* than that of *sorry*.

1880 (Mrs) J. Smith *Booandik Tribe* p.xi [south-east SA] My heart was **sorry** when I left my land—I love it dearly. 1926 L.C.E. Gee *Bush Tracks & Gold Fields* p. 35 [NT] Ole man very **sorry**, very cross that gin go away; so him tell other boss blackfeller him mates. Him yabber longa them. 1950 I. Tonnies (ed.) *Beitrage* p. 72 [Daly River, north-west NT] If the former had sisters, they too, 'because **sorry** for their father's name' would go *ngirawat* with Douglas, though they would not exchange names with him. 1965 F.G.G. Rose *Wind of Change* p. 133 [central Aust.] I have developed and printed the photographs of the funeral ceremony . . but he said he did not like looking at them as they made him 'feel **sorry**'. 1978 J. & P. Read *View of the Past* p. 178 [NT] I bin losem my father, friendly, and old woman go back. Right, find another people, you know, crying everything. We bin **sorry** you know. 1988 J. Harkins *English as 'Two-way' Language* p. 247 [central Aust.] Accurate and comparable statements of the meanings of emotion terms such as **sorry** or *homesick* in Aboriginal and non-Aboriginal usage could help to correct and prevent cross-cultural misunderstandings. 1991 D.B. Rose *Hidden Histories* p. 235 [north-west NT] They stayed out on strike only for a short time, returning because they 'felt **sorry**' for their country.

sorry business, a ceremony associated with a death.

The term **sorry business** is generally used in traditional societies of the north and centre to refer to traditional mortuary ceremonies. The nature of such ceremonies varies widely over Aboriginal Australia and includes particular songs, dances and body decorations. There are displays of overt grief such as ritual wailing and self-inflicted injury. Disposal of the body can be by cremation or burial. In southern Australia, Aboriginal people have utilised the forms of European rituals, though with some variations. Occasionally people in the south will refer to funerals as 'sorry business'.

1981 *Junga Yimi* Yuendumu Sept p. 8 [central Aust.] The School has had many ups and downs this year because of **sorry business**. **1989** G. Knepfer *Nursing for Life* p. 39 The families . . carry out their traditional burials and '**sorry business**' without interruption.

sorry camp, a camp associated with a death or with funeral ceremonies.

1990 *Barrier Daily Truth* (Broken Hill) 17 Dec. p. 5/2 The tortuous, humid build-up to the northern wet season had already contributed to the deaths of a number of the community's elderly, and the township in recent weeks had become a place of '**sorry camps**' and funerals.

sorry cut, a mourning cut. In traditional communities, mourners, especially those closely related to the deceased, will cut themselves, particularly on the head, to express the intensity of their grief.

1988 S. Dunlop *All that Rama Rama Mob* p. 58 'Sorry cut . . She been to *ngangkari* [a traditional healer] said head was mad from **sorry cut**.'

sorry people, people associated with a death.

1983 P. Nathan & D.L. Japanangka *Settle Down Country* p. 101 In the Papunya region one of the five country camps was excluded because it was temporarily vacated for '**sorry' peoples**.

sorry sore, a sore resulting from a 'sorry cut'.

1945 (1991) J. Arthur *Personal File* Aust. Archives 12 July 1945 CRS F1, Item 44/172. 24 [people] had skin lesions ranging from '**sorry sores**' and chronic ulcers.

starve for *verb* To be hungry for; to need; to be in need of. Also **starve**.

The sense is predominantly one of *to need* rather than *to need food*, as in the general English sense.

1936 M. & E. Durack *Chunuma* p. 48 [Kimberley, WA] 'Me only **starve** b'longta lolly, boss,' she said. **1986** B. Shaw *Countrymen* p. 65 [Kimberley, WA] And he carried off that white man's swag . . robbed him of it. He might have been **starved for** blanket. **1989** R.M. Baker *Land is life* p. 224 [Borroloola, north-east NT] **Starving for** tucker, nobody feed them . . . **1990** *Aboriginal History* (Canberra) p. 45 [Borroloola, north-east NT] A number of people have described to me how they walked to Manangoore from surrounding areas when they were '**starving for**' tobacco.

Historically, 'to need' (tobacco) was also expressed in terms of another kind of need, for water rather than food, as in the following nineteenth century example.

1851 J. Henderson *Excursions & Adventures N.S.W.* Vol. II p. 112 [NSW] When they want tobacco, they say they are *murry dry*, that is, very **thirsty** for the weed.

sulky *adjective* Angry.

It is possible that the semantic change arose because the behaviour of Aboriginal people who were *angry* was read as that of people who were *sulky* by non-Aborigines, because of cultural differences in body language and socially acceptable ways of expressing anger. An Aboriginal person who remains silent and sits remote from the group might still be furiously angry. Alternatively, angry

behaviour on the part of Aboriginal people in the early days of contact may have
been described as *sulky* behaviour, as a way of reducing its significance and its
rationality. See also CHEEKY. The recorded use is mostly not current.

1845 C. Griffith *Present State Prospects of Port Phillip* p. 162 [Vic.] 'You pilmillally jumbuck,
plenty **sulky** me, plenty boom, borack gammon', which being interpreted, means—'If you
steal my sheep I shall be very angry, and will shoot you and no mistake.' **1872** Mrs E. Millett
Australian Parsonage p. 84 'Quiet fellow' and '**sulky** fellow' have an almost equally wide range,
the first signifying any conceivable degree of amiability, either in man or beast, and the latter
ferocity to a like extent. **1882** *Instruct. & Rep. Resident Magistrate Murchison & Gascoyne
Districts* p. 13 [Gascoyne, central WA] What right have we to be surprised when we hear
that a native, '**sulky**' with a shepherd for taking his woman away, has put the white man to
death? **1938** V.E. Turner *Good Fella Missus* p. 26 [SA] 'Why for they take our girls? . . These
men make us too much **sulky**-fella, we kill them.' **1988** J. Harkins *English as 'Two-way'
Language* p. 247 [central Aust.] Someone described as **sulky** may well erupt into sudden
violence; non-Aboriginal speakers might describe a person in such a state as *fuming*, but
probably not *sulky*.

tongue for *verb* To long for.

From the sense of *one's tongue hanging out for*, i.e. longing for (something).

1990 Chi & Kuckles *Bran Nue Dae* p. 1 [north-west WA] Hey boy, he **tongueing** for you.
1993 J. Janson *Gunjies* p. 12 [south-west NSW] After a feed, we'll 'ave it eh? I'm **tonguin'
for** a charge'.

winyarn *adjective* [south-west WA] Frightened, pathetic. Also used as a noun: a
frightened person.

From the Nyungar language of south-western WA *wayarn* 'afraid, frightened'.

1982 J. Davis *The Dreamers* p. 97 [south-west WA] Nyoornditj, he's a **winyarn** . . . Wasn't
you ever frightened, when you was little? **1986** A. Weller *Going Home* p. 145 [south-west
WA] Aaaahh, you **winyarn**, bud. Ya couldn't fight if y 'ad eight fists. **1987** G. Ward *Wandering
Girl* p. 93 [south-west WA] 'Choo, I am **winyarn**, big shame!' **1991** G. Ward *Unna you fullas*
p. 96 [south-west WA] In those days us girls either felt **winyarn** or solid.

worry *verb* [Chiefly northern Aust.] To be concerned about, to think about, to grieve
for.

It is generally used with *for* as **worry for**.

1976 *Identity (Sydney)* Jan. p. 14 [Arnhem Land] But why we hate some monanga
(Europeans) . . some balanda **worry** for natives and know little bit of their law. Other ones
don't care and don't worry about it. **1978** J. & P. Read *View of the Past* p. 277 [NT] They
might be hungry, because, you know, army bin **worrying** for people. **1981** *Social Alternatives
(St Lucia)* Vol. II no. 2 p. 26 [Sth Qld] 'Too much **worry** about money, too much talk, too
much worry for themselves' was the succinct comment on Europeans by one old Lockhart
man. **1983** *Yeperenye Yeye (Alice Springs)* Mar. p. 20 [NT] White man's taking all the land.
Which land we going to live on? White man **worries** for land. So he can build houses and
buildings. **1985** I. White & D. Barwick & B. Meehan *Fighters & Singers* p. 209 [NT]
Gurrmanmana said that she still '**worrying** for that baby' who had died. **1985** Borowski
Juvenile Delinquency in Aust. p. 119 'They **worrying** for grog all the time, not that kid.' **1990**
S. Janson & S. Macintyre *Through White Eyes* p. 136 [central Aust.] Though absence from
homelands, from one's place of conception, or father's or mother's conception, could cause
remembrance and anxiety (both captured in the Aboriginal English phrase '**worrying** for
country'), there was no . . sense of a connection between individual and country being lost.

yambilthine *noun* [NSW] Pretence, nonsense. Also **yarmbuldine**.

From the Wiradjuri language of south-western NSW *yaambuuldaayn* 'a liar, a teller of yarns'.

1969 *Koorier* (Fitzroy) p. 5 *Word of the Month* **YARMBULDINE** (wirad-juri)—bulldust, sham, pretense. 1982 E.A. Young & E.K. Fisk *Town Populations* p. 76 [southern NSW] Word: **yambilthine**. Meaning: I'm only joking.

yamble *noun* [NSW] A tall story. Earlier recorded as a 'liar'. Also **yarmbul**.

From the Wiradjuri language of south-western NSW *yaambul* 'nonsense, a lie'.

1906 J.F.H. Mitchell *Aboriginal Dict.* p. 15 [south-west NSW] **Yambler** . . A liar Yamble-yarra . . A red liar. 1991 *Sydney Morning Herald* 16 Dec. p. 1/5 [south-west NSW] The Aboriginal children are of the Wiradjuri tribe, and although none can speak the entire language, some words survive, and are used by all the pupils. In their own playground kidspeak, *narrabung* is silly, a **yamble** is a tall story, a *boori* is a child, a *warjin* is a girl, and so on. Mrs Dianne Strong, their teacher of seven years, said: 'It saddens me that their language has died.'

yarmbul-cryin, pretend-crying.

1975 R.J. Merritt *Cake Man* p. 14 Come on, we see who's the smartest runner, 'round this claypan . . . So the emu gave the knife to curlew and the curlew went off in the bush with it and pretended to be cuttin' off his wings, all **yarmbul**-cryin 'real hard' . . Yarmbul-cryin' means what y'might call foxin' a bit.

CHAPTER 4

Country

The central word in this section is **country**, used all over Aboriginal Australia to name the place where a person or a group belongs. The use of the word 'country' for this 'belonging place' reflects the cultural structure of Aboriginal Australia. It was in fact more like Europe than its occupiers have recognised, with a collection of **countries** with different languages and distinct cultural variations within a recognisably common base.

The relationship of people to country is not only one of history, association, or love of place. Part of the continuing experience of being Aboriginal is holding a spiritual relationship to place. Aboriginal culture was and is place-centred in that the physical and political geography of land is also the spiritual geography. Sacred narratives belong to particular landscapes and personal identities are tied to particular locations. There—that exact spot—is one site of a person's connection to the spirit world. The spiritual beings that created the world walked among known places and the logic of narratives follows the tracks of the dreamings.

The words that Aboriginal people use about country express a living relationship. The country may be **mother** or **grandfather**, which **grows** them **up** and is **grown up** by them. These kinship terms impose mutual responsibilities of caring and keeping upon the land and people. The terms **own** and **owner** are transformed in Aboriginal meaning into mutual interdependence rather than exclusive control.

This chapter also contains the word **camp**, a significant word in Aboriginal/European relations. A camp can be outside a town, on a cattle station, or on a riverbank. A camp can be half a dozen houses or a swag under a tree. The place where someone lives makes the camp, not the physical dwellings. (It would not however so easily be applied to a house in a non-Aboriginal suburb.) Its essential quality is that it is an Aboriginal-controlled environment, psychologically as well as physically outside the non-Aboriginal domain. The camp has often been an asylum for Aboriginal cultural elements such as language. Governments did and do recognise the cultural power of the camp and it might be classified as a threat and liable to abrupt removal and destruction.

For outsiders, the kind of country a people lives in can be a way of categorising them—**saltwater, river, sandstone, flat country**. This use is found in other Englishes such as the American English 'mountain people', but it is not common in Australian English, where people are more commonly defined by political denomination (*Victorian*), or by geography (*southerners*), or by concept (*city slicker*). Aboriginal English of course has these kinds of categories as well as the geographical ones.

belong *verb* [Aust. chiefly in traditional areas] To relate to one's COUNTRY, especially with a sense of spiritual affinity. Also **belonging**.

The sense of 'belonging to' is that the person **belongs** to the country as much as that the country **belongs** to the person. The sense of belonging is based on spiritual and kin associations, and has nothing to do with European notions of property i.e. the sense of being able to dispose of, or do what one wants, with something one 'owns'. The emphasis is one of mutual dependency. See OWN. See also Chapter 8 for the use of **belong** as a grammatical possessive.

1897 W.E. Roth *Ethnological Studies* p. 160 [south-east Aust?] The aboriginal will speak to this Being . . . 'Do not touch me. I **belong** to this country.' **1938** D. Bates *Passing of Aborigines* p. 182 [Ooldea, northern SA] 'Blak-fella king **belong** to this country!' shouted Nyimbana in English. 'We don't want waijela here! This *gabbi* our *gabbi*.' **1978** J. & P. Read *View of the Past* p. 189 [northern NT] My full countryman too. Him **belonga** this land, you know, all over this one now. **1981** *Social Alternatives* (Brisbane) Vol. II no. 2 p. 25 [Lockhart River, northern Qld] Each of these clan territories '**belong**' to particular families and lines of future inheritance are clear. **1983** *Balgo Newsletter* 25 Aug. p. 1 [Western Desert] Last month on July, there was a land claim hearing at Balgo. The judge wanted to hear from the people who **belong** to that country (Warlpiri, Kukatja, and Ngarti). **1985** *Aboriginal Health Worker* (Little Bay) Vol. IX Dec. p. 44 [Tas.] We keep our traditional view of our land as something not only belonging to us, but something to which we **belong**. **1990** A. Schmidt *Loss of Australia's Aboriginal language heritage* p. 24 Aborigines often speak of themselves as 'belonging to that place' or 'belonging to that language'—the land and language come first, and the people come next.

belongin place, a person's country.

1988 R. Langford *Dont Take Your Love to Town* p. 239 [north coast, NSW] I was quietly feeling pleasure from the idea of being back at my **belongin place**.

born place *noun* A person's place of birth. Also **born country**.

This is significant in Aboriginal thinking because of the spiritual links with one's 'country'.

1991 G.R. Langford *Journey into Bundjalung Country* p. 6 [northern NSW] See that tree over there. I was born under that tree. That's my **born place**. **1994** R. & J. Huggins *Auntie Rita* p. 5 [south-east Qld] I was only a small child when we were taken from my **born country** . . . Most of my life has been spent away from my country but . . [it] will always be home, the place I belong to.

brother *noun* A kinship term used to express the intimate nature of the relationship with one's 'country'.

1985 B. Neidjie *Kakadu Man* p. 46 [Arnhem Land] This ground and this earth . . . Like **brother** and mother.

camp *noun* 1 A living place, either temporary or permanent. The term can refer to the living place of either a single person, or a small or large group, and can include in its reference a group of houses or a swag under a tree. Always, it is essentially an Aboriginal-controlled environment. It would not generally be used of a house within a non-Aboriginal environment, such as a suburb. See also HOLIDAY CAMP, RATION CAMP, WALKABOUT CAMP.

The word is recorded in non-Aboriginal Australian English for such a place from

1840. For non-Aboriginal people, the *camp* also had the added sense of being an Aboriginal-controlled environment, which meant that it was often a community to be feared, harried, moved on, or destroyed, and from which fair-skinned Aboriginal children should be 'rescued'. In non-Aboriginal Australian English it is often used with pejorative connotations.

1900 T. Major *Squatter's Note Bk* p. 25 [western NSW] Me think it, blacks' **camp** sit down there. 1909 A.J. Peggs *Aborigines of Roebuck Bay* p. 343 [north-west NT] He .. finally declared him all right now: 'more better come sit down along a **camp**'. 1973 M. Fennel & A. Grey *Nucoorilma* p. 95 [northern NSW] It was one 'miramar' day that several members of the Munro family took their visitor to their **camp** at Bassendean. 1976 J. Mirritji *My People's Life* p. 33 [Arnhem Land] I didn't understand either why so many people were coming to the **camp** and why they were all singing. 1980 P. Pepper *You Are What You Make Yourself* p. 40 [Gippsland, south-east Vic.] .. they took a short cut to the Milly **camp** to warn the blackfellas .. or *gunai* or whatever you want to call 'em. 1980 B. Sansom *The Camp at Wallaby Cross* p. 122 [Darwin, northern NT] The **camp** was now in that state which is having 'dead body business' and, formally, dead body business is concluded in ceremony. 1984 *Puggana News* (Launceston) Feb. p. 3 [Tas.] Not G.T. who hasn't been to the **camp** cause he is too busy with his gub activities. 1986 *Tjakulpa Kuwarritja* (Papunya) Apr. n.p. [central Aust.] If all the children are just left to play around in the **camp** they go mad. 1987 F. Kolig *Noonkanbah Story* p. 97 [East Kimberley, WA] Others were in favour of .. handing over the **camp** and all its facilities to the Djandjoa community, which was composed to a large extent of Bunaba speakers, descendants of the original occupants of the area. 1988 C. Mattingley & K. Hampton (eds) *Survival in Our Own Land* p. 208 [SA] Us kids used to sneak to the **camp** and they gave us rabbits and *guldas* cooked in coals. 1989 B. Morris *Domesticating Resistance* p. 82 [northern NSW] All they needed for sleeping in this **camp** was .. one blanket 'half over, half under and to sleep 'guts on' to the fire'. 1988 J. Harkins *English as 'Two-way' Language* p. 238 [central Aust.] **Camp** and *place* .. refer to a person's or group's present home, both the dwelling itself and the general location .. 1991 G. Ward *Unna you fullas* p. 67 [south-west WA] She was panicking, and crying-way she said 'You two girls go down the bottom **camp** and round up your aunties.'

2 (As adjective) relating to the people who belong to a 'camp'.

1973 *Elliott School Paper* Elliott School p. 10 [central NT] During the easter holiday Mr Ewen took the **camp** mob to Long Reach for a holiday. 1986 A. Weller *Going Home* p. 2 [south-west WA] He bought clean bright clothes and cut off his long hair that all the **camp** girls had loved.

camp black, a person living in a camp as opposed to the town. The term is often used pejoratively, with associations of unsophistication and poverty. See also BAREFOOT.

1951 R. & C. Berndt *From Black to White in SA* p. 160 [Oodnadatta, northern SA] Some of the wages change hands during card games. . . . When the games are held in or near the town part of it may pass into the hands of (town aborigines) who are not above playing with the '**camp blacks**'.

camp English, the dialect of Australian English spoken in a camp.

1987 *D-Bate* Language Education Course, Deakin University p. 36 The **Camp English** that is spoken in the community is not a Kriol, it is simply what they say it is, Camp English, which is a non-standard dialect of Australian English. Others would call this Aboriginal English.

3 (In combinations) a particular kind of camp as in:

lie down camp, a permanent camp.

1982 *Community Capers (Moora)* Oct. p. 26 [NT] The Northern Territory Government . . noted that there were two types of camps. One was the '**lie down**' or permanent **camps** where people sleep or live on a more or less permanent basis.

sick camp, a camp inhabited by the sick.

1990 P. Jacobs *Mister Neville* p. 90 [south-west WA] The 'Spanish Flu' epidemic reached Western Australia in mid-1919 . . Aborigines . . were confined on town reserves, or in '**sick camps**' and supplied with rations.

sit down camp, a temporary camp.

1982 *Parliamentary Papers* (Melbourne) (Commonwealth of Australia) Oct. p. 26 [NT] The other was the '**sit down**' or temporary **camps**. These were camps of convenience and their purpose was a factor influencing their location.

4 (In combinations) an area of a camp divided along gender lines, specifically the **single men's camp, single women's camp, young men's camp**. Also **single boys' quarters**.

Traditionally, an Aboriginal camp has areas open to one gender only. The term **single men's camp** refers to a custom whereby young men leave the family hearth at puberty and move into a particular area of the camp closed to women. It is also a place where male visitors can stay. The **single women's camp** is the place where women who are widowed or for some reason wish to live away from their husbands for a time can stay, and where women can discuss ritual matters closed to men.

1928 B. Spencer *Wanderings in Wild Aust.* p. 585 [Borroloola, north-east NT] The rejected lubra went to the **women's camp**. 1965 F.G.G. Rose *Wind of Change* p. 151 [central NT] I went over to the **young man's camp** to ask (him) to tell me something about the distribution of the parts of a kangaroo. 1983 *Cent. Aust. Land Rights News* (Alice Springs) Spring p. 4 (caption) [central Aust.] Card game at the **single boys' quarters**. 1981 *Ram Paddock Gate* SA Dept of Environment—Minerawuta p. 9 [northern SA] This was the **single men's camp** where Dick lived with his sons . . . Any single man passing through camped with Dick. 1981 *Ram Paddock Gate* SA Dept of Environment—Minerawuta p. 9 [northern SA] This camp was the **single women's camp** and consisted of Lorna, Kitty's daughter and Mavis Patterson, Dick Coulhard's daughter. Kitty's two sons, Jo and Tom lived in their own camp. 1983 H.C. Coombs & M.M. Brandl & W.E. Snowdon *A Certain Heritage* p. 364 [central NT] Among the Warlpiri the **single women's camp** . . is institutionalised in the *tjilimi* . . . It is the focus of women's religious life.

camp *verb* To make a camp, to live at a place for a time.

This is closer to the meaning of the word *live* than the standard English use of the word *camp*, where 'to camp' somewhere is to live in a different way from the way one normally lives.

1924 G. Horne & G. Aiston *Savage Life in Central Aust.* p. 10 [central Aust.] Tradition has that many years ago a moora, wandering over the earth, came to the place and **camped** there. 1936 M. & E. Durack *Chunuma* p. 87 [Kimberley, WA] Im bin **campin'** dere longa ribber three days an' 'im don' come to see me. 1944 M.J. O'Reilly *Bowyangs & Boomerangs* p. 88 That is what he told me: 'that fellow bean tree is one place where big fellow 'Kaditcha' all the time sit down; no white fellow, no blackfellow allowed **camp** alonga that place. **1978**

J. & P. Read *View of the Past* p. 94 [NT] 'Where you gonna **camp**?' You know, not English, but language, you know. **1980** B. Sansom *The Camp at Wallaby Cross* p. 111 [northern NT] By '**campin** close up' and 'campin far' people map current social distances. **1981** *Land Claims in NSW* NSW Aboriginal Land Council n.p. [Bodalla, south coast, NSW] We last **camped** here about 1975 when we were hunted off by rangers. **1986** B. Shaw *Countrymen* p. 207 [Kimberley, WA] He **camps** with her and she comes back full the next month. Well the old bloke looks and reckons, 'No, I don't want you, now you got a white man kid.'

clean *verb* To clean or clear the country by burning. Also **clean up**.

Fire is the traditional tool used by Aboriginal peoples to manage the land. Much of the landscape that the Europeans found when they occupied Australia was not a 'natural' but a managed one, where the varieties of plants and the habitats available for animal life were in part a result of controlled burning by Aboriginal communities over a very long period. When the burning stops, the patterns of animal and plant life change, and some species of both plants and animals are at risk of being lost. Some plants need fire in order to reproduce, and some animals, such as the bilby in the Northern Territory, are affected when the lack of burning changes the vegetation growth.

1980 R. Jones *Cleaning the Country* p. 14 [Arnhem Land] This occurred in thick woodland which had not been visited or burnt for several years . . 'That mob lazy buggers, more better they clean him up.' . . .The fires are said to '**clean up**' the country, to stimulate the growth of fresh new grass, to help get rid of snakes and mosquitoes, and sometimes as part of hunting drives. **1985** B. Neidjie *Kakadu Man* p. 22 [Arnhem Land] '**Cleaning**' the country. [Caption to photograph of grass-burning] **1985** B. Neidjie *Kakadu Man* p. 35 [Arnhem Land] Fire is nothing just **clean up**. When you burn, new grass coming up.

cold *adjective* [northern Aust.] With reference to the dry, cooler season in northern Australia, from about April to August.

The adjective occurs in combinations with nouns such as **season** and **time**.

1978 J. & P. Read *View of the Past* p. 171 [NT] 'We have clothes for you-feller, and blanket too.' Like this time, now **cold** weather time, you know. **1983** A.H. Ross *Aust. Aboriginal* p. 141 [Kimberley, WA] The Gidga and Djaru people distinguish three seasons, a **cold** season . . a hot season . . and a wet season. **1984** K. Benterrak & S. Muecke & P. Roe *Reading Country* p. 109 [north-west WA] That was south-east time too, **cold** time . . **1984** S. Cane *Desert Camps* p. 33 [Western Desert] The 'green grass time' merged into winter or '**cold** time' (yaltaburru). **1987** E. Paddy & M. Smith *Boonja Bardak Korn* p. 6 [WA] Inland bloodwood is good firewood during July, the **cold** season, and for 'married turtle time' in November-December.

country *noun* **1** The tract of land where an Aboriginal person or community belongs, to which they have a responsibility, and from which they can draw spiritual strength.

The use of this word, which dates from the very early time of the British occupation, reflects the cultural structure of Aboriginal Australia at the time of the occupation: it was a collection of peoples with distinct languages and with distinct variations of a recognisably common culture. The power of allegiance to a particular place is vested not only in association, in language, in personal and family history, but also in spiritual knowledge. This knowledge is of the sacred meaning of the landscape, created by the 'dreamings', and manifest in the obligation of a people to sustain the spiritual and physical life of their land. It lies in the understanding of the way the spirit of a person comes from and returns to that particular land.

1843 (1990) Jakelin Troy *Australian Aboriginal contact with the English language in NSW 1788-1845* p. 131 He occasionally wished for his wife and children, saying 'if he had them he would no more go back to his own **country**'. [1843 Thomas Letter in NSW VPLC p. 540] **1844** *Adelaide Observer* 27 Apr. [south-east SA] Let them sit down on the Murray, not here. This is not his **country**. What he do here? **1845 (1990)** Jakelin Troy *Australian Aboriginal contact with the English language in NSW 1788-1845* p. 150 [central coast NSW] Mahroot, the last of the originally four hundred-strong Botany Bay people remarked: 'Well Mither (Mr.) . . all black-fellow gone! All this my **country**! Pretty place Botany! Little Pickaninny, I run about here. Plenty black-fellow then; corrobbory; great fight; all canoe about. **1982** Broome p. 150 **1861** *Rep. Select Committee Native Police Force* p. 90 [Qld] The Government actually broke faith with them twice, Mr Walker having . . undertaken on the part of the Government to return them to their own **country**. **1877** *Jrnl. Anthrop. Inst.* (London) VII p. 291 [WA] Often . . have I heard a native say to another, this is my **country**, yours is Canturbi (a place near New Norsia) go away. **1899** *Rep. Select Committee Aborigines Bill* p. 70 (Minutes of Evidence) Is it not dangerous leaving the aborigines of one tribe in the **country** of another? **1903** *Folklore* (London) XIV. iv. p. 340 [south-west WA] Our Billie and Maggie went, with our permission, to their own **country**, and have not returned yet. **1931** A.P. Elkin *Understanding Austral. Aborigine* (Morpeth Booklet no. 2) p. 12 The spirit-home aspect of a man's 'country' also explains the . . frequent refusals of old people to leave it . . They merely say . . 'This my **country**.' **1937** G.H. Sunter *Adventures Trepang Fisher* p. 93 [northern Aust.] I heard of an old lubra who had run a trepang camp . . . I will call her Milly. Her **country**, I remember, was Port Essington. **1963** D. E. Barwick *Little More than Kin* p. 258 [Vic.] The precipitating cause . . was the refusal of one partner to leave his or her kin and return with the other to 'live in my own **country**'. **1989** B. Neidjie *Story about feeling* p. 150 [Arnhem Land] But **country** e stay . . E give us something to eat, give us life, tree, water, grass, yam. **1990** Davis et al *Paperbark* p. 61 [WA] Oh musta been some NAC people in other **countries**. **1991** *Good Weekend* (Sydney) 16 Nov. p. 68/1 [south-west WA] Some do not want him there and suggest he's out of his **country** and out of his depth. **1995** D. Hodge *Did you meet any Malagas?* p. 52 [northern NT] Darwin is the one place in the world where I feel absolutely relaxed and secure I've been around the world and I've lived around Australia and I think its got to do with I know that this is my place, my **country** and I've known it since I could first think about it.

to country, a phrase used in place of 'his, her, their, or my country'.

The last citation illustrates how the phrase has moved into general use at least in the Northern Territory, although only in reference to Aboriginal situations.

1983 *Upper Daly Land Claim* p. 19 [Daly River, NT] Some children . . are described as 'following father' . . in their primary attachment **to country**. **1984** S. Cane *Desert Camps* p. 118 [Western Desert] They went back **to country**. **1983** *Conference of Abor. Communities* Dept of the Chief Minister p. 33 Does the N.T. Government support traditional owners in trying to control access **to country** e.g.—restrictions on road use.

The concept of 'country' is such that people are able to speak of 'country' being aware of and relating to the humans who inhabit it.

1988 P. Marshall *Raparapa* p. 30 [Kimberley, WA] But Kartiya have different ideas and a different way; and the **country** is feeling very sad as a result. **1988** D.B. Rose *Passive Violence* p. 24 They say they are frightened of their own **country** because their country doesn't know them anymore. **1995** D.B. Rose *Country in flames* p. 59 [Kimberley, WA] My talk to you will be on 'burn grass'. . . It is part of our responsibility in looking after our country. If you don't look after country, **country** won't look after you. **1995** D.B. Rose *Country in flames* p. 30 [Borroloola, north-east NT] A widower or widow may not light country that belonged to their spouse, and the **country** is said not to burn because it is too sad.

2 A greeting given to a fellow countryman or woman. See COUNTRYMAN.

1987 M. Christie et al. *Teaching Aboriginal Children* p. 32 The relatedness of a person and his/her land are so complete that, at Milingimbi, men often greet their relatives by calling them in English '**Country**'.

3 An area of **country** for which an individual has particular rights and responsibilities, usually by right of inheritance.

These rights and responsibilities can include rights in relation to food resources on that land, and the obligation to perform or see carried out rituals which will sustain the land.

1955 M. Durack *Keep him my Country* (1966) p. 75 This was his 'little **country**', the place from which he sprang. **1962** D. Lockwood *I, Aboriginal* p. 31 [north-east NT] We all belong to the Alawa tribe and the Roper River district, but every man among us owns a particular plot of tribal ground which he calls 'My **Country**'. **1975** J.P. Roberts *Mapoon Story* ii. p. 4 [northern Qld] The child's own **country**, its home where it will in the future have the right to hunt and roam, is . . determined not by the place of actual birth, but by the locality where its soul has been held captive.

4 (In combinations) the responsibility deriving from social relationships, as in **father country**, **mother country**, the land belonging to one's father or mother; **marrying country**, the country where one's marriage partner could potentially come from.

1993 E. Young *Aborigines, Land & Society* p. 8 [Western Desert] The social structure is also related to land responsibilities and different 'countries' may be described as '**marrying countries**' or '**father** and **mother countries**'. **1989** B. Neidjie *Story about feeling* p. 41 [Arnhem Land] She started Manganawal tribe . . . Next one . . .Ulbu, my **mother-country**.

countryman *noun* **1** A person from the same area as oneself, having the same allegiances to country. Also **countrywoman**.

Countryman can refer to either sex (as in the 1986 citation); *countrywoman* is used less frequently, and only of women.

1880 (Mrs) J. Smith *Booandik Tribe* p. 25 [south-west SA] She . . came across a *posse* of **countrywomen** lamenting her loss. **1889** *Jrnl. & Proc. of the Royal Soc. NSW* Vol. XXXIII p. 421 [NSW?] It has been remarked that the blacks were exceedingly loth to permit white men to see their sacred objects and they also concealed them from their own **countrywomen**. **1912** Spencer & Gillen *Across Aust.* II p. 499 [central Aust.] You **countryman** along of this boy? **1927** *V & P* (W.A.) I. no. 3 p. 47 [WA] I do not like the police; I think they killed my **countrymen**. **1928** B. Spencer *Wanderings in Wild Aust.* p. 590 [north-east NT] Calls up second witness. 'Now, Peter, you talk straight-fellow longa these gentlemen. You **countryman** longa this boy?' (pointing to prisoner). 'Yes, me countryman all right.' **1978** J. & P. Read *View of the Past* p. 132 [Victoria River, north-west NT] . . they informed me that Gordon Creek Jimmy and Pompey were killed because they had in the past taken a prominent part with the white-fellows in tracking up their **country-men**. **1980** B. Sansom *The Camp at Wallaby Cross* p. 16 [Darwin, northern NT] My own **countrymen** are all those to whom I have social access and who have access to me because we are *known* to one another. **1986** J. Davis *No*

Sugar p. 73 [south-west WA] That one Dargurru, my **countryman**. [In this case the speaker is referring to a woman.] **1995** M. Brady *Giving away the Grog* p. 99 [north-west NT] And you see some of our peoples, that are **countrymen**, mainly around this Northern Territory, they don't get to where my old man is.

2 A living thing from one's country.

c.**1834** (1966) N.J.B. Plomley (ed.) *Friendly Mission* p. 369 [Tas.] The natives make small spears which they throw at and stick into the different trees. Those of Oyster Bay spear the stringy bark trees, pepperment (sic) trees, honeysuckle trees. The gum trees they claim as theirs and call them **countrymen**. The stringy bark trees the Brune call theirs, as being their countrymen, the peppermint the Cape Portland call theirs, and the Swanport claim the honeysuckle. Thus, if the natives of Oyster Bay spear the trees of another native they are much annoyed and go and pull them out. **1977** *Black News Service* Nov. p. 5 He knew the land in an intimate way, showing a real sensitivity for living things—even the cattle he addressed as '**country men**'.

desert *adjective* (Of a person) from the Western Desert or Central Australia.

1988 J. Davis *Barungin—Smell the Wind* p. 31 [south-west WA] Tarney Wallace—he's a little bloke, **desert** bloke. **1990** P. Austin et al. *Lang. & Hist.* p. 251 [Oodnadatta, northern SA] *Mundulu* and Turkey Creek, the same one. A lot of blackfellers are there. That's the doctor country. They have a different language. I can't catch it. Warramala, they're **desert** people. And a different lingo again, Warramanga. **1991** G. Ward *Unna you fullas* p. 1 [south-west WA] There was this fair head kid, a **desert** blonde, crying and grabbing my hand saying, 'My sister, my sister!'

dirty *adjective* (Of country) unburnt, and therefore uncared for. See CLEAN.

Traditional Aboriginal land management practices use fire to control vegetation, and hence the food and habitat available for animals. Burning also reduces the fuel load and minimises wildfires.

1993 E. Young *Aborigines, Land & Society* p. 18 Areas where the vegetation cover has become thick. Aborigines revisiting unburnt country after a number of years often sadly comment that it is '**dirty**' or 'gone to rubbish'.

flat country Aborigine *noun* A person from flat country—in the following citation, from the plains of north-western NSW.

1973 M. Fennel & A. Grey *Nucoorilma* p. 23 [northern NSW] Similarly, the '**flat country Aborigines**' to the west of the Gwydir River were unaccepted.

freshwater *adjective* (Of people) associated with freshwater rivers, i.e. inland people as opposed to a saltwater or coastal people.

1985 B. Neidjie *Kakadu Man* p. 25 [Daly River, NT] The Aboriginal people were **freshwater** river people, occupying the Alligator Rivers areas. **1988** C. Dunne *People Under the Skin* p. 105 [Daly River, NT] My people **freshwater** people. **1989** R.M. Baker *Land is life* p. 183 [Borroloola, north-east NT] As elsewhere in Australia, there is a strong cultural divide in the area between 'salt water' people and '**fresh water**' people.

grandfather *noun* Part of a person's country, defined as kin. See COUNTRY.

This use, and the other family terms applied to material objects in one's country, underline the intense relationship of person and place.

1986 *White Invasion Diary* Invasion Diary Collective 13 Jan. [SA] This is not a rock, it is my **grandfather**. This is the place where the dreaming comes up, right up from inside the ground.

grandmother *noun* **1** An abbreviation of 'grandmother's country'. See COUNTRY.

1991 *Amanbidji Land Claim* 21 Aug. [northern NT] . . what country they follow? . . They got to follow **grandmother**.

2 A kinship term applied to an object within a person's 'country'.

Here the rules of kinship are applied to the inanimate world, marking the continuity between the human and the non-human and the spiritual and the physical.

1981 G.J. Neate *Legal Language Across Cultures* p. 202 [central Aust.] So the spiritual links between a person and an object may have a genealogical component and a person might call an object '**grandmother**' (meaning father's mother) which his father would have called 'mother'.

grandpa country (or **grannie country**) *noun* The country belonging to one's grandfather (or grandmother). See COUNTRY.

1991 *Amanbidji Land Claim* 21 Aug. I was born here, and **Grandpa country**, and **Grannie country**.

granny *noun* A kin term used in reference to an aspect of one's 'country'. See also MOTHER etc.

It indicates the deep personal responsibility a person has to his or her country and the continuity between the animate and inanimate.

1989 B. Neidjie *Story about feeling* p. 25 [Arnhem Land] . . You dig yam? . . Well one of your **granny** or mother you digging through the belly. You must cover im up, cover again.

grow up *verb* [Chiefly traditional areas.] **1** (Of a country) to care for 'country' as one would a child. To GROW UP is the Aboriginal English term meaning raise or rear a child. Also **grow**.

1984 D. Bell & P. Ditton *Law: The Old and the New* p. 53 [central Aust.] We have good country which produces plentiful food—we **grew** it **up**. **1984** P. Toyne & D. Vachon *Growing up the Country* p. 5 [central Aust.] Pitjantjatjara . . '**grow up** the country' just as they 'grow up the kids' with deliberate care and affection. **1988** C. Dunne *People Under the Skin* p. 168 [central Aust.] We are the guardians of the land, we **grew** it **up**. **1988** H. Ross *Community Social Impact* p. 73 [East Kimberley, WA] We bin **grow** (look after) that country. **1989** Lyon & Parsons *We are Staying* p. 58 [south-east NT] They had '**grown up**' Lake Nash. **1994** *Land Rights News* April p. 9/4 The grant of secure title will enable the group to seek funding for basic infrastructure, such as housing, 'to **grow** the place **up**'.

2 (Of a person) to be nurtured by one's country, as by a parent.

In this sense it is the country which nourishes the human being.

1989 B. Neidjie *Story about feeling* p. 30 [Arnhem Land] I look tree but I say . . 'Just like father, mother, brother, grandma.' . . because this earth, this ground, this piece of ground e **grow** you. **1991** D.B. Rose *Hidden Histories* p. 229 [Victoria River, north-west NT] I can't (go) hungry here at the river—fish, turtle, goanna. That thing **grew** me **up**.

The following examples from the people of Ooldea in northern South Australia reinforce the concept of the 'parenting' relationship between people and country; the country is an **orphan** because its people are all dead. It is not clear from the original whether the speakers were using Aboriginal English or their Aboriginal language.

1938 D. Bates *Passing of Aborigines* p. 134 [Ooldea, northern SA] Koolbari called the area 'orphan country' because its own native gooseberry and kangaroo groups were extinct. Ilgamba was also orphaned ground. **1938** D. Bates *Passing of Aborigines* p. 183 [Ooldea, northern SA] 'Which of you owns the water of Yuldil?' I demanded. 'Yuldil **orphan** water. People dead.'

knock em down *adjective* Forceful enough to flatten. Also **knock-im-down.** Particularly as **knock em down rains**, the storms that come at the end of the Wet Season in the Top End.

1946 A. Green *We were (Riff) R.A.A.F.* p. 31 Towards the end of February, and in early March, the '**knock 'em down** rains' flattened the tall spear grass. **1960** J. Glennon *Heart in Centre* p. 240 Another spring had gathered up her remnants of green and departed, followed by a sweltering summer and the '**knock 'em down**' rains which flattened the spear grass that had lately flourished. **1975** R.J. Merritt *Cake Man* p. 47 [south-west NSW] *Ruby*: . . that man just had little heart trouble. *Pumpkinhead*: Pity it weren't big **knock-im-down** sort.

know *verb* To have the ritual and spiritual knowledge (of a place).

1983 *Upper Daly Land Claim* p. 27 [Daly River, northern NT] '**Knowing** country' means that each claimant has a group shared system of knowledge and beliefs about a number of aspects of the landscape: dreaming sites, dreaming tracks, and historical sites connected with birth, death, ceremony, residence and foraging.

look after *verb* [Chiefly northern Aust.] To care for a place in such a way that its spiritual and material life is maintained. See OWN.

1978 C.H. & R.M. Berndt *Pioneers & Settlers* p. 20 [NT] 'Local descent group' was the landowning unit . . . Its members were responsible for **looking after** the stretch of country that they held as a hallowed trust . . 'Looking after' meant caring for and attending to, especially by performing the appropriate rites, prescribed from the past, related (for instance) to the mythical characters who were spiritually part of that country. **1982** *Bunji* (Darwin) Nov. p. 6 [Darwin, northern NT] Do not help to make a list of people called 'traditional owners' . . . The correct words to use are 'the people who **look after** that place'. **1985** S. Cane & O. Stanley *Land Use and Resources in Desert Homelands* p. 100 [Western Desert] . . there is striking evidence of the extent of the traditional custom of '**looking after**' the country by burning it and thus increasing the productivity of the desert landscape . . **1987** *Tjakulpa Kuwarritja* (Papunya) June n.p. [Western Desert] He said people here had to **look after** it . . that this place should be a strong place because it was our grandmothers and grandfathers' place. **1988** P. Taylor *After 200 Years* p. 255 [Cape York, north Qld] It's my responsibility to **look after** the country and the story places. **1990** *Aboriginal History* (Canberra) p. 44 [Borroloola, eastern NT] His son . . has lived his whole life on Vandelin Island and . . has played an important role in '**looking after**' the islands in the eyes of the Yanyuwa people now resident in Borroloola. He has continued traditional burning practices and has safeguarded various sites of significance. **1994** *Encyclop. Abor. Aust.* p. 570 [north Qld] When Kuuku-ya'u people from Lockhart visited their country they said 'Poor old country, come wild now. No-one to **look after** him.'

manager *noun* [northern Aust.] A person who has complementary responsibilities to a piece of land with the OWNER.

1984 M. Gumbert *Neither Justice Nor Reason* p. 88 They have their noetic counterparts broadly throughout Australia and are frequently rendered in the Aboriginal English terms of 'owner' and '**manager**' respectively . . . Another . . problem has lain in a too ready acceptance of the Aboriginal English term 'owner' as being an equivalent of the English word 'owner'. The exclusiveness and supremacy implied in this English word have had an effect of misrepresenting and undervaluing the actual interests in land enjoyed by those who claimed '*manager*' etc. relationship. **1988** C. Dunne *People Under the Skin* p. 108 [central Aust.] In Alice Springs hearings the terms 'Kirda' (owners) and 'kurdongurlu' (**managers**) were used to distinguish two lines of descent of Warlpiri heritage.

mother *noun* A person's 'country', land, earth, called by a kin term to indicate the depth of the relationship between a person and a place.

Other Englishes have terms such as *mother country*, which express something of this emotion. The Aboriginal use is more complex because of the intense and involved spiritual relationship to land.

1989 B. Neidjie *Story about feeling* p. 153 [Arnhem Land] Listen carefully this, you can hear me. I'm telling you because earth just like **mother** and father and brother of you. **1993** E. Young *Land & Society* p. 12 Aborigines have expressed in this saying, 'The land is my **mother**, and I am its protector'. **1993** S. Robinson *Aboriginal Embassy* M.A. Thesis p. 124 The people in riverbed . . . They said the land is our **mother**. **1995** *Koori Mail* Lismore 4 October p. 6/ 3 I have always believed that . . the earth is our **Mother**, our women were created as a continuum of the life of our Mother.

nor'-west *adjective* [WA] Of or from the north-west of Western Australia.

This has also been in non Aboriginal use from the late nineteenth century to refer to non-Aboriginal people.

1981 J. Davis *The Dreamers* p. 93 [south-west WA] An' he used to allus carry a long gidtji, **nor'-west** one. **1989** A. Haebich *For their own Good* p. 241 [south-west WA] (He) recalled seeing one organised by some '**Nor-West** blokes' at Narrogin reserve.

nor'wester *noun* [WA] An Aboriginal person from north-west Western Australia.

Nor'wester has been in non-Aboriginal use to refer to non-Aboriginal people of that area since the late nineteenth century.

1947 D. Bates *Passing of Aborigines* p. 90 [south-west WA] Twenty Bibbulmun and twenty **nor'-westers** had to be collected and . . I camped with them. **1978** H. Dagmar *Aborigines and Poverty* p. 95 [WA] The only wide rift in the Aboriginal community seems to exist between what the Aborigines themselves call the '**Norwesters**' and the 'Souwesters' . . . The Norwesters . . include the people who were born and have grown up in that part of Western Australia which lies north of Geraldton. **1990** R. Bowden & B. Bunbury *Being Aboriginal* p. 109 [WA] The first thing they asked you was where you come from . . and the sou-westers would stick on one side with the **nor-westers** on the other.

own *verb* [Aust. particularly in traditional areas] To have a spiritual and material responsibility for (a place); to acknowledge an identity with one's 'country' and accept one's obligations to it. See BELONG.

The Aboriginal meaning has more of a sense of a kinship relationship, with notions of obligation and care, than does the non-Aboriginal sense, in which *to own land* has a predominant association with exclusive legal possession, and the right of disposal. There is no expectation of such a right in the Aboriginal use.

1851 H. Melville *Present State Aust.* p. 361 [south-east Aust.] I tell you dat, him **own** Wallaby ground—he make 't catamaran, come back so soon as yourself. **1977** R.M. Berndt & C.H. Berndt *World of First Australians* p. 41 [Western Desert] In the Western Desert . . this entitles its members to participate in the system of ritual and myth connected with such beings, and shared by a number of local descent groups which '**own**' certain sites along their tracks.

1984 E. Roughsey *An Aboriginal Mother Tells* p. 136 [Mornington Is., northern Qld] 'That's all my people .. also belong to my brothers who **own** Birri country. 1987 E. Kolig *Noonkanbah Story* p. 81 [Kimberley] Believing is **owning** the land and owning the land, traditionally, means believing. 1990 S. Janson & S. Macintyre *Through White Eyes* p. 137 Being conceived at a place, born at a place, having one's mother, father, grandmother or grandfather buried at a place, being a long term resident of a place, having the same mythological ancestor as that which gave meaning to a place—these have all been found to count as important '**owning**' connections between individuals and places. 1991 *Amanbidji Land Claim* 21 Aug. [north-west NT] Come back to my country .. see old people . . . And we **own** here. 1993 S. Robinson *Aboriginal Embassy* M.A. Thesis p. 18 [south-east Qld] As Dennis Walker put it, 'blackfellas knew that they **owned** the land .. and nothing had been done to redress that'.

own country *noun* The place where a person belongs.

This term is also found in non-Aboriginal Englishes as in 'this is my own country', but here carries the extended or different senses present in the Aboriginal use of the verb 'to own'.

1949 *Oceania* (Melbourne) Dec. p. 106 [western NSW] Amongst the older mixed-bloods one's '**own country**' is the district where one was born. 1975 *Overland* (Mt Eliza) Vol. LXI p. 31 [north-west WA] .. they .. talk to each other in that Ningaloo country. That's their run .. their **own country**. 1977 R.M. Berndt & C.H. Berndt *World of First Australians* p. 97 [NT] However, once entrenched in the system as an employee of one particular station .. it was almost impossible for an Aboriginal to seek employment elsewhere. Apart from the question of '**own country**' .. he or she could (unofficially) be brought back by police. 1978 J. & P. Read *View of the Past* p. 302 [NT] 'Because you were doing, you were doing right way to your **own country**'.

owner *noun* A person who has spiritual and material responsibility for a place.

1983 J.G. Steele *Aboriginal Pathways* p. 38 [northern NSW] Daniel Sambo was the **owner** of the djurebil, and used to visit it until the 1960's. 1984 M. Gumbert *Neither Justice Nor Reason* p. 83 [NT] It should be noted that Aborigines themselves when referring to the patrilineal relationship to land .. frequently did use the Aboriginal English word '**owner**'. 1991 D.B. Rose *Hidden Histories* p.xix [north-west NT] They are **owners** (according to traditional law) of Ngarinman, Mudbura, Bilinara, Ngaliwurru, Karangpurru, Wardaman, Gurindji and Malngin language-defined countries.

As **traditional owner** the term has become an important legal concept in the workings of the Northern Territory Land Rights Act and in the Native Title Tribunal following upon the Native Title legislation.

1983 *Conference of Abor. Communities* Dept of the Chief Minister p. 33 [NT] Does the N.T. Government support **traditional owners** in trying to control access to country e.g.— restrictions on road use. 1991 D.B. Rose *Hidden Histories* p. 251 Now he was a claimant— asking the Aboriginal Land Commissioner to define him as a **traditional owner** within the meaning of the Act, so that he could control a mile-wide strip of land.

paperbark *adjective* [northern Aust.] Of the country and the people of the Daly River country south-west of Darwin, by reason of the predominance of paperbark trees in the area.

The word was also used by non-Aboriginal people of the area, as indicated in the 1991 citation.

1980 T. Donaldson *Ngiyambaa* p. 81 [Daly River, north-west NT] I'm one of the **paperbark** people. **1987** R.M. & C.H. Berndt *End of an Era* p. 162 [NT] He was born in the '**Paperbark**' country near the Daly River, south west of Darwin . . **1991** J. McGinness *Son of Alyandu.* p.xiv [Darwin, northern NT] The Kungarakan Tribal group of the lower Finniss River, referred to by early settlers of Darwin as **Paperbark** People.

right through *adverb* (Of a ritual, a dreaming, or a song) completely mapping the span of its geographical relevance.

Aboriginal narratives often have a logic that is based on place rather than the internal logic of the narrative, because they belong to particular places and the connections between the places provide the connections in the story; the story is there to explain the landscape so that the shape of the landscape is the shape of the story.

1985 E. Malpangka *Aboriginal Women* p. 10 [NT?] But this land is our grandfathers' and grandmothers', their law, their dreaming goes **right through**, strong, its our land. **1986** B. Shaw *Countrymen* p. 147 [Kimberley] He'd sing that one **right through** down and get another one and run it this way now to Halls Creek. **1990** P. Austin et al. *Lang. & Hist.* p. 254 Its a long corroboree. Charlotte Waters that's the middle bit. They're Dreaming people blackfellers and women. I can sing it **right through** to Napperby from Riley Creek down from Napperby not far.

riverbank *noun* [south-east Aust.] An important camping site for many Aboriginal people—along the riverbanks of south-eastern Australia. Also **river**.

The riverbanks, which have always been important camping places, became especially important for Aboriginal people after European land use methods put pressure on available space in the rest of the landscape. Riverbanks provide shady campsites close to a relatively undisturbed food source—the river. They also provide a living place away from missions and towns with their European controls.

1958 J. Becket *A Study of a Mixed Blood Aboriginal Minority* p. 20 [western NSW] 'Home' is either a cluster of weatherboard cottages, built for them by the government and generally known as the 'Mission', or a series of crude wood and iron shacks strung out along the **riverbank** and called the 'Camp'. **1961** *Aborigines in NSW* p. 17 [north-west NSW] At Walgett a well-spoken Aboriginal woman mentioned that she was looking for casual work and staying with friends on the **riverbank** reserve . . . 'I won't live on a station where you get ordered around'. **1981** *Social Alternatives* (St Lucia) Vol. II no. 2 p. 70 [south-east Qld] From the camping area on the **river**, from tents in Orana Park. **1988** *Koori News* Sept. 25 [northern NSW] Strolling down the **river bank** where you dive for binging . . . Bring home some binging And some jubles to eat. Cook in coals with roo meat. **1988** *R. Comm. Aboriginal Deaths in Custody: H.B. Day* p. 535 [northern Vic.] In Echuca the **river bank** no longer provides the refuge it once did for Aboriginals. **1989** *R. Comm. Aboriginal Deaths in Custody: J. Moore* p. 262 [northern Vic.] Does anyone do that—move back on to the **river bank**? **1991** A. Jackomos & D. Fowell *Living Aboriginal Hist. of Vict.* p. 182 [Vic.] . . I am proud of the fact that the address on my birth certificate is 'the **river bank**'.

river people *noun* A people whose lives are centred on a river.

1991 D.B. Rose *Hidden Histories* p. 114 [Victoria River, north-west NT] This was Nyiwanawu people longa river. **River people**, they call (them).

rubbish *noun* See DIRTY.

run *noun* The area where people belong by reason of spiritual and physical association. See Chapter 6.

saltwater *noun* The sea.

There is a similar use in Tok Pisin, from Papua New Guinea, *solwara*, 'the sea'.

1984 C. Allridge *Aboriginal Eng.* p. 107 [Qld] **Saltwater** was the Pidgin word for 'ocean'. **1984** E. Roughsey *An Aboriginal Mother Tells* p. 54 [Mornington Island, north Qld] We call nail food banner. It's a hairy food that grows in the swamp by the creek that the **salt water** flows into. These nail roots are gathered when the salt and fresh water dries up. **1986** B. Shaw *Countrymen* p. 51 [Kimberley, WA] Ground sugar bag is made by little ants. It can be covered by the tide, the **saltwater** everyway right round. And when the tide goes back and the men go down there, oh, you see that sugar bag everywhere. **1989** B. Neidjie *Story about feeling* p. 14 [Arnhem Land] That white chest eagle, that's the one we say e can go billabong, e can go **saltwater**. **1992** D.B. Rose *Dingo Makes Us Human* p. 199 [Victoria River, NT] This world been **salt water** before every way, every land. This world been covered up.

saltwater black, a person who lives by the sea and whose life is dependent on it.

In the 1875 citation, the **saltwater** is an inland salt lake rather than the sea, in this case salt lakes near Strzelecki Creek in northern South Australia.

1875 *Jrnl. Royal Anthrop. Inst. Great Brit. & Ireland* IV. p. 56 These .. I have heard spoken of as the .. **salt water blacks**. **1900** R. Bruce *Benbonuna* p. 347 He also knew perfectly well that the old lubra would attribute their disappearance to the visit of a '**salt-water black**'. **1911** A. Searcy *By Flood & Field* p. 285 [northern Aust.] A strange Myall native reported .. that a number of **saltwater blacks** had a big mob of cattle yarded. **1925** *Bulletin* (Sydney) 15 Oct. p. 24/3 When the banquet is over the jazz begins, the 'pudgeridoo' of the mountain blacks, the rattle of sticks by **salt water** ones .. *c.*1975 J.W. Zillman *Recoll. Early Days* p. 6 [south-east Qld] Two tribes were camped there, the **Salt Water blacks** and our Mountain blacks. [ref. 1860s]

saltwater boy, a boy who is brought up near the sea.

1987 T. Egan *Aboriginals Song Bk.* p. 49 [NT] His mother was an Anmatjira woman from Central Australia. Bob Randall had been reared as a '**salt water boy**' at Croker Island Mission.

saltwater country, the country of a people whose lives are focused on the sea.

1976 *Identity* (Sydney) Jan. p. 18 [Arnhem Land] At last (he) came to the **salt water country** which is called Milingimbi.

saltwater native, a person who lives by the sea and whose life is dependent on it.

1928 B. Spencer *Wanderings in Wild Aust.* p. 565 [Borroloola, north-east NT] Of the two main camps near Borroloola, one was situated close to the river where the '**salt-water' natives** as they are called—that is, the Anula and Mara.

saltwater people, a people who live by the sea and whose lives are dependent on it.

1989 R.M. Baker *Land is life* p. 183 [Borroloola, north-east NT] As elsewhere in Australia, there is a strong cultural divide in the area between '**salt water' people** and 'fresh water' people. **1993** J. Janson *Gunjies* p. 62 [northern NT] I want you to take you up North to my **saltwater people**. **1993** D. Hodge *Did you meet any Malagas?* p. 61 [northern NT] Naturally all our culture is centred around salt water living. So I call myself a salt water person. And you'll find similarities with all **salt water peoples** along the Top End. All the myths and the stories of the Dreaming are centred around salt water culture.

saltwater song, a song from a saltwater people.

1986 B. Shaw *Countrymen* p. 141 [Kimberley, WA] There was a **salt water song** we had one night.

sandbeach *noun* [northern Aust.] The beach.

1981 G. McKenzie *Aurukun Diary* p. 25 [north Qld] The folks at Aurukun always referred to the beach as the **sandbeach**; I suppose because many of the river beaches were more or less mud. **1981** *Aboriginal History* (Canberra) V. i. 13, [north Qld] I was only a good size boy no whiskers yet. My father and I lived . . on top, in the hills . . not **sand beach**.

sandbeach man, **sandbeach people** a person or a people living near a beach; a coastal person, coastal people.

1946 *Jrnl. Royal Anthrop. Institute* Vol LXXVI pt. 2 p. 157 [north Qld] . . later . . I lived among the *Malnkanidji*—the **sandbeachmen** of Eastern Cape York. **1981** G. McKenzie *Aurukun Diary* p. 25 [northern Qld] She had been married first to a **sandbeach man**, a member of one of the clans who lived on the coast. **1994** *Encyclop. Abor. Aust.* p. 570 They were the most northern group of the **sandbeach people** who now live at Lockhart.

sandstone *adjective* [northern Aust.] (Of a people or a country) belonging to the Victoria River district, which has an area of sandstone plateaux and gorges.

The 'sandstone' country was an important area both for local resistance fighters and as a safe haven in the early days of the occupation, because it was difficult for horses to travel through the rugged country.

1987 R.M. & C.H. Berndt *End of an Era* p. 96 [northern NT] In the opinion of the manager and his wife, the **sandstone** family on the station was 'not worth the trouble of having about the place' [i.e. people from the sandstone country] **1987** R.M. & C.H. Berndt *End of an Era* p. 96 [northern NT] The **'Sandstone'** people . . we should investigate the alleged presence of people in the sandstone country. **1991** D.B. Rose *Hidden Histories* p. 114 [Victoria River, north-west NT] This one here **sandstone** people, that's the proper people, Ngarinman.

shade *noun* [Chiefly northern Aust.] A temporary structure of branches to give shade.

There is a non-Aboriginal Australian English word *shade*, but its primary sense is a shelter for plants rather than people.

1929 K.S. Prichard *Coonardoo* p. 29 [north-west WA] She watched Coonardoo swinging down to the uloo one evening when she had left her gina gina in the **shade** miah. **1971** K. Willey *Boss Drover* p. 17 [northern NT] They made a **shade** for him by hanging some bushes in the fork of a tree. **1986** B. Shaw *Countrymen* p. 94 [Kimberley, WA] You can see it on your own eyes in that **shade** there. **1986** S. Wild *Rom* p. 25 [Arnhem Land] When we come to Canberra we will make a **shade** on Rhys' and Betty's land.

sickness country *noun* An area or place that can make people ill or is a source of illness. Also **sickness site**.

1989 *Age* (Melbourne) 27 Sept p. 3/1 [Arnhem Land] An earlier submission from the Jawoyn says there has never been any agreement with the Government on mining in Kakadu, and the Jawoyn want no mining in the Bula '**sickness country**' that covers most of the conservation zone. **1991** *West Austral.* (Perth) 29 May p. 9/5 [Arnhem Land] The Jawoyn has long argued that mining Coronation Hill, which they call the '**sickness country**', would disturb the Bula, an Aboriginal spirit they believe lives underground. When the Bula is disturbed, he spreads sickness and destruction throughout the land. **1991** *Australian*

Weekend Magazine (Sydney) p. 21/22 Dec. 2/4 [north Qld] They are also concerned that sacred sites are being violated out of ignorance or insensitivity. For example, an incident in which a Laura boy fell ill and nearly died this year was blamed by the local Aborigines on tourists intruding on a 'sickness site'. **1991** D.B. Rose *Hidden Histories* p. 75 [Victoria River, north-west NT] He identified the place of origin as a **sickness site**—Dreaming site of origin for illness. **1995** D. Hodge *Did you meet any Malagas?* p. 88 [northern NT] But that country was declared a sacred site. . . that's land that's always been recognised as **sickness country.**

sit down *noun* [northern Aust.] A place where people remain or stay. Also **sit down place.**

1965 L. Haylen *Big Red* p. 68 Their shouts were echoed by the women at the 'sit down' waiting for their men's return. **1981** *Cent. Aust. Land Rights News* (Alice Springs) Dec. p. 13 [NT] They say they're very worried that cattle stations won't be used as cattle stations and become **sit down** places.

sit down *verb* [Formerly widespread now chiefly northern Aust.] To stay or remain at a place, not necessarily permanently, but for a significant length of time.

There is a chiefly nineteenth-century non-Aboriginal Australian English use of *sit down* which was generally applied to those 'squatting' on pastoral land.

1844 *Adelaide Observer* 27 Apr. (page and col. unknown) [SA] Let them **sit down** on the Murray, not here. This is not his country. What he do here? **1863** J. Bonwick *Wild White Man* p. 33 [Vic.] No do that. When blackfellow **sit down** with whitefellow, him say, 'Be off, be off' blackfellow no do the like o' that. **1880** (Mrs) J. Smith *Booandik Tribe* p. 53 [south-east SA] There plenty bullocky **sit down** . . here only piccaninny tuck-out. **1927** M. Terry *Through Land of Promise* p. 174 [NT] Cardiah (white man) **sit down** longa house? **1944** M.J. O'Reilly *Bowyangs & Boomerangs* p. 88 I told one of the old men, who could jabber fairly good English, about the incident. That is what he told me: 'that fellow bean tree is one place where big fellow 'Kaditcha' all the time **sit down**; no white fellow, no blackfellow allowed camp alonga that place'. **1962** V.C. Hall *Dreamtime Justice* p. 160 There was no pension. Rationed and clothed and fed he 'sat down' in the camp by the Station he had served so well and at such cost. **1984** *Aust. Ab. Stud.* no. 2 p. 32 [NT] And Captain Cook come up, see that old fellow **sit down** makeimbad spear there, hunting fish. **1988** J. Collman *Fringe-dwellers and Welfare* p. 128 [central Aust.] Although people insist that others should 'sit down' the good way' and drink quietly, fights are not uncommon.

Mackenzie sit down, poisoned flour.

This historical term comes from the flour laced with arsenic given to some Aboriginal people by a nineteenth-century Queensland squatter by the name of Mackenzie. Poisoned flour or damper was a weapon used by the British side in the frontier wars.

1876 E. Thorne *Queen of Colonies* p. 341 [Qld?] The squatter . . gave them a 200 lb. bag of flour, in which he had mixed a quantity of arsenic or strychnine . . . For many years, on offering a present of flour to any blackfellow, one was met with the enquiry, '**Mackenzie sit down**?'—the name by which the poison became universally known among them for many miles.

southwest *adjective* [Chiefly WA] (Of an Aboriginal person or people) from south-west Western Australia.

1986 A. Weller *Going Home* p. 140 [south-west WA] The two **south-west** boys lit up while Cooley rolled a smoke. **1989** A. Haebich *For their own Good* p. 219 [south-west WA] . .

maban men were accorded considerable respect and many **southwest** people . . followed the policy of 'be nice to them and they'd be nice to you'.

souwester *noun* [Chiefly WA] An Aboriginal person from south-west Western Australia. Also **southwester**.

> **1978** H. Dagmar *Aborigines and Poverty* p. 95 [WA] The only wide rift in the Aboriginal community seems to exist between what the Aborigines themselves call the 'Norwesters' and the '**Souwesters**'. **1978** H. Dagmar *Aborigines and Poverty* p. 96 [south-west WA] I'm a **souwester** you see, my hometown is Albany. **1987** C. Glass & A. Weller *Us Fellas* p. 106 [south-west WA] This photo was taken fifty years ago down the South West at a town called Busselton . . they're all people from down the south—they're all **South Westers**.

sundown *noun* [Chiefly northern Aust.] The west. Also **sundown way**.

> **1976** J. Mirritji *My People's Life* p. 56 [Arnhem Land] When they saw us coming from the eastern sunrise and going towards the western **sundown**, they gathered in a group . . ready to attack us. **1988** P. Marshall *Raparapa* p. 97 [Kimberley, WA] Fitzroy River (the west, **sundown** way). [caption to map]

Hence **sundowner**, a person from the west.

> **1983** *Dark Side of the News* p. 161 [northern Qld] Palm Islanders are full-blood, halfcaste, Thursday Island push, Kanaaka, a **sundowner**, southern, central or far northern black-fella.

sunrise *noun* [Chiefly northern Aust.] The east. Also **sunrise way**.

> **1976** J. Mirritji *My People's Life* p. 56 [Arnhem Land] When they saw us coming from the eastern **sunrise** and going towards the western sundown, they gathered in a group . . ready to attack us. **1986** B. Shaw *Countrymen* p. 126 [Kimberley, WA] In this country when the old people died out the white men, surveyors, came back from the top end (towards **sunrise**). **1988** P. Marshall *Raparapa* p. 164 [Kimberley, WA] Fitzroy River (the east, **sunrise** way)[caption to map]

walk *verb* To travel; travel around an area. Also **walk about, walk (a)round**.

When applied to people walking in their own 'country', as in the 1988 citation, it often includes the sense of living the traditional life, so that *to walk about one's country* is close to the meaning of *living in one's country*. In a nomadic civilisation, 'walking about' and 'living' are experientially almost the same.

> **1828** *Sydney Gaz.* 2 Jan. When the executioner had adjusted the rope, and was about to pull the cap over his eyes . . he said, in a tone of deep feeling, which it was impossible to hear without strong emotion, 'Bail more **walk about**', meaning that his wanderings were all over. **1863** J. Bonwick *Wild White Man* p. 86 Ah! all gone now, all gone; only me left to **walk about**. **1916** S.A. White *In Far Northwest* p. 21 It is a strange thing with camels, once they want (as the natives say) to ' **walk about**' there may be an abundance of their choicest food, yet they will ramble all night long. **1980** N. Mitchell & J.C. Anderson *Kubara* p. 14 [north Qld] *Myall*, wil' fella, if he wanna **walkabout** a lot. **1984** S. Cane *Desert Camps* p. 118 [Western Desert] All the way people been **walking** too much, travelling to home now. **1988** J. Harkins *English as 'Two-way' Language* p. 25 [central Aust.] Just living wild in the bush, then, **walking around** with my families . . . **1991** *Amanbidji Land Claim* 21 Aug. [north-west NT] Well, I been with a mob, included Billy mob **walking round** here, Pumuntu, all that.

walkabout *noun* The area belonging to a person or a people. See also the extended sense of WALKABOUT in Chapter 5.

Now chiefly historical.

1899 W.E. Roth *Rep. to Commissioner Police* 3 [north Qld] Their **walk-about** extends on the one hand up the *Eastern* coast of the Peninsula as far as perhaps as the Stewart River. 1935 M. Gilmore *More Recoll.* p. 34 [south-west NSW] 'The Dead Water' was a . . waterhole at which no black sat, because all the group in whose **walk-about** it had been were killed out. 1981 *Land Claims in NSW* NSW Aboriginal Land Council n.p. [south coast NSW] When I was a boy, I used to walk with my people from Wallaga Lake over Mumbulla Mountain to Bega. From Gallaga to Mumbulla is all part of the one **walkabout**.

come or **go walkabout**, to travel generally through one's country.

1991 *Amanbidji Land Claim* 21 Aug. [north-west NT] *Ginger Packsaddle*: And used to come walkabout here . . . With my father and my grandpa.

CHAPTER 5
Living with whitefellas

The collection of words in this chapter conveys some of the experience of occupation. The words belong to that continuing event: words for different kinds of whitefellows, words for some of the material goods they brought with them, and words for the physical and legislative control that the occupiers have had over Aboriginal people.

After 1788, Australia became culturally divided in a way it had not been before. From this time, Aboriginal people were no longer only Wiradjuri or Wemba Wemba but collectively **blackfellows**, who had to deal with this new group of people, the **whitefellows**. Their perceptions of themselves had changed. The human occupants of Australia were now divided in terms of **colour**. Some words for 'white person' such as **baygal** carry in their etymology the early perceptions of non-Aboriginal people as ghosts or corpses. Others such as **boss**, a term of address for a white man, whether or not he was an employer, clearly indicate the power relation between the two societies. As in any occupied country, there were those who were seen by some of their fellows as betraying their own people by co-operating with the new rulers—these are the **Uncle Toms**, the **coconuts**, the **burnt potatoes**. There are also words for those who have been damaged by the new social structures and by the new European goods—such as the **goomies**, the alcoholics. The British brought of course not only new ways of perceiving and hence organising the world; they also brought new material goods such as **baccy** and **tea leaf**, and new animals such as **bullocky** and **piggy piggy**.

Part of the colonising process has been the use by the governing society of special discriminatory legislation to control Aboriginal people. Words such as **dog tag** and **ticket**, and expressions such as **taken away** (which refers to the removal of Aboriginal children for the purposes of cultural re-education), belong to Aboriginal people's experiences of this situation. The legislation is enforced by the **government** or the **welfare**. Though used by other Australians in a similar sense these terms are included here because of the extent of their use and their significance to Aboriginal Australia. This chapter also contains several words for the police, such as **monaych** and **gunjie**. The police as agents of control of the colonising society have had and continue to have an enormous effect on Aboriginal communities.

bacca *noun* Tobacco. Also **baccy**.

Tobacco was a significant factor in creating a relationship between Aboriginal and non-Aboriginal groups. People would travel to white settlements in order to obtain tobacco, and remain working for non-Aboriginal people in order to maintain the supply. Both secular and religious institutions used tobacco as payment for labour. Later, it became part of the non-monetary wages system on northern cattle stations. See also NICKY NICKY. **Bacca** and **baccy** for 'tobacco' are found in nineteenth-century English colloquial speech. The recorded use of this word in Aboriginal English is mostly historical rather than current.

1853 H.B. Jones *Adventures in Aust.* p. 146-7 He laid down his arms, and walked a few paces with us, asked of course for tobacco, of which we had not any to give him, as we informed him in his jargon. 'Bale (no) **baccy**; white fellow give him black fellow.' 1887 *Overlander: Aust. Sketches* p. 23 A blackfellow had come to the hut door with a boomerang and demanded **bacca**, flour, and chugga. 1909 H.K. Bloxham *On the Fringe* p. 55 S'posem you help this pfeller, this gib it plenty **bacca** and sugar. 1925 A.G. Bolam *Trans-Austral. Wonderland* edn. 4 p. 70 [Ooldea, northern SA] When you observe these blacks at Ooldea begging '**bacca**' or a coin. 1935 F. Birtles *Battle Fronts Outback* p. 29 [northern Aust.] An old gin had been left in charge of the homestead. I squared her with some **baccy**. 1988 C. Mattingley & K. Hampton (eds) *Survival in Our Own Land* p. 130 [SA] They'd just throw some meat down on the wood block for rations, with some flour and **bacca**.

balanda *noun* [Arnhem Land] A white person, white people. Also **ballanda, ballander**.

From Macassarese *balanda*, from the Malay *belanda*, a corruption of Hollander (i.e. Dutch). From about the eighteenth century to the beginning of the twentieth fishing boats from the Indonesian Archipelago used the north-west monsoon to travel to the coasts of northern Australia to fish for trepang. The trepang, or sea slug, was dried and smoked then taken back to South-East Asian ports for sale as food. The Aboriginal people of the area formed social and working associations with the Macassarese who crewed the boats, and adopted some aspects of their culture such as the Macassan pipe and some words from their language. A number of Aboriginal people visited the home islands of the fishermen.

1845 L. Leichhardt *Jrnl. Overland Exped.* 2 Dec. (1847) p. 503 [northern Aust.] They knew the white people of Victoria, and called them **Balanda**, which is nothing more than 'Hollanders'; a name used by the Malays, from whom they received it. 1915 E.R. Masson *Untamed Territory* p. 112 [NT] The blacks rushed up to the house calling '**Ballanda**, Ballanda'—white man—and the Boss and Missus ran out. 1943 W.E. Harney *Taboo* p. 203 [northern Aust.] On the natives' side are . . fear of the **Ballander**-whiteman and the thought of losing their country. 1978 J. Mirritji *My People's Life* p. 48 [Arnhem Land] Then I understood that this '**balanda**' means people with skins like the white clay. 1987 *Land Rights News* Mar. Vol. II no. 2 5/1 [Arnhem Land] Before the boats and the **balanda** (Europeans) came there was a big mob of fish. We are short now. We look for fish but there are not many. 1987 G. Francis *God's Best Country* p. 78 [northern Aust.] That's the only road back for them . . to be rid of all your patronising, domineering **balanda** ways. 1989 B. Neidjie *Story About Feeling* p. 82 [Arnhem Land] **Balanda**! If Aborigine e says something . . . e want to stop im Balanda . . . e might listen. 1993 *Canberra Times* 28 Jan. p. 5/4 There are a lot of fans both **balanda** *white* and yolngu (east Arnhem Land Aborigines).

barabaldain *noun* [western NSW] A policeman.

From the Wiradjuri language of south-western NSW *barramaldaayn* 'a policeman', from *barramal* 'to take, hold'.

1949 *Oceania* Dec. p. 83 **Barabaldain** and its abbreviation *Bara* are some common words for 'policeman' which have remained in use over a large area for many years.

barefoot *adjective* [Chiefly southern Aust.] Without footwear. Also **barefooted**.

This term refers to a time when people lived in poverty or with a lack of European materialism, such that they went *barefoot*. It is sometimes used pejoratively to refer to those lacking European possessions or knowledge of European ways. See also BUSH and MYALL. It was only when a society that wore shoes became the dominant one that being **barefoot** became culturally significant. The identification of 'Aboriginality' with 'lack of material possessions' is a constant theme in non-Aboriginal descriptions and understandings of Aboriginal culture. European society was (and is) one which registered social value and cultural sophistication by possessions, including clothing. See also NO CLOTHES.

1963 D.E. Barwick *Little More than Kin* p. 324 [Vic.] We used to laugh at the old ones talking the lingo, back in our **barefoot** days. **1981** J. Davis *The Dreamers* p. 116 [south-west WA] I dunno why you can't get some decent friends instead of those **barefooted** blackfellas you muck around with. **1993** J. Janson *Gunjies* p. 13 [western NSW] Yeah, an' after you met me, I was **barefoot** and bingel [pregnant].

before *adverb* [northern Aust.] Before the present time i.e. in the past, in the old days, particularly before the time when the country was finally controlled by Europeans. See also EARLY.

1978 J. & P. Read *View of the Past* p. 39 [Nutwood Downs, northern NT] They bin wanta spearem Queensland boy, **before**, wild time. **1989** B. Neidjie *Story About Feeling* p. 68 [Arnhem Land] They never making camp how we camping here. Aborigine **before** . . they use paperbark, stringybark. **1988** H. Ross *Community Social Impact Assessment* p. 23 [east Kimberley, WA] Another bloke spear em white man—that used to be **before**, all over his country in the hills. **1991** D.B. Rose *Hidden Histories* p. 108 [Victoria River, north-west NT] We dont want that law. That's from **before**, old man.

blackfellow *noun* **1** An Aboriginal person. Also **blackfella**, **blackfeller**.

With the British invasion, Aboriginal people were seen and subsequently came to see *themselves* as not only, say, 'Warlpiri' or 'Yindjibarndi' but as **blackfellows**, as an identity separate from non-Aboriginal people. The same change of perception was forced upon other colonised peoples, such as Native Americans. (A similar but of course less violent process is happening in Europe, where the French, British, Germans etc., are beginning to see themselves as *Europeans*, as distinct from *non*-Europeans.) *Black* has been in wider English use to refer to people with a darker skin colour than Europeans since the ninth century. **Blackfellow** was used by both Aboriginal and non-Aboriginal people from the very early days of occupation. It is now generally not used in 'public' Australian English, though it is still used widely by the whole community in northern and central Australia, and by Aboriginal people everywhere amongst themselves. Aboriginal people generally find it offensive to be referred to as a **blackfellow** by a non-Aboriginal person.

1798 D. Collins *Acct. Eng. Colony N.S.W.* I. p. 590 [Sydney, NSW] Car-ru-ey strenuously urged him . . to shoot the Botany Bay **black fellows**. **1825** L.E. Threlkeld *Aboriginal Mission, N.S.W.* p. 13 [central coast, NSW] Massa, you know **black fellow** no tell lies! **1836** J.F. O'Connell *Residence Eleven Yrs. New Holland* p. 87 They appear to have recognised their title '**black fellows**', and in return dub the English 'white fellows', seemingly perfectly content with the distinction, and considering white the worse hue, decidedly. **1859** J.D. Mereweather *Diary Working Clergyman* p. 180 These stupid blacks mistook this poor American black for one of themselves . . . A black expressed . . great indignation at their stupidity, saying, that they ought to have known the difference between '**blackfellow**' and 'white man's blackfellow'. **1952** *Bulletin* (Sydney) 16 Apr. p. 16/2 An aborigine sees nothing offensive in the term '**blackfellow**', but 'nigger' is an insult. **1969** D. Cusack *Half-Burnt Tree* p. 13 Dad got mad when he said '**blackfeller**'. 'Don't use that word, Kem,' he said. 'We've got a name like every other race'. **1980** *Puggana News* (Launceston) May p. 2 [Tas.] The old **blackfellers** gathered their crews, prepared the sheds, arranged transport, all within two weeks. **1985** *Aboriginal History* Vol 9 No. 1 p. 146 [south-west NSW] 'Are you a little **blackfeller**, are you a little blackfeller?' croons a young mother cuddling her baby. When I first heard this, I had just been approached for help in translating a Wiradjuri sentence by someone who remembered a relative cuddling babies with it half a century earlier: 'Burraaydjil-gaa-ndu wirraay', 'Are you a little Wiradjiri kid?' **1988** H.B. Day *Royal Commission into Aboriginal Deaths in Custody* (Transcript) p. 59 [Vic.] You see three **black fellows** walking around and the cops pick them up like that and they're in gaol, especially walking around with a didgeridoo. **1991** A. Jackomos & D. Fowell *Living Aboriginal Hist. of Vic.* p. 64 [Vic.] A lot of them . . might be frightened of **blackfellas**.

The term **blackfellow** has sometimes been used to distinguish between Aboriginal people of the full descent and those of Aboriginal and European descent. See YELLOW FELLOW.

1979 D. Lockwood *My Old Mates and I* p. 35 [northern Aust.] 'Not on your life,' he said. 'I'd hold my own with any blackfeller.' I looked at his black skin again and realised that by '**blackfeller**' he was simply distinguishing between full-blood and mixed-blood.

blackfellow's chair, a bed. This is an indication of the level of material poverty, especially in terms of housing, at which most of Aboriginal Australia lived and still lives. When used by Aboriginal people, the term has some of the ironic humour that is very present in Aboriginal culture but which is not always apparent in the printed texts.

1948 *Oceania* Mar. p. 194 [Moree, western NSW] '**Blackfellow's chair**'—that's what they call a bed. And that's what it is. They haven't got any chairs. **1979** M. Dillon *A Case Study: Kadia Power* p. 7 [western NSW] Some of the huts contain only the '**blackfellows chair**'— the familiar iron bedstead.

2 (In combinations and as an adjective) Aboriginal.

1829 D. Burn *Bushrangers* p. 30 Well, matta, how you like **black fellow** corobbora? **1930** F. Hives & G. Lumley *Journal of a Jackeroo* p. 203 [Qld] Charlie stopped suddenly . . he beckoned the others to come forward, then said in a hushed whisper, 'Some t'ing live for front, I smell im, t'ink he **blackfeller** camp'. **1978** J. & P. Read *View of the Past* p. 164 [Victoria River, north-west NT] 'Whiteman too far you going, trying to pinchem **blackfeller** woman.' That bin all early days do that. **1981** G. Ngabidj & B. Shaw *My Country of Pelican Dreaming* p. 8 [Kimberley, WA] I had to distinguish between the 'white man way' . . and '**blackfeller** Law'. **1991** D.B. Rose *Hidden Histories* p. 80 [north-west NT] They were standing on the Law. They watched that Law, for **blackfellow** Law.

blackfellow country, Aboriginal Australia, particularly the COUNTRY of the speaker.

1863 J. Bonwick *Wild White Man* p. 86 In the evening, at their camp fire, they would sing a mournful plaint about the cruelty of the white man, who 'Take him everything **blackfellow country**.' **1889** *S.A.P.P. Quarterly Report on N.T.* Feb. p. 8 [SA] Now time whitefellow take him bullocky and clear out. This fellow country him **blackfellow country**. **1984** *Aust. Ab. Stud.* no. 2 p. 32 [NT] This no more **blackfellow country**.

blackfella talk, Aboriginal English.

1988 I. Keen *Being Black* p. 68 People of the town acknowledge the use of language as code when they refer to 'gin talk' or '**blackfella talk**'.

blackfeller doctor, a person with spiritual and healing powers. See CLEVER.

1990 P. Austin et al. *Lang. & Hist.* p. 252 [Oodnadatta, northern SA] All the dead fellers were long time ago when I was a young feller. They wanted to be doctors. Some **blackfeller doctors** pull out the bone. There was a doctor woman. She pulled them out like nothing.

blackfeller seats, the seats in the front half of a country town picture theatre where Aboriginal people were compelled to sit. This segregation continued in some parts of Australia until the early 1970s. There is a painting by the Koori artist Robert Campbell Junior entitled *Roped off at the Picture 2* (1987) commenting on this practice.

1990 P. Read *Charles Perkins* p. 104 [Walgett, western NSW] A few of the town's white boys sometimes even joined him in the 2 shilling '**blackfeller**' **seats** in the pictures.

blackgin *noun* An Aboriginal woman.

Aboriginal people sometimes use expressions that are generally considered derogatory when used by non-Aboriginal people but are in these cases merely descriptive or ironic. The term *black gin* is first recorded as being used of an Aboriginal woman in 1837. *Gin* (first spelt *din*) is a borrowing from the Dharuk language of the Sydney region, *diyin*, 'woman, wife', and is first recorded in 1790.

1984 P. Read *Down There With Me on Cowra Mission* p. 104 [south-west NSW] Well, the woman that's got him, she was a **blackgin**; she couldn't have no kids.

blacky *noun* An Aboriginal person.

This is originally an Australian English word for an Aboriginal person, first recorded in 1827. As with the use of BLACKGIN, Aboriginal people are here using a term which would be regarded as derogatory if used by a non-Aboriginal person. Like other minority groups, Aboriginal people sometimes take offensive terms and use them among themselves, often in a self-conscious and ironic way, just as *wog* has now been taken up by the Greek and Italian migrants to whom it was applied.

1990 J. Chi *Bran Nue Dae* p. 7 [north-west WA] Like us I bro, us **blackies** starving.

book *noun* [northern Aust.] European law or laws, characteristically written down, as opposed to Aboriginal law which is contained in oral tradition.

Here the **book** is seen as the icon of the literate culture, significant because it is from this written tradition that the laws used to control Aboriginal society are drawn.

1978 J. & P. Read *View of the Past* p. 221 [northern NT] Carryem up, oh, big **book**, welfare book, you know. **1984** *Aust. Ab. Stud.* no. 2 p. 32 [northern NT] Him bring lotta **book** (law) from Big England right here. **1991** D.B. Rose *Hidden Histories* p. 72 [Victoria River, north-west NT] They got that, **book** all over from Captain Cook. You might see blackfellows anywhere longa this country, you'll have to get them together . . and shoot [the] whole lot!

boss *noun* **1** A form of address from an Aboriginal person to a European man, not necessarily an employer.

This is generally now obsolete except among some older people. It reflects the historical power imbalance between white and black, where most non-Aboriginal people could not imagine a relationship between black and white that was not one of superiority and power on the part of the whites, and powerlessness and dependency on the part of the Aboriginal people. The relative powers of both societies meant that to survive most Aboriginal people had to conform outwardly at least to this expectation.

1924 A.G. Bolam *Trans-Aust. Wonderland* p. 105 [Ooldea, northern SA] **Boss** pfella mucka (no) work like that! **1949** *Oceania* Mar. p. 201 Whites collectively are often referred to as '**bosses**' in the U district, whether they employ Aboriginal labour or not. **1971** *Hope Vale Hotline* Nov. p. 3/1 When I was a kid I used to get a lot of booting from these **bosses** when I did not do anything right. **1983** M. Durack *Sons in Saddle* p. 24 [Kimberley, WA] The term '**Boss**' as used by Aborigines, though an admission of authority in a European-structured economy, did not carry the same undertones of flattering deference as that of 'Master' in an Asian setting. **1988** *R. Comm. Aboriginal Deaths in Custody: H.B. Day* p. 525 [Vic.] He always addressed a policeman as '**Boss**' and spoke courteously. **1994** R.Thomas *Roads Cross* p. 42 [Kimberley, WA] 'What about tobacco?' 'Yeah, we want tobacco, **boss**.'

2 A leader (Aboriginal or non-Aboriginal) in any context.

1979 *Tjaru* (Alice Springs) Aug. n.p. [central Aust.] Students are learning to be **bosses** of some things. They take charge of basketball games and learn to be umpires in other games too. **1987** *The Aim* (Burwood) Dec. p. 7 [northern Qld] She had made the Lord her **boss** about two years ago. She would read her Bible and pray every day. **1988** J. Collman *Fringe-dwellers and Welfare* p. 163 [central Aust.] The person who purchases the bottle and shouts others at a spree is known as 'the **boss**'.

boss boss, the chief boss. Here reduplication is used to intensify the meaning; reduplication is used in many Aboriginal languages for this purpose.

1986 B. Shaw *Countrymen* p. 84 [Kimberley, WA] When we really had that place I put in twenty dollars, **Boss-boss** put twenty dollars.

boss fellow, a boss. Also **boss man**.

1978 K. Palmer & C. McKenna *Somewhere Between Black and White* p. 45 Well, Clancy you young bugger, you a **boss fellow** now, eh? **1974** *Maningrida* Australian Broadcasting Commission p. 8 [Arnhem Land] This **boss man** of Gudgi has nobody to help him stay there and try to make farms.

boss for meself, being independent.

1988 I. Keen *Being Black* p. 188 [central NT] People vigorously protect their right to do their own thing, to be, as Bell (1983, 7) heard, a four-year-old child at Warrabri say, '**boss for meself**'.

3 Something that is of supreme importance in a person's life.

1984 *Nungalinya* (Darwin) no. 28 p. 4 [Kimberley, WA] Those in Hall's Creek who couldn't stay long enough at home to help because 'grog is their **boss**.' **1995** M. Brady *Giving away the Grog* p. 130 [northern SA] From there I bin drinking flagon . . . **Boss** of me then, I was drinking, drinking, drinking.

bottle *noun* [northern Aust.] Broken glass; a piece of glass.

The use of **bottle** for a *piece* of a bottle may be from a characteristic of Aboriginal languages, in which the name for a part is sometimes used as the name of the whole. The choice of **bottle** as the glass object may be because in the early days of Aboriginal and British contact, almost the only glass objects that would have been found in the bush would have been bottles. Glass was one of the European materials that Aboriginal people utilised readily early on in their own cultural tradition of weapon-making, in this case to make spear-heads. People also used ceramic and iron artefacts for the same purpose.

1878 R.B. Smyth *Aborigines of Vic.* Vol. 1 p. 474 [Vic.] **Bottle**, that is broken glass. 1880 Fison & Howitt *Kamilaroi & Kurnai* p. 250 [south-east Vic.] 'Some fellow has put **bottle** in my foot' . . . He explained that some enemy must have found his foot track and buried in it a piece of broken bottle. 1904 A.W. Howitt *Native Tribes S.-E. Aust.* p. 409 [south-east Vic.] For instance, suppose some man has got *groggin* inside him, or **bottle** (that is, a piece of glass) in his arm. 1986 B. Shaw *Countrymen* p. 60 [Kimberley, WA] Sometimes they knock him and leave the **bottle** inside and two or three days after he dies.

bottle spear, a spear with a spearhead made from a piece of broken glass or a glassy stone.

Bottle is here also applied to spearheads made from traditional, non-European material.

1981 G. Ngabidj *Country of the Pelican Dreaming* p. 72 [northern NT] He did not use a shovel spear but a **bottle spear**, an early-day kind made from a white or yellow stone. 1986 B. Shaw *Countrymen* p. 177 [Kimberley, WA] You can make any kind of spear you want from it, shovel or **bottle spear**.

bottle stone, a glass-like stone.

1986 B. Shaw *Countrymen* p. 177 [Kimberley, WA] White stones . . sort of like glass were made there. They were two different **bottle stones**.

bridaya *noun* [south-west WA] A white person in authority, a BOSS. Also **bridaira**, **bridarra**.

Origin unknown, but most probably from the Nyungar language of south-west WA.

1970 J. Davis *First-Born* p. 42 **Bridarra**, important person. 1982 J. Davis *The Dreamers* p. 81 Woops, careful, careful, you gonna look like a real **bridaira**. 1988 J. Davis *Barungin—Smell the Wind* p. 30 [south-west WA] I saw him walkin' up to the **bridaya** office.

bulliman *noun* [Qld] A police officer; the police.

From a nineteenth-century Aboriginal pronunciation of 'policeman'. See GUNJIBLE and POLIGMUN. See also the Introduction for a discussion of pro-nunciations.

1970 *Hope Vale Hotline* Vol. I no. 2 3/1 [north Qld] 'Georgie, Georgie, **bulliman** here!' There he was revolver in hand. 1974 C. Buchanan *We have bugger All* n.p. [Qld] **Bullymen** do not like Aboriginals to be strong and stand together fighting for land rights. But they do like Jacky Jackys. 1976 C.D. Mills *Hobble Chains and Greenhide* p. 144 [NSW?] You come with me now, and we'll ride round these '**bulleman**'. You see this brassy-looking bloke? Well he was culled for lack of quality. 1985 M. Kennedy *Born Half-Caste* p. 24 [northern NSW?] The police are known as '**bulliman**', a name that suits very well.

bullocky *noun* [Chiefly northern Aust.] **1** A bullock; cattle collectively.

The word is less commonly recorded now than in the past.

Aboriginal English

1879 *Native Tribes S.A.* p. 250 [Port Lincoln, SA] Hence arise corruptions like these—knipy for knife, boatoo for boat, **bullocky** for bullock. **1938** D. Bates *Passing of Aborigines* p. 183 [Ooldea, northern SA] White-fellows took it away, and brought their sheep, **bullocky** and pony to hunt our totem meat away. **1988** P. Taylor *After 200 Years* p. 174 [Arnhem Land] In the dry season we take beef to Manmoyi and Gamarrgawan outstations because people there can find no buffalo or **bullocky** in their country. **1991** D.B. Rose *Hidden Histories* p. 195 [Victoria River, north-west NT] That's the way we were making **bullocky** [numbers] bigger and bigger on this country.

2 Beef.

This is an example of an Aboriginal language characterisitic, whereby the same word is applied to an item and what the item is used *for*; see MEAT. This particular term is largely historical.

1839 *S. Austral. Rec.* London (1840) 1 Feb. p. 22 [Adelaide, SA] There was a public dinner given to the Adelaide tribe of Aborigines of roast beef and plum pudding, but they call it **bullocky**. **1846** 'Squatter' *Visit to Antipodes* p. 123 The black fellows have no **bullocky**, or sheepy; but in their stead they have plenty kangaroo. **1923** *Western Star* Roma 3 Jan. p. 2/1 [western Qld?] One day one of these warrigals was up at the Glenormiston stockyard, with others, to get a supply of '**bullocky**', otherwise beef. **1952** A.M. Duncan-Kemp *Where Strange Paths Go Down* p. 16 No pastoralist can afford to pay a pensioned stockman or his dependants, but he is ever willing to give them a home and '**bullocky**' (fresh meat), blankets and tobacco in return for odd jobs done.

bunji-man *noun* [south-west WA] A white man who sexually exploits Aboriginal women, or who particularly seeks out Aboriginal women for purposes of sex. Also **pantji-man**. See also CAPTAIN.

The origin of the word is unclear, but it may be from an Aboriginal pronunciation of *fancy man*. See the Introduction for a discussion of pronunciations.

1975 R. Beilby *Brown Land Crying* p. 4 [WA?] 'When you see one really crawling along you know it's a **bunji-man**.' A bunji-man, an adventurer in sex seeking something exotic. 'Black-velvet, that's what they call us Ab'rig'nes.' **1981** A. Weller *Day of Dog* p. 54 [south-west WA] Ya the cunning one, Val. But ya better not be givin' that ole **bunji man** a bit on the side. **1981** W.J.K. Christensen *The Wangkayi* p. 192 [Kalgoorlie, WA] One offshoot of their developing involvement with **pantji-men** has been their departure from their parents' house. **1985** *Nat. Times* (Sydney) 12 Apr. p. 20/2 They were **Bunji men**. The origins of the term are unclear, but could be related to Bun-gyte, meaning an unbetrothed girl. Today the term, widely used by Aboriginal people around Perth, refers to lonely alcoholic old white men who wander the parks and back streets seeking 'black velvet'—sexual solace from Aboriginal women. The best free translation of Bunji is 'dirty old man'.

pantji-woman, a woman who lives off white men through sexual relationships.

1981 W.J.K. Christensen *The Wangkayi* p. 191 [Kalgoorlie, WA] Casual social and sexual liaisons with European males are also used by some Aboriginal girls to obtain food, drink or money . . there is a small group of girls (often described as **pantji-women**) who maintain themselves in this way.

Hence **bunji-ing**, engaging in a great number of sexual relations, sometimes for economic gain. Also **pantji-ing**. In this sense it applies to both Aboriginal and non-Aboriginal people.

1981 W.J.K. Christensen *The Wangkayi* p. 192 [Kalgoorlie, WA] The different patterns I have identified as 'productive activities'—employment, welfare utilization, begging, scavenging, and **pantji-ing**—have little in common. **1982** J. Davis *The Dreamers* p. 141 [south-west WA] *Peter*: I stopped at Aunt Peggy's. *Eli*: (grinning) **Bunjin'** around, I bet. **1990** Davis et al. *Paperbark* p. 263 [south-west WA] He didn't believe in **bunji-ing** around.

burnt potato *noun* An Aboriginal person who has adopted white Australian attitudes. See also COCONUT.

1986 *Puggana News* (Launceston) Nov. p. 22/9 For **burnt potatoes** are stricken with the plague of white minds . . all burnt potatoes are white inside. **1987** J.C. Altman *Potential for Reducing Dependency at Aboriginal Communities* p. 10 [Kimberley, WA] The second is an option that could be expressed in the following manner in East Kimberley parlance: does one want to remain a 'countryman' or does one want to be a '**burnt potato**', a colloquialism for assimilated Aborigines who are black on the outside but white in the middle.

calici *noun* [northern Aust.] A baby sling.

From an Aboriginal pronunciation of *calico*, from which the sling was originally made. The name of the material the object is made from is used here for the name of the object.

1983 N. Green *Desert School* p. 61 [Western Desert] The babies were usually slung around their hips in cloth **calicis**, leaving their mother's hand free for the steel digging 'stick' and billy can. The calici, a recent innovation, has a sling of linen or calico worn diagonally across the body like a bandola and seemed to have been accepted by most of the mothers.

calico *noun* [northern Aust.] A tent.

This is an example of what something is made *from* being used as the name of the object. See the Introduction for a discussion of this.

1985 *Lang. in Central Aust.* iv. p. 23 [central Aust.] When the English words 'tent' and 'calico' were introduced, they were both used in the actual/potential way . . And '**calico**', (usually pronounced /kaluku/) can mean 'tent'. **1995** M. Brady *Giving away the Grog* p. 72 [northern NT] When I first come out here, I came out with one **calico** and one rubbish old blanket.

captain *noun* [NSW] A white man with money to spend on sex and alcohol.

In general Australian English use, **captain** is someone with money to spend on alcohol, but the term does not have the associations of sex or race which are found in the Aboriginal English sense. See also BUNJIMAN.

1977 K. Gilbert *Living Black* p. 302 [NSW] Have you seen 'em bludging up to a **captain*** who's just come onto the mission with money in his pocket? . . . *The reserve people's name for a white man who visits them to trade money or grog for sex. **1988** A. Rutherford (ed.) *Aboriginal Culture Today* p. 152 [Sydney, NSW] My film, *Nice Coloured Girls*, concerns three Aboriginal girls who go out in the night in Kings Cross, Sydney, pick up a '**Captain**' which is an Aboriginal term for a sugar daddy, have a good night and in the end roll him. **1994** R. & J. Huggins *Auntie Rita* p. 66 [south-east Qld] In those days there were plenty of 'captains' who were willing to share drinks, smokes and their company with us . . . They'd get all goooly up [wild] but who cared?

Captain Cook *noun* **1** The archetypal white man and bearer of European culture and power.

From the name of the navigator, Captain James Cook. Just as **Captain Cook** and his 'discovery' of Australia have become almost an archetypal 'fact' to be taught in school, so has that figure become to Aboriginal people an archetype of the

European invader, whose shadow falling across Aboriginal Australia marks an end of independence.

1988 *Social Alternatives* (St Lucia) Vol. VII no. 1 p. 23 [south-east Qld] When **Captain Cook** came to that land and was ready to put his flag up, and blackfellas was there, watching them from the bush. **1988** *We have Survived* Poster [Arnhem Land] I've finished with the story of old Captain Cook. I'm talking now about all the new **Captain Cooks**. When the old people died, other people started thinking they could make Captain Cook another way. New people. Maybe all his sons. Too many Captain Cooks. They started shooting people then. New Captain Cook people. Those are the people that made war when Captain Cook died; because they didn't care, they didn't know, all those young people. **1989** R.M. Baker *Land is Life* p. 374 [Borroloola, north-east NT] As Eileen Yakibijina puts it, 'Captain Cook been take away all the Aboriginal land and shot all the people'. **1992** P. Taylor *Tell it like it Is* p. 16 In oral cultures . . [it] is impossible to store the names of every single villain and teach them to following generations, so **Captain Cook** has become a symbol of all the invaders, settlers and invaders who tried to destroy Aboriginal life.

2 (In possessive constructions and as an adjective) archetypally European.

1981 *Puggana News* (Launceston) Mar. p. 8 No friend have I in this court you white **Captain Cook** bastard, but my day will come. **1984** P. Read *Down There with Me on Cowra Mission* p. 23 [south-west NSW] They always taught us **Captain Cook's** ways, never taught us our way, the Aboriginal way. **1991** A. Jackomos & D. Fowell *Living Aboriginal Hist. of Vic.* p. 56 [Vic.] It was no good teachers putting something in front of us which was totally irrelevant, out of a **Captain Cook** book. **1991** D.B. Rose *Hidden Histories* p. 138 [Victoria River, north-west NT] Gilruth carried on **Captain Cook's** law in the Northern Territory, as did station owners such as Vestey's.

card *noun* A certificate issued to those Aboriginal people who had become exempted from restrictive legislation. Abbreviation of **exemption card**. See also DOG LICENCE, TICKET.

Exemption cards were issued in most States of Australia from about the 1940s until the 1960s. The intention was to select people seen as 'acceptable' to European Australia and exempt them from the restrictive legislation that applied to people officially listed as 'Aboriginal'. The requirements of exemption were quite rigorous (many non-Aboriginal people would not have qualified), including a stipulation in New South Wales that such a person would succeed in any enterprise he or she would undertake. Many more applied for them than were granted them. In some States, exemption was irreversible; in others it could be lost by what was seen as unacceptable behaviour. In all States the condition of exemption was separation from the Aboriginal community. For further discussion of this see TICKET.

1988 G. Cowlishaw *Black, White or Brindle* p. 84 [NSW] We couldn't drink in the old days. Had to get a **card**. **1988** *Mosa* (Clayton) no. 2, p. 17 Only if you had an **exemption card**, and that's when you received your rights. **1989** D. Walker *Me and You* p. 40 [north coast, NSW] Then later on the **exemption cards** came out. If you had one of them you could go into the pub then.

chooky chooky *noun* A chook, a hen; chooks or hens. Also **juku-juku, tchiki-tchiki, tshukki-tshukki**.

This is one of several examples of reduplication in Aboriginal English of an English (or in this case Australian English) word.

1889 C. Lumholtz *Among Cannibals* p. 369 [south-eastern Aust.] A white man who was out hunting emus asked a black: 'You been see 'im **tshukki-tshukki** big fellow?' The latter indignantly replied: 'I suppose you mean an emu?' **1936** M. & E. Durack *Chunuma* p. 117 [Kimberley, WA] What about where we go findim egg. . reckon **chooky-chooky** bin habbit holiday today? **1949** *Oceania* Dec. p. 83 [north-west NSW] More common. . are the words that have been coined in accordance with the grammatical patterns of the aboriginal dialects e.g. . . **Tchiki-tchiki** (fowl). **1985** *Lang. in Central Aust.* iv. p. 19 [central Aust.] Some English words are repeated or 'reduplicated' in Warumungu. But usually the word is also re-duplicated in Aboriginal English. Many of the (mostly animals), have /i/ added, or /u/ if the vowel of the English word is /u/. . . . jipi-jipi, sheep; **juku-juku**, hen.

Christmas Father *noun* Father Christmas, Santa Claus.

1986 *Kowanyama News* Dec. p. 5 [north Qld] He was an hour and a half late, but there was a big turn up of children who got to meet **Christmas Father** for a friendly word and a cold drink. **1988** C. Mattingley & K. Hampton *Survival in Our Own Land* p. 252 [SA] Further 'Europeanising' continued with '**Christmas Father**' celebrations. In 1957 he arrived in a green bun cart (a four wheeled waggon drawn by two horses).

church married *adjective* Married in a European church, as opposed to married according to Aboriginal law.

1986 J. Davis *No Sugar* p. 43 [south-west WA] Proper **church married**, New Norcia, white dress an' all.

citizenship rights *noun* The **rights** available to all Australian citizens except Aboriginal people, the majority of whom were, until the 1960s, and later in some States, under special legislation which gave them fewer civil rights than non-Aboriginal Australians. Also **citizen's rights** and **citizen**. See also CARD, DOG LICENCE, RIGHTS and TICKET.

The **rights** referred to here are rights such as the right to vote, to control one's own money, to drink alcohol, to move freely around the State, all of which in different ways in different States were denied those who were officially listed as 'Aboriginal'.

1961 *Aborigines in NSW* p. 10 [NSW] Denial of **citizenship rights** and issue of an 'exemption certificate' affects the attitude of Aboriginal people. **1979** J. Davis *Kullark* p. 58 [south-west WA] Be O.K. sir, got my honourable discharge and me **citizenship rights**. **1988** G. Cowlishaw *Black, White or Brindle* p. 80 Many Aborigines who might have been eligible for '**citizen's rights**'. . chose not to do so. **1991** J. McGinness *Son of Alyandu* p. 59 [northern Aust.] They struck again in January, demanding. . **citizenship rights** and freedom of movement. **1995** M. Brady *Giving away the Grog* p. 63 [northern NT] Then going on twenty-one when people got **citizen** for alcohol, like black and white, then everybody start drinking.

civilised *adjective* (Of Aboriginal people) Europeanised; experiencing the British invasion with its physical and cultural consequences.

In its non-Aboriginal sense, there is still an element of a hierarchical concept of human society, with the opposition of *barbarism* and *civilisation*, in which sedentary, technologically complex societies are seen as superior to nomadic, technologically simple cultures.

1978 *Working Together* Qld Aboriginal and Islander Teacher Aide Dev. p. 27 [north Qld] When the first white man landed on the beach the Aboriginal people were uncivilised . . . They changed the Great Grand-parents to **civilised** Australian Aborigines. **1981** *Social*

Alternatives (St Lucia) VII i 23 [south-east Qld?] But . . often they got **civilised** and a lot of them passed on . . our people were the first originals to put their foot on this land.

cockrag *noun* [northern Aust.] A pubic covering for a man.

Traditionally both men and women at times wore pubic coverings made from fur, string, feathers or fibre. Most of the references in this section refer to a covering made from cloth, which became common after the occupation because of European strictures about nakedness.

> **1964** T. Ronan *Packhorse & Pearling Boat* p. 46 [Kimberley, WA] Joe, clad in Malay-style sarong with a grey flannel shirt hanging down outside it . . at night put on the **cockrag** and joined the blacks in their corroboree. **1981** Ngabidj & Shaw *My Country of Pelican Dreaming* p. 82 [Kimberley, WA] Wallambain threw away his woomera and **cock rag** and jumped in. **1991** D.B. Rose *Hidden Histories* p. 11 [central NT] And I dropped that paper from my pocket and threw it away. Grabbed [off] my trousers, and pulled my shirt [off] and put my **cockrag** back [on] and go back to the old time. **1993** G. Koch *Kaytetye Country* p. 11 [central NT] But man bin have a little bit **cockrag** anyway, but woman, he didn't have any clothes.

coconut *noun* [Chiefly south-east Aust.] An Aboriginal person who lives in a manner seen by the community as rejecting Aboriginal identity. See also UNCLE TOM, BURNT POTATO.

> **1980** *N.S.W. Parl. Papers* (1981) 3rd [NSW] When the Premier . . sends non-Aboriginal people out into the country, they talk to people that we call **coconuts** . . . They are assimilated black people who sit about the towns and all they are proud of is how many white friends they have. **1988** *Sunraysia* (Mildura) 9 Jan. p. 1/5 [NSW, Vic.] **Coconut** numbers are thought to be about 20 at this time, but may be getting more as rednecks, and coconuts work full-time to turn more black people into coconuts. **1988** J. Davis *Barungin—Smell the Wind* p. 12 [south-west WA] The **coconut** I'm talking about is two-tone black on the outside, white on the inside. **1988** G. Cowlishaw *Black, White or Brindle* p. 143 [western NSW] The rent collector . . would perhaps be described as a **coconut**, or an Uncle Tom.

colour *noun* **1** A racial group, identified as people of the same **colour** of skin.

> **1975** J.P. Roberts (ed.) *Mapoon Story* i. p. 1 [Mapoon, north Qld] In among our own **colour**, they are fighting against us, instead of coming with us. **1978** J. & P. Read *View of the Past* p. 30 [NT] White man no wantem my **colour**, like blackfeller. **1980** *Visions of Mowanjum* p. 67 [Kimberley, WA] We came to a settlement with a lot of white people there, but also people of my **colour**. **1986** B. Shaw *Countrymen* p. 262 [Kimberley, WA] Well when you see any whitefeller chase after black girls it's because he wants to try to get his **colour**, see? **1988** G. Cowlishaw *Black, White or Brindle* p. 126 [western NSW] He said that he knew others who would 'joke against their own **colour**' just for a bit of peace. **1989** R.M. Baker *Land is life* p. 202 [Borroloola, north-east NT] Aboriginal people working for Europeans likewise were sometimes killed by 'their own **colour**'. **1991** D.B. Rose *Hidden Histories* p. 144 [north-west NT] Anybody interested in Aboriginal people, they can't get through. Their own **colour** [whitefellows] can't get through.

2 (As **the colour**) Aboriginality.

The comment in the following citation was made at a time when to acknowledge one's identity as an Aboriginal was to do so in a climate of opinion that was considerably more racist than that of the present, and to make oneself liable to control by restrictive legislation.

> **1963** D. E. Barwick *Little More than Kin* p. 356 [Vic.] 'Some *kuri* children will be lost, for the **colour** is a heavy burden . . we don't blame the weak who want to pass'.

coloured *adjective* Aboriginal.

This term has been recorded in general Australian English of Aboriginal people and others of non-white descent since 1816. However, it is not as common in Aboriginal English.

1938 *Abo Call* May p. 2 I have been for three years trying to organise the **coloured** people on the Clarence River. 1978 J. & P. Read *View of the Past* p. 278 [NT] We stand back, then, and all these, sergeant and our **coloured** people, and marching out.

compound *adjective* [south-west WA] Of or from the **compound**, part of Moore River Aboriginal settlement in south-west WA.

Moore River was the main Aboriginal settlement in south-west WA. Individuals, families, and even communities were sent there, ostensibly for 'training' (although in fact little of that occurred) but essentially as a form of control and segregation. The **compound** was the area where school-age children were domiciled away from their families in order to inculcate non-Aboriginal values.

1979 J. Davis *Kullark* p. 61 [south-west WA] She was one of the **compound** kids, same as me. 1986 J. Davis *No Sugar* p. 70 [south-west WA] Mary! You should be in the compound . . she can't stay here, Joe, she's a **compound** girl.

cunnichman *noun* A police officer.

Origin unknown.

1977 M. Tucker *If Everyone Cared* p. 35 [NSW] All of a sudden one of our party noticed a police officer . . we all gasped '**Cunnichman**' which means policeman in one Aboriginal language.

dark *adjective* [Chiefly southern Aust.] Aboriginal.

This is used more commonly by older people. Originally it was a euphemism for 'black' (as skin colour) in reference to Aboriginal people, and as such was first recorded in 1838, and as *darkie* and *darkskin* from 1845.

1938 *Abo Call* July p. 2 [north coast, NSW] Our people on the Tweed River have decent homes, and support themselves . . but colour-prejudice is supreme in the towns of Coolangatta-Tweed Heads, and **dark** people are forbidden to attend the cinemas. 1950 *Dark People in Melbourne* (Victorian Council Social Service) p. 25 [Vic.] Although they would prefer to marry darks, a good number of the **dark** boys . . cannot provide the amenities which association with whites leads the girls to expect. 1951 R. & C. Berndt *From Black to White in SA* p. 263 [Adelaide, SA] '**Dark** people' . . this is an expression often used in the city and near-country areas to designate people of aboriginal stock, including those of light skin-colouring. It is common among the people themselves, adults and children, and among certain religions and charitable workers associated with them. 1979 K. Dhougarle *There's More to Life* p. 27 [NSW] When he said I could stay there, I felt good because there was no other **dark** family in the town. 1983 M. Sharpe *Traeger Kid* p. 82 [northern NSW] There were mobs more people there, all **dark** people except for four whites.

dark ward, a segregated hospital ward for Aboriginal people.

1983 *Aboriginal History* (Canberra) Vol. VII no. 1 p. 43 [northern NSW] So we had to go to Kempsey. We didn't like going to the hospital. They'd have special **dark wards**.

darky *noun* An Aboriginal person; a non-white. Also **darkie**.

This is not commonly used by Aboriginal people about themselves. The 1994 citation below is from an older song. **Darkie** is first recorded as being used of Aboriginal people by non-Aboriginal people in 1845.

1969 *Koorier* (Fitzroy) Vol. IX p. 22 A 'Goorie' is a **darky**. Around Bowen, he could be of Aboriginal, South Sea Islander, Singhalese, Malay or a mixture of all these descents—a non-Caucasian. [**1994**] D. Young *Songs* n.p. [western NSW] I'm a happy-go-lucky **darkie** with a swag upon my back. Each year I make a livin' by walkin' along the track. I carry all my cookin' utensils in a worn out sugar bag, An army coat and a gubbie blanket that's what I call my swag.

Day of Mourning *noun* 26 January 1938, the 150th anniversary of the invasion of Australia by the British.

1963 D.E. Barwick *Little More than Kin* p. 171 [Vic.] On January 26, 1938 . . Aboriginal groups throughout New South Wales held a '**Day of Mourning** and Protest'. **1990** A. Markus *Governing Savages* p. 182 In response to the proclamation of a **Day of Mourning** by Aboriginal leaders in Victoria and New South Wales to coincide with the sesquicentenary celebrations, Unaipon . . voiced his opposition. **1992** *Shades of Black* (Carlton) Summer p. 6 I learned only this year that Aborigines first observed a **Day of Mourning** to coincide with Australia Day in 1938 . . organised by the great Koori leader, Mr William Cooper.

dog licence *noun* An exemption certificate. Also **dog certificate, dog collar, dog tag, dog ticket**. See CARD, TICKET, UNDER THE ACT.

Exemption certificates were issued in most States of Australia up until the 1960s and provided the holder with exemption from the special legislation applying to people legally classified as 'Aboriginal'. The intention was to 'select out' those who had succeeded in European terms, especially in employment and housing. The conditions of award were quite stringent and the price of obtaining one was separation from the Aboriginal community. For a more detailed discussion of this subject see CARD. The *Australian National Dictionary* records similar expressions in Australian English to refer to legislation seen as repressive or discriminatory, such as the *Dog Act*, which referred to the power of a publican to refuse to serve inebriated patrons, and the *Dog Collar Act*, which licensed waterside workers.

1955 F.B. Vickers *Mirage* p. 257 Monty wants us to get the paper they give you . . . If we had this paper, me and you could have walked into that pub and stood at the bar all day and none of 'em could have said a word to us . . We'd be as good as the next bloke so long as we could flash the **dog licence**. **1963** *Bulletin* (Sydney) 13 Apr. p. 3/2 The recent amendment to the NSW Aborigines' Protection Act to permit aborigines to drink in NSW hotels without a '**dog licence**' abolishes an iniquitous law and will free aborigines from exploitation by sly groggers. **1977** K. Gilbert *Living Black* p. 297 [NSW] Before the 1967 referendum, before citizenship, Aborigines could receive these exemption cards—**dog certificates**—which enabled them to enter a hotel. **1979** J. Davis *Kullark* p. 59 [south-west WA] We already got a name for these things, we call 'em **dawg collars**. **1981** *Nat. Times* (Sydney) 15 Nov. p. 33/ 2 She carried a **Dog Ticket**—an exemption card which, despite the evidence of the photograph, stated that she was a white person since she had married a man whose father was white. That ticket allowed her to visit hotels, to vote and to assert her status as an Australian citizen. The catch was that she was no longer allowed to associate with her Aboriginal mother, father and sister or she would be charged with consorting. **1985** J. Miller *Koori* p. 174 [NSW] A Koori had to 'behave' to get the **dog licence** then continue with 'acceptable behaviour' in order to keep it. **1989** A. Haebich *For their own Good* p. 270 [south-west WA] He and his family had taken a strong stand against . . exemption . . . 'No Jim, I hope and trust that you have not got one of those **dog collers**.' **1993** D. Hodge *Did you meet* *any Malagas?* p. 54 [northern NT] *What are* **dog tags**? Well, that's a term that Aboriginal people use for these certificates which were issued to people. You had to get such a certificate if you wanted to get a job or if you wanted to basically be able to move around during daylight hours, sunrise and sunset.

dog collar act, an Act containing legislation relating specifically to Aboriginal people. See also DOG LICENCE.

1974 F. Stevens *Aborigines in Cattle Industry* p. 167 I just remember the 'dog collar'—when they were still under the '**dog-collar act**'* . . . *Aboriginals Ordinance.

dry gully *noun* [northern Aust.] Any place where the murdered bodies of Aboriginal workers who caused 'trouble' to their white employers were dumped. The term **dry gully** implied a suitable place where the fold of the land would hide the body from view.

This practice occurred in the violent frontier period in the Victoria River District of the north-west Northern Territory; similar practices were followed in many other areas of Australia as the frontier of European settlement moved across the continent. All the following citations are taken from the same work but are excerpts from accounts by three different people.

1991 D.B. Rose *Hidden Histories* p. 140 [north-west NT] Any man come sick, boy, anything like that, blind man, don't give him medicine. You take him in a **dry gully** and knock him.
1991 D.B. Rose *Hidden Histories* p. 88 [north-west NT] That's finished—dead. Chuck him in the **dry gully**.

into the dry gully, a euphemism for being shot.

1991 D.B. Rose *Hidden Histories* p. 188 [northern NSW] We never get away, never even run away. We know, if we wanted to run we'd be **into the dry gully** [shot].

early *adjective* [Chiefly northern Aust.] **1** Old, olden, of the past. Also **earlier day**, **early day(s)**.

The sense here is not just chronological but cultural. The past is not just a long time ago but a place and a time which is very different from today. The conceptual violence of the invasion can be seen in this usage, where there is now a 'before' and an 'after', with the advent of the Europeans being the central divide. The **early** period can be seen to straddle that divide, so happenings at the time of the invasion are included as well as pre-invasion life. See also BEFORE.

1978 J. & P. Read *View of the Past* p. 164 [Yarralin, north-west NT] 'Whiteman too far you going, trying to pinchem blackfeller woman.' That bin all **early days** do that. 1984 C. Allridge *Aboriginal Eng.* p. 85 [Cherbourg, south-east Qld] (H)e told us about the **early day**. 1986 B. Shaw *Countrymen* p. 47 [Kimberley, WA] That's the **earlier day** Law. You held that daughter to that young feller. 1988 H. Ross *Community Social Impact Assessment* p. 40 [East Kimberley, WA] You know how cruel used to be **early day**?

2 (Of things and people) belonging to this past.

1987 A. McGrath *Born in the Cattle* p. 64 [NT] Watering garden, washem plates, cookem tucker for supper. Make up dinner, stove, **early** feller tucker . . beef. 1981 G. Ngabidj *Country of the Pelican Dreaming* p. 72 [NT] He did not use a shovel spear but a bottle spear, an **early-day** kind made from a white or yellow stone. 1979 *Land Rights News* May p. 8 [NT] Longa that sort of beef him been living **early-day** people. 1981 *Kimberley Land Council* (Derby)

Mar. p. 17 [Kimberley, WA] That's all we mean what we say, not to come in just help himself and put a big oil rig round that sacred place—**early** people not allow people round that block.

feeding outside *noun* The practice of being given food by an employer outside in the open air as opposed to inside a building.

In many rural industries, Aboriginal employees were treated differently from non-Aboriginal employees, including receiving their meals outside, often on the woodheap. The woodheap was used as a kind of social indicator; if you were black you ate on the woodheap and if you were white you ate inside. Sometimes a further distinction was made; people of the full descent ate on the woodheap, part-Aboriginal people ate in the kitchen, and whites ate in the dining room with the boss.

1983 *Mankind* (Sydney) Apr. p. 508 [Arnhem Land] A major area of conflict for Aboriginal men and women and their employers was '**feedin' outside**'. Most employers insisted that their aboriginal employees feed outside. **1989** B. Morris *Domesticating Resistance* p. 45 [northern NSW] What the Aborigines called '**feedin outside**' . . referred to the practice of giving food to Aborigines working on the properties, but making them eat it away from the house i.e. 'eatin' on the woodheap'!

fire bucket *noun* An improvised fireplace consisting of a metal drum in which the fire is lit.

1955 *Oceania* Dec. p. 212 [NSW] The camp-fire of the old days has been replaced by the **fire-bucket** on X. Station. This stands in the middle of the room and the family huddles around it. **1958** *Annual Report* Commissioner of Native Welfare p. 25 [WA] A feature of the improvements was the building of a fireplace inside the home, dispensing with the **fire bucket**. **1981** B. Lennon *Yarns Around the Firebucket* p. 6 [northern SA] The **firebucket** was going well and the station hands were all sitting round ready for a yarn after supper. **1988** R. Langford *Dont Take Your Love to Town* p. 126 [northern NSW] I found a four-gallon drum and two iron bars. We . . cut holes all round the drum . . . I sat it on bricks in the back yard. We built a wood fire in the drum and put the iron bars on top and we cooked on that . . . This was how my sister Margaret learnt to make a **fire bucket**. **1993** E. Crawford *Over my Tracks* p. 24 [western NSW] There was no heatin' in the school, but we had a big **fire-bucket** outside.

flag blanket *noun* [WA] A blanket issued by the government.

Blankets were part of the rations of food and clothing given out by governments to Aboriginal communities. They were usually distinctively marked to identify them as being for Aboriginal people, something that many Aboriginal people resented. Possibly the term **flag** comes from the official appearance of Queen Victoria's crown on the blanket. See also GUBBY BLANKET.

1987 S. Morgan *My Place* p. 328 [WA] There was a government ration we used to get now and then. It was a blanket, we all called it a **flag blanket**, it had the crown of Queen Victoria on it.

flagon *noun* Cheap alcoholic drink, sold by the flagon. Also **plagen**.

Cheaper alcohol is often sold in large glass bottles known as **flagons**. In the first citation it is called a **plagen**—an Aboriginal pronunciation of 'flagon'. For a discussion of Aboriginal sound systems see the Introduction.

1980 B. Sansom *The Camp at Wallaby Cross* p. 222 [Darwin, NT] You Dancin Girl, tellim leave that **plagen**. **1983** P. Nathan & D.L. Japanangka *Settle Down Country* p. 128 [central Aust.] Papunya . . too much **flagon**. We all come back to our own place now. **1988** S. Dunlop *All that Rama Rama Mob* p. 76 [central Aust.] Sometimes *warungka* from grog, wine **flagon**. **1995** M. Brady *Giving away the Grog* p. 61 [northern NT] I was start with **flagon** and with the wine . . . Cask, and box, drinking that . . . When I was drink that flagon.

like flagon, affected by alcohol.

1985 S. Cane & O. Stanley *Land Use and Resources in Desert Homelands* p. 38 The people at Mitukatjiiri said their water was 'no good' and . . 'made you **like flagon**' (drunk or hungover).

flash *adjective* **1** Ostentatious, attention seeking (as in general English use), but with an added suggestion that such behaviour is seen as European rather than Aboriginal.

Aboriginal society is generally more group oriented and cooperative, and less individualistic and competitive than European society, so that behaviour which is outside the norm is often seen in a more negative light than it would be in a non-Aboriginal society. See SHAME.

1958 J. Beckett *A Study of a Mixed Blood Aboriginal Minority* p. 187 [western NSW] It is very difficult to contract out of the system . . people will call one '**flash**' or 'stuck up'. **1963** D. E. Barwick *Little More than Kin* p. 362 [Vic.] My aunty's family have got real **flash**. **1965** *Comparative Sociology* Mar. p. 18 Families . . accumulating property . . will be called **flash**, and will be placed in a humiliating position if they ever find themselves in need. **1966** M. Boney *Bigga-Billa Porcupine* p. 8 [western NSW] This emu, he went and brought all his young ones out. He put his wing out and he ran round the native companion with all his little ones. This old emu, he was getting **flash** and runnin' round with his wing out and showing off all his children. **1977** *Meanjin* (Melbourne) no. 4, p. 543 [Sydney, NSW] Amongst the Aboriginals, there are some . . who regard the speaking of the standard dialect as being **flash**. **1981** G. McKenzie *Aurukun Diary* p. 195 [northern Qld] The black one thought the white one wore all those clothes simply because she was '**flash**', an often used word at Aurukun in the early days. **1984** *Puggana News* (Launceston) Feb. p. 13 [Tas.] The newest black is already acting **flash** with the purchase of a 4 wheeldrive Toyota. The Flash Black added that the machine is available to any lovely dark young ladies. **1984** *New Life for Harpers* n.p. [western NSW?] Yes, he'll say we think we're **flash**, that we trying to be 'white' instead of helping our own people. **1988** J. Harkins *English as 'Two-way' Language* p. 24 [central Aust.] To use his '**flash**' town English to these older men would be disrespectful. **1989** R.M. Baker *Land is Life* p. 202 [Borroloola, north-east NT] Shoot their own colour, they been shoot all about . . their countrymen . . him become **flash** along their colour and shoot all about.

flash talk, using speech or a way of speaking that is seen as European rather than Aboriginal. Also **flash English**, **talk flash**.

1985 *Aust. Review Applied Linguistics* Vol. I no. 1, p. 138 If you talk . . you know, **flash** as they call it at home, that's what they think you are trying to be: stuck up or something you know, and you've got to talk on their level. Interviewer: and they call it *flash*: you're speaking *flash*? . . Yeah. **1988** M.C. Sharpe et al. *An Introduction to the Bundjalung Language and its Dialects* p. 175 [north coast, NSW] They sometimes call school English '**flash talk**'; they also call school English 'gabah', which is a general N.S.W. Aboriginal word for 'white fella'. **1991** G. Ward *Unna You Fullas* p. 80 [south-west WA] She . . **talking flash**-way to that wadjala.

2 Attractive, beautiful.

This sense lacks the pejorative sense of both the general use and the first Aboriginal English sense.

1925 P. Bridges *Walkabout in Aust.* p. 175 Topsy was a picture of industry, perched upon her camel, stitching away at her new dress to be **flash** to enter Alice Springs. **1980** G.F. Brewer *On the Bread Line* p. 41 [central Aust.] We make flowers on table cloths and cut 'em all nice,—crochet around the edge . . I bin do some real **flash** ones. **1986** B. Shaw *Countrymen* p. 144 [Kimberley, WA] Sometimes they had a bone through the nose. That boy would make himself **flash**, nice.

gadia *noun* See KARTIYA.

gnoop *noun* Wine.

From Nyungar *ngoop* meaning *blood*. In the Wiradjuri language of south-western NSW the word for wine is *girri-girri*, 'red'.

1982 J. Davis *The Dreamers* p. 79 [south-west WA] Anybody got any ideas? (Silence.) How about a bottle of **gnoop**?

gnummari *noun* [south-west WA] Tobacco. Also **gnummerai**.

The word for this substance in the Nyungar language of south-western WA.

1981 J. Davis *The Dreamers* p. 79 'Ow about some **gnummari**? **1986** A. Weller *Going Home* p. 88 [south-west WA] 'Grab some **gnummerai**, Murry.' Murry gets a small cardboard box and quickly fills it up with cigars and packets of cigarettes.

gold pass *noun* A pass enabling a non-resident to enter an Aboriginal reserve.

In the past, legally declared Aboriginal reserves were closed by non-Aboriginal authorities to all except those designated to live there; the government-appointed manager had the right to turn away all unofficial visitors. Even relatives could be barred from seeing their families.

1969 *Koorier* (Fitzroy) 18 Apr. p. 11 [Vic.] This sort of thing stinks of the old **Gold Pass** days when one had to go through all sorts of legal channels before being allowed to enter a native reserve.

goom *noun* **1** Methylated spirits, as an alcoholic drink. Also **gum**.

Possibly from *gun*, meaning 'water', hence 'alcohol' from the Gabi-gabi, Waga-waga and Gureng-gureng languages of south-eastern Queensland.

1967 *Kings Cross Whisper* (Sydney) xxxv p. 6/1 [NSW] **Goom**, methylated spirits. **1973** K. Gilbert *People are Legends* p. 2 [NSW] What else is there for me? Except a bottle full of **Goom**, A fire, an old gum tree? **1979** K. Dhougarle *There's More to Life* p. 43 [NSW] We kept looking down at the gummies and we could see that they had beer bottles and milk bottles filled up with water and just a bottle of **gum** alongside . . They were mixing up beer, water and gum. [**1994**] D. Young *Songs* n.p. [NSW] You'll find me beneath the old gum tree drinkin' **goom** and lemonade.

2 An alcoholic who drinks methylated spirits. See GOOMIE.

1984 P. Corris *Winning Side* p. 172 [NSW] You can't inform on your own, Dick. If you do the place'll be finished for sure. No one'll touch it except the **gooms**.

goom camp, a camp of such alcoholics.

1995 M. Brady *Giving Away the Grog* p. 40 [northern NT] I left Perth that is and came up to the north—drinking all the way. . . it was the **goom camp** set which I found quite easily.

goomie *noun* [south-east Aust.] An alcoholic, especially one who drinks methylated spirits. Also **goomee, goomy**. See also GOOM.

1973 K. Gilbert *Because White Man'll Never Do It* p. 87 [NSW] Right at the bottom of the pile are the '**goomies**'. These are the Aboriginal alcoholics, the metho drinkers. 1977 K. Gilbert *Living Black* p. 83 [NSW] My uncle was a **goomee** and when he died it really broke me up. Seeing those people having to go down to the back lane to drink a bottle of meths and the next morning his mate found him dead beside him. 1981 D. Stuart *I think I'll Live* p. 112 [NSW] 'Meself,' he used to say, 'meself, I'm a bit of a **goomy**,' and you two blokes sound just like him; can't keep your minds off your bellies. 1990 R. Bowden & B. Bunbury *Being Aboriginal* p. 50 [south-east Qld] A lot of our old drones, that means old alcoholics, old '**goomies**', old metho kings and queens who've passed on—like my sister who was classed as the Queen of the Drones of Queensland—died in Musgrave Park.

goonya *noun* [southern SA] A white person, white people. Also **gunia**.

From the Narangga language of Yorke Peninsula *koonya* meaning 'excrement'. See GOONA (Chapter 3).

1961 *Polynesian Soc. Journal* (Wellington) June p. 202 [southern SA] Adelaide people . . referring to white people . . most commonly say **gunia**. Gunia is a word made common by Point Pearce people. 1988 C. Mattingley & K. Hampton (eds) *Survival in Our Own Land* p. 4 [southern SA] **Goonyas** came to the country with axe, plough, flock and fencing wire. 1988 C. Mattingley (ed.) *Survival* p. 4 [southern SA] Our ancestors' first impressions of the settlers were not always flattering . . The Ngarinyeri called them *grinkari*, their word for a corpse whose skin had been removed and which was therefore pink. The Kaurna word *kuinyo* means a dead person or a dreaded monstrous being with an immense abdomen whose presence foretells a death. The Narungga word *koonya* means excrement, like the Kaurna word *kudna*. The Adynyamathanha *udnyu* is also the word for dead. The word **goonya** used by Nungas today is derived from the earlier words.

government *noun* [Chiefly northern Aust.] **1** All public authorities and their officials whether State or Federal. See also GUBMENT.

This sense is similar to the standard use but is of special significance because of the enormous impact 'officialdom' has had on Aboriginal lives.

1935 M. & E. Durack *All-About* p. 11 [Kimberley, WA] When 'Missus' left for a holiday the '**Government**' (terrible disembodied spirit of the white man's power) sent its emissaries to take Daffodil [the child of one of the Aboriginal workers] away. 1982 M. Howard *Aboriginal Power* p. 119 The missionaries . . put all the school-aged children into single-sex and spatially segregated dormitories . . invoking '**government**' law' as validation for their actions.

government man, person(s) employed by government bureaucracies. Also **government people**.

1972 E. Kolig *Bi:n and Gadeja* p. 15 [Kimberley, WA] The 'Government' is located in the 'Government-country' or 'Canberra' which is populated by the '**Government-people**'. 1988 C. Mattingley & K. Hampton (eds) *Survival in Our Own Land* p. 24 [SA] (Thats the) first station that was a government station, they call it. An' this man, he was a **government man**.

government time, the period in northern Australia from about the 1970s, when welfare authorities took over from Church organisations in running Aboriginal settlements, until the present.

1981 *Social Alternatives* (St Lucia) Vol. II no. 2, p. 25 [southern Qld] They have a firmly established history . . later through mission times and finally in '**government**' times.

2 (As an adjective) supplied by a government.

1986 J. Davis *No Sugar* p. 27 Did you get married at New Norcia? . . *Jimmy*: An' engaged under a **Government** blanket. **1988** *La Perouse* p. 3 [Sydney, NSW] His shack was painted red and it was the last house built of **government** tin to be demolished. **1989** M. Lennon *That's How it Was* p. 54 [Oodnadatta, northern SA] We never lived on the **Government** ration until my husband was sick in Port Augusta.

gub *noun* [south-east Aust.] A white person.

Abbreviation of GUBBA.

1971 K. Gilbert *End of Dreamtime* p. 8 [NSW] They called me, Kalari, a 'Pommy' and '**Gub**', laughed at my speaking, laughed when I tried to join in their song and dance. **1976** T. Shepherd *Children of Blindness* p. 76 [western NSW] He had . . scorned and verbally lacerated Pete for wanting to become a white man, a **Gub**, as he sneeringly referred to them. **1978** M. Kamien *Dark People of Bourke* p. 5 [western NSW] There is some dispute among Aborigines and white Aboriginologists as to the exact derivation of the word '**Gub**'. Some Aborigines said that it came from 'government' and others that it came from 'garbage'. It is widely used by Aborigines throughout New South Wales as a collective term for whites. Like the white Australian vernacular 'bastard' its use covers a wide emotional spectrum, from hatred to affection. **1983** *Puggana News* (Launceston) Dec. p. 11 [Tas.] When it suits their plea, To the federal **gubs** For funds, you see. **1988** R. Langford *Dont Take Your Love to Town* p. 2 [NSW] The next three I had with Gordon Campbell (**gubb**).

gubba *noun* [south-east Aust.] **1** A white person. Also **gubbah, gubbar**. See also GUB.

The origin of this word is not clear. It is possible that it derives from GUBMENT, an Aboriginal pronunciation of *government*. The use of the word GUBBY in the phrase GUBBY BLANKET for *government blanket* (see below) suggests that this is likely.

1963 *Bulletin* (Sydney) 13 Apr. p. 8/1 [NSW] Any aborigine living in New South Wales who is over the age of 18 can go into a hotel and have a drink like any '**gubbar**' (white man). **1971** K. Gilbert *End of Dreamtime* p. 7 [NSW] Now we wander crying and the **gubbahs** go on lying:- O Land of hope and glory! Southern stronghold of the free! **1975** R.J. Merritt *Cake Man* (1978) p. 12 [south-west NSW] A gubba never had a social welfare cheque in his whole life. '**Gubba**', that's Kuri lingo for whitefella. **1992** R.L. Ginibi *Real Deadly* p. 73 Rita bundled me into her little car and introduced me to her **Gubba** girlfriend, whose name was Dawn.

2 An archetypal white person—the representative of European Australian culture.

1977 K. Gilbert *Living Black* p. 161 [NSW] We go to school, that means the **gubbah** is trying to wipe out the tribal law.

gubbariginal *noun* An Aboriginal person who has internalised non-Aboriginal values. See COCONUT, UNCLE TOM.

1969 *Koorier* (Fitzroy) Vol. 1 no. 12, p. 8 [Vic.] If the Aborigines are being forced to choose between the **Gubbariginal** and the jolly old 'do-gooder' and his 'thirty pieces of silver', surely Aborigines will see through any scheme that tends to show them as being gullible enough to accept the shadow for the substance.

gubbise *verb* To take Aboriginal material and 'Europeanise' it.

1994 *Campus Review* (Canberra) 10 August p. 2/4 She said a lot of past Aboriginal works had been '**gubbised**' by white editors . . . For example, words such as comin' and goin' and gonna were anglicised so they did not reflect the true voice of the Koori people.

gubby *adjective* Government, supplied by the Government. Also **gubbie**.

From early in the nineteenth century, government instrumentalities had issued blankets to Aboriginal communities; historically they were issued once a year, on 'blanket day'. Later, they were supplied, with basic clothing, to inmates of government 'mission' stations. Both clothing and blankets were identified as *Government ration for Aborigines* by a mark, such as a distinctive red stripe on the blankets. Many Aboriginal people spent long hours unpicking the stripe.

1989 B. Morris *Domesticating Resistance* p. 79 Blankets . . and the *betick* were the only essentials for sleeping. The *betick* could be made from **gubby** blankets or old corn bags . . and stuffed with corn husks or blades of grass. **1993** E. Crawford *Over my Tracks* p. 70 [western NSW] All the clothes were . . stamped 'Brewarrina Aboriginal Mission' . . '**gubby**' clothes we used to call them. **[1994]** D. Young *Songs* n.p. [western NSW] I'm a happy-go-lucky darkie with a swag upon my back. Each year I make a livin' by walkin' along the track. I carry all my cookin' utensils in a worn out sugar bag, An army coat and a **gubbie** blanket that's what I call my swag.

gubment *noun* The combined forces of officialdom, State and Federal. Also **gubbment, gubmen**. See GOVERNMENT.

An Aboriginal pronunciation of *government*. For a discussion of Aboriginal language sound systems and their effect on Aboriginal English, see the Introduction.

1928 B. Spencer *Wanderings in Wild Aust.* p. 609 [Darwin, NT] Big **Gubment** come up. **1937** C. Warburton *White poppies* p. 194 [Arnhem Land] The '**gubment**' had sent word to the Arnhem Land tribes that certain country was to be set aside for their use only . . **1986** J. Davis *No Sugar* p. 28 [south-west WA] Yeah, fuckin' **gubment**. Fucks everybody up. **1988** R. Langford *Dont Take Your Love to Town* p. 131 [NSW] We had trouble raising funds from the government (**gubbment**) for any Aboriginal projects. **1993** E. Crawford *Over my Tracks* p. 70 [western NSW] Everyone was scared of the **gubmen**.

gubbermint man, an official from any arm of government. Also **gubb'ment man**.

1927 M. Terry *Through Land of Promise* p. 179 [Kimberley, WA] This one . . no more big fellar **gubbermint** man. **1936** M. & E. Durack *Chunuma* p. 89 [Kimberley, WA] Two fella **Gubb'ment** man . . All day swankin' about, wear'm collar!

gunjabal *noun* [Chiefly NSW] A police officer. Also **gungabul, gunjible**. See GUNJIE.

From a nineteenth-century Aboriginal pronunciation of *constable*. For a discussion of Aboriginal language sound systems and their effect on Aboriginal English, see the Introduction.

1990 S. Watson *Kadaitcha Sung* p. 187 [south-east Qld] '**Gunjibles!**' boonger hissed . . Two uniformed policemen were walking straight across to their table. **1990** Davis et al. *Paperbark* p. 146 [NSW] Nobby was . . accompanied by two young **gungabuls**. **1992** R.L. Ginibi *Real Deadly* p. 26 [Sydney, NSW] There were other pressing things he had to take care of, like keeping out of the way of the **gungabuls**. **1993** E. Crawford *Over my Tracks* p. 137 [western NSW] Someone said "ere comes the **gunjabuls**". The policeman was ridin' a big black high-steppin' horse.

gunjie *noun* [NSW] A police officer. Also **gungie**. See GUNJABAL.

1975 R.J. Merritt *Cake Man* p. 13 [south-west NSW] **Gunjie** is a Kuri word . . means policeman. We say gunjie, it means a white copper animal. Down there at Victoria, now, they got this different word, they say he a berrimaja, the white copper a berrimaja. **1985** *Matto's Koori Writers* p. 10 [Sydney, NSW] Wouldn't it be great if the land was all ours. No government, no **gungies**. No screaming about. **1992** R.L. Ginibi *Real Deadly* p. 27 [NSW] Piss off Nobb, piss off quick, the **gungies** are comin'. **1995** *Koori Mail* Lismore 5 April p. 22/ 4 [NSW] It would be like a black man going to a cemetery and knocking down headstones. I think the **gunjies** . . would put you in gaol, no question.

holiday *noun* [northern Aust.] A time when people live in the bush in a traditional style and away from non-Aboriginal society.

The term originated in the pastoral industry where the 'lay-off' period in the wet season was the time when the Aboriginal communities working on the cattle stations returned to the bush to live more or less in a pre-contact fashion. So the **holiday** became one not only from work but also from the European world, and what had been the central pattern of life now became a holiday from what had become 'real life'.

1915 J.R.B. Love *Aborigines* p. 8 [Flinders Ranges, SA] The rendezvous for the last of the Flinders Ranges tribes is at . . Mt Serles, near Leigh's Creek. Here as many as forty blacks gather at times for a **holiday** to renew old acquaintance, and practice what few of their ancient customs still remain to them. **1978** K. Palmer & C. McKenna *Somewhere Between Black and White* p. 44 [Pilbara, WA] Well you fellows . . perhaps you'd like to take a bit of a **holiday** . . . Think we might have some more business, boss, so we better be off soon. **1978** J. & P. Read *View of the Past* p. 105 [central Aust.] They bin go holiday . . . They go havem **holiday** longa Hanson Creek. **1986** B. Shaw *Countrymen* p. 87 [Kimberley, WA] It wasn't a Big Sunday but a **holiday**.

holiday camp, a camp close in construction and use to a 'traditional' camp.

1986 R.M. Moyle *Alyawarra Music* p. 18 [central Aust.] The present trend . . is for the camp to fragment; single families spend several days at what they call '**holiday camps**'—cleared patches of ground with windbreaks in an area close to water and bush tucker, and away from over-exploited hunting grounds.

holiday rations, European goods such as tea, flour, sugar and tobacco which people would not be able to obtain in the bush.

1991 D.B. Rose *Hidden Histories* p. 155 [Victoria River, north-west NT] We book down longa store . . **holiday rations**.

holiday time, the period when people employed on cattle stations lived in a traditional manner.

1935 M. & E. Durack *All-About* p. 52 [Kimberley, WA] For days there had been a storm brewing in the walkabout camp. In the walkabout camp there usually was . . . Everyone enjoyed them, looked upon them, indeed, as an inseparable part of their **holiday time**. **1992** P. Taylor *Tell it like it Is* p. 89 [Kimberley, WA] We'd get . . hat, trousers, shirt, blanket, boots every year, then **holiday time**, we'd hang 'em all up and go bush. **1991** *Amanbidji Land Claim* 21 Aug. [Amanbidji, north-west NT] They . . returned to their country through mustering activities, returned to their country through **holiday time**, foot-walking with their parents.

home *noun* [NSW] A government-run institution for children removed from their families. Also **homes**.

The **home(s)** referred to in the text are the two NSW children's homes founded early this century to take children removed from their families under the 1905

NSW Aborigines Protection Act. The boys' home was at Kinchela in northern NSW and the girls' home at Cootamundra in the south-west. There the children were trained to be labourers or servants. Significantly for their families, they were brought up with the intention that they would not rejoin the community. The homes were closed in the 1960s. Approximately one in six Aboriginal children in NSW were removed from their families this century; the situation is similar in other States. See also TAKE.

1977 M. Tucker *If Everyone Cared* p. 81 [NSW] When we were naughty, Mother would say, 'I will get the connichman, take you to the **Home** if you don't stop'. 1992 R.L. Ginibi *Real Deadly* p. 40 [NSW] Some were sent to the **homes**, and from boys' homes to the big house (gaol). 1993 J. Janson *Gunjies* p. 39 [NSW] I dont remember Joe . . Narr, you were in the **homes**.

honey bee *noun* [northern Aust.] **1** The European bee; European honey.

1988 J. Harkins *English as 'Two-way' Language* p. 242 [central Aust.] The honey of native bees is usally called *sugarbag*, and the bees themselves are usually called *flies* or *sugarbag flies*, while the introduced bees are always called **honeybee**, never just *bee*, and their honey is called *honeybee sugar*, or just **honeybee**.

2 (In some areas) the native bee.

1985 B. Neidjie *Kakadu Man* p.x [Arnhem Land] Just about daylight e not there / because'll have to give im chance now **honey-bees**. 1991 J. & S. Erbacher *Aborigines of the Rainforest* p. 55 [north Qld] A legend from the Palmer River explains how Ngangkin, the echidna, went out searching for a **honey-bee** nest.

in the white *adverb* [northern Aust.] (Of an Aboriginal person) brought up to be useful to white society.

1987 A. McGrath *Born in the Cattle* p. 61 [NT] The process of being 'reared up' is frequently referred to by Aboriginal station women of the 1920's and 1930's. Winnie Chapman spoke of being 'reared up **in the white**', or assimilated as a presentable domestic.

Jacky *noun* A person subservient to whites. Also **jackie, jacky-boy.**
Abbreviation of JACKY JACKY.

1970 *Koorier* (Melbourne) Vol. 1 no. 13 p. 24 [Vic.] Don't become a **Jackie** (Uncle Tom) for the sake of a few lousy dollars. For God's sake, don't put our noble race of people in a degrading situation by being so undignified as to take part in the white man's coming re-enactment of Captain Cook's landing. 1972 *Identity* (Sydney) Nov. p. 28 While setting about the task like a good '**jackie**' I began to think. (It would have been a shock to my boss if he found out I could think.) 1973 K.J. Gilbert *Because White Man'll Never Do It* p. 18 [NSW] As the blacks are quick to point out, you don't get to be a councillor unless you are a good **jacky** who is totally under the manager's thumb. 1975 R.J. Merritt *Cake Man* (1978) p. 34 [south-west NSW] You know what, Rube . . about me, I ain't never stuck up no white man, and I ain't done not one thing in my whole life is brave. All my life, all I ever done was be a **jacky-boy.** 1982 J. Davis *Kullark* p. 36 [south-west WA] Who are you calling a **Jacky**? The Jackies today are the educated ones like you. 1985 J. Miller *Koori* p. 156 [NSW] The popular Press of Australia makes a joke of us by presenting silly and out-of-date drawings and jokes of '**Jacky**' or 'Binghi', which have educated city-dwellers and young Australians to look upon us as sub-human.

Jacky Jacky *noun* **1** A person who is subservient to whites; an UNCLE TOM. The name is sometimes used as an archetype of this kind of person. See JACKY.

Both **jacky jacky** (first recorded in 1845) and **jacky** (1890) have been used by non-Aboriginal people in Australian English as stereotyping nicknames for an Aboriginal person. The word probably comes from the personal name *Jack*, which can be used as a generic name for a person and was also used in the nineteenth century for a labourer, an odd-job man. The reduplication as **Jacky Jacky** may be from Aboriginal use, being influenced by this practice in Aboriginal languages, or as a parody by whites of Aboriginal linguistic characteristics.

1960 *Realist* (Sydney) ii. p. 10 [NSW?] White men that call us all '**Jacky-Jacky**' are no good white men. **1963** D.E. Barwick *Little More than Kin* p. 65 [Vic.] They . . sometimes become annoyed that the shyness and ignorance of these Gippsland people confirm the stereotype of 'all dark people being **Jacky-Jackys**'. **1977** J. Barker *Two Worlds* p. 59 Now that I was able to read I found that the *Bulletin* and newspapers were full of derogatory stories about blacks and '**Jacky Jacky**'. **1990** S. Watson *Kadaitcha Sung* p. 250 [south-east Qld] I would choose death for myself rather than life as a **Jacky-Jacky**. **1995** D. Hodge *Did you meet any Malagas?* p. 69 [northern NT] I may dress shabbily but it shocks them because they see you with bare feet and they think: 'Oh yeah, just a **jacky-jacky**'. And they get quite a shock because I articulate this very pointed argument back at them.

jacky-jacky talk, speech patterns which seem to present Aboriginal people in a stereotypical light, or are associated with an inferior status.

1985 *Aboriginal History* (Canberra) 9:1, p. 132 [NSW] People who knew the rain-maker react adversely to Cherbury's account as making him speak '**Jacky-Jacky talk**'.

2 A person who is a helper or a drudge for others.

This sense is a comment on the social situation that prevailed when the term was in use; it was the Aboriginal people who were in the subservient, exploited role.

1992 R.L. Ginibi *Real Deadly* p. 55 [NSW] Someone had to look after the house, feed the chooks, and also look after the gardens. Mary was the '**Jacky Jacky**' for them.

kartiya *noun* [north-west Aust.] A white person, white people. Also **cardiah**, **cuddyair**, **cudeha**, **gadeja**, **gadia**, **gadya**, **kardia**.

The term is used widely by Aboriginal people in the Kimberley to refer to white people, when speaking Aboriginal English, Kriol or local Aboriginal languages such as Gooniyandi, Jaru and Walmajarri. The original language and sense of the word are unknown. The various forms in which this word has been recorded testify to the difficulties of representing the sound systems of Aboriginal languages in English. For a discussion of this problem, see the Introduction.

1927 M. Terry *Through Land of Promise* p. 174 **Cardiah** (white man) sit down longa house? **1972** E. Kolig *Bi:n and Gadeja* p. 5 Traditionally, the term **gadeja** does not appear to have been used in any other sense than that of 'European'. **1976** C.D. Mills *Hobble Chains and Greenhide* p. 87 [north-west NT] The reason most '**cuddyairs**' find trouble in this country with the blacks is that they're either muckin' about with their wimmin, or quizzin' 'em about their ceremonials. **1978** J. & P. Read *View of the Past* p. 233 [north-west NT] Aboriginal people sit back now . . not them to go all the way there to meet **gadya** way of life. **1985** *Bulletin* (Sydney) 22 Oct. p. 17/1 Frank Hardy should reside at Wattie Creek . . , that is if the Gurindji will accept the '**Cudeha**' in their community. In the past they have expressed a desire not to have whites there. **1987** R.M. & C.H. Berndt *End of an Era* p. 81 Why should we breed more people for **kardia** or *kardiya* (Europeans) to use the way they use us? **1988** H. Ross

Community Social Impact p. 31 [Kimberley, WA] Stop every **kartiya** doing a cruel thing on a blackfellow. **1991** *Amanbidji Land Claim* 21 Aug. I love to talk **Gadia** language, you know.

kitty kitty *noun* A kid, a young goat. See also PIGGY PIGGY.

1936 M. & E. Durack *Chunuma* p. 12 [Kimberley, WA] Me got to grow 'm up wallaby, steal 'm milk b'longa **kitty-kitty**. **1985** *Lang. in Central Aust.* iv. p. 19 When people, particularly old people, use English or Aboriginal English words in Warumungu, they sometimes pronounce them like Warumungu words. Some English words are repeated or 'reduplicated' in Warumungu. But usually the word is also reduplicated in Aboriginal English. Many of the (mostly animals), have /i/ added, or /u/ if the vowel of the English word is /u/ . . **kiti-kiti**, kid; nani-nani, piki-piki, pig.

know *verb* [Chiefly northern Aust.] Be acquainted with, understand, know about.

All of the examples refer to **knowing** (or not knowing) things, concepts or situations from the European world. This may be an accident of the written nature of the evidence, but it also may give an insight into the sense of alienation, the sense of the disruption of the *known* world caused by the event of colonisation.

1978 J. & P. Read *View of the Past* p. 159 [Groote Eylandt, NT] First time . . old people didn't **know** the Europeans see. **1978** J. & P. Read *View of the Past* p. 158 [northern NT] They don't **know** tea and sugar. He want to stay in the bush . . eat bush tucker. **1988** *We have Survived* Poster [Arnhem Land] Captain Cook was around during the time of Satan. Everybody knows Captain Cook. Old people, not young people. You've got to have a lot of learning to **know** Captain Cook. More culture. I can sing it now for this bark painting. This is the way his song goes. **1989** M. Edmunds *They Get Heaps* p. 29 [Roebourne, north-west WA] When they settle down, Aborigine **know** this white skin, they got plenty food now, they find out. **1990** A. Pring (ed.) *Women of the Centre* p. 154 [central Aust.] I nearly got hit by a car. I didn't **know** the cars. **1991** D.B. Rose *Hidden Histories* p. 80 [north-west WA] And they (Europeans) started separating people when they started to ask people: 'You want to come out (and) work?' 'No, I can't come work. I don't **know**.' **1995** M. Brady *Giving away the Grog* p. 133 [northern SA] Whitefella boss, Madura way, give me drink. I dont **know** drink.

lohan *noun* [south-east Vic.] A white person, white people. Also **loan**, **loon**.

From *lun*, 'a legendary creature', in the languages of the Gippsland area of Victoria.

1880 Fison & Howitt *Kamilaroi & Kurnai* p. 248 [south-east Vic.] The **lo-an** when arrived, was recognised as a 'Mrart' . . . When the Kurnai first beheld white men . . exclaimed, Lo-an! Lo-an! **1904** A.W. Howitt *Native Tribes S.-E. Aust.* p. 390 [south-east Vic.] The *Mrarts* answered questions put to them, as to the movements of the Brajerak and the **Lohan** (white men). **1934** P. Leason *Last of Vict. Aborigines* p. 5 [Lake Tyers, south-east Vic.] The younger people of Lake Tyers know little more of the Lakes dialect than two words: **Loons** (white men—tourists) and Kgunnai (blackfellow). **1963** D. E. Barwick *Little More than Kin* p. 21 [south-east Vic.] They use only two categories: Aboriginal (*Kuri* or 'the dark people'), and white (*gaba* or **loan**). **1963** D.E. Barwick *Little More than Kin* p. 22 [south-east Vic.] In Gippsland the dialect word **loan** . . or *loonies*, is still used. **1980** P. Pepper *You Are What You Make Yourself* p. 8 [south-east Vic.] The **lohans** have come here to our country and they're not gonna go away.

lost *adjective* Of the generation removed from their families in the 1920s and 1930s. See also HOME, TAKE.

The practice of child removal, essentially for the purposes of acculturation, occurred in all States and throughout the history of occupation. The effect on the community of the removal of a certain generation has been particularly traumatic. **1988** C. Mattingley & K. Hampton (eds) *Survival in Our Own Land* p. 215 [SA] This generation of children, the children of the 1920s, and 1930s, are still known as 'the **lost** children'.

maluka *noun* The person in charge, the BOSS. Also **malaga, maluga**.

From the Djingulu language of the central Northern Territory *marluga* 'old man'.

1905 Mrs A. Gunn *Little Black Princess* p. 3 [northern NT] I was 'the Missus' from the homestead, and with the Boss, or '**Maluka**' (as the blacks always called him), was 'out bush', camping near the river. **1928** 'M. Mills' *Montforts* p. 238 'You'd better come and see the **Maluka**.' 'What's that?' ventured Raoul. 'It's aboriginal for headmaster.' **1937** *Oceania* VII. p. 311 The widespread North Australian term **maluka** or **maluga** implies both status and age. **1954** T. Ronan *Vision Splendid* p. 55 To the blacks he was just as often Old Man or **Maluka** as Storekeeper. **1978** R.A.F. Webb *Brothers in Sun* p. 173 As one cheerful Aboriginal said, when he saw one of the Brothers scratching his head over a broken-down Gypsy, '**Maluka** (Boss), 'im all bugger-up proper. No more little bit, eh!' **1994** R. Thomas *Roads Cross* p. 47 [Kimberley, WA] Well that far all I can say **maluka**. [Well that's all I can say, boss].

The word is now used by both Aboriginal and non-Aboriginal people in Darwin, to mean a male, without reference to race. See GAMMON for another example of a word that has entered the speech of the whole community.

1995 *Oral History Journal* no. 17 p. 20 [northern NT] **Malaga** is a word given by the Yangman and Wardaman Aboriginal tribes of northern Australia, and its traditional meaning was old man or elder. It is often heard today, particularly in schoolyards and in everyday parlance, as a reference to a guy or fella.

marta-marta *noun* [WA] A person of Aboriginal and non-Aboriginal descent. Also **mada-mada, mudamuda**.

From *marta*, the word for 'blood' in a number of languages in the Pilbara region of north-western WA. The reduplication of the word is here an attenuation of the sense (as opposed to being an intensification of the word as in DIFFERENT DIFFERENT), so it follows the sense of the generally now obsolete expression *half-blood* (as opposed to a *full-blood*) in that a person is seen as having less Aboriginal blood. The term is now generally considered offensive and would only be applied to someone else, never to oneself.

1964 P. Dalton *Broome* p. 130 [Broome, WA] He was never initiated as a boy . . he is really a '**mada-mada**'. **1978** K. Palmer & C. McKenna *Somewhere Between Black and White* p. 70 [Pilbara, WA] He was a young **mudamuda** fellow who had come from further west. **1980** *Mikurrunya* (Strelley) 23 Apr. p. 12 [north-west WA] They said it was a group of **marta-marta** elected by marta-marta and working for the government. **1991** D. Pilkington (Nugi Garimara) *Caprice – a stockman's Daughter* p. 39 [Pilbara, WA] I want **Muda Muda** (half-caste) boy—same as my girl.

migloo *noun* [Qld] A white person; white people. Also **meggooloo, migaloo, migeloo, migloo**.

From the Mayi-Kutuna language of the Leichhardt River area of north Queensland *miguln* 'a person'. It has been borrowed in this form by many languages of the area.

1891 *Queenslander* (Brisbane) 11 May p. 703/3 [Qld] Murry, a black person; **meggooloo**, a white person. **1978** B. Rosser *This is Palm Island* p. 20 [north Qld] I could see he's not a

migaloo. 1981 H. Reynolds *Other Side of Frontier* p. 3 [north Qld] She looked at me not as an individual, or as a male, or a well meaning academic, but as a white man, a **migloo**, with a fear that was not personal at all but historical and communal and unforgettable. 1983 *Dark Side of the News* p. 160 [north Qld] By the time my grandmother was sent to Palm she was given a **migloo** name from her tribal name which is Muragooloo. 1990 S. Watson *Kadaitcha Sung* p. 41 [south-east Qld] A lost and lonely white prospector had been relieved of his body and his mind so the renegade Kadaitcha could walk more easily in the camp of the **Migloo**. 1994 M.Walsh & C. Yallop *Lang. & Culture Aboriginal Aust.* p. 185 [south-east Qld] Nancy's head was spinning. She hated all their questions. **Migeloos** ask so many questions all the time. It's dangerous to answer them, and it's dangerous not to answer them.

mish *noun* Abbreviation of MISSION.

1991 L.M. Wilkinson *Aboriginality* p. 197 [Vic.] The Framlingham people refer to their home as 'Fram', 'the **mish**' or 'the settlement'.

mission *noun* [Aust. but chiefly in south-east Aust.] An Aboriginal settlement, which may or may not once have been a religious institution. Also used as an adjective.

A person is described as living *on* or *off* a mission, rather than *in* or *at*. The name derived from the original purpose of many Aboriginal settlements—as a mission of one of the various denominations of the Christian Church. When the government and later the communities themselves took over the management the name often remained, or the name was applied to communities that had in fact never been **missions**. The word is also used in general Australian English but has been included here because of its cultural importance in Aboriginal history and society. These institutions, especially in southern Australia, have been very significant as places both of oppression and of cultural survival. Within **missions**, people were offered refuge from the violence of the frontier; often however the price of safety was cultural oppression, especially of aspects of culture such as language and ceremony. **Missions** often provided the place where numbers of Aboriginal people were congregated together, thus unintentionally preserving cultural and community identity against the assimilationist intentions of the majority society.

1979 K. Dhougarle *There's More to Life* p. 24 [Sydney, NSW] We used to call this mill the La Perouse **Mission**, there were so many of us (working there). 1980 B. Sansom *The Camp at Wallaby Cross* p. 121 [northern NT] The poisoner was not one of the mob but an outsider, a **mission** man. 1987 B. Lunney *Mixed Bag* p. 56 Teach him little bit not swear like that alla bout us **mission** boys. 1988 R. Langford *Dont Take Your Love to Town* p. 3 [northern NSW] Dad . . delivered them to the **mission** houses. The houses were four-roomed, no lining, open fire for cooking, and the windows were wooden slats that you prop open. 1989 M. Jackomos Life on Aboriginal Reserve (typescript) p. 5 [Vic.] Sometimes the red **mission** truck would go to Echuca 19 miles away. 1992 R.L. Ginibi *Real Deadly* p. 64 [north coast, NSW] A lot of **mission** folk laboured on that property.

mission ration, an allowance paid to Aboriginal people working on the **mission**, or sent out as labourers. It was below award wages and could be docked if the manager of the mission felt there were reasons to do so.

1978 K. Gilbert *People are Legends* p. 8 Whites didn't pay us wages in those days. Gave us 7/6 **mission ration** a week.

Missions became culturally identifiable places, both for Aboriginal and non-Aboriginal people. In the time when missions were being run by white supervisors, there were varying attitudes held by Aboriginal people both on and off the **mission**. For Aboriginal people living outside the mission, **mission people** might be seen as those who had 'sold out' to non-Aboriginal society. Those raised on missions often had ambivalent feelings about the period, especially on looking back. Terms such as **mission times** encapsulated a range of experiences and feelings, especially to do with survival of culture and lack of personal freedom, but also to do with strong community feelings and memories of good times.

1964 E.G. Docker *Simply Human Beings* p. 6 [western NSW] The station aborigines living under the eye of the . . Board are naturally regarded as . . assimilable prospects. To the people camped over by the Namoi they are simply 'bludgers', 'Depot boys', '**Mission** boots' they are called. Not enough spunk to stand up to European officialdom and spit in its eye. **1964** P. Dalton *Broome* p. 151 [north-west WA] These **mission** girls . . are the worst of the lot. **1990** P. Read *Charles Perkins* p. 208 Naturally there were important differences between north and south, **mission** and city. **1991** *Action Rev.* Oct. p. 13 He told the Assembly about his own background as a **Mission** raised Aboriginal who had lost his language. **1991** L.M. Wilkinson *Aboriginality* p. 216 [Vic.] This may have been the influence of both parents who were raised during the **mission times**. **1992** P. Taylor *Tell it like it Is* p. 31 [SA] In fact, it is going back to the **Mission days** mentality, when we were told whether or not we could practise our cultural ways. **1994** R. & J. Huggins *Auntie Rita* p. 132 [south-east Qld] There's an old saying, 'You can take the Blackfella out of the **mission**, but you can't take the mission out of the Blackfella.' That's so true. Our custom of sharing will never die out as long as we have relations.

missus *noun* A form of address to a white woman, not necessarily an employer.

As with BOSS, its use is more common among the older generation and reflects the power imbalance of the two societies.

1880 (Mrs) J. Smith *Booandik Tribe* p. 48 Very good **missus**—very good massa . . learn un drual Booandik like blackfellow. **1987** A. McGrath *Born in the Cattle* p. 107 [northern NT] Cattle people incorporated the learning experiences offered by the station into the necessary regimen of training which made girls women and boys men . . This is probably one of the reasons for the specially valued relationship with the trainer who is usually described as 'my really boss', or '**missus**' because he [she] 'grew me up'. **1987** A. McGrath *Born in the Cattle* p. 61 [northern NT] When we was a kid we couldn't even talk properly, but the **missus** to tell me fellers: 'You gotta speak! Talk proper English you naughty girls—you'll get a smack!' **1991** D. Pilkington (Nugi Garimara) *Caprice – a stockman's Daughter* p. 39 [Pilbara, WA] Lucy's Auntie Minda . . admonished her for letting 'the **missus**' try to make Peggy into a Wudgebella Wandi (white girl).

monaych *noun* [WA] A police officer; the police. Also **manatj, monarch.**

From the Nyungar language of south-west Western Australia, *manatj*, 'black cockatoo'. The dark uniforms with the peaked caps once worn by the West Australian police probably gave rise to this name.

1961 N. Gare *Fringe Dwellers* p. 35 [south-west WA] Skippy gets off. An ya know the first thing e says ta them **monarch**? E turns round on em an yelps, 'An now ya can just gimme back that bottle.' **1968** W.H. Douglas *Aboriginal Language of south-west Aust.* p. 23 [south-west WA] There are also other words which can be used for 'policeman', **manatj** is the most common term, but most people also know *yutila*. **1975** R. Beilby *Brown Land Crying* p. 10 Myra was terrified. The coppers! **Monaych**! The native word contained a history of oppression: the Men with Chains! **1979** N. Braham *Dwarf* p. 28 When I'm broke I'm just Tommy Caylun, the boong, shuffling down the street, with an eye out for the **monaych**. **1981** A. Weller *Day of Dog* p. 2 [south-west WA] Nuh, gotta go. See Mum. Yeah, well, look out for the **monaych**, budda . . Ard luck if 'e goes back, first day out. **1986** J. Davis *No Sugar* p. 29 [south-west WA] **Manatj** grab us like that. Bastards.

munanga *noun* [northern NT] A white man, a BOSS. Also **mununka**.

Munanga, 'white person' is widespread among the languages of the Arnhem Land region.

1977 *Black News Service* Nov. p. 7 [NT] All the council workers which are now handling all the jobs D.A.A. **munanga** used to do, have been working well for very little money. **1977** K. Maddock *Two Laws in One Community* p. 13 A blackfellow (biji) is a person of Aboriginal descent . . . A whitefellow (**munanga**) is a person of European descent. **1978** J. & P. Read *View of the Past* p. 236 [northern NT] That **munanga** . . bin learnem me, and I bin stop here. **1978** J. & P. Read *View of the Past* p. 244 [northern NT] Where do they keep the dynamite. **Munanga** house? Yeah, munanga house. **1983** *Yulngu* (Katherine) Mar. p. 4 [northern NT] We are printing more and more copies of the Magazine with each issue and getting to more and more people both Aboriginal and **munanga**/kardiya. **1995** M. Brady *Giving away the Grog* p. 82 [northern NT] I explain to them and tell them 'before you gonna come here you gotta see the sign there. You know you're trespassing, that in **mununka** way, you know, and I got every right to kick you out of here.'

myall *adjective* [northern Aust.] Ignorant, especially of European concerns, some-times thereby implying a more TRADITIONAL person, but with negative rather than positive connotations; stupid. See also BAREFOOT and WILD. Also used as a noun.

From the Dharuk language of the Sydney area, *mayal*, 'a stranger'. **Myall** was used in the pidgin of nineteenth-century New South Wales by Aboriginal people to describe foreign Aboriginal groups and by the colonists in a related sense to de-scribe Aboriginal people who were unfamiliar with European ways. This use is illustrated by the 1818 and 1830 citations. It travelled with the frontier to areas where it was not known as an Aboriginal language word but was used by both black and white to refer to people outside the frontier. The recorded historical evidence is generally of non-Aboriginal use but it has survived into contemporary Aboriginal English with the related sense of 'ignorance', especially of European matters. It is also found in contemporary if somewhat old-fashioned general Australian English use to describe TRADITIONAL people. As with WILD, **myall** was also used to describe plants and animals which were either native to Australia or had become feral.

1818 J. Holt *Memoirs (1838)* Vol. 11 p. 148 [NSW?] About fifty natives collected round his house. They are very inquisitive, and said to me, 'Name you? You are **miel**'. That is to say, 'You are a stranger, what is your name?' **1830** R. Dawson *Present State Aust.* p. 103 [NSW?] The fear of meeting strangers, or **Myall** pellows, as they call them. **1983** P. Nathan & D.L. Japanangka *Settle Down Country* p. 17 [central NT] Does the researcher think I'm **myall** (stupid). She knows the answers. What is she asking me these things for? **1984** E. Roughsey *An Aboriginal Mother Tells* p. 2 [Mornington Island, northern Qld] My people never were **myall**, as most people consider we were. **1986** B. Shaw *Countrymen* p. 82 **Myall** fellers, jackeroos, would just sit down on the horse and drown the horse too. **1987** R.M. & C.H. Berndt *End of an Era* p. 123 But some took no notice of any of these, saying they themselves were only ignorant '**myall**-buggas' who knew nothing about such things. **1987** *Junga Yimi*

Yuendumu Sept. p. 26 Men got to sit with women and kids. Warlpiri got to sit with Pintubu . . . Smart Man got to sit with **Myall**.

nicki nicki *noun* [northern Aust.] Coarse chewing tobacco once used as a trade tobacco and as part of the 'wages' on northern cattle stations. Also **nicky, niki-niki**.

Possibly from an Aboriginal pronunciation of *New Guinea twist* or *niggerhead* (both similar forms of tobacco) by reduplication of the first element in either name. Reduplication is a feature of both Aboriginal languages and Aboriginal English.

1938 X. Herbert *Capricornia* p. 137 [northern NT] It was a parcel from a Chinese store, containing . . one pound of **niki-niki**. **1940** W. Hatfield *Into (Great?) Unfenced* p. 101 [northern NT] All they get's flour and tea an' sugar, an' a stick of **Nicky-nick**. **1964** M. Reay *Aborigines Now* p. 11 It was not usually mentioned that he would prostitute his women for a plug of '**nicky**' or a bottle of cheap wine. **1976** J. Mirritji *My People's Life* p. 59 [Arnhem Land] So we went off to the store and got . . two packs of **nikiniki** tobacco (flaked pipe tobacco). **1983** P. Nathan & D.L. Japanangka *Settle Down Country* p. 50 [central NT] He gave them bullocks meat, **nicky**, jam, clothes and soap. **1986** K. Walker *We are Going* p. 140 We used to pay them in tobacco. There were two sorts. One was like a licorice stick and was called 'Nigger Twist', the other was a small plug of black treacle-like tobacco called '**Nikki-Nikki**'. **1988** S. Dunlop *All that Rama Rama Mob* p. 78 [central Aust.] He yells, screams for tobacco, that's the main thing for him, that **nikinik**, that square block for chewing, but people only have that Log Cabin here, for smokes.

niffer *noun* [northern and central Aust.] A sniffer. See also SNIFFING.

From an Aboriginal pronunciation of *sniffer*.

1988 S. Dunlop *All that Rama Rama Mob* p. 114 [central Aust.] My family, living out there looking after homeland, keeping '**niffers**' out there.

no clothes *noun phrase* [northern Aust.] Without clothing, naked, as people were in the time before the British invasion.

Aboriginal society before the European occupation did of course use forms of clothing, but the opposition of *naked* and *clothed* did not have the same meaning as in European society. There, clothing that covers most of the body has been one way in which the 'savage' is distinguished from the 'civilised' person; different kinds of clothing then mark different strata of society. Aboriginal people quickly became conscious of the significance of clothing in non-Aboriginal society, so that the comment **no clothes** encompasses not just clothing but unfamiliarity with European life and European expectations. See also BAREFOOT, MYALL.

1889 *Jrnl. & Proceedings of Royal Soc. NSW* Vol. XXXIII p. 480 What for white-fellow wantum black woman dance likeum that? you askum white lubras jump about mid **no clothes**: you hear what she yabber yabber. **1985** B. Neidjie *Kakadu Man* p. 34 [Arnhem Land] Should be written way Aborigine was live. That floodplain . . my father, my mother, my grandfather all used to hunt there. **No clothes** then. **1991** D.B. Rose *Hidden Histories* p. 37 [north-west NT] That's the police station. Police Hole . . . And policeman was working them people, Aboriginal people. **No clothes**. Just myall times.

old *adjective* Aboriginal; but with an added sense that it is part of Aboriginal culture that belongs to the time before Europeans. See EARLY.

Often the context implies that the present generation is in some sense cut off from that which is **old**, that the **old** ways are no longer a fully functioning part of present society, at least on a day to day basis, although they may be of great value culturally and spiritually. See also OLD (Chapter 1) for another related sense; both have the concept of meaning being derived from the past, rather than the present.

1884 *Jrnl. Royal Anthrop. Inst. Great Brit. & Ireland* Reprint 1971 XIII. p. 195 [Vic.] The 'old' law' which divided the Woi-worng tribe into two classes, *Crow* and *Eaglehawk*, was .. brought down from Bunjil by the wizards. **1964** E.G. Docker *Simply Human Beings* p. 17 [western NSW] There is .. no particular pride or pleasure in knowing the 'old lingo'. **1971** *New Dawn* (Haymarket) May p. 2 I can go up the mountain. I can turn around and ask, in the **old** language, and they'll answer. **1977** A.K. Eckermann *Group Origin and Identity* p. 298 [south-east Qld] They believe that their awareness of the 'old ways' and contact with the 'old people' provides them with extra insights that are not shared with other Aboriginal people. **1988** P. Taylor *After 200 Years* p. 14 Sunday is usually the only day when we have a big cook up of the **old** foods. **1990** *Pemulwuy Dilemma* p. 8 [Sydney, NSW] Most of these sites have a guardian. An old man, one of the ancients who is always in the area of the sites and looks after it and when you go to a site you must always ask the permission of those ancient ones before you go into it. All these sites belong to the ancient ones, the **old** ones. **1992** *Puggana News* (Launceston) Dec. p. 8 [Tas.] As we all know, if the **old** fellas didn't do what they were told by whites, they were shot. **1993** D. Hodge *Did you meet any Malagas?* p. 62 [northern NT] I don't have any say as to how that cut body cicatrices is going to be executed. It could be the **old** way with a stone flint, or it could be with a modern scalpel from the clinic. . . But I suspect it's going to be the old way.

old law, the belief system that governed Aboriginal Australia before the occupation and is still present in Aboriginal understanding today. Also with the additional sense that it no longer influences day to day life. Also **old rule**.

1955 *Oceania* Dec. p. 205 [NSW] It would be tenuous to argue that the present custom among late adolescent girls of going away to work is rooted in the **Old Rule**. **1958** J. Becket *Study of a Mixed Blood Aboriginal Minority* p. 56 [NSW] Today those few old people who still believe in the 'old rule', keep their disapproval to themselves. **1991** L.M. Wilkinson *Aboriginality* p. 215 [south-west Vic.] There is some evidence that the 'old law' is still used with regard to marriage.

old people *noun* People of the older generations, those living and those passed on, holders of traditional ways of living and wisdom, and spiritual guides for those who come after.

See OLD in the previous entry. In the early use, there is sometimes an added sense in which **old people** are those of the full descent, as opposed to their mixed race descendants. This sense is now not as common.

1938 X. Herbert *Capricornia* p. 324 [northern Aust.] Let's consider the **Old People** for a jiffy . . . They're starved and sickened and kicked and stupefied and generally jiggered out of recognition. **1949** *Oceania* Sydney Dec. p. 106 [Vic.] What would the **old people** think? There's — living with — and he's her blood uncle. **1964** K. Willey *Eaters of the Lotus* p. 30 He is a half-caste who, years ago, made his decision to go with 'the **old people**', instead of adopting the white man's way. **1977** *Black Liberation* Brisbane July p. 8 [south-east Qld] Don't be afraid—our **old people** are with us. **1983** *Cent. Aust. Land Rights News* Alice Springs Autumn p. 3 [central Aust.] **Old people** been living there. Grandfather and father, we been in that country ever since sacred sites. **1985** B. Rosser *Dreamtime Nightmares* p. 35 [north Qld] If you ask one of them, they'd know. They're the **old people**. They could tell you what tribe I belong to. **1988** C.Mattingley & K. Hampton *Survival in Our Own Land* p. 4 [northern SA] They took our children and educated them in their ways, deliberately teaching them to forget the ways of the **Old People**. 1990 O. Noonuccal *Aust. Legends and Landscapes* p. 127 [Tas.] My father reckons that Ria Warrawah, the sea spirit, made our **Old People** stop eatin' scale fish. 1994 *Encyclop. Abor. Aust.* p. 485 The Kow Swamp remains were found within the boundaries of the Echuca community. Consequently, the community . . applied for the return of their ancestral remains. Contrary to what most scientists believe, this call was not based on politics, but on a united belief that the community shared a moral obligation to return their **old people** to their land and, in doing so, restore their dignity.

piki-piki *noun* A pig; pigs; pig (as food), pork. Also **biki-biki, piggy, pig-pig.**

1839 *S. Austral. Rec.* (London) (1840) 1 Feb. p. 22 They [i.e. aborigines] call mutton *sheepy*, and pork **piggy**, and bread *bready*. 1895 H. Reynolds *Other Side of Frontier* (1981) p. 130 [Qld] (*Queenslander* 20th of July, 1895) I think altogether we die soon . . **pig-pig** eat him yams; plum fall down, wild pigs too much eat. 1980 N. Mitchell & J.C. Anderson *Kubara* p. 3 [north Qld] They used to eat *kaya* (dog) . . pussy cat too. **Biki-biki** (pig). They used to get a lot of it out there Maytown. 1985 *Lang. in Central Aust.* iv. p. 19 [central Aust.] Some English words are repeated or 'reduplicated' in Warumungu. But usually the word is also reduplicated in Aboriginal English. Many of the (mostly animals), have /i/ added, or /u/ if the vowel of the English word is /u/ . . . jipi-jipi, sheep; juku-juku, hen; kapi-kapi, calf; kiti-kiti, kid; nani-nani, nannygoat (children's talk); **piki-piki**, pig.

poligmun *noun* Policeman. See BULLIMAN.

From a nineteenth-century Aboriginal pronunciation of *policeman*. For a discussion of pronunciations, see the Introduction.

1975 *Identity* (Sydney) July p. 6 Aborigines also have a novel way of changing European words into Aboriginal, such as policeman becomes **poligmun**.

protect *verb* [southern Aust.] To harass, to hound.

This is the Aboriginal understanding of the word used by governmental authorities to describe the control of Aboriginal society.

1983 *Puggana News* (Launceston) Dec. p. 4 All the tribes have gone . . destroyed by their disgusting sickness, pushed and **protected** from the land of our fathers. 1988 *La Perouse* p. 8 [Sydney, NSW] We were constantly **protected** by a manager who lived on the reserve. The manager would just walk into anyone's house without knocking to inspect it.

Hence **protection** is not understood as it usually is in Australian English.

1982 *Aboriginal Children* New South Wales Family and Children's Services Agency. Aboriginal Children's Research Project p. 2 [NSW] This process has been described in government policies in terms of **protection**, assimilation . . but Aboriginal people view it less euphemistically.

puppy dog *noun* [northern and central Aust.] A dog or dingo, often as an item of food.

1936 M. & E. Durack *Chunuma* p. 35 [Kimberley, WA] White fella . . no more like'm lubra **puppy dog**. 1965 F.G.G. Rose *Wind of Change* p. 128 [central Aust.] He became visibly tired and said that this afternoon he was going out to look for '**puppy-dogs**' (dingoes).

pussy cat *noun* [northern Aust.] A cat, often as an item of food.

1936 M. & E. Durack *Chunuma* p. 35 [Kimberley, WA] White fella . . no more like'm lubra **pussy cat**. 1986 B. Shaw *Countrymen* p. 53 [Kimberley,WA] I don't like snake and **pussy cat**. Pussy cat was something like kangaroo, they reckoned. I've never tasted it. 1989 R.M. Baker *Land is Life* p. 245 [Borroloola, north-east NT] Edna Bob recalls . . the hunting of an animal she had previously not heard of, '**pussy cat**'.

rations *noun* **1** A supply of food and sometimes clothing and tobacco given to groups or communities by governments, religious bodies or private agencies such as cattle stations.

The term originated in the *rations* given to military personnel, and was taken into Australian English to refer to the provisioning of white rural workers and Aboriginal people. It is included here because of the significance of the term in the history of Aboriginal people. As Aboriginal people have moved or been forced into European institutions, rationing has been used as a way of attracting people out of the bush, of keeping them within institutions, and as a means of payment for labour. As the social and economic bases of 'bush life' were eroded, the giving or withholding of **rations** became more and more significant as a form of social control. On MISSIONS, for example, 'troublemakers' could have their **rations** withheld. The nature of the **rations** also had an important effect on people's health. Historically, in most institutions and places of employment such as cattle stations, in all areas of Australia, food **rations** were not adequate to maintain good health, consisting largely of highly refined foods such as white flour and sugar.

1983 *Mankind* Apr. p. 491 [north Qld] We used to have to go to Cooktown for **rations**— blanket *kambi* (clothes) little bit tea, sugar. **1988** C. Mattingley & K. Hampton (eds) *Survival in Our Own Land* p. 130 [SA] They'd just throw some meat down on the wood block for **rations**, with some flour and bacca. **1988** J. Harkins *English as 'Two-way' Language* p. 245 Aboriginal and non-Aboriginal speakers share a set of terms specific to, or with specialised meanings in, the contact situation, which can only be briefly mentioned here. These include terms such as . . *mission, dormitory, camp,* **rations**, *taken away,* (of a child, removed from Aboriginal parents by white authorities). **1991** A. Jackomos & D. Fowell *Living Aboriginal Hist. of Vic.* p. 142 [Vic.] If a mother was caught teaching the culture, they cut the **rations** on them.

ration camp, a camp where all the people are living on rations; probably in this case elderly people unable to work, whose families were elsewhere.

1986 B. Shaw *Countrymen* p. 82 [Kimberley, WA] I saw that floodwater go past Argyle when they had a big mob of blackfellers camping below there in a **ration camp**. They came up in the morning to get their rations and came up every afternoon for work, all the old people.

ration clothes, clothes given out as part of rations. In this case the speaker was ineligible for them as her husband was working.

1989 D. Walker *Me and You* p. 37 [north coast, NSW] They were given **ration clothes** those days but I couldn't get any for my kiddies because they're (sic) father worked.

ration paper, an authority given out by the Welfare for someone to obtain rations.

1986 B. Shaw *Countrymen* p. 114 [Kimberley, WA] Well when we get the **ration paper** from Mrs Welfare we go to the store and get our rations.

2 In some areas **rations** have come to be distinguished from other types of food, so that flour, tea, sugar, etc. is contrasted with TUCKER, bread, cooked meat, etc.

1980 B. Sansom *The Camp at Wallaby Cross* p. 59 [Darwin, NT] You got that **rations** (i.e. stored food) and you got that tucker (i.e. prepared food).

read and write man *noun* [northern Aust.] A person who can read and write.

This term encapsulates the new power relationship created by the presence of non-Aboriginal society, where skills in the new society acquired by younger people have unbalanced the traditional power structure of Aboriginal society, in which older people held the power through their greater knowledge.

1979 *Kimberley Land Council* Derby Jan p. 2 [Kimberley, WA] The meeting agreed to elect .. one old law man and a younger **read and write man.**

rights *noun* **1** An abbreviation of CITIZEN'S RIGHTS.

The *Consorting Act* referred to in the first 1988 citation was one employed in South Australia and other States until about the 1960s to prevent association, particularly sexual association, between people officially classified as 'Aboriginal' and non-Aboriginal people. The intention was to prevent an increase in the numbers of children of mixed Aboriginal and non-Aboriginal descent.

1964 P. Dalton *Broome* p. 82 [north-west WA] Even when my brother, who has **rights** came down from Darwin to visit us, the police followed him like a sheep dog. 1987 *Sydney Morning Herald* 18 Dec. p. 4/3 [NSW] This **rights** committee has launched a 'disgraceful attack' on the assistant counsel .. who was called a 'coconut'. 1988 C. Mattingley & K. Hampton *Survival in Our Own Land* p. 53 [SA] The 'Consorting Act' shits you off. You've got no **rights,** you don't get proper award wages. 1988 *Mosa* (Clayton) no. 2, p. 17 Only if you had an exemption card, and that's when you received your **rights.** 1989 J. Thomson *Reaching Back* p. 45 [north Qld] At the time, they didn't want us to be well educated, not like today .. Not until we got the **rights.** 1989 B. Morris *Domesticating Resistance* p. 211 [northern NSW] 'Getting the **rights**' in 1967 removed many of the discriminatory laws and practices.

2 Rights in relation to land; land rights.

1981 *Kimberley Land Council* (Derby) Mar. p. 21 We're boss for our land, we own it, we got **rights.**

run away *verb* [Chiefly northern Aust.] To leave a European situation, particularly a cattle station.

In the past, Aboriginal people lacked the right of free movement; this was particularly so in the more recent past (up to the 1960s) for Aboriginal people employed on northern Australian cattle stations and those ordered to live on particular settlements, especially in Queensland. People were not permitted to leave without permission, whatever their personal circumstances; if they did so their employer or settlement manager could ask the police to find them and bring them back. There is a similar term in Tok Pisin, from Papua New Guinea, *ronewe,* meaning 'run away, desert, remove oneself'. All the citations following refer to people absconding from cattle stations. The first three are from the same work but they are quotations from three different speakers from different areas of the Northern Territory.

1978 J. & P. Read *View of the Past* p. 162 [Groote Eylandt, NT] All right, we're going to go out and **run away** to the bush today. 1978 J. & P. Read *View of the Past* p. 45 [NT] Oh, just people, now eh, different people. People bin **runaway** eh? 1978 J. & P. Read *View of the Past* p. 261 [NT] You got to followem, that native people, what they bin **run away** in the bush. 1983 F. Gale *We are Bosses Ourselves* p. 74 [Borroloola, north-east NT] He **run away** alonga a big city . . . He can't think about mother, send them money, clothes, nothing. 1988 H. Ross

Community Social Impact Assessment p. 46 [Kimberley, WA] We bin sort of work our head very quick, **run away**. **1991** D.B. Rose *Hidden Histories* p. 167 [Victoria River, north-west NT] Settle down, you know. Even that, some old people got a hiding too from white man. Even with a stick. We were frightened we might get shot. Some people used to just sneak away, **run away**, away from that man.

Repetition is used to create emphasis. This use is probably influenced by Aboriginal languages, where reduplication is used to intensify the expression. See also DIFFERENT DIFFERENT, HALF HALF.

1991 D.B. Rose *Hidden Histories* p. 163 [north-west NT] That's one boy, he ran away. Ran away from every drover, you know. He was **run away, run away, run away, run away** every time . . I said: 'Look, my boy. Don't run away. Don't run away. Don't run away . . . Them drovers might turn round and shoot you.'

runner *noun* A white person used to obtain alcohol at the time when most Aboriginal people were unable to purchase it legally.

1988 P. Taylor *After 200 Years* p. 249 [south-west WA] You were Aboriginal regardless of how light-skinned you were, so we had to use a white **runner** to go to the pub. **1989** J. Thomson *Reaching Back* p. 4 [northern Qld] And in those days they used to call them a runner, the man who runs messages. **1991** A. Jackomos & D. Fowell *Living Aboriginal Hist. of Vic.* p. 26 [Vic.] There might be a few Gubbs hanging around the Kooris too in those days. They would be the **runners**. They would go up to town and come back with a couple of bottles of port in a sugar bag.

sheepy *noun* [Aust. in the historical period, now chiefly northern Aust.] A sheep. Most of the recorded evidence is nineteenth-century. Also **yepeyepe**.

Because of the structure of Aboriginal languages, some English names ending in a consonant have had a vowel sound added. See also BULLOCKY etc. and the Introduction for a discussion of pronunciations.

1839 *S. Austral. Rec.* (London) (1840) 1 Feb. 22 They [i.e. aborigines] call mutton **sheepy**, and pork *piggy*, and bread *bready*. **1841** *Port Phillip Patriot* p. 4/5 [Vic.?] The villains laughed at and mocked us, roaring out 'plenty **sheepy**', 'plenty jumbuck', (another name of theirs for sheep). **1993** G. Koch *Kaytetye Country* p. 26 [central NT] And they bin keep teachinem for language. For English Tell him, tobacco, this sort of thing. Like, woman. Not woman, this lubra, and anything tucker—flour, tea—nannygoat, **yepeyepe** (sheep)—not sheep—*yepeyepe*.

sheepy shepherd, a shepherd.

1981 B. Lennon *Yarns Around the Firebucket* p. 26 [northern SA] 'Right', said Bill. 'I remember the days when we were kids and our parents had a '**sheepy-shepherd**' job. There were no motor bikes or horses for us. The whole family took out a flock of sheep and minded them all day'.

sitting down money *noun* [northern and central Aust.] Social security payments. Also **sit down money**.

From SIT DOWN (see Chapter 4) 'to stay in a place for significant length of time', the association possibly being that money was being given for 'being' rather than 'doing'; it is probably also associated with sedentary government settlements.

1985 *Stories from Yuendumu* S.A.L. Literary Workshop n.p. [Yuendumu, central Aust.] They will just be getting '**sitting down money**' and running away into town chasing grog. **1986** B.

Shaw *Countrymen* p. 281 [Kimberley, WA] He used to get money. . child money and **sitting down money. 1989** G. Knepfer *Nursing for Life* p. 56 '**Sitting-down money**' (or social Security cheques) were being handed out. **1990** *Sydney Morning Herald* 2 June p. 71/3 After the dole cheques, the '**sit-down money**', are handed out.

sniff *verb* To sniff petrol.

Petrol sniffing by children and young people has been a serious social problem in some northern and central Australian communities.

1987 *Junga Yimi* Yuendumu June p. 16 [Yuendumu, central Aust.] We are working down in the Ernabella area now where they have lots of kids **sniffing** and sometimes dying. **1988** S. Dunlop *All that Rama Rama Mob* p. 66 [central Aust.] Petrol for years, then head, brains finish . . . Start **sniffing** little, mind becomes like bullet lid.

Hence **sniffing business**, matters concerning petrol sniffing.

1985 R. Gluck *Treatment and Prevention of Substance Abuse* p. 162 [NT] Kids get into trouble—**sniffing business** and court.

take *verb* To remove a child from its family and community, to be raised outside its culture, either by the government, or by private concerns with the tacit consent of the government. Also **take away**.

Child removal, for the purpose of changing Aboriginal culture, has been a characteristic of the European response to Aboriginal society since Governor Macquarie's 'Orphan School' opened in 1814 for the re-education of Aboriginal children. In the twentieth century this was made a major policy in most States of Australia and there is scarcely an Aboriginal family in Australia that does not have a family member who was 'taken away'. In many cases, it was children of fair-skinned appearance who were removed, partly because it was felt that they would assimilate more easily, and partly because of the genetic theory of the time which associated skin colour with supposedly inherited, supposedly superior 'European' mental and moral attributes.

1984 *Cummeragunga* Aboriginal Hist. Program n.p. [Vic.] And when they **took** Marg Tucker I think they took my Aunty too. **1986** *Now and Then* (Aboriginal History Program) p. 16 [Vic.] I believe I was the last person **taken** from the [Framlingham] forest. **1986** *White Invasion Diary* Invasion Diary Collective 12 May [SA] Two men in suits came to **take** the children **away** . . . They pulled the youngest child, my sister and put her in the car. **1991** *Aboriginal History* (Canberra) VX. i. The police used to come along and grab all the half-castes . . the kids in the camp, they used to grab 'em . . . They wanna **take** all the half-caste babies all along the coast. **1991** A. Jackomos & D. Fowell *Living Aboriginal Hist. of Vic.* p. 118 [Vic.] We were frightened in case Welfare might have **taken** us **away**. They took Aunty Nelly's kids away. **1993** C. Jacobi *Evol. & Role Aboriginal Support Groups* p. 39 She was known to the Aboriginal people as the doctor who **took** their children away. **1993** G. Koch *Kaytetye Country* p. 25 [central NT] Only one Kaytetye they bin growem up there . . . From little fella. Half-grown kid, they bin **takem-way** from mother, I think. And they bin growemm up—whitefella bin growem up now. **1994** *Canberra Times* 25 Feb. p. 13/2 *The Hunt*, which depicts the fiercely threatening arrival of a black car at night to **take away** the children. **1994** R. & J. Huggins *Auntie Rita* p. 104 [south-east Qld] To be **taken away** from your family is to me a fate worse than death.

Hence **taken**, removed from the community.

1990 R. Bowden & B. Bunbury *Being Aboriginal* p. 5 Nearly all Aboriginal families in Australia today will know of relatives who were removed as children and put into European care. They're the children the Aborigines refer to as '**taken**'.

taxi plonk *noun* Alcohol delivered by a taxi driver.

In the period up to the 1960s taxi drivers were often used to subvert the legal restrictions preventing Aboriginal people obtaining alcohol.

1957 W.E. Harney *Life Among Aborigines* p. 18 The selling of drink, as well as opium, to aborigines was forbidden by law, but the bottles of '**taxi-plonk**' were planted beside landmarks, such as trees etc. and after the money was paid over . . the purchaser was told where to go to receive his property.

tea leaf *noun* Tea leaves.

Although it refers to the dried leaves rather than the drink, it is used in contexts where the general English use would be *tea*.

1978 J. & P. Read *View of the Past* p. 152 [northern NT] Q: Did he tell the Mangarai people about tobacco? Yes, for tobacco and for sugar, for **tea leaf**, for flour, I think. **1978** J. & P. Read *View of the Past* p. 211 [north-west NT] Old Tom Liddy give him (his father) bag of flour, sugar, tucker, and that **tea leaf**, and that old time treacle. **1981** J. Davis *The Dreamers* p. 103 [south-west WA] *Meena* pours Worru's tea . . Popeye, why do *Nyoongahs* call that one Mahngk? . . You see leaf on a tree, thats a mahngk, that one mahngk, too, **tea leaf**. **1984** E. Roughsey *An Aboriginal Mother Tells* p. 175 [Mornington Island, north Qld] Both Dick and myself went . . travelling through the bush with huge swag and . . flour, sugar, **tealeaf**, milk, rice, frying pan, saucepan, dripping and dish. **1989** D. Walker *Me and You* p. 83 [north coast, NSW] We'll just take some flour and baking powder, **tea leaf** and sugar.

ticket *noun* [NSW] A certificate exempting a person from the restrictive legislation formerly applying to Aboriginal people. See CARD.

1984 P. Read *Down There with Me on Cowra Mission* p. 44 [NSW] So he came down, and he had one of them (exemption) tickets . . 'Have you got a **ticket**?' **1988** P. Taylor *After 200 Years* p. 249 [NSW] To do anything, you had to get a **ticket** from the Welfare Board to say you were exempt.

five mile ticket, a popular name for the former practice of removing those who were deemed by mission managers to be troublemakers and using the police to enforce the decision. The practice was probably not legal.

1988 *La Perouse* p. 15 [NSW] If you broke the law on the mission you would get a **five mile ticket**, and you weren't allowed back on the mission until a certain time. If you were within the five mile limit they would call the police.

titty bottle *noun* A baby's feeding bottle. Also **titi bottle**.

This term has been recorded in British English, but both examples given in the *Oxford English Dictionary* are dialectal rather than general English use. It is possible the use came into Aboriginal English through nineteenth-century British dialect speakers.

1967 May Sellars *Carramar* p. 70 Motherless lambs being fed by aboriginal women out of babies' bottles (**titty bottles** the women call them). **1982** R.D. Eagleson et al. *English and the Aboriginal Child* p. 88 [north-west WA] There are a number of compounds found in

WAACE in northern areas which are not commonly used by SAE speakers .. **titty-bottle**. 1988 J. Harkins *English as 'Two-way' Language* p. 86 [central Aust.] We got that little baby ikwerenhe [tiny] **titty-bottle**? 1988 R. Langford *Dont Take Your Love to Town* p. 87 [Sydney, NSW] The kids fed it with a **titi bottle**.

Tom *noun* A person subservient to whites.

This is a shortened form of UNCLE TOM.

> 1973 K.J. Gilbert *Because White Man'll Never Do It* p. 67 [NSW] A lot of blacks think that the Labor government is going to solve all their problems. The '**Toms**' are going to sit back and let the Labor Party go on its merry way. 1978 K. Gilbert *People are Legends* p. 26 [NSW] Watch for the '**Tom**', With a good career, you know he got it lickin', up that passage dear of a white string-puller.

Tom *verb* To be subservient to whites, to behave like an UNCLE TOM.

> 1978 K. Gilbert *People are Legends* p. 27 [NSW] Watch the traitors with them, Helping them to rob '**Tommin**' for his pay now 'Tommin' for his job.

trouble *noun* Actions or events of a serious nature, such as murder, serious violence, that are likely to lead to intervention by the authorities, particularly non-Aboriginal authorities. Also **big trouble, troubles**.

This is similar to the general English use of *trouble* but often includes the added sense that the **trouble** is something that will mean a European involvement in Aboriginal matters, or will bring about conflict with Europeans. It can sometimes refer to what could also be called a massacre: the 1978 example, for instance, refers to the 1926 Coniston massacre in which approximately 60 Warlpiri were killed by a police punitive expedition. It is similar in this way to the Irish use of the word 'Troubles' to refer to conflict with the British. (Note here though that the British *Oxford English Dictionary* refers to Irish troubles as *civil* wars, etc. The interpretation of such events depends on the perception of Ireland as part of Great Britain or as an occupied nation.) There is a related use in Tok Pisin, from Papua New Guinea, *trabel*, meaning offences associated with females, or sometimes difficulties over any offence.

> 1927 M. Terry *Through Land of Promise* p. 186 [Kimberley, WA] Big fella Gubbermint him send'em big mob police, make'm big mob **trouble**. 1938 *Walkabout* (Melbourne) 1 Apr. p. 16/1 [NT] Constable: 'You all about gotten plenty bush tucker?' Reply: 'No more plenty. Little bit.' Constable: 'Anybody bin come up this country, makem **trouble**?' 1971 J.N. Lickiss *Aboriginal People of Sydney* p. 123 [Sydney, NSW] Strictness on the part of parents concerning truancy varied from extreme severity to permissiveness unless '**trouble**' occurred (i.e. difficulties with the law). 1978 J. & P. Read *View of the Past* p. 105 [central NT] And when people bin .. makem **troubles** and Hanson Creek here, our mob, they didn't know nothing about no trouble. 1978 J. & P. Read *View of the Past* p. 346 [NT] We have a few kids out .. (and) they come here to school, and they go back, and they don't see all this—what you call—**troubles**. 1981 W.J.K. Christensen *The Wangkayi* p. 177 [Kalgoorlie, WA] These sentiments are echoed by some Aborigines who see increasing '**trouble**' coming from growing unemployment and heavy drinking. 1984 P. Read *Down There with Me on Cowra Mission* p. 88 [south-west NSW] We had no **troubles** there, not with the whites. 1984 *Aboriginal Law Bulletin* (Kensington) 10 May p. 6 [central NT] Q6. Can you tell me what a Judge is? A. He listens to that **trouble** and he judges like an old man of the tribe. 1986 B. Shaw *Countrymen* p. 57 [Kimberley, WA] They might lose countryman up here, that sort of **trouble**. 1987 N. Williams *Two Laws* p. 128 [Arnhem Land] When I asked people for a

definition of **big trouble** and we were conversing in English, they usually said it was serious, or it was wounding with a weapon, or killing, and it occurred in public . . . The consistent connecting of remarks about big trouble and Australian legal intervention suggested that the defining attributers of the category were derived from those acts which Yolngu had observed were most likely to be followed by the intervention of white authorities. **1991** D.B. Rose *Hidden Histories* p. 219 [Victoria River, north-west NT] Humbert Tommy made the **trouble**.

police trouble, events that involve the police.

The 'trouble' refers to an attack made by an Aboriginal man on a police tracker. **1980** B. Sansom *The Camp at Wallaby Cross* p. 212 We jus gotta finish up this **police trouble**.

trouble men, men involved in **trouble**.

1991 D.B. Rose *Hidden Histories* p. 45 [north-west NT] Couple of copper there. They used to be hunting for **trouble men**.

tucker *noun* [northern Aust.] Food, particularly European food; sometimes used to refer to prepared food, bread, etc. Traditional Aboriginal food is often distinguished by being called BUSH TUCKER.

Tucker is found in general Australian English to mean 'food', but the particular terms listed below are not widely used except in Aboriginal English. The word was first used by Aboriginal people in the nineteenth century, and its association with pidgin and later Aboriginal English may account for its associations with European food.

1850 *Monthly Almanac* (Adelaide) p. 44 [SA] So hearing that 'plenty **tucker**' was their desire, I let them know by signs that I was not the sort of fellow to offer opposition to their very proper request. **1978** J. & P. Read *View of the Past* p. 84 [NT] They bin give it bullock, **tucker** and tobacco. **1980** B. Sansom *The Camp at Wallaby Cross* p. 59 [northern NT] You got that rations (i.e. stored food) and you got that **tucker** (i.e. prepared food).

baby tucker, food suitable for babies.

1985 *Junga Yimi* Yuendumu Dec. n.p. [central Aust.] The last baby needle is given at 9 months of age; by now the baby is eating **baby tucker**.

dry tucker, dry cereal food.

1964 H.M. Barker *Camels and Outback* p. 102 [NT] Once the swags fell apart, the contents littered the goods on the wagon. They would be crammed with what they call '**dry tucker**', scraps of bread they had been hoarding for weeks at the station. **1987** R.M. & C.H. Berndt *End of an Era* p. 145 [NT] '**Dry tucker**' including rice, and bread or damper, was given out each Sunday.

rubbish tucker, food of low nutritional value, esp. poor quality European food.

1985 S. Cane & O. Stanley *Land Use and Resources in Desert Homelands* p. 100 [central Aust.] Weekend visitors often came to outstations specifically to go hunting and collect bush vegetables and get away from the '**rubbish tucker**' eaten at Yuendumu.

sweet tucker, sweet food.

1978 J. & P. Read *View of the Past* p. 168 [NT] We got to go and have tucker . . . Plenty **sweet tucker**—lollies and biscuit, cake, cool drink, before that grog. **1987** *Tjakulpa Kuwarritja* (Papunya) Oct. n.p. [central Aust.] Emma cooked damper and a cup of tea. We played softball. Then we ate **sweet tucker** by Deborah Napangati Campbell.

tucker dog, a hunting dog. In this case the **tucker** referred to is forms of BUSH TUCKER such as kangaroos.

1978 E. Kolig *Bijdradgen* p. 80 [NT] A few hunting dogs, so-called **tucker dogs** or kangaroo dogs, are proudly pointed out.

weak tucker, food low in nutrition.

1984 *Tjakulpa Kuwarritja* (Papunya) Oct. p. 25 [central Aust.] WEAK TUCKER [caption to drawing of 'junk' food].

Uncle Tom *noun* [Chiefly southern Aust.] A person subservient to whites.

The character of Uncle Tom, from the novel *Uncle Tom's Cabin* by the American writer Harriet Beecher Stowe, came to embody a black person's misguided loyalty and submission to white control. **Uncle Tom** was a slave whose essential virtue as portrayed in the novel was to remain loyal and obedient to his masters despite being treated with violence and contempt. Although the expression originated in America it is now used in other English-speaking countries where there is a black community living with a more powerful white community, to identify those who, in their behaviour, appear to be complicit with an unjust and racist *status quo*.

1970 *Koorier* (Melbourne) Vol. 1 no. 13 p. 24 [Vic.] Don't become a Jackie (**Uncle Tom**) for the sake of a few lousy dollars. For God's sake, don't put our noble race of people in a degrading situation by being so undignified as to take part in the white man's coming re-enactment of Captain Cook's landing. **1976** *Black Liberation* (Brisbane) Apr. p. 7 [Qld] **Uncle Toms** love their controller and will do anything for the white man. **1983** J. Cowan *River People* p. 60 [south-west NSW] Of course there's no black problem . . . Because for white Australians there are no Aborigines left—only tame **Uncle Toms** whose mouths are permanently kept shut by restricting them to a rudimentary education. **1988** G. Cowlishaw *Black, White or Brindle* p. 143 [western NSW] The rent collector . , would perhaps be described as a coconut, or an **Uncle Tom**. **1993** S. Robinson *Aboriginal Embassy* (M.A. Thesis) p. 43 With Bonner's successful candidature for a casual Senate vacancy in 1971 he began a phase of his career which saw him consistently labelled as an **Uncle Tom** by the younger advocates of the movement.

under the Act *adverb* [Aust. but chiefly the eastern States] Of a person or a time when special restrictive legislation applying to Aboriginal people was in force. See also CARD, DOG LICENCE, TICKET.

Such legislation was in force in all States of Australia until the late 1960s, and applied to all those legally identified as 'Aboriginal'. The definition was supposedly genetic (as evidenced in the 1979 example) but was often driven by other non-Aboriginal pressures and preoccupations. These Acts denied Aboriginal people basic civil rights, such as freedom of movement and award wages. Their discriminatory nature was exemplified to many Aboriginal people in the ban it placed on all Aboriginal people being able to enter licensed premises. The term is most commonly recorded in Queensland in reference to the *Queensland Act* as such legislation was still in force there after it had been removed in the other States.

1965 *Tracks we Travel* p. 76 When the publican refused to serve him a drink on the grounds that he was an Aborigine **under the Act**, the town-workers really stacked on a blue. **1979** J. Davis *Kullark* p. 47 [south-west WA] I don't even come **under the Act**. I'm only a quarter native blood. **1980** P. Pepper *You Are What You Make Yourself* p. 33 [Vic.] They had to leave their home at Ramahyuck because of the Act—they always called it '**under the Act**'. 1982 C. Russell (compiler) *People in a Community* p. 8 [Qld] I lived **under the Act** that deprived my people of movement and freedom of speech. **1985** B. Rosser *Dreamtime Nightmares* p. 14 [north Qld] I thought it was terrible but, if you were **under the Act**—the Queensland Aborigines Act—they wouldn't give you anything. **1990** *Koori News* Vol. II no. 1 p. 46 [Sydney, NSW] Although our ancestors had it hard being black. Being tortured and living **under the** white man's **act**.

Hence **out (of the Act)**, free of its restrictions.

1985 M. Kennedy *Born Half-Caste* p. 24 [Qld] I was under the Act for years. Now I will try to explain how I got **out**. **1987** B. Gammage & P. Spearitt (eds) *Australians 1938* p. 102 [north Qld] Being under the Act . . had many restrictions. You couldn't eat with those who were **out of the Act** who had separate eating areas.

uptown *adjective* [Recorded in NSW] Of a person who has moved away from the community, physically and socially, in order to gain greater social prestige with the non-Aboriginal community. Often as **uptown nigger**.

From *uptown*, a more desirable area of town. This is originally and more commonly American English. The term is a derogatory one used of those seen by their community as abandoning Aboriginal values. See also UNCLE TOM.

1986 *Australian Geographic* Jan. p. 76/3 [They] represent Moree's small but expanding middleclass . . . [and] have enjoyed so much success they have earned the epithet '**uptown** niggers' from the other Aboriginal people . . . **1988** P. Taylor *After 200 Years* p. 74 You have to be an **uptown** nigger to get into the clubs—so they say. **1988** G. Cowlishaw *Black, White or Brindle* p. 110 [western NSW] 'Coconut' . . and '**uptown**' nigger' are used by blacks to disparage those who are seen as disloyal. **1993** J. Janson *Gunjies* p. 57 [western NSW] They're too flash for me, those **uptown** gins.

wadgula *noun* [WA] A white person. Also **wadjala, wadjullah, waigella, waijela** and **wetjala**.

From an Aboriginal pronunciation of WHITEFELLOW. For a discussion of the effect of Aboriginal languages on Aboriginal English pronunciation, see the Introduction. See also WALYPALA.

1923 A.G. Bolam *Trans-Austral. Wonderland* p. 76 [northern SA] '**Waijela** bool-ga munda?' (Whitefellow dig big earth?). **1938** D. Bates *Passing of Aborigines* p. 182 [northern SA] 'Blackfella king belong to this country!' shouted Nyimbana in English. 'We don't want **waijela** here! This *gabbi* our *gabbi*.' **1969** L. Hadow *Full Cycle* p. 157 'Hah, ha!' Jimmy Dabchick turned a cartwheel. 'Us all N-Yoongars. What she? Sister Merry Christmas only **Waigella**!' **1975** R. Beilby *Brown Land Crying* p. 2 Pink as a white person's hands . . . Just like a **wadjullah's**. **1981** A. Weller *Day of Dog* p. 7 [south-west WA] We'll go and pick up a woman for ya, Dougo. Would ya like a big fat **wadgula** or a skinny little gin? **1982** J. Davis *Kullark* p. 16 [south-west WA] I'll tell you what 'e'll do, 'e'll finish up marryin' some **Wetjala** *yok*, 'ave blue-eyed kids and 'e won't want nothing to do with us. **1991** G. Ward *Unna You Fullas* p. 80 [south-west WA] She . . talking flash-way to that **wadjala**. **1994** *Encyclop. Abor. Aust.* p. 475 [south-west WA] Written by Jack Davis, his first play primarily for children, *Honey Spot* (1987) is set in a country area of WA. The action centres around the friendship between Tim, a 13-year-old Aboriginal boy, and Peggy, a 12-year-old **wetjala** (white) girl.

walkabout *noun* **1** A periodic return to one's own COUNTRY and a traditional way of life for those otherwise engaged in non-Aboriginal employment. See also HOLIDAY and WALKABOUT in Chapter 4.

Walkabout originally was applied to travel, usually in the traditional manner. See also WALK. In this sense it has most commonly been applied to the lay-off season in the northern cattle industry, when Aboriginal employees (most often living in their own COUNTRY) would leave the station for a period of traditional life. This was the time when ceremonies could be performed, significant sites visited and Aboriginal life in general affirmed. Though it could be a time of hardship in areas where bush food had become scarce, it was very important in maintaining culture. With the changes in the structure of the cattle industry, the term in this particular sense is not so widely used. The word **walkabout** itself has become debased in non-Aboriginal use; when used of, rather than by, Aboriginal people it usually implies an abandoning of responsibility, rather than a return to Aboriginal responsibilities.

1910 *Bulletin* (Sydney) 22 Dec. p. 13/4 Shearing over, black brother was sent off on his **walkabout**, the squatter supplying him with . . a few garments. **1911** E.S. Sorenson *Life in Austral. Backblocks* p. 43 She leaves the station with her followers pretty frequently for a 'walk-about', for the call of the wild comes irresistibly, no matter how long she has mixed with the whites. **1925** M. Terry *Across Unknown Aust.* p. 101 Their explanation is that a 'corroboree' (native dance) must be attended, or a '**walk-about**' taken for their health. **1938** D. Bates *Passing of Aborigines* p. 2 The blacks insisted on a 'pink-hi' or **walkabout** season—they could not live without it. **1947** W.E. Harney *Brimming Billabongs* (1963) p. 101 **Walkabout** time made the natives poor and eager to work when the stock season began. **1959** H. Myers *Regions of Courage* p. 18 The regular boys and their giggling lubras were anxious to start on their **walkabout**, so were lined up at the store and issued dry rations—tea, flour, tobacco, sugar along with many small gifts. Their rations would be supplemented with bush tucker—wildfowl, lily roots, yams, grass-root nuts, snake and other foods. **1962** D. Lockwood *I, Aboriginal* p. 8 It was one **walkabout** time at Mount Saint Vidgeon in the Never-Never Land south of the Roper River that the Medicine Man, the Doctor Blackfellow, tried to kill me. **1970** J.V. Marshall *Walk to Hills of Dreamtime* p. 19 It was the season of **walkabout**: the season-before-the-wet when, from all over the outback, tribes and individuals were making their way to the sites of the corroborees in the lands that had given them birth.

2 A group of people on a walkabout.

1978 K. Palmer & C. McKenna *Somewhere Between Black and White* p. 61 [Pilbara, WA] In the summer when most of the workers had been laid off the **walkabout** came down from Warrawagine again.

walk off *noun* An act of leaving, **walking off** a place, as an act of protest.

It is often used to refer to the mass departure of the Gurindji from Wave Hill cattle station in 1965 to set up an independent community at Darguragu (Wattie Creek), and the move of most of the Cummeragunja community across the river to New South Wales in 1939. Possibly the use of **walk off** rather than **walk out** is influenced by the use of *on* or *off* in relation to missions or cattle stations—a person lives *on* or *off* a mission, and sometimes also stations, although *walk-off* meaning a *walk-out* is also found in general English usage.

1978 K. Palmer & C. McKenna *Somewhere Between Black and White* p. 68 [Pilbara, WA] The Boss was too much concerned . . to argue. He paid off . . most of the other workers . . . It was, in simple terms, a **walk off**. **1984** M. Gumbert *Neither Justice Nor Reason* p. 156 [north-west NT] The **walk-off** by the Gurindji in 1965 from Wave Hill is . . a landmark event in the Aboriginal struggle for land. **1984** *N.T. News* (Darwin) 1 Sept p. 12/2 Gurindji Freedom Day . . [is] . . the 18th anniversary of their historic **walk-off** from Vestey's Wave

Hill Station in protest over appalling working & living conditions. **1991** A. Jackomos & D. Fowell *Living Aboriginal Hist. of Vic.* p. 12 [Vic.] Many of the families who participated in the famous Cummeragunja **Walk Off** in 1939 built a village of humpies. **1991** D.B. Rose *Hidden Histories* p. 233 [north-west NT] When I visited them again in April 1972, following the **walk-off**, they were quite elated over the direct action which they had taken.

walk off *verb* To leave a place as an act of protest.

1978 K. Palmer & C. McKenna *Somewhere Between Black and White* p. 84 [Pilbara, WA] We just want better conditions . . We've been working for the squatters long enough and all we get is a chunk of meat, corned beef, dry bread. We want to **walk off** all that. **1992** *Mikurrunya* (Strelley) Nov. p. 24 [Pilbara, WA] The Strelley Mob were famous for their part in the strike of 1946, when Aboriginal workers all over the Pilbara **walked off** pastoral stations to demand equal wages. **1992** D.B. Rose *Dingo Makes Us Human* p. 39 [Victoria River, north-west NT] We never been **walk off** for grog . . . We never been strike for grog. We been strike for land.

walland *noun* [NSW] Money. Also **wallang, wulling**.

From the Wiradjuri language of south-west New South Wales, *walang*, a 'stone', and by extension, 'money'. In many other Aboriginal languages, the local word for 'stone, pebble, rock' has had its sense extended to cover *money*. Most Aboriginal people's first association with money would be with coins rather than notes.

1949 *Oceania* Dec. p. 85 [north-west NSW] Even six-years-old children on the Murrumbidgee ask their parents and other relatives for **wallang** to buy ice-cream. **1977** *Meanjin* (Melbourne) no. 4 p. 541 [NSW] We find that some Aboriginal words . . are often used . . **walland**—money. **1982** R.D. Eagleson et al. *English and the Aboriginal Child* p. 137 [NSW] We had to elicit deliberately from them any Aboriginal words they might know . . **wulling** or **walland**, 'money'.

walypala *adjective* [northern Aust.] Whitefellow. Also **waipella, walballa**.

From an Aboriginal pronunciation of WHITEFELLOW. For a discussion of the effect of Aboriginal languages on Aboriginal English pronunciation, see the Introduction. See also WADGULA.

1957 F. Clune *Fortune Hunters* p. 55 Then we put *poona* (sticks) all around hole **waipella** (whitefellow) fashion. **1981** W.J.K. Christensen *The Wangkayi* p. i [Kalgoorlie, WA] They contrast their Desert traditions, the 'Wangkayi way', with introduced European patterns of living, the 'Walypala (whitefella) way'. **1990** D. John *Bloody Gold* p. 58 [Kalgoorlie, WA] The Silky Pear . . is here attached to a 'lingi' bush. When young and soft it's eaten straight from the vine. When old and woody, cooked in the ashes. Its native name is 'kwugla' of which 'Kalgoorlie' is a mangled '**walballa**' version.

war *noun* The historical conflict between Aboriginal groups and the invading Europeans.

While the sense here is not obviously different from the general English sense, it is included because most non-Aboriginal Australians have not used the term to describe the conflict between Aboriginal people and the invaders. It has been common in the past for Australian historians to assert that Australia is a land on which no war has been fought.

1978 J. & P. Read *View of the Past* p. 179 [central NT] They bin startem the **war** . . Aborigines and whitefeller bin startem war. **1986** *White Invasion Diary* Invasion Diary Collective 3 Feb. [SA] The resistance that was waged by the Aboriginal people against the Europeans . . clearly indicates that we were in a state of **war**—our country was invaded. **1988** *We have Survived* Poster/n.p. I've got to tell you about the warmaking people. The ones who made **war**. The new ones. Mr White, Bill Harney, Mr Sweeney. They just went after women. All the New Captain Cooks fought the people. They shot people. Not old Captain Cook: He didn't interfere or make a war. **1988** *Social Alternatives* (St Lucia) Vol. VII no. 1 p. 3 [Qld] Deaths in custody today are a progression of this ongoing, undeclared **war**. **1989** R.M. Baker *Land is Life* p. 200 [Borroloola, north-east NT] The wild times is the story of European introduced . . violence. For Aboriginal people in the Booroloola area the violence of this period is well remembered and the term 'war' is often used . . . 'War been fight here, everywhere people ought to know . . war yes.' **1990** *Pemulwuy Dilemma* p. 6 [western Sydney, NSW] When you read about the **war** between the Darug people and the European settlers, it is all recorded by Europeans. **1992** *Puggana News* (Launceston) Apr. p. 45 [Tas.] Later in 1830 a state of **war** existed between black and white.

prisoner of war, an inmate of an Aboriginal settlement.

1984 *Puggana News* (Launceston) Feb. p. 2 [Tas.] Aboriginal **prisoners of war** who had been held at Wybalenna Settlement on F.I. [Flinders Island], were transported to Oyster Cove in 1847.

watjiin *noun* A white woman. Also **wadjin, wijen, wodgin**.

From *white gin*. This is an ironic extension of the word *gin* used, often derogatively, by white people of Aboriginal women.

1949 *Oceania* (Sydney) Dec. p. 83 White women – are still referred to as **Wadjins**, a corruption of 'white gins'. **1957** *Oceania* Sydney Dec. p. 106 [north coast, NSW] They refer to the upper group women in mocking tones as 'Black-**Wodgins**' and speak about their adoption of white ways. **1977** *Meanjin* Melbourne No. 4 p. 541 [Sydney, NSW] We find that some Aboriginal words . . are often used . . *wadjema*—white girl (also **wijen**) **1986** *Austral. Jrnl. of Linguistics* p. 225 [northern NSW] The word wanta originally meaning ghosts, is used to refer to white men, white women being **watjiin** (apparently from 'white gin').

welfare *noun* **1** A government agency, State or Federal, having power over the conditions of life of Aboriginal people, often operating under special legislation.

It overlaps the general use of the word but is significant in Aboriginal communities because of the enormous amount of government intervention in their lives, especially in the past, because of special legislation applying to them, and especially in relation to child removal. In the north, people have mixed reactions to the term, as the interference of government authorities was significant in reducing the physical violence of the contact period, although it introduced new tensions.

1978 J. & P. Read *View of the Past* p. 187 [NT] That **welfare** tellem we got to stop one place now . . . Don't come anymore this side. No more. **1978** J. & P. Read *View of the Past* p. 187 [NT] We had to go and help Welfare now . . **Welfare** bin chasem all over the country, you know. **1982** E.A. Young & E.K. Fisk *Town Populations* p. 154 [Gascoyne, northern WA] A woman who wanted to buy a black dress to attend the funeral of a relative went to '**welfare**' (the Department of Community Welfare) to ask their assistance. **1984** P. Read *Down There with Me on Cowra Mission* p. 87 [south-west NSW] But **Welfare** probably wouldn't bother about it now—although they're still about aren't they? **1985** B. Rosser *Dreamtime Nightmares* p. 32 [north Qld] They might be victimised by the **welfare** for talking about the killings or other information. **1989** R.M. Baker *Land is Life* p. 306 [Borroloola, north-east NT] I think we'll have to go, **welfare** got to cart people down Borroloola. **1991** L.M. Wilkinson *Aboriginality* p. 221 [Vic.] The memory of the '**welfare**' or the police coming to take away children is too great to allow children to be taken to institutions.

welfare bloke, a government employee. Also **welfare man**.

1978 K. Palmer & C. McKenna *Somewhere Between Black and White* p. 88 [Pilbara, WA] Why be afraid of the **welfare blokes**, when all he was interested in doing was supporting the Squatters. **1986** B. Shaw *Countrymen* p. 71 [Kimberley, WA] Me and Mandi gave up work because the **welfare man** told us we were pensioners.

welfare book, an official document. The example below refers to the Northern Territory *Register of Wards*, a list of all people classified as Aboriginal and hence by definition wards of the State. This register was popularly known as the 'stud book'. See also BOOK.

1978 J. & P. Read *View of the Past* p. 221 Carryem up, oh, big book, **welfare book**, you know.

welfare funeral, a funeral paid for by the government.

1974 *Bunji* (Darwin) Feb. p. 2 [Darwin, NT] We are going to bury them . . our way! With a **welfare funeral** we do not know what is going to happen. The members of the Gwalwa Daraniki can not afford a private funeral.

welfare mob, the government and its instrumentalities.

1988 *We have Survived* Poster [Arnhem Land] That last war and the second war. They fought us. And then they made a new thing called 'welfare'. All the New Captain Cook mob came and called themselves '**welfare mob**'.

welfare school, a school run by the department in the Northern Territory responsible for Aboriginal welfare. From the 1950s until the 1970s they were responsible for Aboriginal education.

1984 *Aboriginal History* p. 58 [Borroloola, north-east NT] Her eldest child was taken to Borroloola 'for **welfare school**'.

welfare time, the period in the Northern Territory from about the 1940s to the 1960s, when the physical violence of the contact period was replaced by bureaucratic control. While providing some physical safety it placed other stresses upon Aboriginal society arising from the cultural assumptions of the period, which ascribed little value to Aboriginal society and certainly saw no future for a separately existing society alongside the majority one. Consequently, Aboriginal cultural values were put under pressure and communities fragmented and displaced.

1981 A. Cavadini et al. *Two Laws* p. 70 They talk about the attempted destruction of their Aboriginal law, about police times and **welfare times**. **1988** J. Harkins *English as 'Two-way' Language* p. 245 Aboriginal and non-Aboriginal speakers share a set of terms specific to, or with specialised meanings in, the contact situation, which can only be briefly mentioned here. These include terms such as **welfare-time** (the protectionist era). . . **1989** R.M. Baker *Land is Life* p. 195 [Borroloola, north-east NT] Macassan times, Wild times, War time, Police times, **Welfare times**, Cattle times, Gough Whitlam times, This (tourist time). Figure 7.1 Yanyuwa recognised historical phases.

2 A person employed by a government welfare agency.

1988 G. Cowlishaw *Black, White or Brindle* p. 84 [western NSW] We had some strict **welfares** out here. **1988** H. Ross *Community Social Impact* p. 30 [WA] Welfare come along from Perth, two **welfare**. **1990** A. Pring (ed.) *Women of the Centre* p. 142 [central Aust.] That's when the **welfares** and police came to Ernabella.

3 Legislation regulating intervention by government agencies in the lives of Aboriginal people.

1991 D.B. Rose *Hidden Histories* p. 160 [Victoria River, north-west NT] The Welfare Ordinance of 1953, which Jack referred to simply as Welfare, made a huge difference in his life: When the **Welfare** was come, it was a lot different. When the welfare was come, that's why I got away all the time.

whitefellow *noun* **1** A white person, a European Australian or other person with a similar appearance. Also **whitefella, whitefeller**. See also WADGULA, WALYPALA.

This is likely to have been a response by Aboriginal people to the term BLACKFELLOW used of them by the British. Like the British, Aboriginal people's early response to the 'other' society was often expressed in terms of their physical appearance, hence **whitefellow**. The significance of the skin colour can be seen in the terms for a British or European Australian which were originally an Aboriginal language word for *ghost* or *corpse* (one where the upper dark layers of skin have peeled off). For example, Bundjalung (northern NSW) *dagay* and Nyungar (south western WA) *djanka*, 'ghost', and Kaurna (southern SA) *kuinyo*, 'a dead person, death'.

1826 R. Dawson *Private & Confidential* p. 5 This was not the first time they had seen '**White Fellows**' as they call us. **1836** J.F. O'Connell *Residence Eleven Yrs. New Holland* p. 87 They appear to have recognised their title 'black fellows', and in return dub the English '**white fellows**', seemingly perfectly content with the distinction, and considering white the worse hue, decidedly. **1863** J. Bonwick *Wild White Man* p. 33 [Vic.] No do that. When blackfellow sit down with **whitefellow**, him say, 'Be off, be off' blackfellow no do the like o' that. **1898** D.W. Carnegie *Spinifex & Sand* p. 284 He knew the words '**white-fella**' and 'womany', and had certainly heard of a rifle. **1909** H.G.B. Mason *Darkest West Australia* p. 55 [WA] By and by we'll kill a **whitefellow**. **1936** *Publicist* (Sydney) ii. p. 3/1 His song was unheeded by a crowd of **whitefellows**, who were congregated at that place for the purpose of engaging in S.P. illicit betting, and not for the purpose of hearing Jacky sing. **1980** K. Liberman *Decline of Kuwarra People* p. 80 [Kalgoorlie, WA] *Wangkayis* (Aborigines) always say 'Yes'. We been saying 'Yes' to the **whitefellas** all a' time. **1984** P. Read *Down There with Me on Cowra Mission* p. 77 [south-west NSW] They used to sneak it, you know, get some **whitefeller** to get it for them. **1985** E. Malpangka *Aboriginal Women* p. 10 These **whitefellahs** came and cut the country up with names. They came and they cut it up. **1988** C. Mattingley & K. Hampton (eds) *Survival in Our Own Land* p. 73 [Flinders Ranges, SA] And after that . . we set off . . we went off to have a look, and we took a few **whitefellas** with us, so they'd understand. **1988** P. Marshall *Raparapa* p. 196 [Kimberley, WA] He was the first **whitefella** I was able to have a good look at. First I thought that he might have been a pulya (ghost). **1991** D.B. Rose *Hidden Histories* p. 47 They reckon it's one story, every way. Ngarinmanpurru, Bilinara, Nungaliwurru, Wardaman, Warlpiri, Walman, they know. Because **whitefellow** never do only one place this way. Every way (they were) shooting. All around the Wave Hill, Warlpiri, Walman, Gurindji, Nyining, Jiyal, Walmayarri, Bilinara, Wolayijurung, Ngarinmanpurru, Nungaliwurru, Wardaman, all round. Right up where this Yanyula, Binbinga, Ngalurunga, Jingulu, Wampayi, same thing.

2 (As an adjective) white, European.

1834 G. Bennett *Wanderings N.S.W.* I. p. 210 [NSW] I was accosted by a native black, who asked, whether 'I **white feller** parson, for me want shilling'; but not being of the clerical profession, I did not consider myself liable to be placed under contribution. **1861** *Burke & Wills Exploring Exped.* p. 12 [western Qld?] The flour, 50lb. of which I gave them, they at once called 'white-fellow nardoo'. 1951 E. Hill *Territory* p. 20 [northern NT] No need to promise 'white-fella tucker' when lily-time is here. 1962 D. Lockwood *I, Aboriginal* p. 206, I had put all my tribal ways behind me and attempted to live and behave in the whitefeller way. 1977 X. Herbert *Dream Road* p. 16 Anybody talk whitefeller way here get sick. 1980 Ansell & Percy *To Fight Wild* p. 133 The ranges on the boundary they called High Lonesome. These are all whitefellow names, but they have blackfellow or old-time names for the same places. 1988 S. Dunlop *All that Rama Rama Mob* p.xliii [central Aust.] Some *ngankari* thought that it was not fair that they did lots to help disturbed people (and sick people too) but most health services only pay whitefella doctors, not *ngankari*, the Aboriginal doctors. 1988 *Canberra Times* 8 Mar. p. 3/4 [western Qld] The Charleville Aboriginal Housing Company bought my house . . . Why shouldn't they buy my house? They bought nineteen white-fella houses.

whitefellow business, concerns, occupations and activities of 'whitefellows'; non-Aboriginal matters.

1974 J. Bern *Blackfella Business* p. 27 [northern NT] **Whitefella business** is running the settlement, working for wages, going to school and acting in ways which are outside of and opposed to the obligations of Village relations. 1981 *Tjakulpa Kuwarritja* (Papunya) Oct. n.p. [Western Desert] I went up in the plane and looked down and saw all the white fellow business from the plane. 1982 M. Howard *Aboriginal Power* p. 116 [northern WA] It has become impossible for Aborigines to sustain a clear conceptual distinction between . . 'white fella business' and 'mardu' (Aboriginal) business.

white man *adjective* European.

1936 M. & E. Durack *Chunuma* p. 80 [Kimberley, WA] What about you learn'm me whiteman song. 1981 G. Ngabidj & B. Shaw *My Country of Pelican Dreaming* p. 8 I had to distinguish between the '**white man** way' whereby relationships are described in terms of actual 'blood' ties, and 'blackfeller Law' by which persons become classificatory kin (sometimes referred to as the 'skinning Law'). 1984 *Puggana News* (Launceston) June (cover) [Tas.] They want to cremate them **white man** way. 1986 B. Shaw *Countrymen* p. 207 [Kimberley, WA] He camps with her and she comes back full the next month. Well the old bloke looks and reckons, 'No, I don't want you, now you got a **white man** kid'. 1989 D. Walker *Me and You* p. 53 [north coast, NSW] All the Aboriginal ways are dying out on the North Coast . . . Too much *dagay* (**white man**) in our ways; *yirralee* (white or not good) ways, there's too much of it. 1991 D.B. Rose *Hidden Histories* p. 172 [north-west NT] And did she have another name as well? . . . Yes, she had a **white man** name, Lily Cusack.

whitey *noun* A WHITEFELLOW, a European Australian. Also **whity**.

This is frequently used in a pejorative way.

1827 P. Cunningham *Two Yrs in N.S.W.* Vol. II p. 21 [NSW] The instant *blacky* perceives whity beating a retreat, he vociferates after him . . . Go along, you dam rascal . . should this volley of abuse provoke 'white fellow' to run up and offer to strike him, 'blacky' would dare him 'to the scratch'. 1969 *Koorier* (Fitzroy) p. 1 [Vic.] In a previous edition appeared the terms Whitefella and **Whitey**. Some of our readers seemed to take offence at these two names. 1974 *Smoke Signals* (Melbourne) 10 Apr. (p. 2) So, how about we show these **whities** that we CAN do it? 1979 M. Heppell *A Black Reality* p. 33 The 'transitional Aboriginals' inhabited . . a shadowy half world . . thus the better educated man will, if asked, express a desire for a '**whitey**' house. 1980 *Puggana News* (Launceston) Jan. p. 13 [Tas.] People . . express gut feelings of being Aboriginal and are always prepared to express themselves to '**Whitey**'. 1980 L.G. Fogarty *Kargun* p. 51 [south-east Qld] Turn Abo ways out to be **whitey** ways. 1981 F. Hardy *Who Shot George Kirkland?* p. 102 If I wanted to bug him I just called him **whitey** and reminded him of . . the white Australia policy. 1995 D. Hodge *Did you meet any Malagas?*

p. 79 [northern NT] See if **Whitey** was flavour of the month, so were we too, only because we were two local, dark skinned boys.

yarndi *noun* Marijuana. Also **nyandi, yarndie**.

From the Wiradjuri language of south-western NSW, *nyaandi*, a cover word, 'what's-a-name', for a term that has been forgotten or for something that should not be mentioned. In Wiradjuri, it was a euphemism for menstruation, but in modern usage it almost always refers to marijuana.

1984 L. Fogarty *Ngutji* p. 119 [south-east Qld] **Yarndi** = grass. **1990** Davis et al. *Paperbark* p. 232 He made enough to . . keep himself in **Nyandi** (herb). **1992** *Today* Sept. p. 26 It's just as well it doesn't depend on our feelings. Good feelings just fade like **Yarndi** smoke. **1992** R.L. Ginibi *Real Deadly* p. 101 [NSW] Ya can't work hard, drink, and some **yarndie** too! **1993** *Koori Mail* (Lismore) 10 Mar. p. 4/3 [NSW] I drank and smoked **yarndie** for fourteen years.

yarraman *noun* A horse.

This word was used by both Aboriginal and non-Aboriginal people in the early contact period; each side believed they were using a word from the other's language. There have been several theories as to the word's origin, including a construction on the word for 'tooth' from one of the coastal New South Wales languages, but none of these is conclusive. It was used by both communities in the nineteenth and early twentieth centuries, and is still used by some older people in the rural non-Aboriginal community.

1842 *Legends of Australia* March p. 49 'Got it coat, **yarraman**, and musket just like it soger.' (Meaning that they were equipped with horses, fire-arms, &c., and drest like the mounted police. **1856** W.W. Dobie *Recollections of Port Phillip* p. 61 [Vic.] In stalks a black–fellow, like an emissary of Satan, who . . tells him how that 'two big–fellow bushrangers pull away along o' creek, and look out **yarramen** (horses) belonging to station, and no gammon.' **1892** *Western Champion* Barcaldine 9 Feb. p. 12/2 [NSW] The astonished '**yarraman**' gave one look round . . and started off across the plain like a toboggan slide on the down grade. **1923** J. Bowes *Jackaroos* p. 67 'Lot of pfellers go long here.' 'How many **yarramans**?' **1976** C.D. Mills *Hobble Chains and Greenhide* p. 13 [NT] 'Properly good **yarraman** this one,' seemed to be the undeniable verdict. **1994** R. & J. Huggins *Auntie Rita* p. 133 [south-east Qld] You hardly heard of domestic violence in my time and that's true. . . I think the old **yarraman** got more hits than we did. He never hit the dog because the dog was too fast for him.

yellow fellow *noun* A person of Aboriginal and white ancestry. Also **yella fella, yeller feller**.

This has been used by Aboriginal and non-Aboriginal communities. As with 'half-caste' its use is now generally considered offensive.

c1900 W. Telfer *Wallabadah Manuscript* (1982) p. 87 [northern NSW] He said what names you call that **yellow fellow** i been see him big fella mob. Come along road. **1913** W.J.K. Harris *Out Back in Aust.* p. 115 [northern NSW] We asked how they got on before the advent of the white man. The reply was not quite unexpected: 'Plenty tucker, no **yeller-fellers**' (half-castes). **1935** K.L. Smith *Sky Pilot Arnhem Land* p. 269 [Arnhem Land] The half-caste was the centre of an excited group of blacks and coloured folk. Poor girl! For one brief hour the 'outcaste' was an envied heroine and the once despised '**yellow fellow**' reaped in the darkies' eyes a glory eclipsing that of a film star. **1987** C. Glass & A. Weller *Us Fellas* p. 169 [NT] If someone goes up to the Northern Territory and says to some tribal woman up there

. . 'Did you have a **yella fella**? Did you have a murra murra baby back in nineteen?' **1991** D.B. Rose *Hidden Histories* p. 61 [NT] 'Don't you touch it. You touch it, you look out. I'll shoot you and this **yellow fellow**,' he said.

yirilgan *noun* [south-east Qld, northern NSW] A white woman. Also **jara:limergan**, **yirahligan**, **yiriligan**.

From the Bundjalung language of northern NSW and south-east Queensland, *yirilga* or *yirahlgan* 'a white woman'.

1949 *Oceania* Vol. XX p. 51 [northern NSW] White man, male, *jaral:li* white man, female: **jara:limergan**. **1983** M. Sharpe *Traeger Kid* p. 68 [northern NSW] There were two white ladies near them now . . Them **yiriligans** . . said Jenny. **1983** M. Sharpe *Traeger Kid* p. 70 [north coast, NSW] 'D'ja hear that?' Jenny whispered. 'That **yiriligan** talkin' our lingo!' **1988** M.C. Sharpe et al. *An Introduction to the Bundjalung Language and its Dialects* p.xv [northern NSW] I use the terms that Gidabal and Yugambeh people use, as they are the ones who introduced me to the language. Other Bundjalung people call us whites *yirilis* and **yirilgans**, (or *yirahlis* and **yirahligans**).

yirili *noun* [south-east Qld, northern NSW] A white man, white people. Also used as an adjective: white, European. Also **jaral:li**, **yirilee**, **yirahli**, **yirili**, **yirralee**.

From the Bundjalung language of northern NSW and south-eastern Queensland *yirahli* 'a white man'.

1949 *Oceania* Vol. XX p. 51 [northern NSW] White man, male, **jaral:li** white man, female: *jara:limergan*. **1983** M. Sharpe *Traeger Kid* p. 64 [south-east Qld] 'Balun is language for creek,' Jean said. 'S'pose that's why the **yirilees** called it Pallen Creek,' said Doreen, 'they couldn't say it right.' **1988** M.C. Sharpe et al. *An Introduction to the Bundjalung Language and its Dialects* p. 176 [north coast, NSW] But mostly when white people are around, the Square people will try to speak school English, i.e. gabah/**yirili** or 'flash talk'. **1988** M.C. Sharpe et al. *An Introduction to the Bundjalung Language and its Dialects* p.xv [north coast, NSW] There are the many Bundjalung people who have taught us *dagays* and *waymehrigans* about their language and culture . . . I use the terms that Gidabal and Yugambeh people use, as they are the ones who introduced me to the language. Other Bundjalung people call us whites **yirilis** and *yirilgans*, (or **yirahlis** and *yirahligans*). **1989** D. Walker *Me and You* p. 53 [north coast, NSW] All the Aboriginal ways are dying out on the North Coast . . . Too much *dagay* (white man) in our ways; **yirralee** (white or not good) ways, there's too much of it.

CHAPTER 6
The quiet run and the wild bush

The words in this chapter come from one of the earliest industries of the occupation, the pastoral industry. It was in a pastoral context that many Aboriginal people had their first experiences with English.

These words are not about the experience of the stock camp or pastoral life itself, words such as HOLIDAY, which refer to the period when people returned to the bush and to traditional Aboriginal ways of living. Those words are dealt with in Chapter 5. These are about situations and concepts which originally had a pastoral station meaning but have been taken into Aboriginal English to refer to human situations.

Some are words such as **mob**, **wild**, **quiet** and **tame**, used about pastoral animals in British English and which were applied to Aboriginal people by the colonisers. **Mob**, for instance, was taken from its original meaning, 'a rabble', and applied by the British to a wild herd of cattle and a group of hostile Aboriginal people. Aboriginal people then took these words into their own speech, but used them without the hierarchical and racist meanings that their use for humans implied.

The other words in this chapter are mostly from the regions of the northern cattle industry. This industry was built upon the countries, the labour and the expertise of the Aboriginal people of the area, and it was within this industry that many Aboriginal people learnt a form of English. Within this language were many terms used in the cattle industry; Aboriginal people took some of them and transferred them to human situations. For example, *box up* the Australian expression referring to the mixing of two herds, has been transferred with reference to the mixing of two groups of people, with a similar association of disturbance and confusion. Much of the recorded use has been from the Kimberley and the Northern Territory, but it is likely many of the words are found in other cattle areas such as north-western Queensland.

Cattle station owners would generally have a community of local people, a camp, living on the station property. (Some Aboriginal people did come from other parts of Australia, travelling as drovers with the mobs of cattle, but the majority of the labour was local.) Young men, and sometimes women, were trained as stockriders and in return applied their detailed local knowledge of the country to the care of stock. Women and old men supplied labour for the homestead. In the wet season, the community would move back into the bush, to conduct ceremonies and live off the land in the traditional way, although they often carried with them some European foodstuffs such as tea. The conditions of life were variable, but generally nutrition and housing were poor, and the power of the local station owner was one almost of life and death. Nonetheless, people do have some good memories of this time, for they were living on their own countries, and they had pride in their stockwork skills.

Conditions now are very different; after the 1965 equal wages legislation most Aboriginal cattle station communities were thrown off the stations and their countries. Many of these communities now live in the towns and settlements of northern Australia. More recently, there has been some employment for Aboriginal cattle workers on Aboriginal-owned cattle stations.

beef *noun* [northern Aust.] Meat from any animal.

From *beef*, 'the flesh of cattle'. In the *Oxford English Dictionary* there are two examples of a use meaning 'other kinds of meat' but this is not usually found in other Australian Englishes. In northern Australia **beef**, i.e. cattle meat, would have been almost the only domesticated meat available, which may be why it came to mean 'all meat'.

1935 F. Birtles *Battle Fronts Outback* p. 180 They came streaking towards us . . to share in the supply of 'strong fellah **beef**'. Very seldom would they themselves attack a buffalo. 1951 *Mankind* (Sydney) May p. 243 [northern Aust.] The carapace, or shell, which forms the back of the turtle now becomes a dish, and is full of a rich soup formed by the cooking **beef**. 1979 *Land Rights News* 8 May n.p. [NT] They been all day kill 'm crocodile (warrija) black water goanna (tujangarha) kill kangaroo (wanykurra). Longa that sort of **beef** him been living early-day people. 1986 B. Shaw *Countrymen* p. 53 [Kimberley, WA] They reckon dingo has more fat and **beef**, not like the kangaroo. 1986 B. Shaw *Countrymen* p. 89 [Kimberley, WA] Every day we killed goannas, kangaroos, fish, any sort of **beef**.

box up *verb* [northern Aust.] To mix with people of another group.

Box and *box up*, to accidentally mix two herds or flocks, have been used in Australian and New Zealand English since the mid-nineteenth century. **Box up** has been used in the past in Australian English to mean 'a mixing of people', but only as a self-conscious metaphor.

1983 *Upper Daly Land Claim* p. 42 [Daly River, northern NT] Previous to this, they '**boxed up**' with the people living in the old Pine Creek 'compound' which is on Jawoyn land. 1990 P. Austin et al. *Language & History* p. 24 [Oodnadatta, northern SA] I went with the blackfeller Law in the Walbiri language, dog and everything: chased to another mob again, **boxed up** with another mob again, and go and boxed up again with another different-different tribe.

Hence **box-up**, (of a place) where there has been the mixing of two or more groups of people.

Unlike the verbal form, this term is not found as an adjective in non-Aboriginal English.

1949 *Oceania* Sept p. 12 [NT] *Between* estates and ranges there might be zones of indeterminary, shared by contiguous groups without clash over title . . . The aborigines clearly recognised the existence of indeterminate tracts, which were called 'company' or '**box-up**' places. 1983 C.H. Berndt & R.M. Berndt *Aboriginal Australians* p. 22 [NT] These three sites are shared equally in terms of rights and responsibilities by the two local descent groups and a strip of land approximately 20 km wide joining these sites is a shared or '**box-up**' boundary.

break in *verb* To be taught or given experiences which will make one more fully adult.

From *break in*, to train an animal, particularly to train (a horse) to be ridden.

1987 A. McGrath *Born in the Cattle* p. 166 [NT] '**Breakin' in**' refers to the boys initiation ceremony and the early experiences of the promised bride; it is applied equally to the person learning to ride the horse and the beast being tamed. **1990** *Aboriginal History* (Canberra) Vol. 14:1 p. 34 [Borroloola, north-east NT] Yanyuwa people today use many European expressions . . from their long association with the cattle industry. Individuals have described . . how all the young people 'are very hard to wheel out now' and how 'we're trying to catch him up and **break** them young boys **in**'.

butcher *verb* [northern Aust.] To ritually circumcise. Also used as a noun, the person who performs this task.

From *to butcher*, to cut up a slaughtered beast for eating, and *a butcher*, the person who does this. The immediate understanding of **to butcher** in the cattle station context is one of the performance of a skilled task.

1986 B. Shaw *Countrymen* p. 189 [Kimberley, WA] They do that every year, **butchering** those little boys. **1986** B. Shaw *Countrymen* p. 189 [Kimberley, WA] Oh, he's a champion **butcher**. I tell you, before the kid winks his eye it's gone.

calf *noun* [northern Aust.] A child.

From *calf*, the young of cattle.

1986 B. Shaw *Countrymen* p. 157 Well they have *yudburr* (intercourse), and another time *yudburr*, all the way like that till they find a **calf**.

clean *verb* [north-west NT] To remove a people from their country, either by killing or physical removal.

From Australian English *to clean*, to clear a paddock of stock. The appropriateness of the term in relation to Aboriginal people is evident in much of the history of this area. Although there was violence on each side, the ratio of killing of black to white was approximately 10 to 1. Many groups were wiped out completely and most lost the rights to their ancestral countries.

1991 D.B. Rose *Hidden Histories* p. 16 [Victoria River, north-west NT] Now, when he started to knock (kill) my people up in Sydney, that means he started to **clean** (eradicate) my people. **1992** D.B. Rose *Dingo Makes Us Human* p. 194 [Victoria River, north-west NT] You been like to **clean** the people out from him own country. **1992** D.B. Rose *Dingo Makes Us Human* p. 195 [Victoria River, north-west NT] Captain Cook been **clean** up, bring man, brings book longa this country . . . They say this land belongs Aboriginal people. Captain Cook been stealing this boundary.

cleanskin *noun* An uninitiated, hence uncircumcised, man.

From *cleanskin*, 'an unbranded animal'. Circumcision is part of the initiation ritual for young men entering adulthood in most of the western two-thirds of the continent.

1903 H. Basedow *Jrnl. Govt. N.-W. Exped.* 21 May (1914) p. 111 He is a so-called '**cleanskin**', that is, he has not yet been the victim of any personal mutilation ceremonies. **1985** B. Rosser *Dreamtime Nightmares* p. 71 [north Qld] Yes, same with the men, too, if he's never been done. He's still just a **clean skin**.

cut *verb* [northern Aust.] To circumcise.

From *cut*, 'to castrate'. The *Oxford English Dictionary* does record *cut* meaning 'to circumcise', but notes it as 'rare and obsolete', but common as an adjective. Circumcision is part of the ritual which made a boy into a man.

1981 G. Ngabidj *Country of the Pelican Dreaming* p. 51 [north-west WA] I went into the Law late in life because my mother did not like it. She passed away before they **cut** me. **1987** S. Morgan *My Place* p. 180 [north-west WA] I didn't want to go through the Law . . I didn't want to be **cut** this way and that. **1988** P. Taylor *After 200 Years* p. 169 We could not eat them, they are pets. Here Esau my son is trying to snare a young pig, so that I could **cut** it and make it a 'young man'.

doctor *noun* [Now northern Aust.] A ritual circumciser.

From *to doctor*, 'to castrate an animal'.

1938 D. Bates *Passing of Aborigines* p. 215 [northern SA] The old men and brothers-in-law sometime arrived by trains, wearing felt hats and calling themselves '**dokkatur**', with the initiation knife, whittled from a glass bottle. **1985** O. Stanley *The Mission and Peppimenarti* p. 72 [Daly River, northern NT] There were initiations (circumcisions) of seven local boys. The **Aboriginal doctors** came from Kununurra. **1986** B. Shaw *Countrymen* p. 188 [Kimberley, WA] A good man, that **doctor** boy, won't take long when he's using the blade.

Hence **doctoring**, circumcision.

1986 B. Shaw *Countrymen* p. 189 [Kimberley, WA] We got a black boy to do the **doctoring**. He was a good feller, quick.

drop *verb* [northern Aust.] To give birth to a child.

From *drop*, 'to give birth to', applied generally to domestic animals; although it may be influenced by Aboriginal languages which often have a term equivalent to *to fall* for 'to give birth to'.

1986 B. Shaw *Countrymen* p. 82 [Kimberley, WA] In the early days when they were born, see, the piccaninnies **dropped** and we gave them their blackfeller name and a skin.

gear *noun* [north-west Aust.] Sacred and secret material.

From *gear*, 'equipment'. The speakers would have been familar with the term 'gear' used for stockwork equipment.

1978 K. Palmer & C. McKenna *Somewhere Between Black and White* p. 48 [Pilbara, WA] You got to get through this . . Law now, and he's a big one, big mob songs, plenty **gear** and painting up. **1986** B. Shaw *Countrymen* p. 139 [Kimberley, WA] We keep it away, as long as we can look after the **Gear** . . what we have here . . is the Law. **1986** B. Shaw *Countrymen* p. 165 [Kimberley, WA] Say, if I left that **Gear** of mine on a boat landing and a girl come along and looked, well I'd have to tell all the old people that she'd walked over there.

hunt *verb* **1** To chase (someone), to harass (someone). Also **hunt away**.

1984 P. Read *Down There With Me on Cowra Mission* p. 13 [south-west NSW] They used to talk Wiradjuri, but in them days they'd **hunt** us kids. You know, you weren't allowed to sit down and listen to them talk. **1984** P. Read *Down There With Me on Cowra Mission* p. 66 [south-west NSW] Fuckin' Aboriginal trying to **hunt** another Aboriginal fuckin' where he was bred and born. **1984** *Yeperenye Yeye* (Alice Springs) Jan. p. 19 [central Aust.] We're not going to **hunt** each other **away** from this site. **1992** R.L. Ginibi *Real Deadly* p. 25 Then they'd take off to the pub to play pool, or ogle some dubays . . I scolded the two of them, **huntin'** them home.

2 To chase (something) away, to get rid of.

1986 B. Shaw *Countrymen* p. 137 [Kimberley, WA] The people used to **hunt** the sores away with mud.

3 As **hunt down,** to look for (someone).

1987 A. McGrath *Born in the Cattle* p. 166 Bovine metaphors are wide-ranging, presenting in some cases an explanation from the processes of cattle-colonisation: for example . . 'huntem down' implies the act of looking for someone, while 'huntem' away' is to chase or get rid of someone.

mixed *adjective* **1** (Of a group or community) comprising people originally from different localities or groups, and hence under stress. Also **mixed up.**

It is possible the term with its negative connotations came from the problems associated with *mixing* herds of cattle.

1980 B. Sansom *The Camp at Wallaby Cross* p. 10 **Mixed** in Aboriginal English is not a socially neutral word for it has damaging imputations when applied to mobs. When I was told that the mob I had joined was 'mixed' . . (the speaker) represented the Wallaby Cross mob as perpetually on the edge of dissolution. Then 'mixed' is paired with 'noisy' where noisy stands for fractiousness . . mixed groupings are constitutionally noise prone because their existence must be based on a set of uneasy alliances between people who, because ethnically unlike, will speak in different ways and so have different words for things. They therefore cannot share properly in understandings. The argument is that to join the mob of a mixed camp is to enter Babel. **1988** C. Dunne *People Under the Skin* p. 166 [central Aust.] On other settlements there are a lot of **mixed** people, a lot of trouble.

2 (Of a language) mixed with other languages or dialects.

1984 J. Hudson & P. McConnell *Keeping Language Strong* p. 16 Another way of talking that you can hear a lot around the Kimberleys is 'mixed' language. This is when people put 'language' words or phrases or whole sentences in when they are talking Kriol or Aboriginal English, or put in Kriol or English when they are talking 'language'. **1990** A. Schmidt *Loss of Australia's Aboriginal Language Heritage* p. 33 [northern Qld] The parents themselves are semi-speakers with limited or only partial knowledge of the language. These people . . hesitate to speak such 'mixed-up' language to their children.

mix up *verb* [northern Aust.] To mix with another group.

It almost always has a negative association, in that **mixing up** with another group is seen to be an undesirable thing.

1978 H. Dagmar *Aborigines and Poverty* p. 94 [Gascoyne, central WA] People from town and East Carnarvon **mix up** with the reserve people. **1988** P. Marshall *Raparapa* p. 104 [Kimberley, WA] The Nyikina people and the Yawuru people are all **mixed up** together, nowadays. **1988** S. Dunlop *All that Rama Rama Mob* p. 179 [central Aust.] Lot of people yelling, settlement **mix up.** But when he sit down separate from mob . . he good. **1990** A. Pring (ed.) *Women of the Centre* p. 101 [Oodnadatta, northern SA] Dad didn't want us to **mix up. 1991** *Amanbidji Land Claim* 21 Aug. [north-west NT] *Ginger Packsaddle* . . Then old people, walkabout, you know, **mix up.**

Hence **mix up country,** one shared by different groups.

1984 S. Cane *Desert Camps* p. 46 [Western Desert] This idea of shared or 'mix up country' was in fact alluded to by Berndt.

mob *noun* A group of Aboriginal people, linked by relationship and culture.

The word originated in the term *mob,* meaning 'a rabble, a riotous crowd'. It was applied in the early days of the British occupation to a hostile group of Aboriginal people and to a herd or a flock of animals—both with the sense of a threatening presence. The word is used widely now in Australian Englishes to mean a group of people or animals, or as an expression of number.

The first two examples show the historic origin of the term, applied almost simultaneously to cattle and to Aboriginal groups.

1828 *Hobart Town Courier* 12 July p. 2 [Tas.] The wild **mob** [of cattle] .. content with devouring our grass, walk off with every horn and hoof belonging to us. **1828** *Hobart Town Courier* 13 Sept. p. 3 [Tas.] The tribe of natives who murdered the unfortunate man named Samuel Clarke, at the Lakes last week, consisted of what is generally known as the big river **mob** and another united. **1900–3** W. Telfer *Wallabadah Manuscript* (1982) p. 97 [northern NSW] I been see him big fella **mob** Come along road two fella week ago. **1924** A.G. Bolam *Trans-Aust. Wonderland* p. 80 [Ooldea, northern SA] Big **mob** coming alonga coast. Close up, two days Ooldea. **1938** V.E. Turner *Good Fella Missus* p. 11 [SA, NT] Please tell us properly true what them white fella want black fella **mob** to go Ti-Tree for. **1962** J.H. Bell *Aboriginal Education in NSW* p. 122 [Sydney, NSW] Those .. are described disparagingly as 'wild blackfellers', 'bush natives' and as 'bad **mobs**'. **1975** *Overland* (Mt Eliza) no. 61, p. 31 [Carnarvon, WA] That's their run and that's where they stop you know, in their own lingo **mob**. Yes, they home in their own country. **1978** *Cent. Aust. Land Rights News* (Alice Springs) p. 12 [central Aust.] People had gone to Mission Creek because they were frightened after hearing about shooting which was going on down the Lander River of people, and where a particular **mob** had been in the high school business camp. **1978** *Alyawarra Land Claim* p. 484 [central Aust.] Do the Ukuruputinya **mob** own those places—are they bosses for those places? **1980** B. Sansom *The Camp at Wallaby Cross* p. 14 In the local argot, 'runnin with a **mob**' is related to how one has 'run along with' others in one's life. **1981** M. William *Traditionally My Country* p. 51 [south-east Qld] In some instances a broad sense of focus of identity may be required and one could say that they were from the 'Gooreng Gooreng **mob**' while in another situation where a finer definitive line is required one might say they are 'Miriam Vale mob' or 'Thornhill mob' .. As one gets further afield .. one's focus of identity would extend to being one of the 'Queensland mob'. **1981** W.J.K. Christensen *The Wangkayi* p. 203 [Kalgoorlie, WA] He nodded towards a close 'brother' who had joined him, in Perth, adding simply 'my **mob's** here.' **1988** I. Keen *Being Black* p. 141 [south-west WA] The all one family is divided into a number of sections of approximately forty to 150 people. These sections have no specific term but are variously and interchangeably referred to as 'lots', '**mobs**'.

poddy *noun* [western NSW] A young man before marriage.

From the Australian pastoral English term *poddy*, 'a calf, lamb or foal which is handfed'; the term being originally from the British dialect *pod*, 'a large protuberant stomach'.

1958 J. Becket *A Study of a Mixed Blood Aboriginal Minority* p. 145 Young men or '**poddies**' as they are called, find single life very pleasurable.

quiet *adjective* [Chiefly northern Aust.] **1** (Of a person or people) no longer causing trouble, especially violent resistance to the European occupation of their country.

The term is often used in opposition to WILD where to be 'wild' is to be independent of or in opposition to European control. The word probably came from the use of the term in relation to wild and 'quiet' animals, particularly horses and cattle.

1938 V.E. Turner *Good Fella Missus* p. 26 [central Aust.] We no steal white girl, we sit down **quiet** along station, and no touch white woman or girl. **1978** J. & P. Read *View of the Past*

p. 74 [northern NT] Then people come **quiet** from after that fellow bin get shot now. They all come quiet all the way, now.

2 (Of a place) pacified.

1985 I. White et al. (eds) *Fighters & Singers* p. 80 We all come to that **quiet** country you know [the area now 'pacified'].

3 (Of people or animals) harmless, 'tamed', 'broken in'.

1872 Mrs E. Millett *Australian Parsonage* p. 84 '**Quiet** fellow' and 'sulky fellow' have an almost equally wide range, the first signifying any conceivable degree of amiability, either in man or beast, and the latter ferocity to a like extent. **1978** *Cent. Aust. Land Rights News* (Alice Springs) Jan. p. 2 [southern NT] My dreamtime country, my dreaming is a Storm Bird (Karrakurr) and Brown Snake, the **quiet** one, blackfellows call 'em Coonatjewi. **1986** B. Shaw *Countrymen* p. 90 [Kimberley, WA] When you broke in horses, you had to race them round the yard with all the **quiet** horses. **1988** J. Collman *Fringe-dwellers and Welfare* p. 183 [central Aust.] He presented himself as a '**quiet** man' who did not hit women. **1988** H. Ross *Community Social Impact* p. 30 [Kimberley, WA] New white people bin come in this country now. Some **quiet** mob, not . . hurting native people much.

quiet *verb* [Chiefly northern Aust.] To pacify a community or country in order to end the violent resistance to the European occupation. Also **quiet down, quieten, quieten down**.

As with QUIET the term comes from 'quietening' animals, especially horses and cattle, where the animals were then amenable to control.

1978 J. & P. Read *View of the Past* p. 152 [northern NT] And one old man . . well he was used to white people, and he come all the way along track, quiet them people . . **Quietenem** Mangarai people, yeah. **1978** J. & P. Read *View of the Past* p. 127 [Victoria River, north-west NT] Him mighten be putten that chain longa you-feller (to) **quieten** him. Just makem you-feller, makem little bit quiet, like a dog. **1985** I. White et al. (eds) *Fighters & Singers* p. 81 [central NT] They had tents everywhere, and were **quietening down** all the bush blackfellers. **1989** R.M. Baker *Land is Life* p. 285 [Borroloola, north-east NT] For example, individuals have described to me how the police been '**quieten** us **down**'.

run *noun* The ancestral territory of a person or group; COUNTRY.

From the pastoral Australian English term *run*, an area for the pasturing of sheep or cattle, first recorded in 1804. By the 1830s the term was also being used for the ancestral country of an Aboriginal group, but it is no longer current in this sense in other Australian English. The first citation is an example of this use.

1913 *Science of Man* Sydney) Nov. p. 31 [south-west WA] The number of native names occurring within the area of a small tribal **run** depends upon the many creeks, waterholes, hills, rocks, or other natural features. **1975** *Overland* (Mt Eliza) Vol. LXI p. 31 [north-west WA] They . . talk to each other in that Ningaloo country. That's their **run** . . their own country. **1983** N. Green *Desert School* p. 36 [south-west WA] Most Aborigines worked in loosely defined areas which they called '**runs**', a term originally used to refer to pastoral leases and these were an important feature of Aboriginal life early this century . . . In some cases the runs coincided with traditional territorial divisions. **1988** I. Keen *Being Black* p. 141 [south-west WA] The set of towns within a particular region is referred to by the Nyungar as a '**run**' . . . The concept of a run has no meaning unless it is attached to a particular family community, and a run is usually spoken of in the possessive; for example, our run, their run, or his run. **1989** R.M. Baker *Land is Life* p. 285 [Borroloola, north-east NT] For example, individuals have described to me how the police been 'quieten us down', how 'this . . my country, this . . my **run**'.

run *verb* [northern Aust.] **1** (Of a person) to live in the bush, as opposed to living with Europeans. Also **run wild**. See also QUIET, WILD.

From the predominantly Australian pastoral English term *to run*, '(of sheep and cattle) to live on a tract of land'.

1986 B. Shaw *Countrymen* p. 119 [Kimberley, WA] Those fellers were **running** in the bush, you know, when they were young blokes, kids. **1987** A. McGrath *Born in the Cattle* p. 166 [northern Aust.] Bovine metaphors are wide-ranging, presenting in some cases an explanation from the processes of cattle-colonisation: for example, 'rounding up', 'breakin' in', 'taming' and '**runnin' wild**' are equally applied to human as to animal, in a wide range of situations. **1989** R.M. Baker *Land is Life* p. 200 [Borroloola, north-east NT] He goes on to stress how before Europeans 'him been wild time, people been **running wild** yet longa bush'. **1991** D.B. Rose *Hidden Histories* p. 222 [Victoria River, north-west NT] He continued to work, and to **run** in the bush.

2 To carry or make effective a belief or ceremony over an area.

1981 *Kimberley Land Council* (Derby) Mar. p. 9 [Kimberley, WA] It's our country, for which we **run** our songs—that's why the old men won't agree with those white men. **1984** M. Gumbert *Neither Justice Nor Reason* p. 159 [NT] A travelling dreaming may pass through estates of several clans . . These clans are said in Pidgin to be 'company' for Rain, and may **run** the dreaming together in ritual. **1986** B. Shaw *Countrymen* p. 146 [Kimberley, WA] The girls have to **run** the Emu right up but they can't sing it. Men sing that corroboree. **1989** M. Edmunds *They Get Heaps* p. 143 [north-west WA] How are they going to **run** the law after we are finished?

shy up *verb* [northern Aust.] To act in nervous or frightened manner, like a shying horse.

1986 B. Shaw *Countrymen* p. 279 [Kimberley, WA] We were never frightened. They were like white men. You just said, 'Good morning. Hullo'. They didn't **shy up**.

string *verb* [northern Aust.] **1** To move in a line.

From Australian English *to string*, '(of sheep or cattle) to move in a line'.

1978 J. & P. Read *View of the Past* p. 42 [NT] They bin just go **stringing** longa here. Hid behind, you know, one way.

2 (As a noun) a line of people.

1978 J. & P. Read *View of the Past* p. 66 [NT] But this **string** of blackfeller went bush, you know.

tail *noun* [northern Aust.] The last people in a group.

From *tail*, 'the end of a mob of sheep or cattle'.

1978 J. & P. Read *View of the Past* p. 66 [NT] And when the shooting started, they start to follow them people . . and they could only find the **tail**. All the old ladies couldn't run fast enough.

tame *adjective* [northern Aust.] (Of a person) amenable to control.

Tame, usually used to describe animals, in nineteenth-century colonial Australian English sometimes referred to Aboriginal people who were not a threat to the occupation, as in the first citation.

1843 J. Hood *Australia & East* p. 190 Even the '**tame**' blacks, as they are called, are still a savage race. **1987** A. McGrath *Born in the Cattle* p. 166 [NT] Bovine metaphors are wide-ranging, presenting in some cases an explanation from the processes of cattle-colonisation: for example, 'rounding up', 'breakin' in', '**taming**' and 'runnin' wild' are equally applied to human as to animal, in a wide range of situations. **1988** P. Marshall *Raparapa* p. 57 [Kimberley, WA] I suppose that I got a bit **tame** after the manager said I could have that woman.

taming *noun* [northern Aust.] **1** The making of a person or people amenable to control by Europeans.

From *taming*, the domesticating of an animal.

1987 A. McGrath *Born in the Cattle* p. 99 [NT] 'Quieting down' and '**taming**' processes aimed to achieve a subservient, docile and obedient workforce.

2 The controlling of other non-animal things.

1989 M. Edmunds *They Get Heaps* p. 70 [north-west WA] *Talu* are recognisable places where Aboriginal elders focus ritual action, activating or '**taming** and driving' spiritual forces.

tell off *verb* [northern Aust.] To declare finished.

Possibly from *tell off*, 'to number, reckon, the members of a group, for example the animals in a herd'. *The Oxford English Dictionary* records this term as archaic except in dialect use.

1985 H. Koch *Non-standard English in Aboriginal* p. 183 [NT] A nonstandard use of **tell off** to mean 'declare finished' led to misunderstanding . . . Archie Long: When everything finish, painting turn-out, and kirta finish—finish that business—kurtungurlu going to **tell** him **off**. Mr Howie: You are saying when it finishes . . the kurtungurlu has to **tell** the kirta **off** . . . Archie Long: Yes . . Leave for a while.

wild *adjective* **1** (Of another Aboriginal person or group outside one's knowledge) foreign. By extension a person or group that is unacquainted with European or white ways, hence ignorant. See also MYALL.

From *wild*, 'uncultivated, undomesticated'. It was first used in nineteenth-century Australian English of Aboriginal people who were hostile to or independent of British control. See also TAME, QUIET. For Aboriginal people, **wild** people are objects both of fear (because they may have knowledge of specifically Aboriginal power which the 'insiders' may have lost) and some contempt (because they are ignorant of the European world and incompetent to operate in it). Like the colonial term, it also has the sense of being outside the control of the occupying society, but without the European cultural assumptions about 'wild' versus 'civilised'.

1846 *Portland Gazette* 15 Sept. p. 4/5 [Vic.] Each tribe denominates as '**wild** blackfellows' all others who are beyond the limits of its acquaintance. **1861** *Burke & Wills Exploring Exped.* p. 11 Our black boys are continually in dread lest the '**wild** black fellows' should poison them by some means. **1916** S.A. White *In Far Northwest* p. 36 [northern Aust.] During the afternoon the boys became very excited, and, pointing to footprints in soft sand, repeated '**Wild** Blackfeller' several times. **1927** M. Dorney *Adventurous Honeymoon* p. 34 Consider themselves a peg or two above the '**wild**-feller myall' who roams the bush and is not employed by the whites. **1948** *Oceania* p. 195 [north-west NSW] Upper-class, mixed-bloods dub the lower class . . '**wild** blackfellows'. **1961** *Polynesian Soc. Jrnl.* (Wellington, N.Z.) June p. 203 [SA] Several older Adelaide women have said they would not visit the west coast . .

for fear of unwittingly offending the 'wild blackfellers' who will always have their revenge. **1977** M. Tucker *If Everyone Cared* p. 79 [south-west NSW] We were afraid of the **wild** blackfellows too, but my uncle and aunt would say there are no wild blackfellows now. **1978** J. & P. Read *View of the Past* p. 152 [northern NT] Don't hustlem much to that people you (will) make more **wild**. **1980** T. Donaldson *Ngiyambaa* p. 12 [western NSW] The Marfield mob . . were 'a mob like a little **wild** family' who built miamias outside the tin-roofed huts supplied by the government, in preference to living in them. **1980** G.F. Brewer *On the Bread Line* p. 43 [central Aust.] I'm Christian woman. No church in Alice Springs and too **wild**. They still have corroboree in Alice Springs. Sing all night! **1982** J. Davis *Kullark* p. 57 [south-west WA] Stop it, stop it, Jees, you're acting like a pair of **wild** black fellas.

2 (Of a time, place or people) outside or not yet fully in the control of the occupying society.

This is an inverted use of the nineteenth-century non-Aboriginal Australian English use of the term *wild* to refer to hostile Aboriginal people; this time it is the view from the other side of the frontier and without the European cultural value judgments about 'savagery' and 'civilisation'.

1978 J. & P. Read *View of the Past* p. 39 [NT] They bin wanta spearem Queensland boy, before, **wild** time. **1978** J. & P. Read *View of the Past* p. 20 [northern NT] Still **wild** country and then white man bin come and shootem all the time the blackfeller. **1982** *Cent. Aust. Land Rights News* (Alice Springs) Spring p. 12 [NT] Oh, for a long time, yes, old people, **wild** people, and some other mob people. **1985** I. White et al. (eds) *Fighters & Singers* p. 82 They shot people because they were **wild** and fought back to the policemen. **1989** R.M. Baker *Land is Life* p. 195 [Borroloola, north-east NT] Macassan times, **Wild** times, War time, Police times, Welfare times, Cattle times, Gough Whitlam times. **1990** *Aboriginal History* (Canberra) p. 38 [Borroloola, north-east NT] In some cases such alignment was an important survival tactic during the '**wild** times' when Aboriginal people not associated with a European boss were often indiscriminately killed.

3 Aboriginal as opposed to European. See also BUSH.

In reference to plants, it is related to the originally nineteenth-century Australian English use of **wild** to mean 'Australian' and at the same time 'undomesticated'.

1966 M. Brown *Jimberi Track* p. 67 But first I got to get some **wild** boots—djordi we call 'em . . Ralph knew an old Worgai tribesman who always had a bundle of emu leather boots in his swag. **1980** *Sydney Morning Herald* 24 Jan. p. 2/8 [Murray River, north-west Vic.] We ate a lot of **wild** food. Canary thistles were juicy and sweet when young. **1986** *Aust. Ab. Stud.* no. 2 p. 4 **Wild** oranges (*Capparis spp*) were also, taking into account their lower water content, good sources of protein, fat and carbohydrate. **1989** J. Thomson *Reaching Back* p. 6 [north Qld] That thing what he's got round his head . . all threaded through with **wild** string. **1989** D. Walker *Me and You* p. 39 [north coast, NSW] It was the **wild** food that helped the family get by. **1990** A. Pring (ed.) *Women of the Centre* p. 78 [northern SA] **Wild** tuckers they get off the trees.

CHAPTER 7

Aboriginal way

This chapter traces the obscured patterns that direct the shape of a language—the past history, the social demands that inform and mould the visible present language. The use of these words, or the *way* they are used, manifests the history or the nature of the society in that use.

Some of the terms and usages in this chapter are the ones that people uninformed about Aboriginal Australian history and culture most associate with the idea of 'pidgin'—**plenty, allabout**. Indeed, Aboriginal English is still popularly called 'pidgin', even though in almost all instances that is not so. Some of the words that are found in Aboriginal English are also found in other parts of the world where English has been the contact language. **Plenty, savvy,** and **alonga** (*next to, with*) are found in the post-colonial Englishes of places as far separated as the West Indies, Singapore and North America. Other terms, such as **belong, all the time,** and **by and by** are found in other post-colonial Englishes of the South Pacific, particularly Tok Pisin from Papua New Guinea and Torres Strait Creole. The common colonial history of far-separated countries can be traced in these aspects of their languages.

In some areas of Aboriginal English, Aboriginal people have successfully maintained Aboriginal linguistic forms, so that some of the structural demands or differences found in Aboriginal languages are expressed in particular characteristics of Aboriginal English. Aboriginal languages in general do not have what an English speaker would describe as prepositions. Instead, a suffix is added, usually to the noun. This has meant that prepositions, words such as **to, for, from, in, at,** are sometimes used differently in Aboriginal English. It is also a characteristic of Aboriginal English that the articles **the** and **a** are often treated differently, sometimes being replaced by a demonstrative such as **this** or **that**. Aboriginal languages generally do not have anything that could be described as an 'article'.

Personal pronouns are used differently in Aboriginal languages, with a greater differentiation in number. For example *you* (singular) is distinguished from *you* (plural), *we* (two) from *we* (more than two). In Aboriginal English there is **youtwofeller** (you two) and **metwofeller** (we two or us two). On the other hand there is less distinction in the gender of pronouns, so that there is one third person pronoun, often **e**, for the equivalent of the English *he, she* and *it*. The use of the dual number in Aboriginal languages (English has only singular and plural) is reflected in the Aboriginal use of **two** as in **two hands**, where only one person is involved. In other Englishes there would generally be no mention of number, or the inclusive **both** would be used.

Other characteristics of Aboriginal English are formed out of the needs of the culture which used the language, demands not found in the society which

provided most of the vocabulary. Aboriginal society is one where direct questioning is not generally seen as an acceptable way to obtain information. For
example, to find out where someone else had been that morning, one might
comment that a lot of people had gone over to the football match in the next
town, or make a statement such as '*You been over Aunty Ida's this morning eh*'. To
the *eh* at the end of the sentence, a confirmation, a denial, the supply of further
correct information or no answer at all are all appropriate responses. In this way,
the dignity of the person speaking is preserved, as they are not put into the
situation of being refused information, and the privacy and autonomy of the
person addressed is also maintained. Aboriginal life is one lived 'in public' much
more than in most of non-Aboriginal Australia; this is one way that privacy and
'face' can be preserved in such situations. **Ain't it**, and **true** are other examples
of non-inverted question forms or language 'tags'.

Aboriginal English is also to a very great degree still primarily an oral
language. The number of Aboriginal writers using Aboriginal English is still
relatively small, though it is increasing. As Aboriginal English is still part of a living
oral culture, with the skills and needs of such a culture, it contains characteristics
such as the use of discourse markers in oral narratives to give the audience in-
dications of the structure of the narrative; a kind of oral 'punctuation'. Such
markers are found also in Aboriginal languages. In Aboriginal English **all right**,
now and **finish** are all used as this kind of marker, to give the listener cues as to
the progress of the narrative: when a segment of the story has finished, when a
new 'paragraph' or 'chapter' has begun. English also has some similar narrative
markers for stories that have an oral as well as a written existence, such as *once
upon a time* (which indicates to a listener that a narrative has begun), *now* (which
indicates some new action), and, in a certain kind of narrative, *they lived happily
ever after*, which indicates to the listener that the story has ended.

a *indefinite article* [Chiefly northern Aust.] The indefinite article used here with
collective or plural nouns.

> This use may have arisen for two reasons. Firstly, a use of hypercorrection;
> Aboriginal languages do not have an equivalent of the English articles *a* or *the*,
> and people whose first language does not have articles are likely to use them where
> none are needed. Secondly it could be a use of **a** meaning 'one', where the sense is
> *one lot of* or *one helping of* something which is a 'mass noun'—*ammunition*,
> *dripping, tucker, flour, sugar*, and, to a lesser extent, *seeds*.

> **1978** J. & P. Read *View of the Past* p. 155 [NT] Whitefeller, whitefeller got to pull a gun . . .
> Got **a** ammunition to shoot him. **1984** E. Roughsey *An Aboriginal Mother Tells* p. 68
> [Mornington Island, north Qld] He said 'Get me bushes and **a** dripping'. So we gave him
> bushes and the dripping. **1984** *Aust. Ab. Stud.* no. 2 p. 34 They can just have their bit of **a**
> tucker, flour and sugar. **1984** S. Cane *Desert Camps* p. 74 [Western Desert] Cheeky one
> spinifex . . . He got **a** seeds. **1986** *Kowanyama News* Dec. p. 17 [north Qld] Hey what . . .
> That lot got **a** handcuff!! **1988** C. Mattingley & K. Hampton (eds) *Survival in Our Own Land*
> p. 24 [SA] They'd put a flour in an' **a** water. An' they'd put a brown sugar then. **1991** D.B.
> Rose *Hidden Histories* p. 45 [north-west NT] He made a big stew for those boys, in the big
> oven. And he put **a** strychnine. And that's why they called it Poison Creek.

ain't it *interjection* [Chiefly northern Aust.] A corroborative or interrogative comment. It often functions as a question tag. See EH.

Non-inverted questions with a question tag are more common in indigenised varieties of English because of different rules of social behaviour. In Aboriginal English, it may reflect such different social behaviour in regard to direct questioning; see the introduction to this chapter.

1978 J. & P. Read *View of the Past* p. 60 [northern NT] They used to runaway too gottem you mob, **ain't it**. 1978 J. & P. Read *View of the Past* p. 89 [NT] Somebody might have bin pickem up, **ain't it**? 1986 B. Shaw *Countrymen* p. 285 [Kimberley, WA] We gotta interest that man because we might get caught on some *gadia* one day, **ain't it**?

allabout [northern Aust.] **1** (adverb) Everywhere.

1848 H.W. Haygarth *Recoll. Bush Life* p. 25 All travellers are universally welcome throughout the far districts, literally stopping, as the blacks call it, 'all about'. 1863 *Adelaide Observer* 12 Dec. p. 6/5 The blacks up there say, 'Very good country this one, **all about** flour, sugar, tea, clothes, and sheep.' 1909 H.K. Bloxham *On the Fringe* p. 141 [western NSW] Cobborn (*big*) pfeller white man, plenty wool (*beard*) **all about**, wantem see you longa 'fore. 1951 E. Hill *Territory* p. 443 [NT] **All-about** (Pidgin) . . . Everywhere. 1968 S. Gore *Holy Smoke* p. 17 He's make 'im sun—you call 'im *Yhi*. Make 'im moon—you call 'im *Bahloo*. You tell 'im how that one *Bahloo*, man feller; that one *Yhi*, woman feller—and alladay she's chase 'im that one *Bahloo* longa sky. She's loving him too much, **allabout**.

2 (pronoun) Everybody.

1893 *Report Australasian Assoc. Advancement of Science* V. 505 **All about**, come quick, plenty of kangaroo. 1935 M. & E. Durack *All-About* **All-About**: the story of a black community on Argyle Station, Kimberley. 1956 T. Ronan *Moleskin Midas* p. 235 [NT] 'What this yarn **allabout** got where you going to send my boy to whitefeller school?' she demanded. 1976 C.D. Mills *Hobble Chains and Greenhide* p. 9 [NT] 'All about' employed as gate-openers, we took our first jaunt in the open. 1978 J. & P. Read *View of the Past* p. 39 [central NT] All right we'll fire a shot longa **allabout**. 1989 R.M. Baker *Land is Life* p. 202 [Borroloola, northeast NT] Shoot their own colour, they been shoot **all about** . . their countrymen . . him become flash along their colour and shoot all about.

It now has a distinctive spelling **alabad**.

1991 D.B. Rose *Hidden Histories* p. 70 [north-west NT] This Bilinara, Malngin, they [police] were still chasing **alabad**. All of them, he started there now, chasing *alabad*. Chasing *alabad*.

all day *adverb* All the time, always, habitually. Also **alladay**, **all-day**.

1915 E.R. Masson *Untamed Territory* p. 108 [Arnhem Land] Jim Campbell . . puttem (the trepang) longa boiler . . takem out and killem (hit) longa ground **all day**. 1936 M. & E. Durack *Chunuma* p. 49 [Kimberley, WA] Boss been **all-day** gibbit me lolly, apple, horanch and cake too. 1978 J. & P. Read *View of the Past* p. 243 [northern NT] Him bin what name we two-feller, Jack, they bin callem Jack, but we bin callem . . 'Good boy' Well he bin **all day** like that 'Good boy!' 1979 *Land Rights News* 8 May They been **all day** kill 'm crocodile (*warrija*) black water goanna (*tujangarha*) kill kangaroo (*wanykurra*). Longa that sort of beef him been living early-day people. 1985 H. Koch *Non-standard English in Aboriginal* p. 185 **All day** seems to be used in the sense of 'habitually' . . That's the main waterhole there we been *all day* get im. Early days. 'That's the main water hole from which we would get water—in the early days'.

The term now has an Aboriginal English spelling **alda**.

1978 J. & P. Read *View of the Past* p. 205 [north-east NT] Yeah, I know, but I got all my Bible book in there, that's the way I **alda** . . teach all my grandchildren. 1978 J. & P. Read *View of the Past* p. 20 [north-west NT] Like, then both bin **alda** shoot, you know, spear bin alda come and straightaway—olden time.

all right *interjection* [Chiefly northern Aust.] It is used in a narrative to mark a new event, or a chronological break. Also **righto**. See also FINISH.

See the introduction to this chapter for a discussion of the use of narrative markers in Aboriginal English.

1978 J. & P. Read *View of the Past* p. 136 [Arnhem Land] **All right**, Mr. Robertson go down now, come there, start now that asking. 1978 J. & P. Read *View of the Past* p. 39 [central NT] **All right** we'll fire a shot longa allabout. 1983 P. Roe *Gularabulu* p. 25 [northern NT] **All right** when these womans seen all these, whatname comin' you know the rain. 1986 B. Shaw *Countrymen* p. 149 [Kimberley, WA] **Righto**, we'd fetch up tobacco and material for this *mamul* Business and sell it up Wyndham way. 1984 S. Cane *Desert Camps* p. 81 [Western Desert] **Alright** we can start now. Rock now, grinding put him in grindstone now. 1986 *Kowanyama News* Dec. p. 17 [north Qld] **Alright**, 'That's all eh' (Policeman Brown). Talk he them two. 1991 *Hidden Histories* p. 70 [north-west NT] **All right**, they went away. He shifted from that Midnight, he come to old Bow Hill.

all the same *adjective* Like, similar to. Also **alla same**, **all same**. See also SAME.

As *all same* it is also found in other post-colonial Englishes of the Sino-Pacific area.

1825 J. Troy *Australian Aboriginal Contact With the English Language in NSW 1788-1845* (1990) p. 123 [NSW] 'Oh!' says my guide, '**all the same** as oyster to you, and just as nice!' 1830 R. Dawson *Present State Aust.* p. 142 [central coast, NSW] Murry corbon wool-man, **all the same** like it bullock. 1863 J. Bonwick *Wild White Man* p. 36 [Vic.] We were confidently informed that the proper material came from the mountains, '**All the same** apple tree.' 1909 A.J. Peggs *Aborigines of Roebuck Bay* p. 355 [north-west WA] When a man along a public-house shootem debil-debil, he sing out, **all same** ibis. 1921 Corfield *Reminiscence of Qld* p. 47 [north Qld] He got 'em spear in his hand, and knock about things **all a same** like it duck egg [playing billiards]. 1928 B. Spencer *Wanderings in Wild Aust.* p. 160 [central Aust.] The bird becomes stupefied, or, to use the expressive description given to us by a native who was describing its action, it becomes 'drunk, **all same** white man'. 1982 *Bunji* (Darwin) June p. 11 [Darwin, NT] Fred . . had an initial fear of the desert Aboriginal, being convinced they had three toes '**all-the-same** Emu'. 1987 R.M. & C.H. Berndt *End of an Era* p. 117 [northern Aust.] In station-English phrasing, he said he was '**all-a-same** single-feller now'. He was anxious to know what he could do to recover his wife.

all the time *adverb* Always. Also **all time**.

There is a similar term in Tok Pisin, the post-colonial language of Papua New Guinea, *oltaim* 'always, constantly, all the time'.

1924 G. Horne & G. Aiston *Savage Life in Central Aust.* p. 137 [northern SA] It **all the time** make 'im bad. 1944 M.J. O'Reilly *Bowyangs & Boomerangs* p. 88 [northern Aust.] I told one of the old men, who could jabber fairly good English, about the incident. That is what he told me: 'that fellow bean tree is one place where big fellow 'Kaditcha' **all the time** sit down; no white fellow, no blackfellow allowed camp alonga that place'. 1978 J. & P. Read *View of the Past* p. 20 [northern NT] White man bin come and shootem **all the time** the blackfeller. 1980 S. Kaldor et al. *Language of School* p. 428 [WA] These combinations occur in all areas . . '**all time**' . . 'always'. 1984 *Aboriginal History* p. 56 [Borroloola, north-east NT] **All the time** . . (before) we been tuck out that minja . . bush tucker. 1985 Borowski *Juvenile Delinquency in Aust.* p. 119 They worrying for grog **all the time**, not that kid. 1986 B. Shaw

Countrymen p. 223 [Kimberley, WA] But some blokes don't like the white feller. That's why they give them fight **all the time**.

along *preposition* **1** Next to, with.

The current use is LONGA or LA. It is possible that this was also the pronunciation in the following citations but it was recorded as **along**. This is found in various forms in many post-colonial Englishes throughout the world, such as Sranan in Surinam as well as more local Pacific English languages.

1863 J. Davis *Tracks of McKinlay* p. 100 The 'White fellow what sit down **along** water.' This word the natives use almost indiscriminately. **1863** J. Bonwick *Wild White Man* p. 44 Very nice young man, you go **along** him his country? **1909** A.J. Peggs *Aborigines of Roebuck Bay* p. 349 [north-west WA] I found out soon after he wanted a rake to clear up the grass with—a brush **along** a nail he designated it.

2 To, at, from, for.

Most of the uses in this form are not current. As with the first sense, this may be the result of **longa** being recorded as **along a**. It is also found in post-colonial English languages in Melanesia, including Tok Pisin, the language of Papua New Guinea.

1909 A.J. Peggs *Aborigines of Roebuck Bay* p. 348 [north-west WA] Jack told him he wanted a carved shell to 'put **along** belt'. **1938** V.E. Turner *Good Fella Missus* p. 5 [northern Aust.] We sorry **along** you. **1979** D. Lockwood *My Old Mates and I* p. 172 [NT?] A man earning what was then the award wage of $21 was paid only $3.50 '**along** finger', as they say.

altogether *adverb* [northern Aust.] Completely.

This is also found in post-colonial Englishes in Melanesia.

1882 A.J. Boyd *Old Colonials* p. 205 [north Qld] Oh, Marmy that fellow Ned he kill 'em **altogether** along o' camp. **1928** B. Spencer *Wanderings in Wild Aust.* p. 609 [northern NT] In the end he decided, as he said, to 'chuck 'em **altogether**'. **1978** J. & P. Read *View of the Past* p. 290 [central Aust.] Pow! No good. No good **altogether**. **1986** B. Shaw *Countrymen* p. 184 [Kimberley, WA] They dance, paint up **altogether** right up, and finish. **1986** C.A.V. Priest *Further N.T. Recollections* p. 3 [Borroloola, north-east NT] Dolly had been close up finish then, and **altogether** died at Wearyan. **1990** P. Austin et al. *Language & History* p. 250 [Oodnadatta, northern SA] I was a young feller then. All the young fellers double-banked me all the time. They were cheeky. They attacked me. Their spears never caught me. Only I caught them properly **altogether**.

at *preposition* Used of places, time, etc. where the standard use would be *in*, or no preposition would be used.

Aboriginal languages do not have the equivalent of a preposition but many have a suffix which covers the meanings of *on*, *at*, *in*. This then may become a characteristic of Aboriginal English, even for people whose original language may not have had this feature.

1975 R.J. Merritt *Cake Man* p. 13 [south-west NSW] Down there **at** Victoria, now, they got this different word. **1988** J. Harkins *English as 'Two-way' Language* p. 102 [central Aust.] I live at Anthepe . . I go to picnic and . . dig rabbit, **at** bush. **1988** J. Harkins *English as 'Two-way' Language* p. 189 [central Aust.] Lotta people bin come for Shane birthday **at** yesterday. **1989** R. Comm. *Aboriginal Deaths in Custody: J. Moore* p. 181 [Vic.] She was **at** a totem of the sand storm and the crow.

ay *interjection* See EH.

belong *verb* [northern Aust.] Usually followed by the preposition **to** (with variants such as **belonga, b'longta**), which in turn governs a pronoun (or, less often, a noun), indicating possession. For example, **stockman b'longta you** = 'your stockman'. Also **blung.**

This is also found in other post-colonial Englishes in Melanesia.

1846 *Cumberland Times* 4 Apr. p. 4/1 [Sydney, NSW] Fishook held his bundy over his head, saying 'bail you saucy, or pie cobra **belonging** you,' meaning he would strike me on the head. **1884** *Jrnl. Royal Anthrop. Inst. Great Brit. & Ireland* Reprint 1971 XIII. p. 300 [Qld] That brother **belonging** to me you have killed; why did you do it? **1915** E.R. Masson *Untamed Territory* p. 167 Jim Campbell, Charlie, Dick, . . Fred, lubra **b'longa** him, me, thass all. **1936** M. & E. Durack *Chunuma* p. 47 [Kimberley, WT] By an' bye 'im grow 'm up make 'm good fella stockman **b'longta** you. **1977** N. Kolig *Playing Alonga Mud* p. 15/16 Those who had persevered with the course and had acquired some skill were now almost deferentially called 'Maban (expert) **belonga** clay'. **1986** *Kowanyama News* Dec. p. 17 [north Qld] Them two bin help'm too, and that father **blung** to this one old Frank. **1986** B. Shaw *Countrymen* p. 95 [Kimberley, WA] There's the bloke that's kill that feller, uncle **belong** you an me. **1991** D.B. Rose *Hidden Histories* p. 260 [north-west NT] Get that fire [wood] stacked up like that tree there, that high . . . It wasn't wood **belong** to that fire pile. Might be for station, or somebody else, you know.

bit *adverb* A little, a bit of, slightly.

c.190– R.H. Mathews (Field Notebk.) no.1 n.p. [south coast, NSW] Jallup's head is **bit** straight for Mmumacbumacl. **1949** *Oceania* Dec. p. 102 [north-west NSW] Besides the medicine man himself there are other aborigines in north-western N.S.W. who are believed to be 'a **bit** clever'. They do not possess the same extraordinary powers as the medicine man, but they are believed to be skilled in malevolent magic. **1984** P. Harris *Teaching about Time* p. 11 [north Qld] In Wik-Munkun (Queensland) the English terms are usually used, but brown coins may also be referred to as 'big' and 'small', and the silver (white) coins may be distinguished as 'small', '**bit** big' and 'big'. **1985** B. Neidjie *Kakadu Man* p. 34 [Arnhem Land] When I was growing up good mob of people all around then. Now people **bit** wicked.

bit of (a) prisoner.

This use is probably a response to the circumstance of mentioning a potentially difficult topic (i.e. the situation of being a prisoner) in conversation and attempting to reduce the emotional import of the information.

1984 *Aust. Ab. Stud.* no. 2 p. 33 [NT] And you can have, top of that, couple of men, or big mob men, make him **bit of prisoner**. **1991** D.B. Rose *Hidden Histories* p. 37 [north-west NT] That's the police station. Police Hole . . Girls they had, **bit of a prisoner**, whatever way.

borrow *verb* To lend.

1989 *Koori English* (Vic. State Board Education) p. 9 [Vic.] Don't you know how to bring lawn mower back when I **borrow** it to you = I only lent you that lawn mower.

by *preposition* [northern Aust.] Concerning, from, in relation to.

1978 J. & P. Read *View of the Past* p. 138 [Arnhem Land] Now I'm very sad **by** that business . . what about the Bible by Mr Watson? **1991** D.B. Rose *Hidden Histories* p. 18 [Victoria River, north-west NT] Old people got shot. Why? **By** land. Just stealing the land. **1991** D.B. Rose *Hidden Histories* p. 193 [Victoria River, north-west NT] We always had all them ordinary cattle like. They were born **by** all this country.

by and by *adverb* Eventually. The recorded evidence is mostly not current. Also **bimeby, bimebye, by am by, by-and-bye, bye and bye.**

This is of course also found in general English use, but is used with greater frequency in many post-colonial Englishes derived from pidgins throughout the world. It is found as *baimba* in Tok Pisin, the language of Papua New Guinea. It is also common in the Aboriginal pidgin of fiction.

1830 R. Dawson *Present State Aust.* p. 117 [central coast, NSW] 'What for go dere, massa?' . . I then bid him goodbye, and said, 'Bill no belong to me now I believe I look out another black fellow **by and bye.' 1863** J. Bonwick *Wild White Man* p. 44 [Vic.] **By-and-bye** she say 'when you ready?' **1882** A.J. Boyd *Old Colonials* p. 223 My word! Cobon [very] budgeree [good] pleeceman, you **bimeby? 1900** T. Major *Squatter's Note Bk* p. 109 [north Qld] I . . inquired of an old woman when the corroboree would commence. She answered '**By am by'. 1926** L.C.E. Gee *Bush Tracks & Gold Fields* p. 36 [NT] This blackfeller, him away; him play about him all right, **bye and bye** him go cranky longa head. **1968** S. Gore *Holy Smoke* Glossary p. 104 *Little-bit-time-***bimebye:** Quite soon (Pidgin). **1986** J. Davis *No Sugar* p. 75 [south-west WA] Gudeeah politjman git you, **bye and bye. 1990** P. Austin et al. *Language & History* p. 24 [Oodnadatta, northern SA] I learnt properly that one [circumcision] and **by and by** I had that second cut [subincision].

close up *adverb, adjective, & preposition* Near.

This appears to be more common among older people. There is a similar form in Tok Pisin from New Guinea, *klosop*, 'nearly, almost'.

1845 C. Hodgkinson *Aust. from Pt Macquarie to Moreton Bay* p. 87 [north coast, NSW] They belonged to one of the Manning River tribes and told me that the tribe was '**close up** bulga' (near the mountain). **1895** S. Newland *Aboriginals I have Known* p. 10 The mob of cattle was sold at Swan Hill . . when any doubt was expressed, he retorted ''Wan Hill **close up** Melbourne'. **1928** B. Spencer *Wanderings in Wild Aust.* p. 407 [central Aust.] One day the man walked from the hole . . looked back and said, 'I can see the water, it is '**close up**' yet.' **1966** A.T.H. Jolly & F.G.C. Rose *Field Notes* p. 108 [Kimberley, WA] When someone make cousin to me, I look away when **close up. 1980** B. Sansom *The Camp at Wallaby Cross* p. 111 [Darwin, NT] By 'campin **close up**' and 'campin far' people map current social distances. **1986** C.A.V. Priest *Further N.T. Recollections* p. 3 [north-east NT] Dolly had been **close up** finish then, and altogether died at Wearyan.

close up-close up, very near. As with many other words in Aboriginal English, reduplication is used to intensify the meaning, a linguistic use carried over from Aboriginal languages.

1925 P. Bridges *Walkabout in Aust.* p. 180 [central Aust.] Apparently we were nearing Alice Springs. The boy kept . . saying, '**Close up-close up**'.

different-different *adjective* [northern Aust.] Very different. See also BOSS-BOSS, HALF-HALF.

This is an example of reduplication for emphasis; this usage follows the pattern in Aboriginal languages, and many other languages around the world, where reduplication is used to intensify the meaning

1986 B. Shaw *Countrymen* p. 84 [Kimberley, WA] It comes up together with us Miriwong, Djamindjong, Garamau, and Ngaliwuru, you know, **different-different** languages. **1990** P. Austin et al. *Language & History* p. 24 [Oodnadatta, northern SA] I went with the blackfeller Law in the Walbiri language, dog and everything: chased to another mob again, boxed up with another mob again, and go and boxed up again with another **different-different** tribe.

eh *interjection* An interjection, used as a rhetorical comment, usually at the end of statements. Also **a, ay, aye, hey.**

The use of this interjection, which invites but does not demand a comment from the person addressed, is one of the communication strategies used in Aboriginal society. Direct questioning is often considered inappropriate behaviour; the speaker may attempt to elicit information or opinion by the use of a comment, which the person addressed is therefore free to 'answer' if he or she wishes. In this way, personal privacy in a very 'public' society is protected, and the personal dignity of individuals is preserved by their not being 'put on the spot' with a direct question.

1816 J. Troy *Australian Aboriginal contact with the English language in NSW 1788-1845* (1990) p. 118 (ref. Stanbury 1977) Why Massa Gubernor, said Black Jack:- you Proflamation—all gammon—how blackfellow read him '**eh**! He no learnt him read Book'. **1861** L.A. Meredith *Over the Straits* p. 98 The various expressions conveyed by the peculiar 'ay, ay' so constantly used by the natives in speaking is perfectly indescribable. It is used doubtfully, positively, interrogatively or responsively . . and contains in itself a whole vocabulary of meanings . . Suppose you inquire of a native if he have seen such and such a person pass, as he has gone that way—'**Ay, ay**?' (introspectively). 'Yes, a tall man.' 'Ay, ay.' (thoughtfully). 'A tall man, with great whiskers.' 'Ay, ay (positively). Good way up, cobbra, cabou grasse, ay, ay.' (corroboratively). **1970** *Van Leer Project* Dept of Education, Qld p. 23 [Qld] He big one, **eh**? **1981** J. Davis *The Dreamers* p. 91 [south-west WA] They 'ave lunch, **eh**? Roy: They 'ad pies an' cool drinks. **1982** R.D. Eagleson et al. *English and the Aboriginal Child* p. 133 [NSW] There is one other grammatical tag which seems distinctive of Aboriginal speech: **Eh** . . . [O]ne time me and my uncle were chasing three emus . . . They're not going to take kindly to that *eh*? **1984** P. Read *Down There with Me on Cowra Mission* p. 52 [south-west NSW] Oh well, they reckon you come back to your own dunghill to stay, **eh**. **1984** C. Allridge *Aboriginal Eng.* p. 17 [south-east Qld] Where Ozzie father workin' **eh**. **1987** A. McGrath *Born in the Cattle* p. 71 [NT] We all felt sorry for that girl, cruel **eh**? **1987** *Junga Yimi* Yuendumu Sept. p. 26 [Yuendumu, central Aust.] Can't be too hard to work out **ay**? **1987** J. Davis *Honey Spot* p. 19 [south-west WA] **Eh**, gneen baal? (Who's that?) **1988** *Social Alternatives* (St Lucia) Mar. p. 24 [south-east Qld] JB: That was a mission too, hey? **1988** J. Davis *Barungin—Smell the Wind* p. 23 [south-west WA] No thanks, cob, but you can gives us a lift to the session on your way back. **Hey.** **1988** *Dusty Creek Comic Bk. no. 2* p. 37 [western NSW] Great film, **aye** Sam? **1988** R. Langford *Dont Take Your Love to Town* p. 206 [northern NSW] That's all that matters '**a**'. **1989** *R. Comm. Aboriginal Deaths in Custody: J. Moore* Sect. 2.13 [Vic.] It's alright here, **eh**. **1989** D. Walker *Me and You* p. 45 [north coast, NSW] Douglas was the biggest, he ran that kangaroo down **eh**! **1991** L.M. Wilkinson *Aboriginality* p. 260 [south-west Vic.] The use of '**eh**?' on the end of statements and questions is common . . it is posited more as a statement of fact rather than requiring an answer. Often a statement such as 'Good, eh?', or 'This is the blackfella way, eh?' do not require an answer. **1992** R.L. Ginibi *Real Deadly* p. 37 [Sydney, NSW] Though the whole history of white Australia is one of fiction, **eh**!

fellow *noun* **1** A person, either male or female, though usually male. Also **fella, feller, fulla,** and many other variant spellings. See also BLACKFELLOW, WHITEFELLOW and YELLOWFELLOW.

Fellow has been and is used in general English colloquial and informal speech, but it was taken up very early in the occupation by Aboriginal people to mean 'a person' (generally a man).

1848 T.L. Mitchell *Jrnl. Exped. Tropical Aust.* p. 110 'Those **fellows** were murry coola' (very angry). **1900** T. Major *Squatter's Note Bk* p. 25 [western NSW] My word, me catch him that **fellow. 1949** *Oceania* Dec. p. 95 [north-west NSW] 'I don't like that **feller.** He's too *gwaan-gwaan*' a half-caste woman said, referring to a white man of obviously subnormal intelligence. **1978** K. Palmer & C. McKenna *Somewhere Between Black and White* p. 70 [Pilbara, WA] He was a young *mudamuda* **fellow** who had come from further west. **1978** J. & P. Read *View of the Past* p. 249 [northern NT] Cheeky **feller** . . Killem (i.e. hit) boy, little boy, brokem up you know, makem good boy. **1982** J. Davis *Kullark* p. 94 [south-west WA] Yeah, lotta **fellas** finish there, Mogumber. **1984** *Puggana News* (Launceston) Feb. p. 9 [Tas.] Christ you **fullas** that ball hurt. **1984** P. Read *Down There with Me on Cowra Mission* p. 108 [south-west NSW] I haven't been in jail with these new **fellers** now. **1990** S. Watson *Kadaitcha Sung* p. 189 [south-east Qld] Beer for us **fullahs** and one bottle of rum for our deadly sister! **1990** O. Noonuccal *Aust. Legends and Landscapes* p. 108 [Tas., Qld] One day the Oyster Bay Tribe was trading with the Big River Mob when an argument started over who owned the ochre, the Oyster Bay **fullas** wanted more ochre, and for no cost. **1993** E. Crawford *Over my Tracks* p. 138 [western NSW] He come over and jumped all over me. I could hear my mother's voice sayin' 'Who's that **feller** the dog's jumpin' all over? The dog must know him'.

somefellow, some person or some people.

1978 J. & P. Read *View of the Past* p. 103 [NT] Well that's why some people, old people bin setting up camp . . waiting for **some feller** go out hunting. **1980** L.G. Fogarty *Kargun* p. 98 [south-east Qld] Also billy is hairy Wowee . . **somefella** call him YOWIE. **1980** B. Sansom *The Camp at Wallaby Cross* p. 149 [Darwin, NT] I dunno, **somefella** you jus caan understand.

Other combinations include: **little fellow**, a child; **old fellow**, an older person (but see also OLD); **young fellow**, a young person, usually a young man. For the combination **poor fellow** see Chapter 3.

1978 K. Palmer *Somewhere Between Black and White* p. 20 [Pilbara, WA] The years passed, Clancy was no longer a child, and ceased to have the benefits and privileges of being a '**little fellow**'. **1991** *Amanbidji Land Claim* 21 Aug. [north-west NT] Pick **little fellow** up, bring little fellow here. **1977** M. Tucker *If Everyone Cared* p. 31 [south-west WA] She was such a tiny old woman, and old *Nkuppa* was a bent **old fellow.** They always spoke together in the language. **1978** J. & P. Read *View of the Past* p. 101 [NT] They bin findem one **old feller** . . longa Dingo Hole, longa Hole. **1978** *Yura Wangkanyi* June p. 3 [north-east SA] Namana (uncle) was a greedy man and whenever any **young fellows** caught anything he would tell them that they shouldn't eat it. **1988** A. Moffatt (ed.) *Aboriginal Deaths in Custody* (Transcript) p. 134 [south-east Vic.] That **young fellow** up the back might tell me the name. **1990** A. Schmidt *Loss of Australia's Aboriginal Language Heritage* p. 22 [north-west WA] Them **young fella**, he dry up, spilt. He empty person. Without identity, without language, he got nothing left.

2 Any animate or inanimate thing.

1884 *Jrnl. Royal Anthrop. Inst. Great Brit. & Ireland* Reprint 1971 XXIII. p. 292 [Qld] The blacks do not attribute much malice to these *Limbeen*, but say they are 'good **fellows**', although they can work evil at times. **1914** F.A. Fitzpatrick *Peeps Into the Past* p. 28 [north coast, NSW] He . . threw the gun down on the verandah and remarked 'That **fellow** no good . . I bin put im up gun, that fellow bin snap'. **1986** B. Shaw *Countrymen* p. 240 [Kimberley,

WA] They had to bring the outside cattle into the paddock and pass them over to other **fellers**. 1990 S. Watson *Kadaitcha Sung* p. 210 [south-east Qld] That **fullah** is my tucker! He my minnu, you know? 1993 E. Crawford *Over my Tracks* p. 125 [western NSW] When I'd stand straight in the water, it'd move me, rock me, lift me up, off the bottom! I said to meself, 'This's no water like I know. This **feller's** *alive!*'

3 In combination with adjectives. This is similar to the use of ONE or WAY used with adjectives; Aboriginal languages generally do not distinguish between nouns and adjectives and this use may be a consequence of this, by making the adjectives nounlike. Thus **big fella business** = 'important business'.

1872 'Resident' *Glimpses Life Vic.* p. 195 [Vic.] The word 'fellow' was always used as an additional qualification of the noun; as for instance '**fine fellow** horse', or 'big fellow river', which meant simply 'a fine horse', or 'a big river'. 1889 *S.A.P.P. Quarterly Report on N.T.* Feb. p. 9 [SA] Now time whitefellow take him bullocky and clear out. **This fellow** country him blackfellow country. 1893 *Transactions Royal Society S.A.* (Adelaide) XVII p. 244 [Borroloola, north-east NT] First time rain came on we call'm 'Meewidgie' By-and-bye rain go away, **cold fellow** come on . . . Then dry fellow come up we burn'im grass. Then big fellow hot come on. 1924 G. Horne & G. Aiston *Savage Life in Central Aust.* p. 117 [north-east SA] No good make 'em rain this time. Too much **dry fella**. 1944 M.J. O'Reilly *Bowyangs & Boomerangs* p. 88 That is what he told me: 'that fellow bean tree is one place where **big fellow** 'Kaditcha' all the time sit down; no white fellow, no blackfellow allowed camp alonga that place'. 1978 J. & P. Read *View of the Past* p. 172 [Borroloola, north-east NT] We bin gettem out at night time, you know . . . We bin jump down, at night time, you know. Oh proper **dark-feller** too, too cold too. 1986 B. Shaw *Countrymen* p. 129 [Kimberley, WA] They all settled down and went straight back to the bone fat. 'Oh, oh very good, e **sweet feller**' . . . They ate it and finished it till there was nothing left. 1987 A. McGrath *Born in the Cattle* p. 64 [NT] We go back to work again. Watering garden, washem plates, cookem tucker for supper, **ready feller**. 1989 R.M. Baker *Land is life* p. 282 [Borroloola, north-east NT] They come up **big fella** business. 1984 *Aust. Ab. Stud.* no. 2, p. 34 [NT] That's for the **me fellow** Aboriginal people.

The combinations **good fellow** and **silly fellow** are especially common.

1935 K.L. Smith *Sky Pilot Arnhem Land* p. 50 To Dan everything that flew, or walked, or creeped, or swam was '**good fellow** tucker'. 1947 W.E. Harney *Brimming Billabongs* (1963) p. 92 They told me that this boss of theirs was a '**good fellow** man'. 1968 S. Gore *Holy Smoke* p. 16 Make 'im goanna too, and snake—**goodfeller** tucker longa you binjy, eh? 1977 *Up Beat* Aug. 7 Him **goodfella**, but jus' keep 'im 'way from me. 1911 A.L. Haydon *Trooper Police of Aust.* p. 399 One man whom the boy described as '**silly fellow**' because he had gone in his socks . . and gone lame. 1936 M. & E. Durack *Chunuma* p. 29 [Kimberley, WA] 'Chunuma **silly fella**!' he said sternly. 1980 B. Sansom *The Camp at Wallaby Cross* p. 80 [northern NT] Youfellas you jus **sillyfellas**. Siddown.

4 In combination with numbers and quantity.

1856 W.W. Dobie *Recoll. Visit Port-Phillip* p. 91 [Vic.] The flattering compliment meant for my brother and myself, that 'there was no gammon along o' **two fellow** Dobie'. 1870 C.H. Allen *Visit to Qld.* p. 182 [Qld] 'Fellow' is a very important word in their English vocabulary, and expresses number; as '**six fellow** yarraman', six horses. 1884 A.W. Stirling *Never Never Land* p. 93 Everything is a 'fellow'; '**one fellow** bob', the black calls a shilling; 'me got three fellow gin', meaning 'I have three wives' and so on. 1928 B. Spencer *Wanderings in Wild Aust.* p. 590 [NT] Then **two fellow** walk. By and by him come back. Him been bring 'em three fellow bag longa potato. Doctor been carry 'em two fellow bag, him (pointing to prisoner) 'been carry one fellow. Two fellow been sit down and tuck out.' 1953 L. & C. Rees *Spinifex*

Walkabout p. 125 The homestead itself is . . storeyed—as the natives say 'him **two-fella** house'. 1978 J. & P. Read *View of the Past* p. 244 [northern NT] I bin oughta (used to) makem **three feller** hole, you know, inside. 1978 J. & P. Read *View of the Past* p. 121 [NT] They bin meetem **one-feller** girl, longa creek.

5 In combination with pronouns.

me feller, me, us, we.

1989 R.M. Baker *Land is Life* p. 189 [Borroloola, north-east NT] I been find all my boy long Borroloola . . **me fella** and Banjo find big mob girl too and boy. **1984** *Aust. Ab. Stud.* no. 2 p. 34 [NT] That's for the **me fellow** Aboriginal people. **1987** A. McGrath *Born in the Cattle* p. 61 [NT] When we was a kid we couldn't even talk properly, but the missus go tell **me fellers** 'You gotta speak! Talk proper English you naughty girls—you'll get a smack!' **1993** G. Koch *Kaytetye Country* p. 47 [central NT] This my wife here because **mefella** family, mefella bin gettin married.

me two-feller, we two, us two.

1896 *N.T. Times (& Gazette)* (Darwin) 11 Dec. n.p. **Me two fellow** kill em at Timlet. **1987** R. Baker *Borroloola Area Contact History* p. 2 [north-east NT] **Me two feller** been yabber, 'They are going to fight me two fella.'

them fellows, them.

1963 D.E. Barwick *Little More than Kin* p. 48 [Melbourne, Vic.] We heard that two of **them fellows** are stopping down Gore Street.

us feller, us.

1984 *Black Voices* (Townsville) Apr. p. 39 Most of **usfella** don't know how to pray. **1986** B. Shaw *Countrymen* p. 52 [Kimberley, WA] The way we learned to kill a kangaroo, the old father for **us fellers** showed us. **1993** G. Koch *Kaytetye Country* p. 123 [central NT] More bigger than **usfellas** any way.

we feller, we, us two.

1986 *Wangkany* SA Dept of the Environment n.p. [northern SA] There were no Afghans or Chinese, only **we fellers**, Aborigine stockmen, running the camp.

we two-feller, we, us two.

1978 J. & P. Read *View of the Past* p. 243 [NT] Him bin what name, **we two-feller**, Jack, they bin callem Jack, but we bin callem . . 'Good boy.' Well he bin all day like that 'Good boy!'

you feller, you.

1993 G. Koch *Kaytetye Country* p. 27 [central NT] **Youfella** come a little bit close. Wefella— we might give youfellas a little bit—youfella gotta eatem tucker. And meat. **1986** J. Davis *No Sugar* p. 59 [south-west WA] **You fella** got them doothoo tied up? **1978** J. & P. Read *View of the Past* p. 93 [NT] You know, poor fellers, you might go, **you-feller** perish.

you two feller, you two.

1978 J. & P. Read *View of the Past* p. 127 [NT] **You two-feller** mightem be pullem me-feller leg. For nothing.

6 In combination with adverbs and adjectives, usually with adverbial force. Thus: **true fella** 'truly'; **quick-fellow** 'quickly'.

1896 *N.T. Times (& Gazette)* (Darwin) 11 Dec. n.p. [north-west NT] Jaydeadda told me killed a white fellow little bit, Wallagoola killed him **hard fellow**. **1927** M. Terry *Through*

Land of Promise p. 201 [NT] When a black says someone has 'bin kill 'em' he means someone has been knocked about or hurt; he says 'bin kill 'em **dead fellow**' when he refers to death. **1936** M. & E. Durack *Chunuma* p. 117 [Kimberley, WA] '**True fella**?' he asked. **1950** A.S. Bird *Scarlet Pillow* p. 41 [WA] Her queer little merry laugh could always be heard when she succeeded in alarming the roosters and making them 'sing out **big fella**'. **1963** I.L. Idriess *Our Living Stone Age* p. 30 They would . . seriously paint the doll, boy or girl, with stripes of red or yellow ochres, 'dressing' them thus for various corroborees; all had to be done '**proper feller**'. **1978** J. & P. Read *View of the Past* p. 89 [NT] Policeman bin catchem **quick-feller**, straightaway. Him bin catchem now, that's right. **1986** J. Davis *No Sugar* p. 76 [southwest WA] He bin knock me **silly fella**, with a big stone.

fetch *verb* To go.

1989 R. Comm. *Aboriginal Deaths in Custody: J. Moore* p. 93 [Vic.] The rents are too high for Aboriginal peoples. It **fetches** it back to poor jobs. All these sort of things come into it.

finish *verb* [northern Aust.] The end, an end.

This is a marker used in narratives to mark endings of parts or wholes. See also ALL RIGHT, OH, NOW and the introduction to this chapter for a longer discussion of narrative markers.

1978 J. & P. Read *View of the Past* p. 137 [Arnhem Land] He talk like that, 'Oh you go away now. **Finish**'. **1984** S. Cane *Desert Camps* p. 118 [Western Desert] More people coming behind; my husband . . eating up bush potato; **finish**. **1986** B. Shaw *Countrymen* p. 303 [Kimberley, WA] Glossary . . **finish** . . In oral literature the expression is often used to mark the conclusion of a tale or an episode within it.

first time *adjective & adverb* [northern Aust.] First.

This is also found in Melanesian post-colonial Englishes.

1928 B. Spencer *Wanderings in Wild Aust.* p. 590 **First time** him sleep, then him wake up. Moon longa top of sky. Him say you and me go longa Price potato. Doctor been first time yabber this. Me no been go. Then two fellow walk. By and by him come back. **1931** *Bulletin* (Sydney) 15 Apr. p. 21/3 From the moment one of them knows that she is to have her '**first-time** piccaninny', she carries everywhere with her what is meant for a doll or effigy of the small expected. **1991** D.B. Rose *Hidden Histories* p. 39 [north-west NT] But I know a lot of *ngumpin* got shot at Police Hole now . . I saw that place. That's the **first-time** police mob made that place there.

for *preposition* 1 Concerning, about, because of, for the reason of.

Many Aboriginal languages have a suffix which indicates that entity to which the activity is directed; the goal, the beneficiary, the recipient which this action *will be for*. These citations would have employed this suffix if they were translated into Aboriginal languages.

1930 F. Hives & G. Lumley *Journal of a Jackeroo* p. 173 Then, for no apparent reason and without previous 'symptoms' they will suddenly revert to the most primitive savagery, throwing off their clothes and going '**for** bush'. **1976** *Identity* (Sydney) Jan. p. 14 [Arnhem Land] How about the other mobs? They do not interested **for** swimming. **1978** *Cent. Aust. Land Rights News* (Alice Springs) June p. 6 [central Aust.] Roy Hammer added: 'Yeah, Mr Viner been fooling us **for** that country.' **1978** J. & P. Read *View of the Past* p. 57 [NT] They sat there, they didn't say anything, nothing. They were very careful **for** each other. **1978** J. & P. Read *View of the Past* p. 152 [northern NT] 'Did he tell the Mangarai people about tobacco?' 'Yes, **for** tobacco, and for sugar, for tea leaf, for flour, I think'. **1982** *Tjakulpa*

Kuwarritja (Papunya) Aug./Sept. n.p. [central Aust.] On picture nights and concert nights please do not use the side of the Town Hall **for** toilet because there has been a lot of sickness. **1985** O. Stanley *The Mission and Peppimenarti* p. 43 [Daly River, north-west NT] Yes, all been get killed **for** a fight, you know? All been die. **1989** M. Lennon *That's How it Was* p. 16 [Oodnadatta, northern SA] After my mother died, I found it very hard **for** food. **1980** B. Sansom *The Camp at Wallaby Cross* p. 122 [Darwin, NT] The Singing Man froze in a squatting position when he 'went **for** that toilet'. **1984** *Tjakulpa Kuwarritja* (Papunya) Dec. n.p. [central Aust.] We stop in Threeway **for** buy some food for eat. **1988** S. Dunlop *All that Rama Rama Mob* p. 42 [central Aust.] She's wrong in the head, *rama rama*, she's *rama rama* **for** head. **1989** *Koori English* (Vic. State Board Educ.) p. 9 [Vic.] You **for** eating = You eat too much. **1991** D.B. Rose *Hidden Histories* p. 72 [Victoria River, north-west NT] He's frightened **for** whitefellow.

for drunk, for drunkenness, on a drunkenness charge.

1988 R. Langford *Dont Take Your Love to Town* p. 154 [northern NSW] We left feeling ashamed of ourselves for being pinched **for drunk. 1988** H.B. Day *Royal Commission into Aboriginal Deaths in Custody* (Transcript) p. 97 [Vic.] They said, 'Don't be silly, you're under arrest **for drunk**, now come on'.

2 There is a particular use where the **for** refers to a ritual or spiritual relationship. One member of a family may fast, or dance in a ceremony, **for** another member of the family, because that person is undergoing some stage in a ritual. This is similar to general English use in an expression such as *he died for his country.* The relationship can also be between a person and non-human thing.

1979 G.K. Cowlishaw *Woman's Realm* p. 277 [Arnhem Land] A husband and son sat down in front of a whole roast bush-turkey and his wife and daughter chewed damper. They simply said 'We don't eat that **for** our brother/son'. That is, a classificatory kinsmen . . was undergoing his initiation, and during many months this fact placed restrictions on his 'M's ['mothers'] and 'Z's ['sisters']. **1987** *D-Bate* Language Education Course, Deakin University p. 12 [central Aust.] Sasha: And what they gotta dance for na? Antronese: **For** our brother, they gotta make-em strong man na. **1989** B. Morris *Domesticating Resistance* p. 141 [northern NSW] She didn't dance **for** me while I was out in the bush. **1986** B. Shaw *Countrymen* p. 34 [Kimberley, WA] There was this barramundi down here at the dam **for** my mother and father, and *Yiralalan* the Dream for that tree belonged to my father. **1988** *We have Survived* Poster/np [Arnhem Land] Everybody knows Captain Cook. Old people, not young people. You've got to have a lot of learning to know Captain Cook. More culture. I can sing it now **for** this bark painting. This is the way his song goes.

3 Of, from, belonging to.

Most Aboriginal languages can have a suffix which is related in some sense to the suffix mentioned in **1** above, with a possessive sense, 'belonging to, of'.

1984 *Aboriginal History* p. 57 [Borroloola, north-east NT] When they been eat that tucker **for** whitefella, they couldn't live in the bush. **1985** S. Kaldor et al. *Aboriginal Children* p. 422 [Kimberley, WA] Rachel mob-**for** dog bin die (Rachel's people's dog died) (Fitzroy Crossing 9). **1985** S. Kaldor et al. *Aboriginal Children* p. 232 [WA] I know who-**for** birthday was last night. **1986** B. Shaw *Countrymen* p. 214 [Kimberley, WA] Somebody might be short **for** beef. We could kill our own beef. **1988** P. Marshall *Raparapa* p. 204 [Kimberley, WA] That's where I met up with the boss **for** Kungkarakarta (Jubilee Downs). **1988** I. Keen *Being Black* p. 151 [south-west WA] The foundation of authority . . expressed in the Nyunga maxims: 'a mother is boss **for** her children'. **1991** *Amanbidji Land Claim* 21 Aug. [north-west NT] And what country that father **for** you, where did he come from? *Ginger Packsaddle* My father he for Watitj.

from *conjunction & preposition* [northern Aust.] Because, because of, at.

Many Aboriginal languages have a suffix which has the sense of *this was the reason for it* (in the past). It is similar to the sense of FOR, which relates more to the future. There is a causative sense in the Aboriginal English use of *from* which is not usually present in other Englishes, except occasionally, as in *she became ill from overwork*.

1986 B. Shaw *Countrymen* p. 44 [Kimberley, WA] I not givin you cheek. Your fault **from** hit me. **1988** J. Harkins *English as 'Two-way' Language* p. 104 [central Aust.] She frightened, **from** the boys. **1988** H. Ross *Community Social Impact* p. 31 [Kimberley, WA] They shooting and poisoning people, most of the people got killed **from** the *kartiya*. **1989** J. Thomson *Reaching Back* p. 15 [northern Qld] There's a big creek—Karpa Creek—well just on the other side there was a big camp . . while he was still alive. He died **from** there. **1991** D.B. Rose *Hidden Histories* p. 90 [Victoria River, north-west NT] I'll talk **from** Lingara this morning. **1991** D.B. Rose *Hidden Histories* p. 218 They never forget that law. **From** (because) they (trackers) shot him—Old Gordon.

get *verb* Become.

This is also found in other post-colonial Englishes in North America, West Africa, and the West Indies (Jamaican Creole), as well as the South Pacific. It is similar to the general English use of *get* as in *get old, get tired,* but it is found in a wider range of contexts.

1962 T. Ronan *Deep of the Sky* p. 187 [northern NT] Young man **get** properly shame then. **1978** J. & P. Read *View of the Past* p. 111 [NT] We **get** happy, old people was coming back again. **1980** B. Sansom *The Camp at Wallaby Cross* p. 144 [Darwin, NT] Besides, they had to '**get** clear', redeem their debt to the dead girl, cleanse and purify themselves. **1985** H. Koch *Non-standard English in Aboriginal* p. 183 [NT] To **get** *young man* is to become a young man or be initiated . . Billy Pumper: Hatches Creek . . . After I *get young man*, he ('my father') brought me back to Murray Downs. **1989** M. Lennon *That's How it Was* p. 49 [Oodnadatta, northern SA] Say if I **got** in love with a full blood I suppose I wouldn't have been allowed to [marry]. **1990** *Austral. Jrnl. of Linguistics* Dec. p. 294 The Aboriginal English term *shame* differs from non-Aboriginal uses of *shame* and *ashamed* not only in meaning but also in syntactic form. The most common syntactic frames are *be shame* (with optional surface copula, Harkins 1988:120), **get** *shame* and *make (someone) shame*.

get accident, to become involved in an accident, to have an accident.

1980 B. Sansom *The Camp at Wallaby Cross* p. 185 [Darwin, NT] The story is that the person damaged got into a fight, got bashed or 'bin **get** that **accident**'. **1986** B. Shaw *Countrymen* p. 195 [Kimberley, WA] Every time you have to watch that place because a lot of trucks **get accidents** there. **1995** M. Brady *Giving away the Grog* p. 98 [north-west NT] I got a young fella driver, he drive us back to the Bulla community, and big mob of young fella driving home and that's when they **got accident**.

get (one's) age, to become old.

1989 R. Comm. *Aboriginal Deaths in Custody: J. Moore* p. 167 [northern Vic.] He was a good worker until this business happened like, you know, till he **got his age**.

he *personal pronoun* [Chiefly northern Aust.] The third person singular pronoun: **he**, **she**, **it**.

Many Aboriginal languages do not differentiate in pronoun use for gender, as does English with *he/she/it*, whereas both Aboriginal languages and English do so for number, as in the English *I/we*. Harkins (1993) says that the modern version *ee* is really an undifferentiated pronoun, which should not be interpreted as being '*e* (he). The use of an undifferentiated personal pronoun is also found in other post-colonial Englishes. In many cases this is the result of the influence of the structure of the original or first language of the speaker. **1839** W. Mann *Six Yrs' Residence* p. 72 [Sydney, NSW] 'Well, please your Majesty . . are not these fine houses . .?' 'Yes please your Excellency,' exclaimed King Bungaree, 'de be vera good, pose (suppose) **he** rain'. **1909** *Folklore* (London) p. 360 [north-west WA] White womane go away now, **he** no good. **1914** R.S. Newall *Stone Implements from Millstream Stn, WA* p. 303 [WA] **He** good fella stone, he cut'em spear. **1978** J. & P. Read *View of the Past* p. 201 [Ali Curung, central NT] Topsy's not here. He's gone . . . And **he** went to be with his mother and father. **1978** J. & P. Read *View of the Past* p. 153 **He's** same like bush rice, yeah, lily seed, and when you grind him and make a damper, well, that one same. **1983** A.H. Ross *Aust. Ab. Perceptions* p. 269 [Kimberley, WA] This house, **he's** buggered up now. **1984** S. Cane *Desert Camps* p. 73 [Western Desert] Gunamarradja (Scirpus dissachanthus) . . Hard one, **he** got to stop in water. **1985** B. Neidjie *Kakadu Man* p. 41 [Arnhem Land] Tree, **he** change with rain. He get new leaf, he got to come because rain. **1986** *Wangkanyi* n.p. [northern SA] Broke em like that, cook him. Just like potato. And **he's** got a flower, yellow one, big leaf. **1988** H. Ross *Community Social Impact* p. 44 [Kimberley, WA] They say that government **he** didn't allow for him. **1990** J. Chi *Bran Nue Dae* p. 47 [Broome, WA] I got this girl Rosie . . . **He** in Broome now, he bin kicked outta Mission too. He different one from me . . . I don't know if he like me. **1993** G. Koch *Kaytetye Country* p. 15 [central NT] He's—**he's** my daughter. I bin give him promise to that old man there, he's my lamparra (son-in-law).

On Cape Barren Island, Tasmania, **he** is used for **it** (but **she** is not similarly used).

1975 *Linguistic Communications* Melbourne Vol. XIII p. 88 [Bass Strait, Tas.] Pronouns: regular use of 'he', 'him' for 3 pers. impersonal pronouns ('it' very rare) of Standard English in reference to 'middle sized' objects—eg. animals, tools, etc.

him *personal pronoun* [northern Aust.] **1** The third person pronoun (objective case): **him, her,** and **it.**

1978 K. Palmer & C. McKenna *Somewhere Between Black and White* p. 52 [Pilbara, WA] 'I heard something about you riding back from Moolyella with a bucket of tea balanced on your head or something.' 'Well', replied Clancy quickly, 'Put **him** on the handle bars really'. **1980** B. Sansom *The Camp at Wallaby Cross* p. 115 [Darwin, NT] We bin try to break that Rose **him** arm. **1985** B. Neidjie *Kakadu Man* p. 41 [Arnhem Land] I tell kids. When you get yam, leave hole. I say 'Who leave that hole? Cover **him** up'. **1988** H. Ross *Community Social Impact Assessment* p. 75 [Kimberley, WA] Even woman, woman could say that **himself**. **1987** R. Baker *Borroloola Area Contact History* p. 2 [Borroloola, north-east NT] They been flog that woman now, no more little bit, they been kill [hit] **him** some way again.

2 The third person pronoun (subject case), where the non-Aboriginal use would be **he, she,** or **it.**

1909 *Folklore* (London) p. 326 [WA] **Him** good pfeller boomerang. **1929** Wm T. Hill *Magic Spear* p. 14 **Him** moon libbit on ground long time before. **1950** A.S. Bird *Scarlet Pillow* p. 120 [northern WA] They stayed chattering and laughing and scolding their many dogs till 'bacca **him** all finish'. **1978** J. & P. Read *View of the Past* p. 243 [Barunga, northern NT] But my wife he bin all day hanging up there, look look while **him** bin young girl.

in *preposition* [northern Aust.] On, about.

1984 C. Allridge *Aboriginal Eng.* p. 47 [Qld] Hey something touching me **in** the leg. **1987** T.S. Dixon *The Wizard of Alice* p. 332 [central Aust.] That man was sitting **in** the side of the beach. **1989** M. Edmunds *They Get Heaps* p. 148 [Roebourne, north-west WA] They like to sit down and talkin with Aboriginal people, talkin **in** the land.

la *preposition* [northern Aust.] In, at, on, to. See also ALONG, LONGA.

1980 B. Sansom *The Camp at Wallaby Cross* p. 118 Young Jack bin bash ol Frank **la** head kad (by means of a) bottle. **1978** J. & P. Read *View of the Past* p. 89 [Borroloola, north-east NT] When that thing went click, that means the rifle went bang. Finish him off. They chucked him **la** fire. Chuck a kerosene. Light him. Burn. **1985** *Black Voices* (Townsville) p. 22 [north Qld] 'We go **la** this Point', said Horace. **1986** *Kowanyama News* Dec. p. 17 [north Qld] What you call'm . . Jack Lefthand where he bin dead **la** Palm Island. **1988** H. Ross *Community Social Impact Assessment* p. 44 [Kimberley, WA] They bin take her **la** Moola Bulla, now, little fella time (when she was small) my sister.

little bit *adverb & adjective* **1** (In relation to quantity, such as time, age, distance, temperature), quite (a), a bit of (a).

1968 S. Gore *Holy Smoke* Glossary p. 104 **little-bit**-*long-time*: Fairly soon . . . **little-bit**-*time-bimebye*: Quite soon. (*Pidgin*) **1978** J. & P. Read *View of the Past* p. 89 [Borroloola, north-east NT] I bin see him (when I was) **little bit** young feller. Havem whisker today. I bin little young feller. **1978** J. & P. Read *View of the Past* p. 111 [Western Desert] Old people was coming back again—what they bin run away. That way, Western Australia, **little bit** long way. **1983** *Upper Daly Land Claim* p. 48 [Daly River, north-west NT] The Wagiman people divide the annual cycle into five seasonal periods: . . '**little bit** warm, hot time'.

2 Used as a diminisher, which reduces either the intensity of the action referred, or the intensity of the statement itself.

The distinction may not always be clear. It is sometimes used when reporting facts or situations which might potentially be disturbing for the listener and hence disrupt social relations. See also BIT OF.

1896 *N.T. Times (& Gazette)* (Darwin) 11 Dec. n.p. [north-west NT] Jaydeadda told me he killed [hit] the white fellow **little bit**. **1984** *Aust. Ab. Stud.* no. 2 p. 32 [NT] I know Captain Cook been **little bit** wrong for these people. **1984** P. Read *Down There With Me on Cowra Mission* p. 24 [south-west NSW] We didn't swim, just drown a **little bit**, and they'd come and pull us out, give us a rest, and just throw us in again. **1986** J. Davis *No Sugar* p. 105 [south-west WA] GRAN: Bit crook. (Rubbing her leg.) Me leg get tired, **little bit**, this one. **1991** D.B. Rose *Hidden Histories* p 217 [north-west NT] Humbert Tommy a wild [one], **little bit** . . That's his son, Old Gordon's [he's a] big wild looking fellow like Gordon, too. **1995** M. Brady *Giving away the Grog* p. 71 [northern NT] I had a good name, **little bit**. That grog bin sort of pulled me into the town. And I lost me all sort of licence . . . Lose everything.

3 Small, short, (a) bit (of).

1910 (1975) E. Hassell *My Dusky Friends* p. 44 [south-west WA] Nothing Missus, I see **little bit** fire so I walk up see what *nunghas* down here. **1936** M. & E. Durack *Chunuma* p. 10 [Kimberley, WA] The older members of the camp had set themselves assiduously to the task of smearing charcoal and fat over the new born, lest he grow up '**little bit** white fella'. **1938** *Walkabout* (Melbourne) 1 Apr. p. 16/1 [NT] Constable: 'You all about gotten plenty bush tucker?' Reply: 'No more plenty. **Little bit**'. **1978** J. & P. Read *View of the Past* p. 288 [northern NT] You can see only a **little bit** machine gun, then after they got all bombed out. **1980** R. Davidson *Tracks* p. 180 [central Aust.] There seemed to be several categories of distance, divided up like this: **little bit** way, little bit long way, long way. **1985** B. Neidjie *Kakadu Man* p. 36 [Arnhem Land] Alright, . . from Oenpelli they bin walk, bring smokes,

little bit tea and sugar. 1990 P. Austin et al. *Lang. & Hist.* p. 249 [Oodnadatta, northern SA] I didn't like it in the Army. I couldn't sleep, nothing. No tucker. A **little bit** of dog biscuit, a little bit of bottle there for water.

longa *preposition* [northern Aust.] **1** Next to, with. Also **longe**. See also ALONG (sense 1), LA.

This is found in various forms in many post-colonial Englishes throughout the world, such as Sranan in Surinam as well as in more local Pacific English languages. 1861 *Rep. Select Committee Native Police Force* p. 162 [north-west Vic.] My word, my picaninny keep him prayer **longe** blackfellow; not longe station but longe bush. 1955 F. Lane *Patrol to Kimberleys* p. 215 [Kimberley, WA] **Longa**, aborigine pidgin for 'at' or 'with'. 1980 B. Sansom *The Camp at Wallaby Cross* p. 55 [Darwin, NT] A pitch is a place . . from which one can launch a foray against a wanted person spotted in the crowd, to 'catch up **longa** that fella and (ar)rest im'. 1993 G. Koch *Kaytetye Country* p. 104 [central NT] Cause not many people bin come in, Kaytetye, **longa** him because they had another church bin come round closer and from Hermannsburg.

2 In, at, to. See also ALONG (sense 2), LA (sense 2).

This use is found in other south-west Pacific post-colonial languages, for example in Tok Pisin of Papua New Guinea as *long*. 1861 *Rep. Select Committee Native Police Force* p. 162 [north-west Vic.] My word, my picaninny keep him prayer longe blackfellow; not **longe** station but longe bush. 1926 L.C.E. Gee *Bush Tracks & Gold Fields* p. 23 [northern NT] 'Might be I come too?' . . 'No more; more better you stop **longa** Pine Creek. Jack come back all right'. 1943 W.E. Harney *Taboo* p. 83 [northern NT] I take you **longa** court, you cheeky fellow. 1978 J. & P. Read *View of the Past* p. 85 [Western Desert] And they, they picked two old blokes up here **longa** Mt. Doreen . . doctor man you know. 1991 D.B. Rose *Hidden Histories* p. 72 [Kimberley, WA] They got that, book all over from Captain Cook. You might see blackfellows anywhere **longa** this country, you'll have to get them together . . and shoot [the] whole lot! 1995 M. Brady *Giving away the Grog* p. 101 [north-west NT] Every time I start to get up for drink of water or something like that, start to get giddy **longa** head.

might be *adverb* Perhaps, possibly; it may happen or may have happened (like this).

This is found of course in non-Aboriginal English, but it appears to be more common in Aboriginal English. The term is used to reduce the assertiveness of a statement, so that it functions socially more as a suggestion than a statement; as with EH. For a longer discussion of this aspect of Aboriginal English, see the introduction to this chapter. 1976 *Cent. Aust. Land Rights News* (Alice Springs) Spring p. 12 [central Aust.] **Might be** I know that already. They don't like the people to stop down there. 1978 J. & P. Read *View of the Past* p. 190 [NT] And I reckon, **might be**. 'Oh, that, that going to be bad, you know.' 1978 J. & P. Read *View of the Past* p. 45 [north-east NT] Them kid . . hittem longa tree. Bashem longa stone . . **Might be** too cruel. 1981 *Kimberley Land Council* (Derby) Mar. p. 17 [north-west WA] **Might be** trouble Wiluna, Yeelirrie, Leonora or Kalgoorlie way—we're all in one area, one country. 1981 B. Lennon *Yarns Around the Firebucket* p. 10 [northern SA] The boss employs stockmen to go to the dam every day to save the sheep. **Might be** one stockman dies or clears out—the boss has to employ another man in his place to keep pulling out the sheep. 1982 R.D. Eagleson et al. *English and the Aboriginal Child* p. 172 [WA] What would you like to be when you grow up?: Workin' . . I can't hear. E **might be** working. 1986 B. Shaw *Countrymen* p. 214 [Kimberley, WA] Somebody **might be** short for beef. We could kill our own beef. **1986** A. Weller *Going Home* p. 156 [south-west WA] If you 'ear someone call out to ya and ya turn around, then **might be** that ya die. **1988** I. Keen *Being Black* p. 106 [south-east Qld] Von Sturmer . . discusses the use of the expression '**might be**' (as a model qualifier) to distance the speaker from the certainty of the idea he is presenting. **1988** I. Keen *Being Black* p. 109 [south-east Qld] 'They gone fishin?' '**Might be**.'

my word *exclamation* Goodness, gracious me.

This is also found in general English use, although it would be considered somewhat old-fashioned in Australian English. It is recorded as a feature of pidgin and Aboriginal English in periods earlier than the present; it is found less frequently in the current records. It is sometimes used as a stock phrase for Aboriginal characters in fiction.

1887 W.H. Suttor *Austral. Stories Retold* p. 128 [western NSW] You hear him that one that fellow find him little boy . . Jim sit down there where that one cattle make it that one row . . We find him now, **my word**! budgeree that one! baal gammon. **1900** T. Major *Squatter's Note Bk* p. 25 [western NSW?] **My word**! Black fellow close up. **1909** H.G.B. Mason *Darkest West Australia* (1980) p. 54 [WA] **My word**, plenty me peer 'em up. **1933** E.R. Gribble *A Despised Race* p. 93 [north-west WA] **My word**, boss, I been make 'em. **1936** M. & E. Durack *Chunuma* p. 154 [Kimberley, WA] **My word** me chorry longa you! **1986** J. Davis *No Sugar* p. 65 [south-west WA] *Billy*: **My word** you fellas pr retty fellas. *Bluey Wee-ah*, plenty wilgi.

never *adverb* An emphatic negative.

This is also found in other post-colonial Englishes, such as that of Singapore, and other varieties of English.

1909 H.G.B. Mason *Darkest West Australia* p. 55 [WA] Nothing, **never** more. You see 'em that one? Jinghie man kill 'em. **1983** A.H. Ross *Aust. Ab. Perceptions* p. 264 [Kimberley, WA] We **never** been in school, we been schooling our law. **1984** E. Roughsey *An Aboriginal Mother Tells* p. 54 [Mornington Island, north Qld] My people **never** knew to call our weathers by their seasons . . . It was by certain food . . 'water lily time, we dig for and eat them', or 'Palm nut time is on'. **1985** S. Kaldor et al. *Aboriginal Children* p. 228 [WA] We **never** pushed it but he did it by himself. **1989** R.M. Baker *Land is Life* p. 329 [Borroloola, north-east NT] 'Sit down quiet' they been tell him . . . Him bin sleep quiet he couldn't move nothing, he **never** cried nothing. **1988** H. Ross *Community Social Impact Assessment* p. 44 [Kimberley, WA] We don't know where she is . . . We **never** see her again, nothing. **1991** D.B. Rose *Hidden Histories* p. 47 [Victoria River, north-west NT] That's the story we know from Top End—old people were losing all the people every way. Aboriginal **never** got away. **1992** R.L. Ginibi *Real Deadly* p. 39 [northern NSW] Sometimes he **never** had the fare to go to and from, so he'd have to, as we Kooris say, 'put the long ones in' and walk all the way.

no more *adverb & adjective* Not, no, in no way.

1874 G. Taplin *Narrinyeri* p. 61 [south-east SA] My father, my mother **no more** help me. **1906** W.A. Horn *Notes by a Nomad* p. 134 [north-east SA] **No more** me want em pizzic, me big fellow all right now. **1938** X. Herbert *Capricornia* 1956 p. 205 [NT?] 'Do you like the job?' '**No-more**!' she cried, wrinkling a pretty nose. 'All dem sister proper humbug.' 'How's that?' 'All time roustin'. All time tink we go out wid boys.' **1938** *Walkabout* (Melbourne) 1 Apr. p. 16/1 [NT?] Constable: 'You feller gottem plenty tobacco?' Reply: '**No more**. Nothing.' Constable: 'All right. You all about sit down and I'll gibbit you tobacco and tucker!' **1946** D. Barr *Warrigal Joe* p. 82 '**No more**' said Warrigal Joe, using a favourite expression of the . . blacks, which the white man has picked up and uses freely. **1971** *Hope Vale Hotline* Nov. p. 3/1 [north Qld] **No more** one month, two months spell (meaning when on holiday). **1978** *Cent. Aust. Land Rights News* (Alice Springs) Jan. p. 3 [central Aust.] We **no more** want 'em somebody taken land from me fellow. 1984 *Aust. Ab. Stud.* no. 2 p. 32 [NT] This **no more** blackfellow country. No more. 1987 R. Baker *Borroloola Area Contact History* p. 2 [Borroloola, north-east NT] They been flog that woman now, **no more** little bit, they been kill him some way again. 1991 *Amanbidji Land Claim* 21 Aug. [northern NT] Oh, I used to walk around this country—**no more** house this country yet.

This also has an Aboriginal English spelling **numore**.

1983 *Dark Side of the News* p. 158 [northern NT] **Numore** go there! I tell you numore go there. You fela hard head I tell you numore go there.

nother *adjective* Another. Often as **this** or **that nother**.

From an Aboriginal pronunciation of *another*. It is likely the use came about through the influence of the structure of Aboriginal languages, where in many cases it is not possible to begin a word with a vowel. Aboriginal English has a range of distinctive accents and pronunciations; most are not registered by the printed versions, but in this case the use is sometimes recorded.

1890 J. Watts *Family Life in SA* p. 179 [SA] At last he came into the hut and in an excited way said:—'Me must have flour, '**nother** one blackfellow tell me you bring 'em. Suppose you no give, me take it'. 1926 L.C.E. Gee *Bush Tracks & Gold Fields* p. 36 Suppose blackfeller bin take away gin belong ole man or any man and then him go away long way, **nother** place altogether. 1938 *Walkabout* (Melbourne) 1 Apr. p. 16/1 Reply: Constable: 'Well, when all about '**nother** boy come back from catchem kangaroo, you tellim, suppose policeman come up any time, no more frighten.' 1978 J. & P. Read *View of the Past* p. 335 Now I tell you, this '**nother** Kormilda business, 'nother Kormilda problem. 1978 J. & P. Read *View of the Past* p. 43 [NT] 'No, he just come up look,' another old man talk longa that '**nother** old man. 1984 E. Roughsey *An Aboriginal Mother Tells* p. 73 [Mornington Island, north Qld] The skin or body of the man was just as it was before it was banded by this '**nother** bloke. 1988 H. Ross *Community Social Impact Assessment* p. 44 [Kimberley, WA] When the half-caste girls bin breed up here now, they bin take it away long **nother** school. 1991 D.B. Rose *Hidden Histories* p. 197 [Victoria River, north-west NT] Some, one down to Yarralin, **nother** two out to Bulla, one on Katherine, one on Timber Creek. I got all the daughters here, by Pigeon Hole. 1995 M. Brady *Giving away the Grog* p. 70 [northern NT] Me '**nother** uncle over there. . . He's not drink any more.

These are some other examples of the dropping of an initial *a*.

1978 J. & P. Read *View of the Past* p. 341 [NT] I used to sendem every fortnight that telegram . . to this '**ccountant**. 1978 J. & P. Read *View of the Past* p. 278 [central Aust.] Do not get away, or bullet'll '**tack** you, bullet going to (be) stuck for you today. 1983 M. Sharpe *Traeger Kid* p. 52 [central Aust.] If I'm '**llowed** to, that is. 1980 B. Sansom *The Camp at Wallaby Cross* p. 55 A pitch is a place . . from which one can launch a foray against a wanted person spotted in the crowd, to 'catch up longa that fella and (ar)**rest** im'. 1993 G. Koch *Kaytetye Country* p. 49 [central NT] Well he they bin still fight for that one. From wrong skin because he not '**llowed** to takem anybody's wrong woman.

nothing *adverb* **1** An emphatic negative (usually at the end of statements, and often intensifying a negative statement).

1909 H.G.B. Mason *Darkest West Australia* p. 55 [WA] **Nothing**, never more. You see 'em that one? Jinghie man kill 'em. 1978 H. Dagmar *Aborigines and Poverty* p. 77 [Gascoyne, central WA] They're supposed to settle down, but **nothing**. 1978 J. & P. Read *View of the Past* p. 75 Long time ago, olden time, no white people bin here, **nothing**. 1982 R.D. Eagleson et al. *English and the Aboriginal Child* p. 133 [NSW] In negation, the tag turns up as *and/or* *nothing*. The toilets *weren't* open *or* **nothing**. 1984 S. Cane *Desert Camps* p. 82 [Western Desert] That the different one, he got no law. We can't cooking damper; **nothing**. 1986 B. Shaw *Countrymen* p. 176 [Kimberley, WA] Righto, 'Cooee', **nothing**. He couldn't hear an answering cooee. 1988 P. Taylor *After 200 Years* p. 27 [northern NSW] I heard the word of God . . and since that day I've not touched the grog, **nothing**. 1988 H. Ross *Community Social Impact* p. 44 [Kimberley, WA] We don't know where she is. We never see her again, **nothing**. 1989 R.M. Baker *Land is Life* p. 329 [Borroloola, north-east NT] 'Sit down quiet' they been tell him . . . Him bin sleep quiet he couldn't move **nothing**, he never cried nothing. 1991 D.B. Rose *Hidden Histories* p. 202 [north-west NT] Even my mother was born here, and she was working for bread and beef. Same work. Early days work. She was working in the stock camp, cooking. She never get any money, **nothing**.

2 No.

1982 R.D. Eagleson et al. *English and the Aboriginal Child* p. 93 [WA] The negator nothing may be used instead of no . . when a speaker contradicts a previous speaker and says no in the sense of nonsense. Child 1: And I bin com las'. Child 2: (J) **Nothing**. I bin come fin'.

3 The equivalent of 'I have none', 'I got none' etc.

1979 G.K. Cowlishaw *Woman's Realm* p. 113 [Arnhem Land] 'Give me tucker' or 'Give me tobacco' are common phrases . . A fairly common response is '**Nothing**' meaning 'I have none'. 1987 C. Glass & A. Weller *Us Fellas* p. 52 [south-west WA] I've got a trophy and sash— I thought I'd win some money—but **nothing**.

now *adverb* A marker in a narrative of a sequence of events, either in the past or in the present, so it can sometimes be equivalent to *then* or *at that time/point in the narrative*.

While often adverbial, this is one of a series of punctuation terms used in oral narratives to mark changes in the narrative. See also ALL RIGHT and the introduction to this chapter for further discussion.

1980 N. Mitchell & J.C. Anderson *Kubara* p. 11 [north Qld] They pick up that whole crowd one time, only from that opium **now**. 1984 C. Allridge *Aboriginal Eng.* p. 108 [Palm Island, north Qld] *Now* was frequently used in the Palm Island data . . . Its meaning in sentences marked for the past though was equivalent to the SAE 'then'. . I climbed up there **now**. 1984 S. Cane *Desert Camps* p. 81 [Western Desert] Alright we can start now. Rock **now**, grinding put him in grindstone now. 1984 C. Allridge *Aboriginal Eng.* p. 32 [Palm Island, north Qld] He chasin' that butterfly **now**. That butterfly get on that trophy . . . Them two big fella rush over. 'Look—trophy'. 1986 *Wangkanyi* n.p. [northern SA] This water **now** from Hamilton Station creek and Stevenson Creek, comes down one now and this Alberga Creek comes in this creek now. Three come into one creek here now. 1989 M. Edmunds *They Get Heaps* p. 121 [Roebourne, north-west WA] From that, we put in for this Mawarukarra **now**. 1991 D.B. Rose *Hidden Histories* p. 202 [north-west NT] Well, my name [is] Ivy, la Pigeon Hole station. I'm talking for the girls' words **now**.

number one *adjective* [northern Aust.] Best.

There is a similar term in Tok Pisin, from Papua New Guinea, *namba wan*.

1951 E. Hill *Territory* p. 38 [NT] Turtle eggs on damper, toast for breakfast, curried crayfish and dugong steak for supper—'**Number One** tucker all the year round, free.' 1978 J. & P. Read *View of the Past* p. 245 [northern NT] Don't puttem but some lump. **Number One!** 1981 G. Ngabidj *Country of the Pelican Dreaming* p. 50 [northern NT] A big mob there had a play for me called *mandiwang* . . . It was good too; **number one**. 1980s A. Laycock *Glow with Fruit and Veg.* p. 11 [NT] Fruit and vegetables are good food. They are '**number one**' tucker because they are 'glow' foods which protect us from getting sick, and help us to get well fast when we are sick.

oh *interjection* An exclamation, marking the beginning of a statement, or functioning as a kind of 'punctuation mark' in oral narrative. Also **ah**.
One of a series of rhetorical devices used to mark changes or stages in a narrative. For a further discussion of this, see the introduction to this chapter.
1830 R. Dawson *Present State Aust.* p. 60 [central coast, NSW] **Oh**! plenty bark, massa . . make plenty bark for white pellow, massa. **1880** Fison & Howitt *Kamilaroi & Kurnai* p. 249 [south-east Vic.] **Oh**! that fellow dead boy long ago! **1893** *Transactions Royal Soc. S.A.* (Adelaide) Vol. XVII p. 262 [Daly River, north-west NT] '**Ah** too much long time; me been lose'im'. i.e. I have forgotten. **1970** R. Robinson *Altjeringa* p. 52 [south-east Aust.] The women looked out into the night and whispered together, '**Oh**, look, what is that 'something' over there?' 'Oh, it is like a shadow'. **1978** J. & P. Read *View of the Past* p. 171 [Borroloola, north-east NT] Go with, **oh**, big mob, big mob, and Island boy, too, from Torres Strait, you know, oh, big mob bin come up too. **1978** J. & P. Read *View of the Past* p. 86 [NT] Something about, **oh**, it must be over women, something. **1980** N. Mitchell & J.C. Anderson *Kubara* p. 2 [north Qld] When I come Mareeba, **oh**! There was hundreds of them. **1981** *Cent. Aust. Land Rights News* (Alice Springs) Dec. p. 9 [central Aust.] When he come there, he found the place—'**Oh**, we'll found a place here. We live here'. **1986** B. Shaw *Countrymen* p. 51 [Kimberley, WA] Me and Mandi were talking, talking talking talking talking. **Oh**, we were kids now. **1988** I. Keen *Being Black* p. 187 [southern NSW] '**Oh**! No more!' That was it then. He downed em. **1989** B. Morris *Domesticating Resistance* p. 212 [northern NSW] People come and (**ah**!). You put the kettle on. **1991** D.B. Rose *Hidden Histories* p. 260 [north-west NT] 'Where's that old man?' 'He's over here'. '**Ah**, you come over here'. **1991** A. Jackomos & D. Fowell *Living Aboriginal Hist. of Vic.* p. 106 [Vic.] People were sick of moving back and forwards . . and some of them said, '**Ah**, look, we will stay at the Mooroopna Flats permanently'.

on *preposition* **1** Used in the sense of *with, for, about*, or where the standard use would not have a preposition.
1978 H. Dagmar *Aborigines and Poverty* p. 96 [Gascoyne, central WA] We are commoners, we help **on** another. **1978** J. & P. Read *View of the Past* p. 235 Some of them young fellers, they bin going too much **on** European. **1980** P. Pepper *You Are What You Make Yourself* p. 56 [east Vic.] They all poached **on** these animals because they got a bit of money from the skins too. **1983** *Mankind* (Sydney) Apr. p. 508 That dog came right up there till he shot 'im bang . . . Yea he could bring 'em right up to 'im. He was good **on** them. He'd just know when their gonna come too. He said they give that little bark, yelp. **1984** E. Roughsey *An Aboriginal Mother Tells* p. 190 [Mornington Island, north Qld] No one has respect **on** them, which is one of the greatest law of our tribes. **1988** P. Taylor *After 200 Years* p. 112 [north Qld] They tried to shift us before you know. We gave them a fight **on** that and told them we're not going to move. **1988** *Social Alternatives* (St Lucia) 23 Mar. p. 7 [south Qld] JB: aunty Ettie, what I would really like to talk to you about, is the Bicentenary . . . Would you like to say something about that? EM: . . I don't agree in making money **on** it. **1988** H. Ross *Community Social Impact Assessment* p. 31 [Kimberley, WA] Stop every *kartiya* going round doing cruel thing **on** a blackfella.

2 A related but slightly different sense, closer to *in relation to*, and similar to the somewhat archaic English *think on these things*.
1987 T.S. Dixon *The Wizard of Alice* p. 412 [central Aust.] I have been look . . for the people like that and thinking **on** it. **1988** D. Tunbridge *Flinders Ranges Dreaming* p. xxviii [Flinders Ranges, SA] When one says in English: 'There is a big history (*muda*) **on** that one' means

Aboriginal way 213

that there is an account which puts a special meaning on to that thing which may outwardly appear commonplace. **1989** B. Neidjie *Story About Feeling* p. 1 [Arnhem Land] This story e can listen careful and how you want to feel **on** your feeling. **1990** R. Bowden & B. Bunbury *Being Aboriginal* p. 62 [south-west WA] He was a very hard man and he was very prejudiced **on** the Aboriginal People. **1991** D.B. Rose *Hidden Histories* p. 196 [Victoria River, north-west NT] Chase them cattle longa bush. Not **on** the paddock.

3 Used with reference to life on a mission, where people are described as living **on** a mission, where the general English use would be *at* or *in*. This is similar to the general English use of *on the farm, grew up on a cattle station.*

1984 P. Read *Down There With Me on Cowra Mission* p. 93 [south-west NSW] There was just one little paddock . . . Just one little strip, then you got **on** the Mission. **1988** C. Mattingley & K. Hampton (eds) *Survival in Our Own Land* p. 188 [south-east SA] At that time there was quite a lot of families still **on** Point McLeay. **1991** A. Jackomos & D. Fowell *Living Aboriginal Hist. of Vic.* p. 56 [Vic.] I was . . brought up **on** the Manatunga Mission.

one [northern Aust.] **1** (As an adjective) used instead of the indefinite article *a* or where in general English use there would be no article.

Aboriginal languages do not have an equivalent of the indefinite article *a* so that the numeral **one** now functions as an indefinite article, but often with an added sense of differentiating one known entity from another.

1880 (Mrs) J. Smith *Booandik Tribe* p. 48 [south-east SA] There come drual: **one** black man there kill my father. **1984** C. Allridge *Aboriginal Eng.* p. 78 [Palm Island, north Qld] I seen **one** book about Phantom. **1987** T.S. Dixon *The Wizard of Alice* p. 205 [central Aust.] 'Who did you see?' '**One** girl.' (N.T. English for 'a' girl). **1988** J. Harkins *English as 'Two-way' Language* p. 74 [central Aust.] SINGULAR . . a dog **one** dog. **1991** D.B. Rose *Hidden Histories* p. 187 [north-west NT] I was going to bring out what they did to that **one** girl [who] passed away there with the family way.

2 (As a noun) used with adjectives, with the resulting combination, while appearing noun-like, still functioning as an adjective. Thus **new one puppy dog** = 'new puppy dog'.

Aboriginal languages generally do not differentiate between nouns and adjectives, so it may be, as suggested in the 1985 citation, that there is some sense that the use of **one** is to give a kind of prominence or emphasis to the adjective. This use is also found in other post-colonial Englishes such as Singaporean English and Norfolk Island English.

1880 (Mrs) J. Smith *Booandik Tribe* p. 25 [south-east SA] Heard about big **one** whaleboat. **1927** M. Terry *Through Land of Promise* p. 179 [Kimberley, WA] This **one** . . no more big fellar gubbermint man. **1936** M. & E. Durack *Chunuma* p. 91 [Kimberley, WA] 'New **one** puppy dog!', they exclaimed delightedly. **1984** S. Cane *Desert Camps* p. 90 [Western Desert] *C. notabilis* was considered to be 'a rubbish **one**'. **1985** B. Neidjie *Kakadu Man* p. 91 [Kimberley, WA] He want new water, then fish and turtle, make him new **one**. **1985** M. Clyne *Aust.: a meeting place of languages* p. 83 [north-west NT] In Warlpiri, there is no part of speech adjective; adjective-like meanings are expressed nouns, so when English adjectives are borrowed into Warlpiri, it is not surprising that they are nominalised with the suffix **one**, sometimes pronounced wani. We should point out, however, that the use of one with adjectives is common in Aboriginal English. Examples follow (English spelling): black/black-one, hot/hot-one, sweet/sweet-one, slippery/slippery-one, short/shorty-one, good/good-one, new/new-one, same/same-one. **1985** S. Kaldor et al. *Aboriginal Children* p. 230 [WA]

'E good tucker, sweet **one**. 1987 *D-Bate* Language Education Course, Deakin University p. 12 [central Aust.] I like eat-em weetbix, rubbish **one** kandirr.

oughta *verb* [northern Aust.] (Usually with the past tense marker *bin*) used to. Also **ought to**.

It is possible that this is a transcription of an Aboriginal pronunciation of *used to*. Aboriginal languages do not have an *s* sound.

1978 J. & P. Read *View of the Past* p. 251 [northern NT] (We have) horse tailer and camp cook. I bin **oughta** horse tailer. **1978** J. & P. Read *View of the Past* p. 244 [northern NT] I bin **oughta** makem three feller hole, you know, inside. **1989** R.M. Baker *Land is Life* p. 200 [Borroloola, north-east NT] The wild times is the story of European introduced . . violence. For Aboriginal people in the Booroloola area the violence of this period is well remembered and the term 'war' is often used . . 'War been fight here, everywhere people **ought to** know . . war yes.'

plenty 1 (As an adjective) much (of), many. It does not necessarily include the sense of 'sufficiency' or of 'abundance beyond one's needs' that the general Australian or British English sense has.

It is found in this form in other post-colonial Englishes such as Torres Strait Creole, Cameroons Pidgin and Jamaican and Guyanese Creole. **Plenty** as an adjective was first recorded in the late nineteenth century; it is found in non-colonial Englishes in this form but it is not as common.

1863 J. Bonwick *Wild White Man* p. 86 [NSW] When I little fellow, **plenty** blackfellow—plenty gin—plenty piccaninny—great corrobory—plenty fight. Ah! all gone now, all gone; only me left to walk about. **1936** M. & E. Durack *Chunuma* p. 42 [Kimberley, WA] Me got **plenty** langwige. **1975** *New Dawn* (Haymarket) p. 15 [northern NSW] They were a very happy people for there were **plenty** fish in the river . . plenty everything. **1986** J. Davis *No Sugar* p. 60 [south-west WA] GRAN: I brought **plenty** *kooloongah* into this world, Matron. **1989** M. Edmunds *They Get Heaps* p. 29 [north-west WA] When they settle down, Aborigine know this white skin, they got **plenty** food now, they find out. **1992** R.L. Ginibi *Real Deadly* p. 1 [Sydney, NSW] **Plenty** bush tucker around, bunihny, binging, burbi.

2 (As an adverb) very, very well.

This use does not appear to be as common now in Aboriginal English as the first form. Again the Aboriginal English use does not have the sense of 'excess over mere necessity' that other Australian English use possesses. It is occasionally used as an adverb in other Englishes, as in *It is plenty big enough*.

1845 C. Griffith *Present State Prospects of Port Phillip* p. 162 [Vic.] 'You pilmillally jumbuck, **plenty** sulky me, plenty boom, borack gammon', which being interpreted, means—'If you steal my sheep I shall be very angry, and will shoot you and no mistake.' **1890** J. Watts *Family Life in SA* p. 165 [SA] 'Me **plenty** know your father; him Mr. Company;' and then, extending his arms, 'him big one like 'em bullock; him cocoanut all same bag of flour.' **1928** B. Spencer *Wanderings in Wild Aust.* p. 590 [Borroloola, north-east NT] 'You been see 'em anyone track?' 'Yes, me been see 'em that one fellow track' (pointing to prisoner). 'You savee him track?' 'Yes, me **plenty** savee'. **1935** *Hist. Soc. of Queensland* (Brisbane) Nov. p. 233 [south-east Qld] In the old days, '**plenty** long before whiteman bin come-up' . . the country bordering on this watery tract was high and dry. **1957** F. Clune *Fortune Hunters* p. 55 [Western Desert] Mick told me how Lasseter was found by the tribe, south of Lake Amadeus, after his camel had bolted. 'We carry 'im,' said Mick; 'I carry 'im **plenty** on my back. He very sick, his eyes *oona* (inflamed) and *peeka-boolka* (properly sore). His belly *peeka-booka*. He *goona-goona* (dysentery) all day'.

As with other words in Aboriginal English, the sense can be emphasised by extending the vowel. This example is taken from a nineteenth-century report from the captain of the Victorian Native Police Force. For other examples see BIG and LONG in Chapter 3.

1988 M.H. Fels *Good Men and True* p. 184 'Captain Dana come down .. with him black police, shoot him blackfellow there, black lubra there, black piccanniny there, shoot him **plaaanty** .. me tell true .. me see up tree'. Plaaanty needs explaining . . . One of the verbal ways in which they conveyed this kind of information was by the emphasis or stress on the vowel sound of the word used. Thus 'planty' (plenty) had a meaning, 'plaanty', meant more still: 'plaaanty' meant an even greater number.

put *verb* Apply, make, do (something) with (something). Also **puttem**.

Unlike the general English use of the word, it can be used without a preposition. Aboriginal languages do not have the equivalent of prepositions in their structure, and this has probably affected the Aboriginal English use of verbs such as this one.

1968 W.H. Douglas *Aboriginal Language of south-west Aus.* p. 20 [south-west WA] '**Put** 'em' 'Apply the ointment.' **1978** J. & P. Read *View of the Past* p. 172 [Borroloola, north-east NT] He bin **puttem** me captain you know . . . I bin telling all the black boy. **1982** R.D. Eagleson et al. *English and the Aboriginal Child* p. 173 [WA] The answer is not simply repeated, it is completed and 'standardised' . . Jan's response to Matron (3) is relayed to the class as A matron. (4). '**Put** the bandage' (8) becomes 'Put the bandage on it and clean it all up I hope' (9). **1983** *Conference of Abor. Communities* Dept of the Chief Minister p. 27 [NT] Why is the NT Government **putting** its law on Aboriginal people, like poking Aboriginal people with a stick at Barret Drive in Alice Springs. **1986** B. Shaw *Countrymen* p. 38 [Kimberley, WA] All right, we made a yard, **put** rails, posts, wire. **1989** B. Morris *Domesticating Resistance* p. 85 [northern NSW] Instead of **putting** the dry yeast, you'd put the lemon yeast. **1990** P. Austin et al. *Language & History* p. 245 [Oodnadatta, northern SA] We came up to Wingelee—Pitjantjara country—and from there we sat down at Docker River. Ah not Docker River—that's only lately. *Kadjikadjidjarra* that's the name. The whitefellers **put** it on. There we no white men. Only blackfellers. **1991** D.B. Rose *Hidden Histories* p. 203 [Victoria River, north-west NT] And we used to go and **put** them nanny goat.

put the long ones in, go by foot.

1992 R.L. Ginibi *Real Deadly* p. 39 [Sydney, NSW] Sometimes he never had the fare to go to and from, so he'd have to, as we Kooris say, '**put the long ones in**' and walk all the way.

really *adjective* Genuine, complete; actual.

1978 J. & P. Read *View of the Past* p. 319 [NT] That's my **really** eldest brother. **1978** J. & P. Read *View of the Past* p. 281 [central Aust.] You got to take the **really**, you know, sight, let you get really sight (i.e. take very careful aim). **1982** N.M. Williams & E.S. Hunn *Resource Managers* p. 164 [Arnhem Land] In Aboriginal English usage, primary territory in this sense is referred to as . . '**really** country'. **1984** *Aust. Ab. Stud.* no. 2 p. 34 And this is the one that's troubling for the **really** Aboriginal people. **1984** S. Cane *Desert Camps* p. 71 [Western Desert] The local Aborigines said they burnt the landscape within the study area frequently and explained that it was once '**really** desert' whereas now it has turned into 'jungle'. **1985** B. Neidjie *Kakadu Man* p. 57 [Arnhem Land] Three or four kind of eagle here. Proper one **really** that black one. **1987** A. Newstead & C. Watson *Dalkuna Mnunuway Nhe Rom* n.p. [Arnhem Land] I was born into a big family, one father, two mothers **really**. **1986** B. Shaw

Countrymen p. 267 [Kimberley, WA] Then the next morning we got on the bus and went up to **really** Adelaide, right on the city. 1987 A. McGrath *Born in the Cattle* p. 107 [NT] Cattle people incorporated the learning experiences offered by the station into the necessary regimen of training which made girls women and boys men . . this is probably one of the reasons for the specially valued relationship with the trainer who is usually described as 'my **really** boss', or 'missus' because he 'grew me up'. 1991 *Amanbidji Land Claim* 21 Aug. [north-west NT] He fought everything again, Gordon. He didn't want [Aboriginal] woman and white man [together] . . . fight anything. **Really** murderer. Something about like about Ned Kelly.

same *adjective* [northern Aust.] Similar to, like. See also ALL THE SAME.

1978 J. & P. Read *View of the Past* p. 153 [northern NT] He's **same** like bush rice, yeah, lily seed, and when you grind him and make a damper, well, that one same. 1982 R.D. Eagleson et al. *English and the Aboriginal Child* p. 187 Child: (showing a picture to the teacher) Two girls, Miss Shaw . . **Same**. Miss S: Two girls the same, that's right. 'Two girls' in this case was initially 'read' by the teacher as 'Look at these two girls' yet the intention was rather to suggest to the teacher that these were 'two members of a set. 1985 H. Koch *Non-standard English in Aboriginal* p. 177 [NT] During the research stage misunderstandings sometimes arise . . from the fact that **same** was used with a meaning closer to SE *similar*. Thus, for example, it was asserted that two people had the 'same father' when in fact their fathers were brothers. (To express the meaning 'same father' they would say 'one father'). 1986 B. Shaw *Countrymen* p. 93 [Kimberley, WA] He was the biggest brother to Jerry from the **same** mother.

something *noun* [northern Aust.] This term is used as a 'filler' in a narrative or account. See also THING.

This is found in other post-colonial languages, such as Jamaican Creole and Sranan from Surinam.

1876 J.A. Edwards *Gilbert Gogger* p. 115 Baail that fellor-**something** fool; yarraman plenty cooler. 1978 J. & P. Read *View of the Past* p. 185 [central Aust.] Come up and get a feed. Tea and sugar and tobacco, **something**, for his relations, you know. 1978 J. & P. Read *View of the Past* p. 66 [central NT] He couldn't see any fire or fresh turn-out nothing, you know, **something**. 1986 B. Shaw *Countrymen* p. 88 [Kimberley, WA] Ah, this must be **something** crocodile. 1989 M. Lennon *That's How it Was* p. 27 [Oodnadatta, northern SA] We used to go out every Friday or **something**. 1995 M. Brady *Giving away the Grog* p. 93 [north-west NT] And I didn't know but already I got crook, I might be crook **something** inside, from that liver.

suppose *verb* Introducing hypothetical situations, as a form of proposal etc.: what if, if. Also **pose, s'pose**.

This is of course also found in general English use, but it is found with greater regularity of choice over alternative possibilities in many post-colonial Englishes such as Chinook Jargon and American Indian Pidgin from North America. In Aboriginal English it seems to be more common historically than it is in contemporary times. It is also a term used frequently as part of stereotyped Aboriginal English in fiction.

1830 R. Dawson *Present State Aust.* p. 12 [NSW] Belonging to me all about, massa; **pose** you tit down here, I gib it to you. 1839 W. Mann *Six Yrs.' Residence* p. 72 [NSW] 'Well, please your Majesty . . are not these fine houses' . . . 'Yes please your Excellency,' exclaimed King Bungaree, 'de be vera good, **pose** he rain'. 1893 *Transactions Royal Soc. S.A.* (Adelaide) Vol. XVII p. 234 [SA?] '**Suppose** you cut him Dymboo, you no more get him sore fellow' . . 'Yah no more get him sore fellow'. **1904** A.W. Howitt *Native Tribes S.-E. Aust.* p. 194 [western NSW] When the question was put to several men . . 'what would be done if a Mukwara took a Mukwara for his wife? the reply was an emphatic 'No good—**suppose** that, then we kill him'. **1926** L.C.E. Gee *Bush Tracks & Gold Fields* p. 36 [NT?] **Suppose** blackfeller bin take away gin belong ole man or any man and then him go away long way, nother place altogether. **1936** M. & E. Durack *Chunuma* p. 35 [Kimberley, WA] **S'pose** me tak'm Dingyerri long house, 'im gibbit two fella lolly. **1938** *Walkabout* (Melbourne) 1 Apr. p. 16/1 Constable: 'Well, when all about 'nother boy come back from catchem kangaroo, you tellim, **suppose** policeman come up any time, no more frighten.' Reply: 'All right. We tellim all about.' **1986** A. Weller *Going Home* p. 46 [south-west WA] **S'pose** the demons come too soon, 'e won't never see 'is girl again.

that *adjective* Used to designate the thing named, indicated or understood. See also THIS.

It is used more extensively than in standard English, either where there might be no pronoun at all, as in **going to that Sydney** as opposed to *going to Sydney* or where the standard use would be **the**. Aboriginal languages do not have the equivalent of articles (*a* and *the*) and hence they are used differently in Aboriginal English. However, *that* in this sense is more common in spoken than in written English, and this is possibly also the case here, as most of the evidence is transcriptions of spoken Aboriginal English. For further discussion see THIS.

1975 R.J. Merritt *Cake Man* p. 32 [south-west NSW] Rube, I'll just go down to **that** Sydney. **1975** *Overland* (Mt Eliza) No. 61 p. 31 [north-west WA] They meet close together and talk to each other in **that** Ningaloo country. **1978** *Cent. Aust. Land Rights News* (Alice Springs) p. 10 [central Aust.] We were born there, not only myself but my big brother and my big sisters were born before **that** Wildlife (Sanctuary). **1978** J. & P. Read *View of the Past* p. 44 [NT] They bin takem, they bin takem longa **that** six mile. **1980** N. Mitchell & J.C. Anderson *Kubara* p. 3 [north Qld] Chinaman would eat **that** *minya* (meat foods) then. **1984** *Tjakulpa Kuwarritja* (Papunya) June p. 7 [Western Desert] We used to go for **that** wangki. **1985** S. & M. Kaldor & I.G. Kaldor *Aboriginal Children* p. 422 [goldfields, WA] We was playing with that Andrew. **1986** B. Shaw *Countrymen* p. 34 [Kimberley, WA] I stayed on Ivanhoe till I was a big man and had learnt everything . . all **that** one thing and another. **1988** I. Keen *Being Black* p. 46 [northern NSW] They had that boomerang or two sticks and hit it like **that**, you know. **1989** J. Thomson *Reaching Back* p. 3 [north Qld] They go back but when they make that fire (it's) just a little fire. **1991** G. Ward *Unna you fullas* p. 81 [south-west WA] They got all them mans in one family and **that** little boy.

the *definite article* It is used more widely in Aboriginal English than in standard English in cases where there would be no article.

Aboriginal languages do not have an equivalent of the English articles *a* or *the*; hence they tend to be used differently in Aboriginal English. See the introduction to this chapter for a further discussion of articles. In Australian English in general, there is an increased use of *the* in reference to towns, mostly those which belong to rivers, water sources, or mines, as in *the Katherine, the Alice* or *the Isa*.

1971 *Bunji* (Darwin) Sept p. 1 [Darwin, NT] If the people want to keep **the** Bagot, I don't know what they going to do. **1984** *Tjakulpa Kuwarritja* (Papinya) Dec. n.p. [central Aust.] We went swimming at **the** Mataranka and . . swimming at the Katherine. **1988** H.B. Day *Royal Commission into Aboriginal Deaths in Custody* (Transcript) p. 173 [northern Vic.] Well, at the moment she's coming over to Echuca because **the** husband and I are staying at his mother's place because we're getting a house built. **1988** P. Marshall *Raparapa* p. 182

[Kimberley, WA] **The** brother had to go and chip them about it. **1990** C. Zagar *Growing up Walgett* p. 32 [north-west NSW] I might be there with him one day if I keep up **the** trouble, but its hard to give it up.

thing *noun* Thingumebob, a meaningless substitute for a word.

> **1926** L.C.E. Gee *Bush Tracks & Gold Fields* p. 35 Before him make um mud him bin make big fire all same bake um damper, then spread out fire, then him take um mud **thing** put him longa middle fire and cover—then go away. **1980** S. Kaldor et al. *Language of School* p. 428 [Goldfields, WA] We went to **thing**.. Kalgoorlie. **1980** N. Mitchell & J.C. Anderson *Kubara* p. 6 [north Qld] They brought that **thing** (gold) over a lot cheaper than we'da brought it over. **1985** A. Schmidt *Young People's Dyirbal* p. 39 [north Qld] She'll probably— she'll say **thing** 'Gee, you talk half, half English, half Guwal'. **1988** R. *Comm. Aboriginal Deaths in Custody: A. Moffatt* p. 406 I got it from the canteen.. from that shop **thing** on the train.

Hence **thingy**.

> **1991** S. Romaine (ed.) *Lang. in Aust.* p. 79 [north-west NT?] All rain comin' on, comin' on and.. he got **thingy** and he bin cry really hard.

thing *verb* A substitute for an understood verb, or for a verb which momentarily escapes the speaker.

The substitution of a meaningless word for a verb is not as common in other Englishes.

> **1977** E. Brumby & E. Vaszolyi *Language Problems* p. 79 [south-west WA] We went buy some chick chicken and we **thing** dinner out. **1977** E. Brumby & E. Vaszolyi *Language Problems* p. 80 [south-west WA] Me and Basil and Michael and Kookie and Robert.. was **thinging** and.. Basil was doing somersault in the water in swimming in the creek. **1980** S. Kaldor et al. *Language of School* p. 428 [goldfields, WA] Put it in the frying pan and **thing**.. mix them. **1982** R.D. Eagleson et al. *English and the Aboriginal Child* p. 97 [WA] The word **thing** (usually in the form *ting*) is used with great frequency as a 'stand-in' for any word of any grammatical class when the word desired momentarily escapes the speaker: .. put it in the frying pan and **thing**.. mix them.

this *adjective* Designating the person or thing indicated or understood. It is often used in positions where non-Aboriginal English would use *a* or *the*.

The sense of the word is not different from its use in other Englishes, but it is used with greater frequency in Aboriginal English. This is probably because the absence in Aboriginal languages of articles (the equivalents of the English *a* or *the*) has meant a different use of not only articles but words used in their stead, such as **this** and THAT. It is also a feature of other post-colonial Englishes, such as those of Singapore and Norfolk Island. However, as with THAT, it is more common in all spoken Englishes than it is in written forms.

> **1975** *Overland* (Mt Eliza) No. 61 p. 31 [north-west WA] They wouldn't let all **this** Ningaloo mob come in. **1975** R.J. Merritt *Cake Man* p. 13 [south-west WA] Down there at Victoria, now, they got **this** different word. **1978** J. & P. Read *View of the Past* p. 37 [north-west NT] We bin know after **this** tobacco coming. **1980** N. Mitchell & J.C. Anderson *Kubara* p. 1 [north Qld] Most of them had **this** long hair and that long moustache for a long time and then they gradually give it up. Some of them later used to cut themselves baldy. **1985** S. Kaldor et al. *Aboriginal Children* p. 227 [WA] **This** uncle come back from this pub. **1986** B. Shaw *Countrymen* p. 35 [Kimberley, WA] That was my own country, Dunham River and **this** Ord River right up to Argyle country, and all that big blue hill. **1988** I. Keen *Being Black* p. 46

[northern NSW] I don't think that there is anybody (left) that I can think of . . none here on **this** Macleay. **1989** D. Walker *Me and You* p. 78 [north coast, NSW] She even planted (hid) the water away from **this** Balugan so she could have it all herself. **1989** M. Edmunds *They Get Heaps* p. 121 [Roebourne, north-west WA] From that, we put in for **this** Mawarukarra now. **1995** M. Brady *Giving Away the Grog* p. 99 [north-west NT] And you see some of our people, that are countrymen, mainly round **this** Northern Territory, they don't get to where my old man is.

this one, used to indicate something with particularity, often alongside the name of the thing indicated, and to distinguish it from another in the same category.

1863 *Adelaide Observer* 12 Dec. [SA] They said, 'They no care long a mucketty (that is, a gun)' . . The blacks up there say, 'Very good country **this one**, all about flour, sugar, tea, clothes, and sheep'. **1927** M. Terry *Through Land of Promise* p. 179 [northern NT] **This one** . . no more big fellar gubbermint man. **1935** R.B. Plowman *Boundary Rider* p. 267 'What name **this one**?' asked the white man. 'Stick him yahba long Jimmy.' (A letter-stick with a message for Jimmy) . . . The stick was about three-quarters of an inch wide, an eighth of an inch thick, bevelled at the edges and oval top and bottom. **1984** S. Cane *Desert Camps* p. 90 [Western Desert] No stopping **this one**, this place. No stopping. Keep going, keep going. **1986** *Kowanyama News* Dec. p. 17 Them two bin help'm too, and that father blung to **this one** old Frank.

The term has also an Aboriginal English spelling, **dijwun**.

1990 J. Chi *Bran Nue Dae* p. 84 [north-west WA] Us people bin waiting for **dijwun** for 200 years now.

to *preposition* Of, from, at. This preposition is used in Aboriginal English in ways which differ from general Australian English. Thus: welfare and policeman **to** this country, 'welfare and policeman *of* this country'; that daughter **to** you, 'that daughter *of yours*'; cat got sick **to** die, 'cat got sick *and died*'.

1978 J. & P. Read *View of the Past* p. 302 [NT] Because you were doing, you were doing right way **to** your own country. **1982** R.D. Eagleson et al. *English and the Aboriginal Child* p. 183 [WA?] I 'ad a cat got sick **to** die. **1983** *Upper Daly Land Claim* p. 47 [north-west NT] One dead **to** Daly. Another one too [sic] Claravale and one to Darwin. Me last. **1986** B. Shaw *Countrymen* p. 151 [Kimberley, WA] The welfare and policeman **to** this country said no law to marry that woman to that young feller. **1988** J. Harkins *English as 'Two-way' Language* p. 26 [central Aust.] Our language is, see, it's strong **to** our culture. **1988** H.B. Day *Royal Commission into Aboriginal Deaths in Custody* (Transcript) p. 141 [Vic.] That was sister **to**— do you know Pearl Joyce? . . Yes. Pearl Joyce's sister? . . Yes. **1989** M. Lennon *That's How it Was* p. 29 [Oodnadatta, northern SA] There was Arabanas, Antakarinjas, Arandas. I took notice **to** all that. **1991** *Amanbidji Land Claim* 21 Aug. [north-west NT] Your sisters might be able to help me with that name for that daughter **to** you. **1991** D.B. Rose *Hidden Histories* p. 197 [Victoria River, north-west NT] Some one down **to** Yarralin, nother two out to Bulla, one on Katherine, one on Timber Creek. I got all the daughters here, by Pigeon Hole.

too *adverb* Very, very much.

This does not always have the sense of an *excessive* amount found in most other Englishes.

1983 A.H. Ross *Aust. Ab. Perceptions* p. 371 [Kimberley, WA] '**Too** many people' . . In Kriol, it means 'lots of people'. **1987** N. Williams *Two Laws* p. 31 [Arnhem Land] Missionaries occasionally demanded change in work behaviour which was sometimes resentfully characterised as . . '**too** hard' ('Too' is an intensifier, best translated as 'very' where English is used by Yolngu not fluent in English or who have had contact with whites speaking 'pidgin English' to them.) **1987** T.S. Dixon *The Wizard of Alice* p. 392 [central Aust.] He thought Joan was '**too** fresh' and said this really to compliment her on her lovely skin. In Northern Territory English 'too' means 'very'. **1991** D.B. Rose *Hidden Histories* p. 39 [north-west WA] They were shot while they walked along. Some were running. Some got shot, broke their legs, broke their arms. Some just rolled around trying to climb up. Some just kept running, trying to beat them, and they brought them back. Bad . . . **Too** cruel, that time.

too much, very, very much; a great deal (of), a lot (of).

This is also used in other post-colonial Englishes such as Sranan in Surinam, as well as more local Pacific languages, for example *tumas* from Tok Pisin, from Papua New Guinea. There is the same use in creoles formed from Spanish and French. **1862** W.R.H. Jessop *Flindersland and Sturtland* p. 49 [SA] Me **too much** old, me plenty very bad. **1893** *Transactions Royal Soc. S.A.* (Adelaide) Vol. XVII p. 262 [Daly River, north-west NT] 'Ah **too much** long time; me been lose'im'. i.e. I have forgotten. **1924** G. Horne & G. Aiston *Savage Life in Central Aust.* p. 117 [north-east SA] No good make 'em rain this time. **Too much** dry fella. **1976** L.J. Dwyer *Language Program for Aboriginal Children* p. 13 [Qld] 'My uncle in jail. 'e steal **too much** money' . . that expression 'too much', when used by the children in that school was equivalent to 'a lot of' so that the uncle was in jail because he had stolen a lot of money. **1984** S. Cane *Desert Camps* p. 118 [Western Desert] All the way people been walking **too much**, travelling to home now. **1987** E. Kolig *Noonkanbah Story* p. 87 [Kimberley, WA] I have often come across the belief that atrocities committed in earlier years would not be possible today because there is 'too much government'. **1987** *Junga Yimi* Yuendumu Sept. p. 26 [central Aust.] 'Clean Clothes' got to sit with '**Too Much** I got No Soap'. **1991** D.B. Rose *Hidden Histories* p. 207 [Victoria River, north-west NT] I taught them **too much** (everything).

true *adverb* An intensifier of a statement or response to a statement, meaning 'it's really so' or 'is that really so', 'truly'.

1924 A.G. Bolam *Trans-Aust. Wonderland* p. 106 [Ooldea, northern SA] Mucka (not) me, boss, I never been see 'em, **true**! **1981** B. Lennon *Yarns Around the Firebucket* p. 16 [northern SA] '**True**?' said Tom, 'Didn't you give him proper directions?' **1988** K. Gilbert *Inside Black Australia* p. 14 [north-west NT] She listens to the radio from 8.30 in the morning until 7.30 in the night. She keeps listening, listening, **true**. **1989** D. Walker *Me and You* p. 46 [north coast, NSW] That's where the kangaroo ran straight across the road. Within five minutes that kangaroo was dead, oh **true**! **1993** J. Janson *Gunjies* p. 10 [western NSW] So you went for a drink, **true** eh? **1993** E. Crawford *Over my Tracks* p. 15 [western NSW] No one been actin' up, Mum. **True**. She just cries.

two *adjective* Used to specify number, sometimes with the sense of *both*, but sometimes also where in most other Englishes no number would be used.

In other Australian Englishes, a speaker might say *both* in reference to someone's hands, for example, but he or she is unlikely to say *two* hands when referring to one person. Harkins (1993) suggests that the use comes from the dual number in Aboriginal languages. English has only singular and plural number, so that one might speak of *one* of something or *more than one* of something, by using the singular form or the plural ending (usually *s*) but there is no way of registering *two* of something.

1982 R.D. Eagleson et al. *English and the Aboriginal Child* p. 187 Child: (showing a picture to the teacher) **Two** girls, Miss Shaw . . . Miss S: Two girls the same, that's right. 'Two girls' in this case was initially 'read' by the teacher as 'Look at these two girls' yet the intention was rather to suggest to the teacher that these were two members of a set. **1983** N. Green *Desert School* p. 11 [Western Desert] The spear went right through the legs and broken his **two** leg and we were happy. **1984** D. Hynes *Young Aboriginal Aust. Writes* p. 37 [central Aust.] The police said, 'That your **two** daughter?' **1985** B. Rosser *Dreamtime Nightmares* p. 99 [north Qld] Aw, Yes. I got kicked in the leg—**two** legs. One was broken here. **1988** K. Gilbert *Inside Black Australia* p. 14 [north-west NT] Her **two** eyes don't even hurt and she doesn't even get cramp from watching video. **1991** *Amanbidji Land Claim* 21 Aug. [north-west NT] No, well, **two** place Bamboo is here. **1993** E. Crawford *Over my Tracks* p. 291 [western NSW] When he met another Aboriginal who wasn't me the **two** hands went straight in the pockets.

unna *interjection* [south-west WA] Isn't it; wouldn't you say; don't you think. See also AIN'T IT, EH, MIGHT BE.

This word is used, like the English equivalents, as a comment to another speaker. However, as with EH, MIGHT BE, etc. the use is significant because of the conventions of interpersonal communication in Aboriginal society, where direct questioning is seen as possibly offensive. Instead, a comment with query added, which provides an invitation rather than a request for a reply, is a common form of interpersonal communication.

1977 *Identity* (Sydney) Jan. p. 29 Aw, jeez, Nick, not so soon. Maybe next week, **unna**? **1981** A. Weller *Day of Dog* p. 59 [south-west WA] 'Ya wanna go to Meeka, Doug? Plenty of yorgas up there, mate. Meekatharra womans rock like a rattlesnake, **unna**, Floyd?' Charley chuckles. **1986** J. Davis *No Sugar* p. 25 [south-west WA] *Joe*: Let's have a look. *David*: Moorditj, **unna**? **1991** G. Ward *Unna you Fullas* p. 9 [south-west WA] I never heard nothing, **unna**, Sally? **1991** G. Ward *Unna you Fullas* p. 182 [south-west WA] **Unna**: isn't that right, do you think so too?

up *adverb* This is used in verbal phrases more frequently than in other Englishes.

It is possible that the use came about from the influence of an Aboriginal language or languages, which commonly marked actions which were completed. (*Up* in English has this sense of a 'completed action'.) It is possible then that it became a characteristic of Aboriginal English, even when it was used by people whose original languages did not have this particular feature.

1909 H.G.B. Mason *Darkest West Australia* (1980) p. 54 [WA] My word, plenty me pear 'em **up**. **1915** E.R. Masson *Untamed Territory* p. 167 [northern NT] Blackfella come **up**, him sing out. **1978** J. & P. Read *View of the Past* p. 132 [north-west NT] They informed me that Gordon Creek Jimmy and Pompey were killed because they had in the past taken a prominent part with the whitefellows in tracking **up** their countrymen. **1982** P.C. Neal *Appellant to the Queen* p. 312 [north Qld] He . . called out to some youths who were on the roadway . . outside the boundaries of the property to 'come **up**'. **1984** P. Read *Down There With Me on Cowra Mission* p. 22 [south-west NSW] They were going to get the police **up** because I was forever fighting, swearing and everything. **1986** B. Shaw *Countrymen* p. 201 [Kimberley, WA] I still gotta foller you. I'm lovin' **up** with you now. **1988** P. Marshall *Raparapa* p. 58 [Kimberley, WA] Our people just used to live together 'married **up**' and that was it. **1988** H. Ross *Community Social Impact Assessment* p. 44 [Kimberley, WA] When the half-caste girls bin breed **up** here now, they bin take it away long nother school. **1990** A. Pring (ed.) *Women of the Centre* p. 131 [northern SA] They used to dig a hole and bury the money **up**. **1990** C. Zagar *Growing up Walgett* p. 30 [western NSW] When the time came to have her funeral, I couldn't stand **up** to go to it so I stayed at her place. **1995** M. Brady *Giving* *away the Grog* p. 111 [north-west NT] When the season used to finish at station we used to go into town and get drunk **up**.

want (to) *verb* (Usually with the past tense marker *bin*) used to. Also **wanta, wantem**. See also OUGHTA.

1909 H.K. Bloxham *On the Fringe* p. 54 [western NSW] Dickey-dickey, these pfeller **wantem** yan (go) across spinifex—long way—right through—that away. **1978** J. & P. Read *View of the Past* p. 39 [north-east NT] They bin **wanta** spearem Queensland boy, before, wild time. **1978** J. & P. Read *View of the Past* p. 39 [central NT] That's olden days. They bin **want to** killem.

way *noun* Used with adjectives. See also FELLER.

1847 *Maitland Mercury* 20 Nov. p. 2/6 [NSW] Who will deny that great changes have taken place since the white man took possession of Australian soil. The native tribes are unanimous on this position, that the seasons are altered to the 'dry **way**' in comparison of what they were antecedent to that eventful period. **1978** J. & P. Read *View of the Past* p. 260 [central Aust.] We got plenty tucker home, little boy gottem, we cookembat, sort of rubbish **way**. **1986** *Kowanyama News* Dec. p. 17 [Qld] Too true **way**, all that where they bin shoot 'm bout together. **1988** H. Ross *Community Social Impact Assessment* p. 18 [Kimberley, WA] They read about it in a book or something, what we done, hard **way**. **1991** G. Ward *Unna you Fullas* p. 67 [south-west WA] She was panicking, and crying-**way** she said 'You two girls go down the bottom camp and round up your aunties'. **1991** G. Ward *Unna you Fullas* p. 80 [south-west WA] She .. talking flash-**way** to that wadjala. **1988** J. Collman *Fringe-dwellers and Welfare* p. 128 [central Aust.] Although people insist that others should 'sit down the good **way**' and drink quietly, fights are not uncommon.

what for *adverb* Why.

It is possible that this form came about because of the different rules of interpersonal relationship that operate in Aboriginal society, where direct questioning is seen as inappropriate behaviour; possibly *what for* appeared a less aggressive form of language.

1830 R. Dawson *Present State Aust.* p. 117 [central coast, NSW] '**What for** go dere, massa?' . . I then bid him goodbye, and said, 'Bill no belong to me now I believe I look out another black fellow by and bye.' **1863** J. Bonwick *Wild White Man* p. 33 [Vic.] **What for** you do the like o' that. No do that. **1882** A.J. Boyd *Old Colonials* p. 180 [north Qld] **What for** you bin cooey like it that, Joe? **1926** S. Newland *Memoirs* p. 96 [western NSW] **What for** 'no'! That one only makum paper. **1983** M. Sharpe *Traeger Kid* p. 8 [central Aust.] **What for** Mis' Seaton boy get sick for? **1988** *Tjakulpa Kuwarritja* (Papunya) Apr. n.p. [central Aust.] Judge called out and in came Dennis Nelson. Dennis said '**What for** come and talk at Judge'. **1991** D.B. Rose *Hidden Histories* p. 96 [Victoria River, north-west NT] **What for** some of those *ngumpin* agree to go longa *kartiya* and shoot up their own people?

CHAPTER 8

Survival

The words in this chapter are manifestations of aspects of the indigenous Australian culture of the late twentieth century. They are the words of a people who have been confronted with violent change, and who, out of a struggle for survival, have created new concepts of Aboriginality. For many non-Aboriginal people, Aboriginality remains in time-warp, forever locked in the images of pre-European Aboriginal life. But like all ways of life, Aboriginal life changes, absorbs the pressures and influences that are brought to bear upon it, and becomes the Aboriginal societies of the 1990s. This chapter marks some of these new cultural changes.

One of these new cultural concepts has been the use of regional names for Aboriginal peoples that cover a greater geographical area and refer to a larger group of people than did the original language names. For example, **Koori** is used for the people of NSW and Victoria; it includes those who still use language names such as Wiradjuri, Yuin or Wathaurong, and also those who have lost their language identity through the violence of colonialism. Other such names are **Murri** for the people of northern NSW and south-east Queensland, **Bama** for those of northern Queensland, **Anangu** for people of the Western Desert, **Yolngu** for eastern Arnhem Land, **Nunga** for southern South Australia, **Nyungar** for south-west Western Australia, **Wongi** for the Western Australian goldfields, and **Yammadji** for the Gascoyne area of that State. All these terms have their origin in a local Aboriginal language word for 'person' or 'man'. Aboriginal people will use a word such as **Murri** to mean Aboriginal but they will also use it to distinguish Aboriginal people from southern Queensland and northern NSW from Aboriginal people from elsewhere. The use of these names acknowledges the massive changes that have taken place in Aboriginal social organisation, particularly in the south, but it also recognises that Aboriginal culture was not and is not identical over the Australian continent, and that there were and are cultural variations within a recognisably common cultural base. The geographical and cultural locations of the use of such names also testifies to the variety within contemporary Aboriginal Australia; these names are not generally used within traditional communities. The use of local language words, which gives Aboriginal English its regional identity, is another example of this variation, which is in part a heritage of the pre-colonial local culture, and also in part a result of the different colonising experiences that Aboriginal people in different parts of Australia have had.

This chapter also recognises new cultural and social structures that have emerged in the interaction of European and Aboriginal cultures; for example, **homeland centre** refers to the small communities created by people moving away from large settlements in Arnhem Land and central Australia back to their

ancestral countries. But the way people live in these ancestral countries is somewhat different to the way they lived there before colonisation. People might go
hunting for bush tucker, hold ceremonies and speak an Aboriginal language, but
there will probably also be a permanent collection of shelters, a Toyota, and maybe
a generator and a video player. People will travel in and out from the larger centre
for non-Aboriginal medical services and education and also to make contact with
a wider society. Ancestral country is now a region where people have established
a permanent centre, rather than a place with a range of camping places, some
used for longer periods, some for shorter. This is not to say that the way people
relate to country is 'less Aboriginal' than it was; it is simply the way of Aboriginal
culture in the late twentieth century. Similarly, a **keeping place** is a way of keeping
culture alive, but it is keeping it alive in a new way, in a new kind of institution.
Keeping places are used for a variety of purposes—as a place for cultural teaching, as a local resource centre, and for displays of art and craft. These places owe
something in their conception to non-Aboriginal cultural concepts, such as the
museum or community centre.

There is also a collection of words arising out of the political movements of
the last decades, some of which are now used by the whole community. I have
included words which seem to be particularly significant to the Aboriginal
community and which are used with greater frequency and with greater importance—words such as **identity**, which carries with it the history of the attempt
to destroy Aboriginal Australia as a people and a culture, by assimilating it totally
into non-Aboriginal society. Other words such as **Invasion Day, pay the rent**,
and **Aboriginal Embassy**, are part of the rewriting of history by Aboriginal and
non-Aboriginal people, so that events and institutions that were created out of
the colonising process have been re-understood in Aboriginal terms; for example,
the 'settlement' becomes an 'invasion'.

Not all the words are heavy with politics. Some refer to new ways of 'playing'.
There is a game involving wheels which is played over large areas of northern
Australia called **rollers, trucks**, or **buggies**. In NSW, the **knockout** refers to the
Aboriginal rugby football competition, and going to the knockout is an important
socialising event in Koori life.

Aboriginal *adjective* Of the indigenous culture of Australia, both the TRADITIONAL
and the contemporary culture.

Included here are examples of the use of *Aboriginal* to distinguish concepts or
events that are distinctively indigenous, from non-Aboriginal concepts or events
etc. In the 'post-colonial' society, Aboriginal culture has become to some extent
self-conscious, as opposed to the pre-colonial time when it was the medium within
which people lived and thought. Also included here are terms which refer to
contemporary indigenous events such as **Aboriginal Embassy**, a term coined by
Aboriginal activists but now used by the whole community.

Aboriginal is first recorded as used of the indigenous people of Australia by the
British colonial government in 1824 and as a word for *indigenous inhabitant* in
1828. Aboriginal people now use the term of themselves, although many prefer

to use a word such as MURRI which recognises the regional nature of Aboriginal Australia, or 'indigenous'.

Aboriginal business, Aboriginal spiritual powers, especially as expressed through ritual. See BUSINESS.

1988 S. Dunlop *All that Rama Rama Mob* p. 128 [central Aust.] Lot of people dying of **Aboriginal business**.

Aboriginal Embassy, the continuing demonstration set up by a group of Aboriginal people on the lawns of Old Parliament House on 26 January 1972, in response to the Prime Minister's Australia Day address.

The **Aboriginal Embassy** was established as a demonstration for land rights and expressed for many the sense of alienation and dispossession felt by Aboriginal people. The embassy 'building' was at first a beach umbrella, and later a collection of tents. It was destroyed by official order the same year and re-erected in 1992 to mark the twentieth anniversary of its establishment. In using the term *embassy* Aboriginal people have used traditional structures of European society to present their own society's relationship to the dominant non-Aboriginal one, and underlined their dispossession by the irony of having an 'embassy' in their own country.

1972 *Bulletin* (Sydney) 5 Aug. p. 16/3 Aborigines throughout Australia have found common cause in the federal government's removal of the **Aboriginal embassy** from the lawns of Parliament House. **1983** *Koories* AIAS Canberra p. 49 It was eventually decided that I go to Canberra and seek political asylum in the **aboriginal embassy** down there. **1984** M. Gumbert *Neither Justice Nor Reason* p. 23 This '**Aboriginal Embassy**', as it came to be known, forcefully made the point that Aborigines were aliens in their own country. **1990** P. Read *Charles Perkins* p. 129 Perkins had suggested to two radicals, Michael Anderson and Kevin Gilbert, that they erect a couple of tents outside Parliament House and call them the **Aboriginal embassy**.

Aboriginal Night, a night of celebration of Aboriginal culture.

1988 P. Taylor *After 200 Years* p. 259 [north Qld] We . . brought the balls of arrowroot back to Weipa South for the celebrations on **Aboriginal Night**.

Aboriginal paint, traditional body paints such as clays and ochres.

1988 P. Taylor *After 200 Years* p. 90 We used ordinary paint but when we do business we use proper **Aboriginal paint**.

Aboriginal way, customs, beliefs, habits, practices and so forth that belong to Aboriginal society, particularly those that relate to traditional life. See also WAY.

1988 C. Dunne *People Under the Skin* p. 125 Nelson and Terry go to bush school where they learn 'dancing and painting and **Aboriginal way**'. **1989** D. Walker *Me and You* p. 53 [north coast, NSW] All the **Aboriginal ways** are dying out on the North Coast . . Too much *dagay* (white man) in our ways; *yirralee* (white or not good) ways, there's too much of it. **1989** M. Edmunds *They Get Heaps* p. 98 [Roebourne, north-west WA] He was swearing at us in the **Aboriginal way**. *Counsel*: Can you tell us in the English way. **1995** M. Brady *Giving away the Grog* p. 46 [northern NT] If I just walk out, and don't talk to anybody, then **Aboriginal way**, in our way, if they call out to me and I just walk past . . they think it's a white man you know.

Aboriginal work, work that is relevant and appropriate to Aboriginal culture.

1988 J. Downing & M. Smith *Ngurra Walytja, Country of my Spirit* p. 100 The people talked a lot about doing **Aboriginal work,** by which they appeared to mean ceremony, teaching their young people fencing, gardens and any work associated with the building up of their homeland communities; but done with Aboriginal priorities and at their own pace, and in ways that fit in with a total lifestyle.

Anangu *noun* [central Aust.] An Aboriginal person from the Western Desert of central Australia; the Aboriginal people of this area. Also used as an adjective: of or relating to the Anangu, Aboriginal.

From the Pitjantjatjara, *anangu,* 'a person'. For a discussion of the use of such terms, see KOORI.

1984 P. Toyne & D. Vachon *Growing up the Country* p. 5 They (Pitjantjatjara) are known to themselves as **anangu,** the human beings who belong with the earth. **1984** P. Toyne & D. Vachon *Growing up the Country* p. 4 **Anangu,** glassy-eyed with tiredness, stare out at peak-hour traffic. **1985** D. Smyth et al. *Aboriginal Ranger Training* p. 63 **Anangu** always specify the need for Rangers and Community members to 'work together level' on all aspects of Park management. **1987** R. Folds *Whitefella School* p. 57 On the other hand, there are forceful demands made by their own people that they enter the **anangu** world and accept the responsibilities which accompany this. **1995** M. Brady *Giving away the Grog* p. 127 [northern SA] Oh, not married whitefella's way, **anangu** way you know. **1995** *Koori Mail* Lismore 23 August p. 11/1 [central Aust.] The new graduates . . are working in **Anangu** Schools. The success of the graduates is ensuring that Anangu Schools become more reflective . . of Anangu culture and wishes.

Bama *noun* [north Qld] **1** An Aboriginal person of north Queensland; the Aboriginal people of this area. Also used as an adjective: of or relating to the Bama people, Aboriginal. Also **Pama.**

From *bama* 'person' or 'man' in many north Queensland languages. For a discussion of the use of such terms, see KOORI.

1978 *Bloomfield River News* Aug. p. 14 When the roots provided by a strong and real relationship with their own *bubu* (land or country) are restored that **Bama** will be able to stand proud . . again. **1978** *Bloomfield River News* p. 17 You older people know how to . . make a kurrima. You still know . . **bama** law. **1980** N. Mitchell & J.C. Anderson *Kubara* p. 3 Big **Bama** camp, too, later on. **1981** *Social Alternatives* (St Lucia) Vol. II No. 25 p. 2 There is a distinction . . between **pama** or all Aboriginal people . . and *para,* the Europeans who through their late migrations fail to possess this distinctive belonging to the Australian continent.

2 People, particularly indigenous people, from elsewhere.

1979 *Bloomfield River News* no. 1 p. 8 This boat was made by Indonesian **Bama** in Bali.

Baryulgil Square Talk *noun* [northern NSW] The Aboriginal English used by some Bundjalung people of Baryulgil in northern NSW. For another example of local names for forms of Aboriginal English, see also JAMBUN ENGLISH.

This form of Aboriginal English contains words and phrases from Bundjalung, and ways of saying things which are based on Bundjalung constructions rather than English ones. The word **Square** comes from the name of the original land grant made to some Bundjalung people on Yulgilbar Station.

1988 M.C. Sharpe et al. *An Introduction to the Bundjalung Language and its Dialects* p. 175 **Baryulgil Square Talk** has been developed as a special Community language by the people of the Square, Baryulgil.

B.C. *adjective* The time before the British invasion and occupation of Aboriginal Australia.

The end of this time is marked by the arrival of Captain Cook on the shores of eastern Australia. See also CAPTAIN COOK.

1988 J. Lee Burgmann *Staining the Wattle* p. 189 [NSW] Something like 800 million Aboriginal people lived and died in Australia **B.C.** (Before Cook). **1995** *Koori Mail* Lismore 31 May p. 6/3 In the days **B.C.*** we roamed this land, wild and free . . . *Before Cook.

black *adjective* Aboriginal.

Black as applied to a darker skin-colour first recorded in English in the tenth century, and *a black* meaning a person with a 'black' skin in 1625. The British are recorded as describing Aboriginal people as *blacks* by 1809, and using *black* to describe them (as in *black camp* or *black girl*) by the 1820s. Aboriginal people have in the past generally referred to themselves as BLACKFELLOWS. **Black** as used by Aboriginal people to refer to Aboriginal matters appears to be a more recent use.

1974 M. Gillespie *Into Hollow Mountains* p. 53 [Vic.] The Builder's Arms is supposed to be Melbourne's '**black**-pub', although . . a black activist from Sydney says it doesn't deserve the title. 'A black pub is full of black people talking about black topics.' **1984** *Puggana News* (Launceston) Feb. p. 12 [Tas.] When is **Black** Night going to be held in Hobart? **1993** B. Bunbury *Reading Labels Jam Tins* p. 52 [south-west NSW] We were never taught **black** things, like if we used Aboriginal words at the home we were punished, or if we spoke black, we were punished. **1994** *Canberra Times* The Guide 21 Nov. p. 5/1 [NSW] **Black** perspective is not talking about colour of skin or religion—it's a way of life. It's in your heart.

blackout *noun* An event at which almost everybody present is Aboriginal; an Aboriginal gathering.

1992 R.L. Ginibi *Real Deadly* p. 16 [Sydney, NSW] There was a picture theatre called the Lawson in Lawson Street, Redfern; there was a **blackout** there every Saturday night, meaning it was full of us Aboriginal people there to enjoy the movies. **1994** *Canberra Times* The Guide 21 Nov p. 5/1 [NSW] **Blackout** [an Aboriginal television program] was not designed so much to make strong political statements about Aboriginal culture . . but was aimed at helping people come to terms with it.

Hence **to black out**, to fill a place with Aboriginal people.

1988 R.Langford *Dont Take Your Love to Town* p. 205 [Sydney, NSW] They said the place was **blacked out** Koories everywhere.

buggy *noun* [north Qld] See MOTOR CAR.

bush school *noun* [northern Aust.] A place and a time where children learn traditional Aboriginal matters.

The pressures of European style schooling, which removes young people from the community for long periods, have meant that there must now be a self-conscious attempt to teach Aboriginal children things that they would have once learnt by participation and observation.

1988 C. Dunne *People Under the Skin* p. 125 Nelson and Terry go to **bush school** where they learn 'dancing and painting and Aboriginal way.'

chuck-in *noun* [northern Aust.] Communal money raising. Also used as an adjective: of or relating to communal money raising.

This term derives from the custom in some northern and central communities of pooling monies such as welfare or unemployment benefits, to fund community projects, such as buying supplies or community vehicles.

1983 A.H. Ross *Aust. Ab. Perceptions* p. 283 [Kimberley, WA] They preferred the heavy contributions they had made during the '**chuck-in**' period of raising the money. **1987** A. Bolger *Effect Public Sector Activity on Aborigines E/Kimberley* p. 6 [Kimberley, WA] Support for the Community Homemaker Program was minimal and many people refused to pay the '**chuck-in**' suggested by the Council to help fund community activities. **1987** A. Bolger *Effect Public Sector Activity on Aborigines E/Kimberley* p. 31 [Kimberley, WA] Otherwise both DAA and DCW officers made sure that they were receiving pension and unemployment entitlements . . and encouraged the adoption of a '**chuck-in**' system to enable them to buy bulk stores.

chuck-in *verb* [northern Aust.] To raise money communally. See the previous entry.

1984 D. Bell & P. Ditton *Law: The Old and the New* p. 60 [central Aust.] All '**chuck in**' for their maintenance and all ride on them to town for supplies.

claypan dance *noun* [south-east Aust.] A dance held in the open area on a hard ground such as a claypan.

This was a new cultural form resulting from the destruction of traditional dance ceremonies and the exclusion of Aboriginal people from the places where dances for the general community were held. The dancing was European ballroom-style dancing, often to the music of an accordion. As Aboriginal people were allowed access to community facilities, these dances became less common and are today no longer held.

1987 A.I.A.S. *Photographic Exhibition* Recorded 19/9/87 [NSW] Denied access to halls, dances were very often held out of doors, the ground being swept and watered to make the surface hard, and light being provided by fire in winter and lanterns in summer. These '**claypan**' dances were still being held in many communities as late as the early 1970s. **1988** C. Sullivan *Non-Tribal Dance Music* p. 66 [NSW] Open air dances were regularly held on mission stations, in some cases up until the early 1970s. By that time the '**Claypan dance**', dance on the flat or the bank of a river, had been a dominant feature of Aboriginal social life for more than a century. **1992** P. Taylor *Tell it like it Is* p. 108 [south-west Qld] My uncle can still remember the **claypan dances** that were still there when he was a child in the 1930s. **1993** E. Crawford *Over my Tracks* p. 73 [western NSW] Sometimes they'd have **claypan dances** at night, but they needed the permission of the Manager. [**1994**] D. Young *Songs* n.p. [western NSW] There's no more **claypan dances**, all the accordions are still.

community *noun* **1** A settlement or place where the majority of the inhabitants are Aboriginal. The distinction between this sense of a *place*, and the second sense of a community of *people* (see sense 2), is not always absolute.

Although this sense is found in other Englishes, it is included here because of its significance in Aboriginal English. This significance and its wide use among Aboriginal people reflect a culture where in general community opinion and social cohesion are given a higher priority than individual achievement. It also highlights the different groupings of Aboriginal people brought about by colonisation and social change. Sometimes the **community** will be coterminous with a pre-invasion group, but the movements of people, both voluntary and enforced, have greatly altered the sense of *who is us*. Moreover, the non-Aboriginal community has produced the concept of an Aboriginal **community** which cuts across traditional boundaries.

1979 L. Andrews *Kinship & Community at Wreck Bay* p. 29 [south coast, NSW] One solution to this problem is to marry people from outside the **community**. **1983** *Conference of Abor. Communities* Dept of the Chief Minister p. 5 [NT] In general, a '**community**' has been regarded as a stable fully serviced group established for some time and having a capacity, through an elected council, to undertake a range of local government type of functions. **1988** G. Cowlishaw *Black, White or Brindle* p. 133 [NSW] These **communities** are so fractured, so fragmented, so mixed up that the entire concept of representation is nonsense! **1991** *ATSIC News* Autumn 7/1 [Aust.] Woorabinda could well become a model for many **communities** seeking to provide good lifestyles and futures for their people.

2 The Aboriginal community as a community of people (as in *the community has responded to the statement*). The 'community' may be regional and specific (as in *La Perouse Community*), or general and non-specific.

Community in this sense is used among non-Aboriginal people, but the sense is included here because of the significance its use has in Aboriginal Australia.

1977 A.K. Eckermann *Group Organisation and Identity* p. 308 [south-east Qld] A number of Aboriginal words . . are still used by the whole **community**. **1984** B. Swanton *Aborigines and Criminal Justice* p. 95 [Kimberley, WA] The police aide, they explained worked for the 'police' and was not part of their '**community**'. **1989** *Aboriginal Children* p. 4 [Arnhem Land] Children talk about . . things in the **community** . . names, skins, family, country, animals, plants etc. **1990** *Wreck Bay Koori Newsletter* Aug. p. 4 [south coast, NSW] The **community** organisations are one way Kooris have been standing up and saying that the welfare days are over. **1993** J. Janson *Gunjies* p. 35 [NSW] Thanks for coming everyone, it's great to see so much **community** interest in the sovereignty issue.

community elder, a leader in the community. See ELDER.

1988 *Us Mob* Aboriginal and Islander Studies Unit June p. 11 [Qld] **Community elders** and other community members spoke.

community leader, a leader in a COMMUNITY.

1991 *Action Rev.* Oct. p. 6 I felt it was a most worthwhile and rewarding experience to be able to participate in a conference whose skilled . . **Community Leaders** . . were freely . . sharing their personal concerns.

community school, a school controlled by an Aboriginal community.

1979 M. Dillon *A Case Study: Kadia Power* p. 2 [Kimberley, WA] Fr. Kriener went on to denigrate the idea of a **community school** as a 'bush school' and therefore not good enough.

concentration camp *noun* A term now sometimes applied to former missions and reserves, because of the level of oppression and lack of freedom suffered by the inmates.

The use of this term is part of the writing of Australian history from the perspective of the occupied NATIONS that is taking place among Aboriginal and non-Aboriginal people today—although in this case, the comparison between Nazi concentration camps and missions had been made by Aboriginal activist William Cooper in 1939.

1988 *Social Alternatives* St Lucia, Qld Vol. VII no. 7 p. 49 [south-east Qld] Europeans . . really did disturb and destroy things by their tactics like . . missions like **concentration camps** . . germ warfare (the dropping of small pox scabs). 1990 *Aboriginal History* Canberra Vol. XIV i p. 1 Most Aboriginal speakers today are adamant that the reserves were **concentration camps** where . . their experience was of . . segregation, repression and cultural assault. 1993 *Koori Mail* Lismore 5 May p. 15/2 Contact history . . colonial occupation, the pearling boom and slavery, colonial prisons and **concentration camps.** 1993 D. Hodge *Did you meet any Malagas?* p. 49 [northern NT] I refer to places like Kahlin [Aboriginal Compound] as **concentration camps**, because that's what they were. People had no freedom, they weren't allowed to go outside.

cultural *adjective* (Of places, people, activities) concerned with Aboriginal culture, especially TRADITIONAL culture.

In contemporary Australia, Aboriginal TRADITIONAL culture is often presented, preserved, and handed on in a different way from that in pre-contact Aboriginal Australia. See CULTURE in Chapter 1.

cultural camp, a place where Aboriginal people, particularly children, can learn aspects of Aboriginal culture. Also **culture camp**.

Such institutions are mostly found in areas where Aboriginal people are very much in the minority, as in most of southern Australia, and where traditional methods of handing on particular aspects of culture are no longer available.

1984 *Puggana News* (Launceston) Feb. p. 2 The **Cultural camp** began on Monday 16th of January. 1989 M. Edmunds *They Get Heaps* p. 147 [Roebourne, north-west WA] A **culture camp** for kids . . has become the Gurru-Bunjya Youth Culture Camp.

cultural centre, a place where aspects of Aboriginal culture are presented and preserved.

The focus is usually on traditional rather than contemporary aspects of culture. Cultural centres are often also seen as a place for informing non-Aboriginal people of aspects of local culture. See also KEEPING PLACE.

1986 *Aboriginal Newsletter* June p. 4/2 [Tas.] The Commonwealth's interest in putting in a keeping-place and **cultural centre** for Aboriginal people would . . form part of Tasmania's heritage. 1991 L.M. Wilkinson *Aboriginality* p. 269 [Vic.] The proliferation of . . **cultural centres** . . is an indication of the level of interest in Aboriginal history.

cultural heritage, the TRADITIONAL Aboriginal inheritance of an area expressed in cultural sites. The emphasis is on sites of traditional rather than recent historic or contemporary culture.

1989 J. Moore *Aboriginal Deaths in Custody* (Transcript) p. 80 [Vic.] I do the **cultural heritage** for this area. Over . . this area . . you are going to find a lot of Aboriginal sites.

cultural officer, a person employed to look after the Aboriginal cultural sites of a particular region.

1988 P. Taylor (ed.) *After 200 Years* p. 88 [south-east Qld] I've got a **cultural officers'** meeting here on Monday and I'm going to get some bush tucker to feed them.

cultural track, a walk, usually through the bush, designed to display aspects of Aboriginal culture, particularly TRADITIONAL ones.

1990 *Puggana News* (Launceston) Dec. p. 6 [Tas.] Oyster Cove. We have a caretaker's hut, a keeping place . . a **cultural track**.

2 Traditional.

1992 *Puggana News* (Launceston) Apr. p. 27 [Tas.] The **cultural** food was wonderful specially going out on the rocks getting abalone.

cut a rug *verb* [NSW] To have a good time, to let off steam (especially in contexts where alcohol is involved).

From American English *cut a rug*, 'to dance'. This is known also in standard English but is not in general use.

1992 R.L. Ginibi *Real Deadly* p. 79 [NSW] Then her brother Dougie got up and sang an old Koori song called '**Cutta Rug**'. 1994 D. Young *Songs of Dougie Young* n.p. [NSW] I was **cuttin' a rug**, they threw me in the jug, as the magistrate looked down. He said, 'Youngie, Doug, you're a wine lovin' mug and you're a menace to the town.'

Hence, **cutting a rug**, having a good time, letting off steam.

1958 J. Becket *A Study of a Mixed Blood Aboriginal Minority* p. 232 [western NSW] Summing up the various aboriginal attempts to interpret it one may say that '**cutting a rug**' corresponds to our 'letting off steam', 'breaking out', 'cutting a dash'. 1964 M. Reay *Aborigines Now* p. 41 [western NSW] '**Cutting a rug**' means ostentatious drunkenness and carries with it the connotation of 'letting off steam'.

gibberish *noun* [south-east Aust.] Aboriginal English. The word is also used to mean Aboriginal language, see GIBBERISH in Chapter 1.

The Aboriginal English sense lacks the pejorative associations of the non-Aboriginal use of *gibberish*, which is defined in the *Australian Concise Oxford Dictionary* as 'unintelligible or meaningless speech; nonsense.' Aboriginal people have taken a word used about them and used it for their own purposes.

1949 *Oceania* Dec. p. 93 [western NSW] On the Murrumbidgee . . they survive only in the memory of a few 'old hands' to be used only when these individuals meet and converse in 'the language' as distinct from 'the **gibberish**.'

The origin of the Aboriginal English word can be seen in the following citation.

1859 H. Kingsley *Recoll. Geoffry Hamlyn* II. p. 185 'Make a light', in blackfellow's **gibberish**, means simply 'see'.

glass bottle cemetery *noun* The Aboriginal cemetery at Angledool, where the local community devised a new set of mortuary symbols, using arrangements of pieces of broken glass over the graves, to reflect the spirits away from the earth. See also BOTTLE.

This is an example of a new cultural practice using non-traditional sites (a public cemetery) and non-traditional artefacts (glass).

1938 *Abo Call* Sept. p. 1 [NSW] Why should they exchange their home-town, where their ancestors lie buried in the famous '**glass-bottle' cemetery**, to go to a Government Station to be bullied and half-starved?

Goorie *noun* An Aboriginal person of northern NSW; (as **Goories**) Aboriginal people of northern NSW. Also **Goree**. Also used as an adjective: of or relating to the Goorie people, Aboriginal.

A pronunciation of KOORI. In Aboriginal languages, there is generally no semantic distinction between voiced and unvoiced consonants; however in contemporary Aboriginal English, the distinction is now sometimes made, as in this instance. **1969** *Koorier* (Fitzroy) Vol. 1 no. 9 p. 22 [Vic.?] 'You gurrum' is the Islanders' way, in a half-joking, half-admonishing way (but still friendly in the way that only **Goories** can) of saying 'That's what you get!' or 'I told you so!' **1988** K. Gilbert *Inside Black Australia* p. 85 [northern NSW] You tell of love and sharing and giving. That is a big part of **Goree** living. **1989** B. Morris *Domesticating Resistance* p. 155 [northern NSW] Young people . . felt embarrassed, to see older people 'spinning the leg', as dancing in the **goorie** way was commonly referred to. **1995** *Koori Mail* Lismore 17 May p. 16/2 [northern NSW] A **Goori** fella from Bowraville, on the NSW Mid-North Coast, is taking the airwaves by storm.

homeland *noun* A person's or community's ancestral COUNTRY.

1985 *Aboriginal Health Worker* (Little Bay) Dec. p. 17 [Tas.] In May this year we held a traditional ceremony cremating our ancestors remains and setting their spirits free in their **homeland. 1988** S. Dunlop *All that Rama Rama Mob* p. 114 [central Aust.] My family, living out there looking after **homeland**, keeping 'niffers out there. **1990** S. Janson & S. Macintyre *Through White Eyes* p. 135 [central Aust.] Though absence from **homelands**, from one's place of conception, or father's or mother's conception, could cause remembrance and anxiety (both captured in the Aboriginal English phrase 'worrying for country'), there was no . . sense of a connection between individual and country being lost. **1992** *Action Rev.* Oct. p. 8 [central Aust.] The band hails from the tribal **homelands** around Yirrkala.

homeland centre, a small centre in northern Australia set up by a group moving away from a large settlement in Arnhem Land or central Australia back to their ancestral COUNTRY, at the same time maintaining some connection with the large centre for non-Aboriginal food, medicine and education. Also **homeland place**. **Homeland centres** enable people to make contact again with ancestral country, remove themselves from the tensions of settlements, and educate their children in their own culture. Such places were originally called *outstations*, a term derived from the subordinate settlement on a grazing property, away from the main homestead. The term **homeland** is closer to the central meaning of these places, which is that people have *gone home* rather than *moved out*. The term demonstrates the continuing but changing relationship that contemporary Aboriginal people have with their countries.

1978 H.C. Coombs *Kulinma* p. 150 The descriptive term 'outstation' is increasingly used for such settlements, reflecting probably the use of this term for settlements around Elcho Island which for many years had been serviced by Harold Sheppardson. However, the term somewhat misrepresents the Aboriginal conception of them, for each clan appears to consider its settlement as existing in its own right and not as an off-shoot from a larger unit, although some sense of affiliation with the central unit continues. The Yirrkala community now refers to these settlements in English language contexts as **homeland centres**. This phrase probably reflects more accurately the Aboriginal conception. **1979** M. Heppell *Black Reality* p. 3 Why are so many remote Aborigines leaving government and mission settlements to set up small **homeland centres** away from European influence? **1983** M. Sharpe *Traeger Kid* p. 106 [central Aust.] 'It's a **homeland place**,' she said. 'But they got electricity an' TV too.'

identity *noun* Aboriginal identity.

This word has been very significant in Aboriginal thinking because of the assimilationist pressures placed on Aboriginal people, particularly in the last sixty years. Aboriginal people, particularly those not of the full descent, and even more particularly those of European appearance, had many pressures put upon them not to 'identify'; others chose not to identify because of the restricted options that were open to those known to be 'Aboriginal'. Tasmanian Aboriginal people have had particular problems because their **identity** as Aboriginal people has been denied.

1980 *Puggana News* (Launceston) July p. 4 [Tas.] We must stop thinking of our **identity** the way white people do. **1985** *Aboriginal Health Worker* (Little Bay) Dec. p. 17 Every day, people and especially the government, put us through the pain and anger of denying us our **identity**. **1986** *Aboriginal Newsletter* June p. 3/3 [Tas.] Mutton birding is very closely linked with the Tasmanian Aboriginal **identity**. **1988** R. Langford *Dont Take Your Love to Town* p. 255 [NSW] Aboriginal **identity**, both traditional and city dwellers, is alive and strong. **1990** A. Schmidt *Loss of Australia's Aboriginal Language Heritage* p. 22 [north Qld] This is the reason why we want to keep our language. It shows our **identity**.

Invasion Day *noun* The 26th of January, the day in 1788 when the fleet of British soldiers and prisoners landed in Sydney Cove, an event which marked the end of independence for Aboriginal Australia. See also DAY OF MOURNING in Chapter 5.

The re-naming of significant events in Australian history in Aboriginal terms is part of the new cultural consciousness.

1986 *Treaty '88* n.p. [central Aust.] Wear a black armband for Aboriginal year of mourning 1987. **Invasion Day**, 11 am. January 26th 1987. **1987** *Invasion 88* n.p. 200 years on stolen ground, Isn't it time to come around? Australia Day = **Invasion Day**.

Jambun English *noun* A variety of Aboriginal English spoken by the Jambun people of northern Queensland.

1990 A. Schmidt *Loss of Australia's Aboriginal Language Heritage* p. 34 For example, in the Dyirbal language of North Queensland, speakers do not lose all features of their weakening language, nor do they adopt Standard Australian English as their first language. Instead, **Jambun English**, a non-standard variety of English, is used as a common code of communication within the community.

keeping place *noun* An Aboriginal cultural centre, where cultural artefacts are held, and which may also be a teaching and local community centre. The focus is usually on TRADITIONAL culture.

Such centres present a new way by which a community holds, engages with, and represents its culture. At a **keeping place** there may be displays of local art or history, language classes, community meetings and a library of material on local culture. Some of these facilities are available for non-Aboriginal people, so that the place becomes a way of presenting Aboriginal culture to the rest of the community. The name 'keeping place' suggests some of the tensions present in an Aboriginal Australia whose cultures are under threat from that of the majority, and where there is also a determination to keep local cultures alive. One of the first keeping places was built in Shepparton, Victoria.

1981 J. Mulvaney et al. *Aboriginal Aust.* p. 40 [northern Vic.] An Aboriginal '**Keeping Place**' at the Shepparton Museum Complex and an associated craft industry in the adjacent town of Mooroopna . . were specifically initiated to provide resources for this growing movement towards self identity among the local Aborigines. [1984] L. Reed & E. Parr *Keeping Place* title page [north-east NSW, south-east Qld] **The Keeping Place** An annotated bibliography and guide to the study of the Aborigines and Aboriginal culture in northeast New South Wales and southeast Queensland. **1984** *Koorie Information Centre* n.p. [Vic.] Rough map of **keeping places**, historical sites and important known Aboriginal areas in Victoria. **1986** *Aboriginal Newsletter* June p. 4/2 [Tas.] The Commonwealth's interest in putting in a **keeping-place** and cultural centre for Aboriginal people would . . form part of Tasmania's heritage. **1987** *Wellington* p. 10 [south-west NSW] The Corporation has just received $200,000 to build on the Reserve a cultural centre, a **keeping place**, and a holiday camping area. **1990** *Puggana News* (Launceston) Dec. p. 6 [Tas.] Oyster Cove. We have a caretaker's hut, a **keeping place** . . a cultural track. **1991** A. Jackomos & D. Fowell *Living Aboriginal Hist. of Vic.* p. 76 [Vic.] Now I give classes every year at the Hamilton **Keeping Place**. **1994** *Encyclop. Aboriginal Aust.* p. 541 [Bathurst Island, NT] External and internal views of the **Keeping Place** at Nguiu, Bathurst Island, NT. **1995** *Koori Mail* Lismore 1 November p. 25/ 1 [northern NSW] 'The Art of Utopia' currently on display at the University of New England's Aboriginal Cultural Centre and **Keeping Place**, is the first comprehensive record of the work of a community of Aboriginal artists from Central Australia.

knockout *noun* [NSW] A rugby football competition.

This is also in general Australian use, but is significant in the NSW Aboriginal community (and similarly elsewhere) as a social event which works to strengthen community and family connections. This is particularly important in areas such as NSW where reasons for other large group activities such as ceremonies are not as common. Such occasions are an important element in contemporary Aboriginal life.

1988 *La Perouse* p. 57 [Sydney, NSW] We won the South Sydney **Knockout**. **1993** J. Janson *Gunjies* p. 17 [western NSW] Is 'e goin' up to Wilga for the **knock-out**? **1993** J. Janson *Gunjies* p. 25 Can't wait to get to the **knockout**. I wanna see the Redfern Allblacks. **1995** *Koori Mail* Lismore 20 Sept. p. 30/2 [NSW] The club's big test next year is the NSW Annual Aboriginal Rugby League **Knockout** in which teams come from all over NSW.

Koori *noun* An Aboriginal person, especially one of NSW or Victoria; (as **Koories**) the Aboriginal people of NSW or Victoria. Also **Koorie**. Also used as an adjective: of or relating to the Koori people, Aboriginal.

From *gurri*, the word for 'Aboriginal man' or 'Aboriginal person' in the Awakabal language of eastern NSW, and neighbouring languages. It was first recorded by the Reverend Lancelot Threlkeld in 1834, in his grammar of the Awakabal language. The term was also used in Tasmania, but has recently been been replaced by PALAWA. This is one of a group of words that have gained wider currency in recent years to refer to groups of Aboriginal people from a particular region— see also ANANGU, MURRI, etc. The use of such terms acknowledges the regional cultural variations within Aboriginal culture, while recognising the changes to the original structure of language groups or 'tribes'. In contemporary Aboriginal Australia, some people have lost their original group origin, and the larger but still local identity of being a **Koori** or a MURRI fits their cultural situation. Others who still have their traditional identity, recognise the common cultural needs of people from certain regions. In other areas, especially the more traditional ones of northern Australia, such groupings of people have not replaced the local traditional language names, such as *Jawoyn* or *Kaytetye*, with which people identify. **1834** L.E. Threlkeld *Austral. Grammar* p. 87 **Ko-re**, man, mankind. **1845** C. Hodgkinson *Aust., Port Macquarie to Moreton Bay* p. 54 They . . informed me that the Bellengen **corees** (black fellows), were belcoula, (not angry). **1892** J. Fraser *Aborigines N.S.W.* p. 2 [NSW] The **kuri**, *or* 'blackman' is usually kind and affectionate to his jin, 'wife'. **1973** D. Wolfe *Brass Kangaroo* p. 306 You should get rid of the white bosses here and let us **koories** run the station. **1977** K. Gilbert *Living Black* p. 201 [NSW] How many **Kooris**, town or mission, would be prepared to come out here and put up signs saying 'This is an Aboriginal Burial Ground. Keep Off. This is a Sacred Area' Who'd be in it? **1983** *Awabakal* Sept. p. 7 [north coast, NSW] The two groups have performed in front of crowds as big as 1,000 people and their latest performances were at the Newcastle City Hall for the 'Carnival 83'. Only one word can describe these **koorie** kids . . 'solid'. **1985** J. Miller *Koori* p. 218 [NSW] Since I believe in **Koori** land rights and no dams on the Franklin River, that makes me a black, greenie, pinko. **1986** *Puggana News* (Launceston) no. 8 p. 22 [Tas.] I am a **Koori** and I will survive. **1989** *La Trobe Library Journal* Vol. XI no. 43 (Autumn) p. 5 [Vic.] **Koori** was probably in use then, but not in front of whites. Aboriginal people between the 1930s and 1950s, preferred to be called by whites, 'the dark people'—not 'natives', 'blacks' and so forth. Koori was, as Diane Barwick discovered in 1960, a semi-secret word used among the people themselves. Indeed the first newspaper reference to 'Koori' that I have so far discovered is a *Sun* report of 7 January 1969, referring to the creation of an 'Aborigines only' Koori Club in Fitzroy. Since then Kooris have used this word openly to define themselves. **1991** L.M. Wilkinson *Aboriginality* p. 196 [Vic.] Generally in Victoria, **Koorie** is spelt with an 'e', rather than as spelt in New South Wales as 'Koori'.

Koori English, Aboriginal English.

1985 J. Miller *Koori* p. 73 [NSW] Many Kooris today speak this dialect which I call **Koori English**.

Kriol *noun* The language, originally derived from pidgin, of parts of northern Australia.

Both Kriol and Aboriginal English are derived from the pidgin that was used as a form of communication between Aboriginal and non-Aboriginal people in the contact period. Kriol developed from the Northern Territory Pidgin English, which was used in the nineteenth and twentieth centuries as a form of communication between the Aboriginal, Chinese and European populations of the area. It first developed into a 'full' language early this century at the Roper River Mission in the north-east of the Territory, where the children of eight different language groups were brought together in the mission school and expanded the pidgin they were all familiar with into a language. Other areas, such as Fitzroy Crossing in the Kimberley, also have a form of Kriol. Kriol now has its own spelling system and an increasing body of literature. It is spoken by over 20,000 people and is the first language of many people in northern Australia; areas where it is used are sometimes called *Kriol Kantri*. Like Aboriginal English, it has been and often still is the object of prejudice and misunderstanding, being seen as a 'deficient' or bastardised form of language.

1982 *Yulngu* (Katherine) Dec. p. 31 [northern NT] This idea is to have tapes . . so as people can hear in their own language or in **Kriol** what is being talked about. **1983** A.H. Ross *Aust. Ab. Perceptions* p. 371 [Kimberley, WA] 'Too many people' . . . In **Kriol**, it means 'lots of people'. **1984** J. Hudson & P. McConnell *Keeping Language Strong* p. 16 [Kimberley, WA] Another way of talking that you can hear a lot around the Kimberleys is 'mixed' language. This is when people put 'language' words or phrases or whole sentences in when they are talking **Kriol** or Aboriginal English, or put in Kriol or English when they are talking 'language'. **1986** *Nugget News* (Halls Creek) Oct. 20/1 [Kimberley, WA] There is now a new language in Hall's Creek called **Kriol**. Most Aboriginal people and one or two White people know how to speak it.

Mardu *noun* [north-west WA] An Aboriginal person of the Pilbara, WA; the Aboriginal people of this area. Also **martu**. Also used as an adjective: of or relating to the Mardu, Aboriginal.

From the name for 'person' in the languages of the area. This, like other terms such as KOORI or MURRI, serves to identify a local group; it is, however, a term that encompasses a wider range of people than do the original language or 'tribal' names.

1980 *Mikurrunya* (Strelley) 23 Apr. p. 10 The whiteman brought in their animals; cattle, sheep and horses, and the **martu** were taught how to muster, and how to cut posts and build fences and yards. **1982** M. Howard *Aboriginal Power* p. 116 It has become impossible for Aborigines to sustain a clear conceptual distinction between . . 'white fella business' and '**mardu**' (Aboriginal) business. **1991** D. Pilkington (Nugi Garimara) *Caprice – a stockman's Daughter* p. 73 I now converse and communicate in **Mardu** Wangka and listen more intently as the Dreamtime stories are told. **1991** L.M. Wilkinson *Aboriginality* p. 351 It is culture, rather than colour, that draws the distinction between those that are mardamarda (of mixed descent) and those who are **mardu** (black people). Those who are of mixed descent are also referred to as *mardu*, indicating that while they are described separately, they are also incorporated into the notion of 'black people'.

motor car *noun* [northern Aust.] A toy used by children and young people. Also **buggy, roller, truck.**

There are several different names for this toy, which is found over a wide area of northern Australia. They are all based on the idea of making some form of push-along wheel.

1965 F.G.G. Rose *Wind of Change* p. 91 [central NT] One interesting phenomenon at Angas Downs as in other parts of Central Australia is the practice of both un and initiated young men making a toy composed of an empty or partly sand filled treacle tin which they roll along the ground, sometimes for hours together, at the end of a length of fencing wire the upper extremity of which is bent into the shape of a steering wheel. This the Aborigines call '**motor-car**'. **1975** I. Robertson *Sport and Play* p. 4 [NT] Another type of **roller** is the discarded wheel rim of a motor car or truck. These are either pushed by a stick, pulled by a rope or rolled like a hoop . . . The activity is commonly referred to as '**roller**' or 'trucks'. Since the mid-1950's children have been observed at many different settlements playing with round objects such as treacle tins and motor car rims. Keen observation by the children of the steering mechanics of a motor vehicle has enabled them to build toys with steering wheels that are quite functional. The steering wheel is made of fencing wire which is fashioned into a circular shape and leads down on either side of the treacle tin. **1991** J. & S. Erbacher *Aborigines of the Rainforest* p. 27 [north Qld] The children make toys called '**buggies**' from powdered milk tins. They poke a hole through each end of the tin, thread a string through it, and then fill the tin with sand.

Murri *noun* An Aboriginal person from southern Queensland or northern NSW; the Aboriginal people of the area. Also **murree, murrey, murrie**. Also used as an adjective: of or relating to Murris, Aboriginal. For a discussion of regional names for Aboriginal people, see KOORI.

From the Kamilaroi language of northern NSW and many southern Queensland languages, *mari*, 'an Aboriginal person'.

1884 J.B. Gribble *Black but Comely* p. 125 [Qld] It has been the misfortune of the **Murri** . . to be found in the way of European colonisation. 1896 *Bulletin* (Sydney) 18 Apr. p. 27/2 [northern NSW] Crossing the range we enter the two great and widespread dialects of Kamilroi and 'Wiradhuri'. . . Here we have the generic word '**murri**' (murree) for all blacks. 1930 K.G. Taylor *Pick & Duffers* p. 49 'I bet it's someone dressed up to frighten the blacks.' 'No fear; **murreys** never come to Yeller Cap in the moon.' 1975 *Black Knight* (Brisbane) 11 Oct. p. 10 [south-east Qld] Hasten to the fight my friends Every Narrinyerie, Wik and **Murrie** And soon we'll live in dignity. 1982 J. Davis *The Dreamers* p. 144 [south-west WA] Nyoongah . . Aboriginal, literally 'man' in the languages of the South West. Some time after 1829 it entered common usage as a term denoting Aboriginality, similar to *Wongai* in the eastern goldfields, *Yamatji* in the Murchison and *Koori* and **Murri** in the eastern states. 1983 *Sydney Morning Herald* 14 Feb. p. 7/8 [NSW] There are two Aboriginal words for the races in Moree. One is '**murri**', an Aboriginal word for themselves, which is quite acceptable. 1989 *La Trobe Library Journal* Vol. XI no. 43 (Autumn) p. 5 [Vic.] The only difficulty with 'Koori' is that it is a regional word for people in the south-east of Australia. People in Queensland prefer '**Murri**'; those in the West, 'Nyunga'; in the North, 'Yolngu'. We may be forced to rely on 'Aborigine' for some time yet, when referring to the descendants of the first Australians throughout the whole of the continent. 1990 R. Bowden & B. Bunbury *Being Aboriginal* p. 52 [south-east Qld] The first thing they said was, 'You'll see all the **Murris** down at Musgrave Park'. So I went down there and met all my people.

gulf murri, a person from the Gulf of Carpentaria region in Queensland.

1990 S. Watson *Kadaitcha Sung* p. 139 [south-east Qld] He look like one of them **gulf murries**.

nation *noun* **1** The people of Aboriginal Australia.

This word is not commonly used by non-Aboriginal Australians to describe Aboriginal Australia. The significance of the term lies in the preservation of the concept of a separate identity and sovereignty for Aboriginal Australia despite the facts of invasion and colonisation.

1987 *Puggana News* (Launceston) June p. 5 [Tas.] I stood up and spoke as a member of the Aboriginal **nation**. 1988 *Mosa* (Clayton) no. 2 p. 37 [Tas.] By going to Libya we also encouraged them to allow us into their country on the Koori passport which meant that for the first time ever in the history of the Koori people—over 50,000 years—has a foreign government recognised that we are a **nation** of people.

Hence **nationhood**.

1986 *White Invasion Diary* Invasion Diary Collective 13 Mar. [SA] This state of warfare was apparent to the early colonial authorities but it was not in the interests of the British Home Office to recognise and accord **nationhood** to the Aboriginal tribes.

2 A group of people identifying with a particular COUNTRY within Aboriginal Australia.

This is similar to the use of *nation* for Native American groups. The term is not generally used by non-Aboriginal people to describe individual language groups, although it has been used by some observers, such as George Taplin, in his 1874 account of the Narinyeri of South Australia, 'They . . call other nations of Aborigines wild blackfellows' [p. 1] and A.E. Howitt in his *Native Tribes of South-East Australia* of 1904. Its significance lies in the recognition of the continuity of cultural difference and local identity that was present at the time of the occupation, but which the occupiers have in general not acknowledged.

1980 R. Dixon *The Languages of Australia* p. 36 [north Qld] Each Australian tribe (or as my insightful informant preferred to call them, '**nation**') is looked upon as a distinct political entity, that is characterised by having its own language. **1986** M. Coe *Windradyne* p. 3 [NSW] This is a true story of a warrior named Windradyne and the Wiradjuri people, who lived within an area known as the Wiradjuri **nation**. **1992** *Shades of Black* (Carlton) Vol. VI (Summer) p. 2/3 [Vic.] I dedicate this article to the descendants of the 500 Aboriginal **Nations** that lived in Australia for over 40,000 years. **1995** *Koori Mail* 31 May p. 4/2 [SA] It was through this that my grandmother, Pukanu Pinky, saved her traditional title as Queen of the Ngarrindjeri **nation**, since she was then the oldest living Ngarrindjeri woman. **1995** *Koori Mail* Lismore 4 Oct. p. 29/1 [NSW] A feast of entertainment has been organised for the 'Strength through Unity' festival in Brewarrina . . . Originally a meeting place for more than 10,000 people, from many Aboriginal **nations**, a festival of this nature will recreate the energy of this tradition.

Nunga *noun* An Aboriginal person of southern South Australia; (as **Nungas**), the Aboriginal people of this area. Also used as an adjective: of or relating to Nungas, Aboriginal. For a discussion of regional names for Aboriginal people, see KOORI.

From the Nhangka language of south-western South Australia, *nhanga* meaning 'a person'.

1924 A.G. Bolam *Trans-Aust. Wonderland* p. 85 [Ooldea, northern SA] Following upon the death of one young **nunga** at 2 o'clock one morning . . preparations were immediately made to shift camp. **1961** *Polynesian Soc. Jrnl.* June p. 202 [Adelaide, SA] Adelaide people . . use . . different native words to refer to aborigines . . . Point Pearce people say **Nunga**. **1980** D. Milera *Walkabout to Nowhere* p. 30 [SA] The Aboriginal comes from a different environment altogether. There are city **nungas**, country nungas and outback bush nungas. **1981** M. Brusnanhan *Gateway* n.p. [SA] Come on you **Nungas**, lift your feet. Swing along now. **1984** *Mikawomma Nungas* Croydon High School Jan n.p. [Adelaide, SA] Hey You **Nungas**! Would you like to be involved in the 'Aboriginal History Volume'. **1987** N. Barber *How to become a successful Derelict in Adelaide* p. 22 [Adelaide, SA] Aboriginal is the white people's name for **Nungas**. They call themselves Nungas. Always have.

Nyungar *noun* An Aboriginal person from south-west Western Australia; (also as **Nyungars**) the Aboriginal people of the area. Also **Noong-ah, Noongar, Nyoongah, N-Yoongar, Nyunga, Nyungah.** Also used as an adjective: of or relating to Nyungars, Aboriginal. For a discussion of regional names for Aboriginal people, see KOORI.

From the Nyungar language of south-western WA *nyungar* 'a person'.

1954 *Coast to Coast 1953-4* p. 105 [south-west WA] **N-Yoongars** not black. Most all us N-Yoongars brown. **1969** L. Hadow *Full Cycle* p. 157 [south-west WA] Jimmy Dabchick turned a cartwheel. 'Us all **N-Yoongars**'. **1975** R. Beilby *Brown Land Crying* p. 3 You're as much coloured as white, as much **Noong-ah** as wadjullah. **1977** K. Gilbert *Living Black* p. 88 [south-west WA] The most effective means of communication . . we call . . the '**noongar** grapevine' . . . It used a sort of communication that can only be understood by Aborigines and it's highly functional. **1981** A. Weller *Day of Dog* p. 58 [south-west WA] Every **nyoongah** gets itchy feet and feels restless, like a cat or a moonstruck dog, sooner or later. **1988** *South Western Times* (Bunbury) 28 Jan. p. 2/5 He represented a small group of **Nyoongar** people who had been invited by Bunbury Jaycees. **1988** I. Keen *Being Black* p. 247 He said that if it were '**Nyungar** way' they would have acted differently. **1991** R. Rebera & M. Richards (eds) *Remembering the Future* p. 112 [south-west WA] The Wangal is the name given by the **Nyungahs** (Aboriginal people of the southern region of Western Australia) to the spiritual being who is believed to be the creator and sustainer of all water rats and life. **1994** *Encyclop. Abor. Aust.* p. 814 [south-west WA] The **Nyungar** have preserved their identity in many ways. In some towns a local Aborigines advancement association provides a focus for Nyungar endeavours, and a collective voice for speaking out on issues of concern to Aboriginal people.

Palawa *noun* An Aboriginal person of Tasmania; the Aboriginal people of Tasmania. Also used as an adjective: of or relating to the Palawa, Aboriginal. For a discussion of regional names for Aboriginal people, see KOORI.

The Tasmanian Aboriginal people formerly called themselves *Kooris* but recently they have decided their distinctive cultural history should be marked by a distinctive Tasmanian name. Tasmania was separated from the mainland some 8,000 years ago, which meant that its Aboriginal culture has differed somewhat from that of the mainland peoples.

1994 Tasmanian Aboriginal Centre Inc. *Origins of Palawa* n.p. [Tas.] It has been suggested for some time that the Tasmanian Aboriginal community find a name to call ourselves instead of Koori which is used by Victorian and New South Wales Aborigines. Through the establishment of the Tasmanian Aboriginal Languages project now called the 'Palawa Karni' Program, meaning Tassie Blackfella's talk, research has reinforced that **Palawa** was recorded by early historians as meaning 'native'. Fanny Cochrane Smith was recorded singing in 1903 and in those recordings Fanny refers to her people as Palawa and through consultation with the Tasmanian Aboriginal community people growing up on the Bass Strait islands remembered being called Palawa. **1995** *Koori Mail* Lismore 20 September p. 18/3 In Tasmania there is a four-member **Palawa** (indigenous) health-care team to advise on . . aged-care services.

Fanny Cochrane Smith (1834-1903) is a significant figure in Tasmanian history. She survived the death camps of Flinders Island and Oyster Cove to become well-known in both the Aboriginal and non-Aboriginal communities; she was a prominent member of the Methodist Church, while at the same time retaining pride in her Aboriginal identity and traditional culture. In 1899 and 1903 she was recorded singing songs in her language; these recordings are the only ones ever made of any of the Tasmanian languages.

pay the rent *catch phrase* [south-east Aust.] A phrase recognising and asserting the original and continuing ownership of Australia by Aborigines, and the obligation owed to the original owners by those who now hold control.

This has become a slogan in the land rights movement. It marks the sense of the continuity of Aboriginal ownership—that occupation has not destroyed the moral right of Aboriginal people to their country.

1986 *White Invasion Diary* Invasion Diary Collective p. 3 [SA] We should live on the '**pay the rent**' system . . that's why I say the diary should have the last say on the last page . . that is *pay the rent*. **1989** *Signs of Survival* [western Sydney, NSW] **Pay the rent**—*you* are on Aboriginal land.

roller *noun* [northern Aust] A child's toy. See MOTOR CAR.

slang *noun* [northern NSW] (Usually as **the slang**) Aboriginal English of the Baryulgil area. Also known as BARYULGIL SQUARE TALK.

1988 M.C. Sharpe et al. *An Introduction to the Bundjalung Language and its Dialects* p. 184 When the people from the Baryulgil Square began to go to school . . they learnt 'school English', i.e. 'flash talk', and realised that this was different from the type of English they spoke at the square. They therefore sometimes refer to the English in Baryulgil Square Talk as '**the slang**' to show that . . it is different from school English.

survival *noun* The continuing existence of Aboriginal people, particularly as **Aboriginal** people, despite the destructive effects—physical, spiritual and cultural—of the colonising society.

The **survival** in recent times refers not so much to physical survival, as to the spiritual and cultural survival of Aboriginal people (with the notable exception of 'deaths in custody' and of very poor community health). This survival is set against the enormous assimilationist pressures on the Aboriginal community, particularly in the period from the 1930s until the 1970s, and especially upon the people of southern Australia. The assimilation policies of the Australian Government assumed that there would eventually be no distinctive Aboriginal community or culture. There was no concept in official thinking of *Aboriginal* cultural change and development. This official understanding of the future of Aboriginal Australia is expressed in the following statement from the 1963 Conference of Commonwealth and State Ministers on Aboriginal Welfare: 'The policy of assimilation means that all Aborigines and part-Aborigines will attain the same manner of living as other Australians and live as members of a single Australian community, enjoying the same rights and privileges, accepting the same responsibilities, observing the same customs, and influenced by the same beliefs, hopes and loyalties as other Australians.'

1986 *White Invasion Diary* Invasion Diary Collective n.p. [Adelaide, SA] Aborigines were still resisting around Port Lincoln. Aboriginal resistance did not only relate to economic survival but also the spiritual **survival** of our people. 1989 *Signs of Survival* [western Sydney, NSW] Signs of **survival** . . an exhibition of Aboriginal art in the west. 1991 A. Jackomos & D. Fowell *Living Aboriginal Hist. of Vic.* p. 124 [Vic.] Percy Clarke during the **survival** celebrations of 1988. 1993 S. Robinson *Aboriginal Embassy* M.A. Thesis, ANU p. 32 Perhaps even more important . . was the foundation of the '**survival**' programme, community services operated for and by Aboriginal people. 1993 *Sydney Morning Herald* 22 Jan. (Suppl.) 3/3 [Sydney, NSW] A roll call of artists won't reveal any Iggy Pops or Sonic Youths, but **Survival** *'93* at La Perouse features an almost definitive line-up of Aboriginal musicians. These are as diverse in their muse as the points on the map from whence they hail— Warumpi Band, The Tiddas, Kev Carmody, Bangarra Dance Theatre, Mixed Relations, Toni Janke, Dead Heart, Djaambi, Roger Knox, Auriel Andrew and Amunda.

survive *verb* To survive as Aboriginal people. See SURVIVAL.

The sense includes physical survival from the violence of the frontier times, and survival from the more subtle but psychologically as violent assimilationist forces, whereby authorities attempted to make people see Aboriginality as a thing of the past. There was no attempt to support cultural inheritance through educational or other means, and the cost of identifying as Aboriginal was often paid in institutionalisation and the removal of children. Tasmanian Aboriginal people **survived** in the face of official denial of their existence.

1982 L. Fogarty *Yoogum Yoogum* p. 19 [south-east Qld] The worker who, the human who, the Abo who **survived**. 1984 *Puggana News* (Launceston) Feb. p. 5 [Tas.] We have **survived**! We want our land! We want it Now! 1986 M. Coe *Windradyne* p. 84 [NSW] It is a long and bitter battle for us to **survive** but we have survived as a nation of people. 1986 *White Invasion Diary* Invasion Diary Collective 24 Mar. [Adelaide, SA] We're concerned about our own survival, if we're not going to **survive** whey should we give a fuck about them? 1986 *White Invasion Diary* Invasion Diary Collective (inside back cover) [SA] We have **survived** the white man's world And you know you can't change that. 1987 *We have Survived* Poster [NSW] We have **survived**! White Australia has a black history. 1992 P. Taylor *Tell it like it Is* p. 108 [western Qld] Shaw thought we could die out, but we didn't we **survived**.

Hence, **survivor**.

1985 *Aboriginal Health Worker* (Little Bay) Dec. p. 47 [Tas.] *We are the* **survivors**. We have a sense of pride and identity in being Aboriginal.

toyota *noun* [northern Aust.] A four wheel drive vehicle.

This term is used to refer to four wheel drive vehicles in general, because of the number of Toyota four wheel drives used in northern Australia.

1982 *Bunji* (Darwin) Mar. p. 2 [Darwin, NT] We really want a **toyota** . . we want to go hunting. 1985 S. Cane & O. Stanley *Land Use and Resources in Desert Homelands* p. 92 [Western Desert] Outstation **toyotas** are also used on grog runs. 1985 B. Neidjie *Kakadu Man* p. 19 [Arnhem Land] He say 'Oh, somebody there' Him frightened, too many **Toyota**. Make me worry too. 1988 S. Dunlop *All that Rama Rama Mob* p. 102 [central Aust.] Before his family had own **toyota**, before and used to visit him. 1988 S. Dunlop *All that Rama Rama Mob* p. xxxiii [central Aust.] Other people get angry or upset; they might swear all the time . . smash up **Toyotas** or buildings.

truck *noun* [NT] A child's toy. See MOTOR CAR.

two ways *noun* [Chiefly northern Aust.] A combination of Aboriginal and European Australian knowledge, concepts, behaviours, etc. Also **two laws**, **two way**. Also used as adjective: (of people, events, situations, etc.) accommodating both Aboriginal and European Australian knowledge, concepts, and behaviours. See also WAY.

This term acknowledges the necessity of some non-Aboriginal concepts and information being included in modern Aboriginal life, while at the same time affirming the value and importance of retaining Aboriginal customs and knowledge. Non-Aboriginal Australians have often assumed that it is an 'either/or' situation, where Aboriginal knowledge is extinguished by European knowledge. In **'two-way** thinking', for example, Aboriginal and non-Aboriginal understandings of disease and its treatment can both be present and active in a community. **Two** is used here with the sense of *both*; for this sense see TWO in Chapter 7.

1977 K. Maddock *Two Laws in One Community* p. 27 [northern NT] My opinion is that **two-laws** talk is significant, not so much as a description of what life is actually like . . but as an affirmation of the dignity and value of Aborigines themselves and their traditional culture. 1980 *Aboriginal Health Workers Conference* p. 7 We encourage people to use both Aboriginal and Western medicine. We call it **two way** medicine. 1984 *Aust. Ab. Stud.* no. 2 p. 27 [north-west NT] Yarralin people now speak of themselves as having '**two-way**' brains, meaning that they know how [to] operate in both European culture and their own culture. **1984** *Yeperenye Yeye* (Alice Springs) Jan. p. 18 [central Aust.] Oh, that Aboriginal school is going to be teaching **two ways**. It'll teach the Aranda way and it'll teach the English way. **1988** C. Mattingley & K. Hampton (eds) *Survival in Our Own Land* p. 114 [northern SA] It is a wonderful honour to be a **two-way** person. But it is costly as well. **1988** J. Harkins *English as 'Two-way' Language* p. 4 [central Aust.] In studying a '**two-way** language' a language variety whose main purpose and function for its speakers is one of cross-cultural communication, a cross-cultural method of describing meaning is needed. **1991** D.B. Rose *Hidden Histories* p. 71 [Victoria River, north-west NT] And that tracker he still got a **two way** (two loyalties, torn in two directions). **1995** *Koori Mail* Lismore I November p. 26/3 The book contains 10 articles describing different kinds of programs . . covering different issues such as bilingual education, **two way** education, curriculum development.

Warbo *noun* An Aboriginal person of the Warburton Ranges area of Western Australia; (as **Warbos**) the Aboriginal people of this area. Also used as an adjective: of or relating to the Warbos, Aboriginal. For a discussion of regional names for Aboriginal people, see KOORI.

1987 S. Morgan *My Place* p. 223 [north-west WA] You're lucky you didn't come lookin' for your relations any earlier, we've only all just been converted. Those **Warbos*** people came through and held meetings. It's made such a difference . . not many drunks, now . . *Warbos—name used by Aboriginal people of the Port Hedland/Marble Bar area of Western Australia for the Aboriginal people of the Warburton Ranges area.

way *noun* **1** The manner in which one lives as an Aboriginal person, uses language, and performs social and personal activities; the beliefs and customs which provide meaning for this way of living. See also TWO WAYS.

This is not significantly different from the meaning of *way* in other Englishes, but is used much more widely and with more *cultural* significance in Aboriginal Australia. A society that has been colonised by another and hence has become the minority society, will find the **way** that it believes, thinks and behaves, is perceived as problematic, its **ways** often challenged or opposed by the majority, and the solutions to questions of manner of life or social problems often becoming a matter of cultural survival.

1979 *Cent. Aust. Land Rights News* (Alice Springs) Dec. n.p. [central Aust.] We hold the land in a stronger **way** than white fellers. We hold it from our fathers and grandfathers. We hold it as Kurtingurlu. **1988** P. Marshall *Raparapa* p. 30 [Kimberley, WA] But Kartiya have different ideas and a different **way**; and the country is feeling very sad as a result. **1991** D. Pilkington (Nugi Garimara) *Caprice – a stockman's Daughter* p. 40 [Pilbara, WA] We don't want Peggy to go 'nother **way** . . and lose 'em for good (go away and not return).

head way, the belief system of a people.

1984 E. Roughsey *An Aboriginal Mother Tells* p. 216 [Mornington Island, Qld] Some got married and forgot about their head **way**, which meant so much for them and their people.

2 Sometimes the reference is to Aboriginal life in general. See also ABORIGINAL.

Aboriginal way. Also **Aboriginal ways**.

1978 J. & P. Read *View of the Past* p. 176 [Lajamanu, north-west NT] All right, we bin come out now. Marching, you know, **Aboriginal way**, marching. **1984** P. Read *Down There With Me on Cowra Mission* p. 23 [south-west NSW] They always taught us Captain Cook's ways, never taught us our way, the **Aboriginal way**. **1987** *Aboriginal Health Worker* (Little Bay)

Sept. p. 9 [central Aust.] **Aboriginal way** by the Grandmother's law is directed and carried out by Aboriginal women in the security and ancestral tradition and the warmth of the *Alukura*. **1991** A. Jackomos & D. Fowell *Living Aboriginal History* p. 198 [Vic.] I went to Cummeragunja Sunday School and if you started doing anything in the **Aboriginal way** they'd say the Devil would get you.

blackfella way. Also **blackfella ways.**

1966 *Oceania* June p. 274 [SA] Asked what Herry had to do with her mother's death, she answered '**blackfellow's way**'. **1988** I. Keen *Being Black* p. 58 [northern NSW] The notion of shame . . was also applied to 'old **blackfella ways**'.

bush way, Aboriginal way. See also BUSH.

1988 H. Ross *Community Social Impact* p. 72 [east Kimberley, WA] My mother born there, la creek. **Bush way** you know.

3 Sometimes the reference is to a smaller local group.

Adnyamathanha way, the traditions of the people of the Flinders Ranges in South Australia.

1989 M. Lennon *That's How it Was* p. 52 [northern SA] In **Adnyamathanha way** we call the oldest one *Buka*, the name stuck to him.

baygal way, the traditions of the people of northern New South Wales.

1983 M. Sharpe *Traeger Kid* p. 81 [northern NSW] Jenny's father called it Gurigay, and said 'That's the **baygal way** to say it'.

Nyoongah way, the traditions of the people of south-west Western Australia.

1987 J. Davis *Honey Spot* p. 5 [south-west WA] Now I am brother to the plura. *Peggy*: What's the plura? *Tim*: The bees. That's our law, **Nyoongah way**.

4 Sometimes the reference is to non-Aboriginal ways.

balanda ways.

1987 G. Francis *God's Best Country* p. 78 [Arnhem Land] That's the only road back for them . . to be rid of all your patronising, domineering **balanda ways**.

English way.

1986 B. Shaw *Countrymen* p. 144 [Kimberley, WA] The Miriwong call barra *ingurung* (subincision) and we call it *rran*. In all the places around town they call it barra the **English way**.

gadya way.

1978 J. & P. Read *View of the Past* p. 233 [north-west NT] Aboriginal people sit back now . . not them to go all the way there to meet **gadya** [European] **way** of life.

white ways.

1957 *Oceania* Dec. p. 106 [north coast, NSW] They refer to the upper group women in mocking tones as 'Black-Wodgins' and speak about their adoption of **white ways**.

Wongi *noun* An Aboriginal person from the goldfields area of Western Australia; the Aboriginal people of this area. Also used as an adjective: of or relating to the Wongi, Aboriginal. For a discussion of regional names for Aboriginal people, see KOORI.

From the word *wangayi* 'a person' in the Western Desert group of languages.

1950 K.S. Prichard *Winged Seeds* p. 161 [WA] Bob Brown'd never forgive us if he heard we'd been calling on the **wongi** and hadn't paid him and his missus a visit, Dinny chuckled. **1981** A. Weller *Day of Dog* p. 61 [south-west WA] Charley's woman, a shy dark **wongi** from Kalgoorlie, comes out and takes the baby. **1981** *Goldfields Weekender* (Esperance) 15 May p. 1/3 [goldfields, WA] Kalgoorlie fringe-dwelling Aborigines have claimed they are discriminated against . . . 'The white fellow has been driving out the **Wongi** all the time'. **1986** A. Weller *Going Home* p. 68 [south-west WA] He was still a **wongi** even after eleven years in this bushy green-brown country. **1995** *Koori Mail* Lismore 1 Nov. p. 40/4 Veteran **Wongi** surfer Sam Sadler who represented WA in the 1975 Australian Titles, finished fourth.

Yamagi *noun* An Aboriginal person from the Gascoyne and Murchison Rivers region of Western Australia; the Aboriginal people of that area. Also **Yamadji, Yamatji, Yamidgee, Yammogee**. Also used as an adjective: of or relating to the Yamagi, Aboriginal. For a discussion of regional names for Aboriginal people, see KOORI.

From the Watjari language of that area, *yamaji* 'a person'.

1925 J.E. Liddle *Selected Poems* p. 89 They talked of '**Yammogees**' and 'Jinns'. **1937** E. Morrow *Law Provides* p. 145 You know 'em **yamagi** called Spider? **1965** R. Stow *Merry-Go-Round* p. 186 'What's **yamidgees**?' said the boy. 'Boongs. Noogs. Coloured folk'. **1975** *Overland* (Mt Eliza) No. 61, p. 31 [north-west WA] Another **yamadji** speared one of these whitefellers. **1983** G.E.P. Wellard *Bushlore* p. 55 [WA] I was standing outside the humpy discussing the days work with three of the **Yamagee** musterers. I use the word 'Yamagee' because that is the name they call themselves in that district. They never say 'Blackman' or 'Aborigine', it is always 'Yamagee'. **1995** *Koori Mail* Lismore 1 Nov. p. 32/3 Despite teething problems, Yamatji Media has a small but dedicated team of wadjulas (white people) and **Yamatjis** running the station.

Yolngu *noun* An Aboriginal person from eastern Arnhem Land and nearby areas; the Aboriginal people of this area. Also used as adjective: of or relating to the Yolngu, Aboriginal. For a discussion of regional names for Aboriginal people, see KOORI.

From the word *yuulngu* 'a person' in the Yolngu languages of Arnhem Land.

1977 *Black News Service* Nov. p. 9 [Arnhem Land] So I was working for Nangalala to Ramingining making a really good road and all balandas and **yolngu** were really glad that I was forming the road. **1987** W.H. Edwards (ed.) *Traditional Aboriginal Society* p. 2 [Arnhem Land] From a **Yolngu** point of view, there need be no direct connection between what he does and what he promises to do. **1987** W.H. Edwards (ed.) *Traditional Aboriginal Society* p. 9 [Arnhem Land] *Balanda* and **Yolngu** are the terms the people of north east Arnhem Land use to refer to white people and themselves respectively. **1994** *Encyclop. Abor. Aust.* p. 1230 When the mining company Nabalco entered **Yolngu** land in 1968, the Yolngu were so concerned that they took out an injunction to try to stop the mining. Although the 1971 decision went against the Yolngu, the case led to a royal commission and eventually the Aboriginal Land Rights (NT) Act of 1976.

yolngumatha, Aboriginal language of the Yolngu.

1978 *Nungalinya* (Darwin) p. 8 [northern NT] A group of yolngu women keen to write stories in **yolngu matha** (Yolngu language). **1987** M. Christie et al. (eds) *Teaching Aboriginal Children* p. 145 [Arnhem Land] They understood only that we would use **yolngumatha** (Aboriginal language) in the school.

Yolngu war, traditional PAYBACK killings.

1987 N. Williams *Two Laws* p. 151 Yolngu often referred to the suppression of revenge killing, which they sometimes called 'Yolngu war' that followed the imposition of Australian law in terms that implied they were grateful.

Yura *noun* An Aboriginal person from the Flinders Ranges area of northern South Australia; the Aboriginal people of that area. Also used as an adjective: of or relating to the Yura, Aboriginal. For a discussion of regional names for Aboriginal people, see KOORI.

From the word for 'person' from the Adnyamathanha language of the area.

1977 *Yura Aboriginal* (Kent Town) Aug. p. 6 [SA] It has been good at Quorn that other **yura** people besides the teachers have come to help us learn. **1988** D. Tunbridge *Flinders Ranges Dreaming* p. 10 [SA] Now the white men are taking Akurna's fat and making big money out of it. It was the **Yuras** who showed them that big history. **1988** C. Mattingley & K. Hampton (eds) *Survival in Our Own Land* p. xii [SA] In Pitjantjatjara and Adnyamathanha sections their own words for themselves—Anangu and **Yura**—are used. **1988** C. Mattingley & K. Hampton (eds) *Survival in Our Own Land* p. 227 [SA] Despite hostilities, pastoralists were often glad to employ **Yura** because they knew the terrain.

yura ngawarla, Aboriginal language, specifically the language of the Adnyama-thanha people. Also **yura nawala**, **yura ngowala**.

1977 *Yura Aboriginal* (Kent Town) Apr. p. 2 [SA] In teaching **yura ngowala**, or describing the kinship system, she had . . wide knowledge and a good memory. **1977** *Yura Aboriginal* (Kent Town) Nov. p. 2 [SA] The method of spelling we use writing in **yura nawala** is that of John McEntee. **1988** D. Tunbridge *Flinders Ranges Dreaming* p. xliv [SA] **Yura Ngawarla** literally 'Aboriginal people's talk'. This is the term for the language of the Adnyamathanha people most commonly used by the people themselves.

yura-wungi, a spiritually powerful person among the Adnyamathanha people, a CLEVERMAN.

1978 C. Coulthard *Mt Chambers* p. 14 [SA] There might be a witch-doctor man, 'yura-wungi', he goes into a dream to follow the eagle who has left a red mark along his trail.

SELECT BIBLIOGRAPHY

Abo Call Sydney 1938

Aboriginal Health Worker Little Bay, NSW 1977–

Aboriginal History Canberra 1978–

Aboriginal Law Bulletin Kensington, NSW 1981–

Action Review Aborigines Friends Association, Adelaide 1991–92

Allridge, Clare 'Aboriginal English as a Post-pidgin' BA Hons thesis, Canberra 1984

Austin, Peter, Dixon, R.M.W., Dutton, Tom, & White, Isobel *Language and history: essays in honour of Luise A. Hercus* Pacific Linguistics Series C-116, 1990

Australian Aboriginal Studies Canberra 1983–

Australian Journal of Anthropology Sydney 1990—see also *Mankind*

Australian Journal of Linguistics St Lucia, Qld 1981–

Awakabal: Newcastle Aboriginal Co-op Newsletter Newcastle NSW 1983–85

Baker, Margaret 'A Social Survey of Tingha' MA thesis np, 1943

Baker, Richard 'Borroloola Area Contact History' np, 1988

Balgo Newsletter Balgo WA 1982–3

Bardsley, Rosemary *David's Story—Book 3* Lawson, NSW 1991

Barwick, Diane E. 'A Little More than Kin: Regional Affiliation and Group Identity Among Aboriginal Migrants in Melbourne' Ph D thesis, Canberra 1963

Bates, Daisy *The Passing of the Aborigines* London 1938

Beckett, Jeremy 'A study of a mixed-blood Aboriginal minority in the pastoral west of New South Wales' MA thesis, Sydney 1958

Bell, Diane Robin *Aboriginal women and the religious experience* Bedford Park, SA 1982

Berndt, Ronald & Berndt, Catherine *From black to white in South Australia* Melbourne 1951

Berndt, R.M. (ed.) *Aborigines and change: Australia in the 70s* New Jersey, USA 1977

Berndt, Ronald M. & Berndt, Catherine H. *End of an Era: Aboriginal Labour in the Northern Territory* Canberra 1987

Black, Paul David (ed.) *Growing in language* Batchelor NT 1986

Bloomfield River News Bloomfield River Mission, North Queensland 1978–79

Bolam A.G. *The Trans-Australian wonderland* Melbourne 3rd Edition 1924

Bonwick, James *The wild white man and the Blacks of Victoria* Melbourne 1863

Bowden, Ros & Bunbury, Bill *Being Aboriginal* Crows Nest, NSW 1990

Brady, Maggie (ed.) *Giving away the grog; Aboriginal accounts of drinking and not drinking* Canberra 1995

Brumby, Ed & Vaszolyi, Eric (eds) *Language problems and Aboriginal education* Mt Lawley, WA 1977

Bunji Darwin 1971–83

The Bulletin Sydney 1880–

Byno, Josephine & Wright, Doreen *Mundagudda and Warwai* Western Reader Committee, 1979

Cane, Scott 'Desert camps; a Case Study of stone artefacts and Aboriginal behaviour in the Western Desert' Ph D thesis, Canberra 1984

Cane, Scott & Stanley, Owen *Land use and resources in Desert Homelands* Darwin 1985

Central Australian Land Rights News Alice Springs, NT 1976–

Chi, Jimmy *Bran Nue Dae* Paddington NSW and Broome, WA 1990

Clyne, Michael *Australia: a meeting place of languages* Canberra 1985

Collman, J. *Fringe-dwellers and welfare* St. Lucia, Qld 1988

Cowlishaw, G.K. 'Woman's realm: a study of socialisation, sexuality and reproduction among Australian Aborigines' Ph D thesis, Sydney 1979

Crowley, Terry *The middle Clarence dialects of Bundjalang* Canberra 1978

Curr, Edward M. *Recollections of squatting in Victoria then called the Port Phillip District* Melbourne 1883

Dagmar, Hans *Aborigines and poverty* Nijmegen, the Netherlands 1978

Daly, Mrs Dominic *Digging, squatting and pioneering in the Northern Territory of South Australia* London 1887

Dark side of the news Aboriginal Task Force, Darwin 1981–85

Davis, Jack *The first-born and other poems* Sydney 1970

Davis, Jack *Kullark* Perth 1979

Davis, Jack *The Dreamers* Perth 1981

Davis, Jack *Honey Spot* Sydney 1987

Davis, Jack et al. *Paperbark: a collection of Black Australian writing* St. Lucia, Qld 1990

D'Bate: Aboriginal teachers write about their community languages Batchelor, NT 1987

Dhougarle, Koorie *There's more to life* Chippendale, NSW 1979

Dillon, Michael *A case study: kadia power in an Aboriginal community* CFOA Research and Information Service, Canberra 1979

Dixon, Thomas Sidney *The wizard of Alice: Father Dixon and the Stuart case* Morwell, Vic. 1987

Docker, E.G. *Simply human beings* Brisbane 1964

Donaldson, Tamsin *Ngiyambaa: the language of the Wangaaybuwan* Cambridge 1980

Douglas, Wilfrid H. *The Aboriginal language of the South-West of Australia* Canberra 1968

Duncan, Pearl 'Shame in Australia' B Litt thesis, Canberra 1986

Dunne, Clare *People under the skin: the Irish immigrant's experience of Aboriginal Australia* Carlingford NSW 1988

Durack, Mary & Durack, Elizabeth *Chunuma* Sydney 1936

E., W. A. *The blacks of Beagle Bay* Melbourne [1930]

Eades, Diana ' "You gotta know how to talk ..." Information seeking in South-East Queensland Aboriginal society' in Pride, J.B. *Cross-cultural encounters: communication and miscommunication* Melbourne 1985

Eagleson, Robert D. & Kaldor, Susan *English and the Aboriginal child* Canberra 1982

Eckermann, A-K 'Employment patterns among Aboriginal people in Rural Town, South-East Queensland' in *Australian Economic Papers* 18 (33) Adelaide 1979

Edgar, Lucy Anna *Among the Black boys* London 1865

The encyclopaedia of Aboriginal Australia David Horton (ed.) Canberra 1994

Erbacher, John & Sue *Aborigines of the rainforest* Cambridge, UK 1991

Fennel, M. & Grey, A. *Nucoorilma* Sydney [1973]

Fesl, Eve 'Melbourne Aboriginal English' BA Hons thesis, Melbourne 1977

Fison, Lorimer & Howitt, A.W. *Kamilaroi and Kurnai* Melbourne 1880

Fogarty, Lionel *Yoogum Yoogum* Melbourne 1982

Fogarty, Lionel *Ngutji* Spring Hill, Qld 1984

Folds, Ralph *Whitefella school* Sydney 1987

Gale, Fay *A study of assimilation* Adelaide 1964

Gale, Fay *We are bosses ourselves* Canberra 1983

Gammage, Bill & Spearritt, P. (eds) *Australians 1938* Broadway, NSW 1987

Gee, Lionel C.E. *Bush tracks and gold fields, reminiscences of Australia's 'Back of Beyond'* Adelaide 1926

Gilbert, Kevin *End of dreamtime* Sydney 1971

Gilbert, Kevin *Living black* Melbourne 1977

Gilbert, Kevin *People are legends* St Lucia, Qld 1978

Gilbert, Kevin *Inside Black Australia: an anthology of Aboriginal poetry* Ringwood, Vic. 1988

Ginibi, Ruby Langford *Real deadly* Pymble, NSW 1992

Glass, Colleen & Weller, Archie *Us fellas: an anthology of Aboriginal writing* Perth 1987

Graham, Duncan *Dying inside* Sydney 1989

Green, Neville (ed.) *Nyungar—the people: Aboriginal customs in the southwest of Australia* Perth 1979

Green, Neville *Desert school* Fremantle, WA 1983

Gribble, J.B. *Dark deeds in a sunny land or Blacks and Whites in North-West Australia* Perth [1886]

Gumbert, Marc *Neither justice nor reason: a legal and anthropological analysis of Aboriginal land rights* St Lucia, Qld 1984

Haebich, Anna *For their own good: Aborigines and government in the Southwest of Western Australia 1900–1940* Nedlands, WA 1989

Hammond, J. E. *Winjan's people: the story of the South-West Australian Aborigines* Perth [1933]

Harkins, Jean 'English as a 'two-way' language in Alice Springs' MA thesis, Canberra 1988

Harney, W.E. *Taboo* Sydney 1943

Harney, W.E. *North of 23 deg* Sydney [1946]

Harris, Pam *Teaching about time in tribal Aboriginal communities* Darwin 1984

Hassell, Ethel *My dusky friends* [1910] Fremantle, WA 1975

Haygarth, Henry William Esq. *Recollections of bush life in Australia* London 1848

Heppell, M. (ed.) *A black reality: Aboriginal camps and housing in remote Australia* Canberra 1979

Hercus, Luise *The languages of Victoria: a late survey* Canberra 1969

Hercus, Luise & Sutton, Peter *This is what happened: historical narratives by Aborigines* Canberra 1986

Hodge, Dino *Did you meet any malagas? A homosexual history of Australia's tropical capital* Nightcliff, NT 1993

Hope Vale Hotline Hope Vale, Qld 1970–75

Horne, G. & Aiston, G. *Savage life in Central Australia* London 1924

Howard, M. (ed.) *Whitefella business* Philadelphia, USA 1978

Howitt. A M. *Native tribes of south-east Australia* London 1904

Hudson, Joyce & McConvell, Patrick *Keeping language strong* Report of the pilot study of the Kimberley Language Resource Centre, Broome, WA 1984

Huggins, Rita & Huggins, Jackie *Auntie Rita* Canberra 1994

The Invasion Diary Collective *The white invasion diary* Flinders University, SA and Fitzroy, Vic. 1986

Jackomos, Alick & Fowell, Derek *Living Aboriginal history of Victoria: stories in the oral tradition* Cambridge, UK 1991

Janson, Julie *Gunjies* [Sydney] 1993
Jones, Elsie *The story of the falling star* Canberra 1989
Junga Yimi Yuendumu, NT 1984–87
Kaldor, Susan & Malcolm, Ian G. 'Language of school and schoolchild' in Berndt, R. M. & C. H. *Aborigines of the west: their past and present* Perth 1980
Keen, Ian *Being black: Aboriginal cultures in 'settled' Australia* Canberra 1988
Kennedy, Marnie *Born a half caste* Canberra 1985
Kimberley Land Council Newsletter Derby, WA 1979–87
Koch, Grace *Kaytetye country* Alice Springs, NT 1993
Kolig, Erich *Bi:n and Gadeja—Oceania* Reprint Sydney 1972
Kolig, Erich *The Noonkanbah story* Dunedin, New Zealand 1987
Koori English Aboriginal Languages Project Steering Committee, Melbourne 1989
Koori Mail Lismore, NSW 1991–
Land Rights News Darwin, NT 1976–
Langford, Ruby *Dont take your love to town* Ringwood, Vic. 1988
Langford, Ginibi Ruby *A journey into Bundjalung country* Kempsey, NSW [1991]
La Perouse: the place, the people and the sea A collection of writings by members of the Aboriginal community, Canberra 1988
Libermann, Kenneth 'The decline of the *Kuwarra* people' in *Ethnohistory* 27/2 1980 Canberra 1968
Lyon, Pamela & Parsons, Michael *We are staying: the Alyawarre struggle for land at Lake Nash* Alice Springs 1989
McGrath, Ann *Born in the cattle* Sydney 1987
McGinness, Joe *Son of Alyandu: my fight for Aboriginal rights* St Lucia, Qld 1991
McKenzie, Geraldine *Aurukun Diary* Melbourne 1981
Mankind Sydney 1931– see *Australian Journal of Anthropology*
Marshall, Paul *Raparapa—all right, now we go 'longside the river: stories from the Fitzroy River drovers* Broome, WA 1988
Masson, Elsie R. *An untamed territory* London, 1915
Mattingley, Christobel & Hampton, K. (eds) *Survival in our own land: Aboriginal experiences in South Australia since 1836* South Adelaide, SA 1988
Matto's Koori writers Writings from the Aboriginal Students Writing Camp, Gerroa 1985 [Sydney] 1985
Meredith, Mrs Charles *Notes and sketches of New South Wales* London 1861
Messagestick Cairns, Qld 1986–
Meyer, H.A.E. *Vocabulary of the language spoken by the Aborigines of the southern and eastern portions of the settled district of South Australia* Adelaide 1843
Mikawomma Nungas Croydon High School, Croydon, SA 1984
Millet, Mrs Edward *An Australian parsonage* London 1872
Mirritji, Jack *My people's life* Milingimbi, NT 1978
Mitchell, Norman & Anderson, J.C. *Kubara: a Kuku-Yalantji view of the Chinese of early north Queensland* St Lucia, Qld 1980
Mosa Monash Orienteering Scheme for Aborigines, Clayton, Vic. 1987–9
Visions of Mowanjum—Aboriginal writings from the Kimberley Adelaide 1980
'Mt. Penang's young men go west' in *YACS News* 1982 [Sydney]
Muecke, Stephen 'The good oil company and the bad oil company' in *Art and Text* vol 9 1983, Prahran, Vic. 1981–

Nathan, Pam, & Japanangka, Dick Leichleitner *Settle down country: pmere arlatywele* Malmsbury, Vic 1983

Neidjie, Bill *Kakadu man* Canberra 1985

Neidjie, Bill *Story about feeling* Keith Taylor (ed.) Broome, WA 1989

Nelen Yubu Melville Island, NT 1980–88

New Dawn Haymarket, NSW 1970–75

Newland, Simpson *Memoirs of Simpson Newland* Adelaide 1926

Newstead, Adrienne & Watson, C. Dalkuna *Mnunuway Nhe Rom* Melbourne 1987

Ngabidj, Grant & Shaw, Bruce *My country of the pelican dreaming* Canberra 1981

Northern Territory Government *Amanbidji Land Claim—Transcript of proceedings* Darwin 1991

Palmer, Kingsley & McKenna, Clancy *Somewhere between black and white: the story of an Aboriginal Australian* South Melbourne, Vic 1978

Pepper, Phillip *You are what you make yourself to be: the story of a Victorian Aboriginal family 1842–1980* Melbourne 1980

Pepper, Phillip with Araugo, Tess de *The Kurnai of Gippsland Vol 1* South Yarra, Vic. 1985

Plomley, N.J.B. *Weep in silence: a history of the Flinders Island Aboriginal Settlement* Hobart 1987

Portland Guardian Portland, Vic. 1842

Puggana News Launceston, Tas. 1975–

Read, Jay & Read, Peter (eds) *A view of the past: Aboriginal accounts of Northern Territory history* Canberra1978

Read, Peter 'A history of the Wiradjuri people in New South Wales 1883–1969' Ph D thesis, Canberra 1983

Reid, Janice & Trompf, Peggy *The health of Aboriginal Australia* Marrickville, NSW 1991

Roberts, J. P. (ed.) *The Mapoon story: by the Mapoon people* Melbourne 1975

Robinson, Roland *Altjeringa and other Aboriginal poems* Sydney 1970

Robinson, Scott 'The Aboriginal embassy, 1972' MA thesis, Canberra 1993

Roe, Paddy & Muecke, Stephen *Gularabulu' stories from the West Kimberley* Fremantle, WA 1983

Romaine, Suzanne (ed.) *Language in Australia* Cambridge, UK 1991

Rose, Deborah Bird *Hidden Histories: black stories from Victoria River Downs, Humbert River and Wave Hill stations* Canberra 1991

Rose, Deborah Bird *Dingo makes us human* Cambridge, UK 1992

Rose, Deborah Bird (ed.) *Country in flames: proceedings of the 1994 symposium on biodiversity and fire in Northern Australia* Canberra & Darwin 1995

Rose, Frederick G.G. *The winds of change in Central Australia* Berlin 1965

Ross, Helen *Just for living* Canberra 1987

Ross, Helen *Community social impact assessment at Turkey Creek* East Kimberley Working Paper, Canberra 1988

Rosser, Bill *This is Palm Island* Canberra 1978

Rosser, Bill *Dreamtime Nightmares: biographies of Aborigines under the Queensland Aborigines Act* Canberra 1985

Roughsey, Elsie Lebumore *An Aboriginal mother tells of the old and the new* Fitzroy, Vic. 1984

Royal Commission into Aboriginal Deaths in Custody—transcript of proceedings *Day, Barney Harrison.* Melbourne 1988

Royal Commission into Aboriginal Deaths in Custody—transcript of proceedings *Moffatt, Arthur* Melbourne 1988

Royal Commission into Aboriginal Deaths in Custody—transcript of proceedings *Moore, James* Swan Hill, Vic 1989

Science of Man Sydney 1898–1912

Scott, William *The Port Stephens blacks: recollections of William Scott* prepared by Gordon Bennett, Dungog, NSW 1929

Sansom, Basil *The camp at Wallaby Cross* Canberra 1980

Schmidt, Annette *Young people's Dyirbal* Cambridge, UK 1985

Sharpe, M.C. 'Alice Springs Aboriginal English' in Wurm, S.A. (ed.) *Australian Linguistic Studies* Canberra 1979

Sharpe, Margaret *The Traeger kid* Chippendale, NSW 1983

Shaw, Bruce *Countrymen: the life histories of four Aboriginal men as told to Bruce Shaw* Canberra 1986

Skrzynecki, Peter (ed.) *Joseph's coat: an anthology of multicultural writing* Marrickville, NSW 1985

Small, Mary & Ingpen, Robert *Night of the muttonbirds* Sydney 1981

Smith, Mrs James *The Booandik tribe of South Australian Aborigines* Adelaide 1880

South Australian Department of the Environment *Minerawuta—Rum Paddock Gate—an historic Adnyamathanha settlement in the Flinders Ranges, South Australia* Adelaide 1981

South Australian Record London 1838–41

Stanley, Owen *The mission and Peppimenarti: an economic study of two Daly River communities* Darwin 1985

Stevens, Frank *Aborigines in the Northern Territory cattle industry* Canberra 1974

Stories from Yuendumu SAL literacy workshop, Darwin 1985

Strelley Community School *Primers in English* Strelley, WA 1976

Sunny and the dark horse dir David McDougall, Canberra 1986

Taplin, Rev. George *The Narrinyeri* Adelaide 1874

Telfer, William Jr *The Wallabadah manuscript: recollections of the early days by William Telfer, Jr. The early history of the Northern District of New South Wales* 1900–03 introduction and notes by Roger Milliss, Kensington, NSW 1982

Terry, Michael *Across unknown Australia* London 1925

Tilbrook, Lois *Nyungar tradition: glimpses of Aborigines of South-Western Australia 1829–1914* Perth 1982

Tiwi talkabout Melville Island, NT 1970–75

Tjakulpa Kuwarritja Papunya, NT 1979–88

Tjaru Yirara College, Alice Springs, NT 1979–82

Tonkinson, Robert *The Mardudjera Aborigines* New York, USA 1978

Tonnies, Ilse (ed.) *Beitrage zur Gesellungs- und Volkerwissenschaft* Berlin 1950

Toyne, Phillip & Vachon, Daniel *Growing up country* Ringwood, Vic. 1984

Tracks Nelen Yubu newssheet [NT?] 1978

Troy, Jakelin *Australian Aboriginal contact with the English language in New South Wales 1788 to 1845* Pacific Linguistics Series B—no 103, Canberra 1990

Tunbridge, Dorothy *Flinders Ranges dreaming* Canberra 1988

Turner, Violet E. *The 'Good Fella Missus'* Adelaide 1938

Upper Daly Land Claim Northern Land Council [Darwin 1983]

Us Mob Aboriginal and Islander Studies Unit, St Lucia, Qld 1988

Vaszolyi, Eric G. *Aboriginal Australia Speaks* Perth 1976

von Eckert, Dennis *Muttonbirding on Trefoil* [Hobart] 1986

Walker, G. W. *Notes on the Aborigines of Tasmania, extracted from the manuscript journals of George Washington Walker* Hobart 1898

Walker, Della *Me and you: the life story of Della Walker as told to Tina Coutts* Canberra 1989

Walker, Kath (Oodgeroo Noonuccal) *Stradbroke Dreamtime* Sydney 1972

Ward, Glenyse *Wandering girl* Broome, WA 1987

Ward, Glenyse *Unna you fullas* Broome, WA 1991

Watson, Sam *The kadaitcha sung* Ringwood, Vic 1990

Weller, Archie *The day of the dog* Sydney 1981

Weller, Archie *Going home* Sydney 1986

West, Ida *Pride against prejudice: reminiscences of a Tasmanian Aboriginal* Canberra 1987

White, Isobel, Barwick, Diane & Meehan, Betty *Fighters and singers: the lives of some Australian Aboriginal women* Sydney 1985

Wilkinson, George *South Australia* Adelaide 1848

Wilkinson, Linda M. 'Aboriginality: the Framlingham experience' Ph D thesis, Bundoora, Vic. 1991

Williams, Nancy *Two laws: managing disputes in a contemporary Aboriginal community* Canberra 1987

Willshire, W.H. *The Aborigines of Central Australia* Port Augusta, SA 1888

Willshire, W.H. *A thrilling tale of real life in the wilds of Australia* Adelaide 1895

Wreck Bay Koori Newsletter [Wreck Bay, NSW] 1990–